Smoking and
Human Behavior

Smoking and Human Behavior

Edited by

TARA NEY
University of Victoria, British Columbia, Canada

and

ANTHONY GALE
University of Southampton, UK

JOHN WILEY & SONS
Chichester · New York · Brisbane · Toronto · Singapore

Library of Congress Cataloging in Publication Data:

Smoking and human behavior.

  Bibliography: p.
  Includes indexes.
  1. Smoking—Psychological aspects. I. Ney, Tara.
II. Gale, Anthony.
BF789.S6S66 1989   616.86′5   88–33844
ISBN 0 471 92138 6

British Library Cataloguing in Publication Data:
Smoking and human behavior.
  1. Tobacco smoking
  I. Ney, Tara II. Gale, Anthony
  613.8′5

  ISBN 0 471 92138 6

Phototypeset by Input Typesetting Limited, London
Printed and bound in Great Britain by Bath Press Ltd, Bath

List of Contributors

Heather Ashton, *Clinical Psychopharmacology Unit, Department of Pharmacological Sciences, University of Newcastle upon Tyne, Newcastle upon Tyne, Tyne and Wear NE2 4HH, UK*

Timothy Baker, *Department of Psychology, University of Wisconsin, W.J. Brogden Psychology Building, 1202 West Johnson Street, Madison, Wisconsin 53706, USA*

Karl Bättig, *Comparative Physiology and Behavioral Biology Laboratory, Swiss Federal Institute of Technology, Turnerstrasse 1, CH-8092, Zurich, Switzerland*

Thomas Brandon, *Department of Psychology, University of Wisconsin, W.J. Brogden Psychology Building, 1202 West Johnson Street, Madison, Wisconsin 53706, USA*

Robert E. Church, *Department of Psychology, University of Southampton, Highfield, Southampton, Hampshire SO9 5NH, UK*

Robert B. Coambs, *Behavioral Research on Tobacco Use, Addiction Research Foundation, 33 Russell Street, Toronto, Canada M5S 2S1*

Roberta G. Ferrence, *Prevention Studies Department, Addiction Research Foundation, 33 Russell Street, Toronto, Canada M5S 2S1*

Ray Fleming, *Department of Psychology, University of Wisconsin, Milwaukee, Wisconsin, USA*

Anthony Gale, *Department of Psychology, University of Southampton, Highfield, Southampton, Hampshire SO9 5NH, UK*

David G. Gilbert, *Department of Psychology, Southern Illinois University at Carbondale, Carbondale, Illinois 62901, USA*

John F. Golding, *Institute of Naval Medicine, Alverstoke, Gosport, Hampshire PO12 2DL, UK*

Dorothy K. Hatsukami, *Department of Psychiatry, Box 393 Mayo Memorial Building, University of Minnesota, 420 Delaware St SE, Minneapolis, Minnesota 55455, USA*

Murray E. Jarvik, *Department of Psychiatry and Biobehavioral Sciences, The Neuropsychiatric Institute and Hospital School of Medicine, University of California at Los Angeles, Los Angeles, California 900 24, USA and Veterans Administration Medical Center, West Los Angeles, Brentwood Division, Los Angeles, California 90073, USA*

Verner J. Knott, *Clinical Neurophysiological Services and Department of Research, Lady Grey Building, Royal Ottawa Hospital, 1145 Carling Avenue, Ottawa, Ontario, Canada K1Z 7K4*

Lynn T. Kozlowski, *Behavioural Research on Tobacco Use, Addiction Research Foundation, 33 Russell Street, Toronto, Canada M5S 2S1*

Howard Leventhal, *Department of Psychology, University of Wisconsin, W.J. Brogden Psychology Building, 1202 West Johnson Street, Madison, Wisconsin 53706, USA*

Haydn Morris, *Department of Psychology, University of Southampton, Highfield, Southampton, Hampshire SO9 5NH, UK*

Tara Ney, *Cooperative Education, University of Victoria, Victoria, British Columbia, Canada V8W 2Y2*

Rico Nil, *Comparative Physiology and Behavioral Biology Laboratory, Swiss Federal Institute of Technology, Turnerstrasse 1, CH-8092, Zurich, Switzerland*

Kieron O'Connor, *Psychiatric Research Center, Hôpital Louis-H. Lafontaine, University of Montreal, 7401 rue Hochelaga, Montreal, Quebec, Canada H1N 3M5*

Cynthia S. Pomerleau, *Behavioral Medicine Program, Department of Psychiatry, University of Michigan School of Medicine, Ann Arbor, Michigan 48109, USA*

Ovide F. Pomerleau, *Behavioral Medicine Program, Department of Psychiatry, University of Michigan School of Medicine, Ann Arbor, Michigan 48109, USA*

Roy J. Shephard, *School of Physical and Health Education and Department of Preventive Medicine and Biostatistics, Faculty of Medicine, University of Toronto, 320 Huron Street, Toronto, Ontario, Canada M5S 1A1*

Stephen Sutton, *ICRS Health Behaviour Unit, Institute of Psychiatry, 101 Denmark Hill, London SE5 8AF, UK*

Anne C. Walters, *Department of Psychology, University of Reading, Earley Gate, Whiteknights, Reading, Berkshire RG6 2AL, UK*

David M. Warburton, *Department of Psychology, University of Reading, Earley Gate, Whiteknights, Reading, Berkshire RG6 2AL, UK*

Richard Welser, *Department of Psychology, Southern Illinois University at Carbondale, Carbondale, Illinois 62901, USA*

Contents

Foreword

Not long ago, cigarette smoking was so pervasive that it was regarded as a natural behavior—socially acceptable, physically harmless, and culturally attractive. The hero in the Hollywood movie, male or female, displayed confidence and sophistication when lighting up and exhaling smoke. The cigarette was a symbol of strength, status and well-being.

But things have changed. No longer will you be offered a cigarette at every social encounter. Coffee tables are not adorned with the paraphernalia of smoking—cigarette boxes, lighters and ashtrays. While in the recent past there were smoking sections on airplanes, now there are smokeless flights. In public buildings and on public transport smoking is becoming progressively prohibited. Many people maintain smoke-free zones not only at work but at home. Manufacturers of cigarettes are now facing costly litigation in the courts.

What accounts for these changes in individual and group attitudes, individual behavior and public policy? Statements by the US Surgeon General have underlined three general points: that smoking has adverse affects on several aspects of health; that secondary smoke affects the health of the non-smoker; and that nicotine meets the criteria for addiction in a way similar to other addictive behaviors. The notion that smoking is addictive colors our view of the smoker.

The reaction of the non-smoker is no longer neutral. While objecting to the behavior of smokers in restaurants and other public places, the non-smoker may also believe the smoker to not only be irresponsible but pathological. Thus, the hero has now become stigmatized and smoking, in a short space of time, has moved from being an everyday habit and custom towards social designation as a pathological behavior.

Smoking and Human Behavior reviews biological, experimental psychological and social psychological aspects of smoking, from models of causation and maintenance, to studies of prevention and cessation. This volume brings together a variety of approaches to the problem of smoking as part of the search for understanding. Does smoking have benefits as well as costs? What are the reasons for smoking? Do different individuals have different motives for smoking? How does smoking relate to performance and mood? What evidence is there for the deleterious effects of passive smoking? How do expressed attitudes about smoking relate to individual behavior? What is the best way to design anti-smoking interventions? What is the future for the smoker and for smoking research?

We wish to thank all our authors for their cooperation and perseverence in producing this book. We know they will agree that the final product is worthy of their labors.

Tara Ney wishes to thank her family for offering their support wherever and whenever it was needed: her husband Kim Blank for his enthusiasm and ideas, and her children Acia and Jenner, who somehow made the book possible and worthwhile. Anthony Gale joins her in thanking colleagues at John Wiley & Sons, particularly Wendy Hudlass, for her resilient support. Liz Gale endured more than one holiday in Scotland, where time was devoted to editing rather than having fun; to her thanks also.

TARA NEY *Victoria, Canada*
ANTHONY GALE *Southampton, UK*

October 1988

1

Introduction: The Key Questions about Smoking Behavior

ANTHONY GALE
and
TARA NEY

ABSTRACT

This introductory chapter provides a rationale for the book and its structure. It summarizes each of the remaining chapters and identifies relationships between them. Research into smoking occurs within a socioeconomic context in which governments are faced by the conflicting demands of the health dangers of smoking and the revenue potential of cigarettes. The psychological sciences have explored smoking behavior from biological, behavioral, cognitive and social perspectives. It is explained that a number of persistent themes and questions continue to be the preoccupation of researchers into the smoking habit.

INTRODUCTION

Cigarettes are a wonderful commercial product. Made from essentially natural raw materials which are harvested with cheap labor, the cigarette is manufactured in large quantities by automated equipment and at low unit cost. The product is easily packaged, easily transported by manufacturer and wholesaler, and then sold without great difficulty from multiple outlets in virtually every urban and rural retail center and from vending machines for 24 hours per day. Persistent levels of sale and minimal seasonal fluctuations

Smoking and Human Behavior, Edited by T. Ney and A. Gale

in popularity make shelf-life and storage a relatively minor problem. While there are national preferences in brand and taste, the cigarette and its manufacturers are hardly affected by national frontiers, and every country has a large proportion of smokers (Office of Population Censuses and Surveys, 1981; United States Surgeon General, 1979). No preparation of the product is required before use; it slips into the customer's pocket or handbag and can be used immediately in virtually all environments.

The smoker ensures that a constant supply is available since it is hard to cope with life's pressures without it; the cigarette is a natural companion to many of the smoker's working and leisure activities. Smokers say that smoking reduces feelings of anxiety and anger, provides hedonic pleasure and improves concentration and attention (Russell, Peto and Patel, 1974; Spielberger, 1986). Only sleep interrupts smoking. Customers apparently become so committed to the product that they are willing to pay a price which includes a large tax element; they are also willing to endanger their health. A large proportion of the population of both sexes smoke; they begin the habit early in life and find it very hard to stop (Clark, 1976; McKennell and Thomas, 1967; United States Department of Health and Human Services, 1987). Even where governments in developed countries, in the face of evidence of the threat to health, are evolving positive policies towards cessation, markets are expanding in the Third World. It would be hard to find a more profitable product.

CHALLENGES TO CHANGES IN HEALTH POLICY

Governments in developed countries must confront a number of contradictions. The cost of smoking to health has been clearly demonstrated (Royal College of Physicians, 1977). Yet the taxation imposed on such a popular product provides a ready source of government revenue. Tobacco companies are multinational multiproduct corporations with major benefits to convey across a wide range of diversified manufacturing and commercial enterprises. They provide employment and stimulation to the local economy. Their advertising budgets far exceed those allocated to health promotion bodies (Sutton, 1984). Even where traditional advertising routes are closed, tobacco companies are willing to sponsor sports and the arts and to fund basic research. They therefore have considerable power to act as pressure groups and influence government policy, as well as potential customers. Tobacco companies, in spite of extensive diversification of commercial activity, are reluctant to forgo the ready profits which the cigarette brings.

While state welfare benefits to the elderly can consume close to 50 percent of all government social welfare benefits (Slater, 1984) the life expectancy of a middle-aged patient with a diagnosis of inoperable lung cancer is between six months and one year (Royal College of Physicians, 1977); thus the cost of terminal care for such a short period is much lower than the cost of providing for the health and well-being of an aging person over two or more decades. A cynical view of current public health policy in many advanced countries would be that smoking both creates government revenue and saves long-term expenditure.

The association of the smoking habit with increased risk of contracting a variety of diseases has been well established and is now rarely challenged (Royal College of Physicians, 1977; Wald, 1978). The imposition of crippling taxes to put the price out of the reach of average disposable incomes or, indeed, the imposition of firm restrictions on outlets and sales, would be likely to have a major impact on health and to remove the dangers associated with the largest preventable cause of death in the western world (Peto, 1974; Lewit and Coate, 1982; Sutton, 1984). However, such action on the part of governments seems most unlikely. In spite of health promotion campaigns and reductions in overall levels of consumption significant proportions of the population continue to smoke.

It is important for researchers into smoking to appreciate that changes in public policy could be a rapid route to cessation. High prices or lack of access to the cigarette could well have a far greater impact on the smoking habit than the results of any psychological research into smoker motivation or smoking cessation. In a sense, researchers into smoking could themselves be accused of helping to sustain the habit, since the focus of their concern has typically been the nature of the smoker, rather than the social and economic structures which support the tobacco industry. As with other forms of deviance, the problem has been taken out of the social and interpersonal domain and translated by many researchers into an intrapersonal problem or even a psychopathological disease state (Szasz, 1961).

THE ROLE OF THE PSYCHOLOGICAL SCIENCES IN EXPLAINING SMOKER MOTIVATION

In the absence of dramatic changes in social and health policy a major focus of scientific research must nevertheless be to understand why some people smoke and some do not. For those who smoke, what are the primary sources of motivation? How does the habit become established and then sustained? What particular aspects of the smoking habit are reinforcing for the individual? What strategies are available, on the basis of our understanding of motivation for smoking, to help us in devising programs to assist in cessation? Essentially, by understanding this habitual yet self-destructive behavior, can we devise means of preventing it?

For the psychological sciences, smoking presents a unique challenge. The psychological sciences extend from the exploration of basic bodily mechanisms, including brain function and biochemistry, through learning processes, human performance, subjective and cognitive appraisal of the world, and social interaction between individuals and groups. They are also concerned with developmental processes and individual differences in habits and personal preferences which arise from aptitude and personality. Psychologists have also developed an armamentarium for measuring and experimenting upon human behavior and attitudes. Applied psychologists seek to apply, in the real world, the knowledge acquired in the laboratory about human psychological processes.

Typically, expertise in one of these areas of psychological research (for example, brain mechanisms) does not guarantee either expertise or interest in other areas (say, human memory, attitude development). The rate of gain of research information is so rapid that it is hard for an individual researcher to keep pace with developments in other fields. Yet research into smoking motivation and smoking cessation has drawn upon several psychological disciplines. The problem of smoking as an established habit resistant to change has been tackled from biological, behavioral, cognitive and social perspectives (Ashton and Stepney, 1982). Potentially, therefore, research questions about smoking can be integrative for the disciplines of psychology, drawing together a variety of expertise in both pure and applied fields.

The present volume is organized to reflect the continuum from brain mechanisms to interpersonal and social behaviour. Part One focuses on biological mechanisms and the claim that smoking has its effects on mood and behavior through the impact of nicotine on brain biochemistry. Evidence is examined to test the claim that smoking is addictive, that smokers become tolerant of nicotine and experience withdrawal symptoms when in a state of abstention.

In Part Two the biological focus shifts to the measurement of physiological and subjective responses in smoking and nonsmoking subjects. Electrodes may be placed on the human cranium to measure electrical changes in the brain while the smoker performs various tasks. Variations in mood following smoking can be measured by questionnaires and other devices used to measure subjective response and report on individual experience. An important issue is whether smokers vary in their temperament or personality, use smoking for different purposes and, indeed, smoke in different ways. This theme is extended in Part Three, which is concerned with human performance. First, smoking itself is considered as an elaborate behavior. For example, if smoking is driven by the smoker's need for nicotine, will variation in the nicotine content of the cigarette affect the way in which the smoker smokes? If the cigarette is used as a psychological coping tool, will the imposition of different levels of stress affect the frequency and intensity of smoking? A variety of techniques have been developed for measuring smoking patterns and for manipulating the smoker's reactions by introducing changes in the nature of the cigarette. Secondly, major claims have been made for the effects of smoking on concentration and the efficiency of cognitive performance. Part Three considers whether such claims are justified, and indeed whether the experimental procedures which have been used by researchers are adequate to the testing of precise hypotheses about smoking and performance.

Passive smoking and its effects on individual discomfort and working efficiency provides a link to Part Four, which is concerned with attitudes, interventions and social policy. Awareness that passive smoking is deleterious for health has come relatively recently (Hirayama, 1981; Shephard, 1982; United States Surgeon General, 1986). It has led to changes in our views of what is acceptable in social contexts, and to restrictions on the freedom of smokers to smoke in public places (Shephard and LaBarre, 1978).

Part Four considers both individual and group aspects of social psychology and influence. How are the individual's attitudes to smoking related to actual patterns of smoking and the ability to cease smoking? Several strategies of intervention are considered, including reports of a number of large-scale prevention and cessation studies in American schools. Finally, and projecting forward through the next two decades, we consider the implications of current trends in smoking behavior and the growing power of the health lobby, both for society's attitude to the smoker and for the future of psychological research on smoking.

In the remainder of this Introductory section we consider the key themes which emerge from contemporary theory and research into human smoking behavior. We survey each chapter briefly, identifying some of the enduring problems for research into smoking. But before turning to a brief review of the contents of the book we should mention the problem of bias and the dangers of oversimplification. Smoking researchers fall roughly into two camps, those who are concerned with the dangers of smoking to health and who wish to develop and facilitate programs of cessation, and those who, by virtue of research funding by the tobacco industry, have focused on the psychological benefits of smoking and the possibility of producing a safe cigarette. It is difficult to conduct research into smoking and not be affected by the vested interests and controversies in the field. For example, it is easy to take evidence which is not truly robust and invest it with more authority than is justified. There is also a danger of undue commitment to one particular approach; for example, the nicotine addiction model versus a social influence model. The approach adopted influences the style of study, the ways in which key variables are manipulated, and the type of explanatory models which are used to explain the outcome. Particular theoretical approaches lead to particular varieties of intervention procedures.

But there is no theory of smoking which is able to deal conclusively with the facts, or which can generate hypotheses which lead to an exhaustive modeling of experimental or survey data. Typically, most theoretical notions can account for only a modest proportion of the observed variance. Our view is that the contributors to this volume have been able to adopt a disinterested, balanced and objective view of the current state of smoking research. Generally speaking, while our authors have been able to come to conclusions, they are typically cautious in making claims about the nature of smoking and its causes. As the book reveals, in spite of a long history of research into smoking a great deal is still to be learned. The most secure knowledge we have is about the deleterious health consequences of smoking. In contrast, our understanding of its causes, the demonstration of its benefits, and the development of means for securing cessation without relapse, are still dogged by uncertainty. There are few authorities in the field of smoking behavior willing to make confident pronouncements.

BIOLOGICAL APPROACHES AND THE PROBLEM OF ADDICTION

Reward and punishment are basic motives for higher organisms and underlie our ability either to operate purposively on the world or to retreat from external influence through anxiety and fear (Gray, 1982). It has been claimed both that smoking is inherently rewarding and that it is negatively reinforcing either through reducing negative affect or by reducing the negative consequences of withdrawal. Initially, the smoker may smoke for reward in the form of the positive affect which smoking is alleged to induce; subsequently, once the smoker has become addicted, smoking may become an imperative, driven by the negative feelings created by withdrawal symptoms. The rationale for biochemical approaches to smoking includes the notion that nicotine acts upon reward and punishment centers in the brain. Reward and punishment centers have been implicated in several models of addiction.

In Chapter 2 Heather Ashton and John Golding begin their review of motivation for smoking with an account of research into the reward and punishment areas of the central nervous system. Nicotine is a drug which has been shown to reinforce or reward behavior in animals; it can also bring about reward indirectly by blocking nicotinic receptors in cholinergic punishment pathways. Models of addiction include the notion that punishment systems can be overactive and reward systems underactive, leading to withdrawal symptoms. Thus administration of the addictive drug can act as its own reward by returning the system to temporary equilibrium. Natural bodily substances which protect the organism against pain can also be released by nicotine. Reward and punishment systems act in concert, and are linked also with mechanisms which sustain wakefulness and arousal. Deviation from an optimum level of arousal is considered to be punishing and actions or substances which return the organism to its optimal arousal level acquire the property of reward. Again, nicotine appears to have the power to modulate arousal level. Thus there is a prima-facie case for the view that nicotine is the active substance in cigarette smoke which accounts for persistence of the habit.

However, the psychopharmacology of nicotine is complex, and Ashton and Golding demonstrate how difficult it is to interpret existing studies of the effects of nicotine on brain and behavior and upon subjective positive hedonic responses to smoking. They say: 'although nicotine is clearly a drug of addiction, it must be admitted that its evident effects on reward systems are probably the least understood of its many pharmacological actions' (page 32). Similarly, the role of nicotine as a tranquilizer and a means of reducing anger, pain and negative affect is not altogether clear.

Abstinence from smoking produces withdrawal effects and craving. The nicotine addiction model would predict that nicotine chewing gum should reduce craving; however, it does not do so, even though other withdrawal symptoms are reduced. There is controversy as to whether nicotine creates tolerance and this issue is considered in subsequent chapters in Part One. Certainly, dose escalation does not occur with smoking, since smokers acquire a stable level which appears to satisfy their needs on a continuing basis.

The arousal manipulation model mentioned earlier implies that smoking can be used either to arouse the individual or to sedate and tranquilize. Again there is controversy over such alleged biphasic effects, and it appears that nicotine dosage level, personality type and situational stress combine in complex ways, there being considerable individual variations both in optimal arousal level and the means employed to modulate state. A recurrent theme in the present volume is the demonstration that smoking is arousing in some situations and for some people, and dearousing for others.

In concluding their discussion Ashton and Golding reject simple addiction or arousal models since the nervous system operates in a complex integrative fashion; reward, punishment, arousal and learning have elaborate integrative and reciprocal relationships.

A more generous view of findings relating to dependence and tolerance is taken in Chapter 3 by Murray Jarvik and Dorothy Hatsukami. They draw analogies between smoking and dependence upon other substances such as opioids. Having defined dependence as involving repetitive self-administration of a chemical substance which the person cannot resist, they argue that smoking falls within their definition. Difficulty in cessation and high relapse rates are given as evidence. Similarly, they argue that smoking provokes tolerance given, for example, the fact that the initial response to smoking involves severe irritation of the respiratory tract, which the smoker subsequently comes to tolerate and even enjoy. Jarvik and Hatsukami also describe studies which demonstrate withdrawal symptoms in smoking with a return to physiological, subjective and behavioral normality once smoking is resumed. Nevertheless, smoking withdrawal does not involve the debilitating illness associated with opioids. Moreover, evidence concerning relapse in the presence of withdrawal is contradictory, with poor correlations between the extent of reported withdrawal and the disposition to relapse. Indeed, much relapse occurs long after the physiological signs of withdrawal have disappeared.

Like Ashton and Golding, Ovide and Cynthia Pomerleau (Chapter 4) reject the simple physiological addiction model. They demonstrate that the necessary conclusive evidence for addiction in the form of dependence, tolerance and withdrawal phenomena is not yet forthcoming. The addiction model seems to play down the more positive aspects of smoking, given its reliance on smoking as a means of reducing the negative consequences of withdrawal. Pomerleau and Pomerleau are also critical of behavioral models of smoking and the strategies for cessation which they generate, since such approaches focus on antecedent and consequent events, without paying due attention to the pharmacological effects of nicotine.

They cite evidence for the effects of nicotine on a variety of endogenous substances, effects which include the synthesis, release and turnover of such substances in the central nervous system. These substances are involved in a variety of functions including: learning and memory; pain inhibition; arousal modulation; selective attention and facilitation of information processing. The endogenous substances work naturally and independently of nicotine; however, since nicotine increases their bioavailability it is used by the smoker as a means of self-regulation. Pomerleau and Pomerleau demonstrate that, in a variety of ways, nicotine has the same effects on behavior as do these natural neuroregulators. They cite evidence which demonstrates that smokers can adjust nicotine intake to match dose to environmental demands and achieve either stimulant or sedative effects. Finally, Pomerleau and Pomerleau present an integrative model which both explains the ways in which smoking can enhance performance and subjective state, and suggests possible approaches to intervention for cessation. Their biobehavioral model is considered by several authorities to be the current model with the most potential for explaining the smoking habit. They point out that some authorities, preoccupied with the hazardous consequences of smoking, have failed to appreciate the nature of its beneficial effects; such understanding should hold the key to successful intervention.

HUMAN PSYCHOPHYSIOLOGY, EMOTION AND INDIVIDUAL DIFFERENCES

Psychophysiologists study the relation between bodily processes and human performance. With the development of powerful computers the study of the electrical activity of the brain has been revolutionized over the past 20 years. It is possible to measure discrete changes in brain activity in response to external events, and large quantities of data may now be captured and subjected to statistical appraisal. When smokers report that smoking induces pleasant feelings, or that their concentration is enhanced by smoking, it is reasonable to assume that such reactions are mediated by brain processes. The event-related potential or ERP enables us to plot the course of external stimuli as they are processed by the central nervous system. The challenge to researchers has been to see whether brain patterns are altered by the inhalation and absorption of cigarette smoke, and whether there are correlative changes in performance or subjective state.

Verner Knott's review of ERP research (Chapter 5) leads him to the cautious conclusion that abstinence from smoking reduces the brain's sensitivity to sensory input. Smoking arouses the brain and increases sensitivity not only to simple properties of stimuli but to their evaluation for significance to the person; thus the effects of smoking are both general in arousing the person but also specific, in facilitating cognitive processing. The key to such effects is the impact of nicotine on the brain. Knott is critical of the research which he reviews: few studies include measures of both brain response and performance, so that relationships between the two domains are inferred rather than demonstrated; the technical quality of brain measurement and the associated experimental procedures is not universally high; and few studies of ERPs and smoking have exploited recent advances in our understanding of these complex waveforms and their relation to psychological processes. Nevertheless, Knott is optimistic about future research.

Robert Church (in Chapter 6) is even more critical in his evaluation of research upon smoking and the electroencephalogram or EEG. Like Knott he appeals for an improvement in the quality of research. He is particularly concerned that laboratory studies should simulate natural conditions of smoking; otherwise the research findings may be more related to special laboratory conditions and the requirements imposed upon subjects, than to the effects of nicotine or smoking *per se*. For example, it is likely that the many studies which show that smoking has an activating effect on the electrical activity of the brain are actually reflecting special conditions within the laboratory. It is possible that laboratory smoking, particularly under the direction of the experimenter, largely represents a change in the pace of the subject's activity following a boring and monotonous pre-experimental rest period, during which the smoker has not been allowed to smoke. Church's own studies, in which smokers smoke their own cigarette at their own habitual pace, shows reliable EEG indications of *lowered* activation following each puff on the cigarette. After reviewing more than two dozen research studies from other laboratories, which typically obtain results different from his own, he appeals for a new style of research, in which the microstructure of smoking acts is studied during natural smoking, along with discrete measurement of EEG, together with performance at well-defined tasks.

Kieron O'Connor's early research on ERPs represented a revolution in research strategy because he studied small groups of subjects on more than one occasion and in considerable detail, exploring the relations between brain responses, smoking acts, personality and performance (O'Connor, 1986); several of his studies are considered in Knott's review. In Chapter 7 in the present volume he proposes a radical theoretical view of smoking which challenges the nicotine motivation model, which he seeks to replace by a motor model. Smoking is seen to stimulate the sensory-motor system, releasing energy for motor routines, which in turn are deployed to reduce stress and the effects of distractors. The emphasis thereby shifts from nicotine as the key factor in smoking, to the motoric aspects of smoking. Thus his views are in radical contradiction to those of several authors in the book, and they also challenge the view that nicotine has bimodal effects (Gilbert, 1979) since O'Connor's claim is for *activation* effects rather than for sedation. But the notion of activation is specific to sensory-motor acts and does not imply support for a *general* arousal model. He is particularly critical of the findings of titration studies (as reviewed in Chapter 9 by Nil and Bättig), which he sees as far from conclusive evidence of the smoker's dependence on nicotine. Titration studies have helped to promote an emphasis on pharmacological effects rather than self-regulatory behavior, with a consequential neglect of the functional roles of smoking. O'Connor is also reluctant to accord much importance to sensory function as such, for he considers motor and sensory properties of the nervous system as virtually indivisible; his emphasis is on motor aspects and the integration of sensory and motor information within a self-regulatory loop. Mild doses of nicotine are seen as minor stressors, mobilizing motor-action patterns, which are experienced by the smoker as substitutes for real action: 'smokers use smoking as a portable, stationary activity generator, to produce the effects of required action under conditions where the opportunity for such action is lacking' (page 161). Smoking therefore enables a smoker to create an illusion of action and thereby to resolve conflicts between alternative patterns of motor activity. He shows how his theory can be tested by exploring the relationships between smoking styles, personality and situational demands. Like the research studies upon which it is based, O'Connor's theory is radical, subtle and complex, and merits careful reading.

In the final chapter of Part Two David Gilbert and Richard Welser focus upon smoking as a regulator of mood, and in particular as a means of reducing negative affect. The need to remove anxiety and negative mood states is seen as the primary motivator for the smoking habit, and a key reason why cessation is so difficult and relapse so frequent. They stress the need to replicate natural environmental conditions when studying the effects of smoking on mood, since context can affect whether the individual reacts with positive or negative emotion. If the habitual smoker is prevented from smoking, anxiety and negative mood are experienced and subsequent availability of nicotine typically releases the stressful effects. Studies which induce negative affect through aversive stimulation must pay attention to the nature of the stressor used and its salience to the smoker; otherwise contradictory findings emerge. Apart from the effects of nicotine on mood, there is now evidence that smoking may shift the individual's cognitive or perceptual bias from negative to positive thoughts. Gilbert and Welser underline the need for appropriate measures of mood and emotion, sampling physiological, behavioral and subjective aspects of mood and using reliable and well-validated measurement instruments. Like Ashton and Golding, they speculate about the brain mechanisms affected by nicotine and the interaction of brain biochemistry with environmental demands. They suggest that different doses of nicotine may bring different brain mechanisms into operation. It is not clear whether nicotine works by alleviating the negative consequences of withdrawal, or itself has intrinsic mood-enhancing effects; nevertheless, there are several empirical demonstrations of enhanced mood in the absence of signs of withdrawal. Gilbert and Welser indicate that their own future research focus will be on careful manipulation of nicotine levels within the habitual range of smokers, varying stress and context in systematic ways and employing multiple measures of emotional response.

SMOKING AND PERFORMANCE AND SMOKING AS PERFORMANCE

Smoking is a complex behavior involving a series of interrelated actions: lighting the cigarette, drawing upon it, inhaling and exhaling, all the time manipulating the cigarette, sometimes in stereotypical or idiosyncratic ways, including smoking-related behavior such as tapping off the ash and apparently independent, personalized rituals. Included in this sequence is the absorption of smoke constituents into the blood. In Chapter 9 Rico Nil and Karl Bättig describe the techniques which have been developed to provide precise measurement of smoke absorption, and consider the advantages and disadvantages of different methods. They then report their own studies in which they have explored the relationships between a variety of measures of smoking. Because of the relatively low correlation between various measures they conclude that single components of smoking behavior are independent. This is an important conclusion, since many laboratories have their preferred approach to measurement; given the lack of correlation between measures it is unlikely that different researchers are measuring common processes. Failure to reconcile discrepant findings may well be explained by reference to the different techniques employed to measure smoke absorption. At the same time, it is clear that individual smokers vary from one another even when smoking cigarettes of a similar type in terms of nicotine and tar delivery.

Again, Nil and Bättig conclude that for different smokers different nicotine regulation mechanisms are in operation. Studies in which the nicotine delivery of cigarettes is switched enable us to see whether the smoker is titrating, varying smoking behavior to compensate for upward or downward shifts in delivery. Nil and Bättig offer a detailed review of titration studies which, on the whole, demonstrate incomplete compensation for nicotine and, in some cases, compensation more for tar than nicotine (recognizing that the two are closely correlated).

While it is clear that nicotine has an important role in the maintenance of smoking behavior, Nil and Bättig suggest that smokers compensate by titrating within a range of tolerance. The relative failure of alternative methods of nicotine delivery (such as by chewing gum) indicates that non-nicotinic factors play an important role in sustaining the habit. Finally, Nil and Bättig remind us that little is known about the relationships between individual patterns of smoking and smoke absorption and the development of respiratory disease. It is clear, from their very careful reviews of earlier work and their own multivariate studies, that simple or straightforward assertions about the nature of smoking and the impact of cigarette smoke on the smoker are not supported by the evidence.

If we cannot make simple statements about the nature of smoking itself are we free to draw conclusions from studies of the effects of smoking on human information processing? In Chapter 10 David Warburton and Anne Walters review evidence for the effects of smoking on attention and concentration. They draw largely upon laboratory studies, but also report relationships between smoking and aspects of efficiency in working life. Several research studies from their own laboratory demonstrate that smoking can have positive effects in sustained attention or monitoring tasks and in selective attention, reducing errors and increasing speed of response. They review studies reporting improved performance in smokers in certain aspects of academic achievement, confirming the assertion by smokers that smoking enables them to think and concentrate. Warburton's group have also studied smoking patterns in a variety of working contexts, showing that smoking can occur at times when the need for concentration is high. Unlike the laboratory studies, the field studies, which are cross-sectional and correlational in nature, make it difficult to draw causal paths between smoking and performance.

Warburton and Walters conclude that nicotine improves attentional processing by influencing acetylcholine release and changing the level of arousal of the brain. The smoker uses smoking and nicotine as a device for coping with stress and environmental demands; smoking is therefore seen as a personal resource which is deployed by the smoker in a purposeful manner.

The second contribution to consider the effects of smoking on human information processing is by Tara Ney, Anthony Gale and Haydn Morris. Their review of the effects of smoking on learning and memory suggests that smoking prior to learning can have long-term effects; while performance at the time of initial learning is not enhanced (and may be inferior), there is a measurable improvement in retention after a delay. They attribute this intriguing result to special properties of the consolidation process; smoking induces an arousing state, which can disrupt immediate performance but which protects the consolidation of the memory trace in the long run (Walker, 1958). There is also some evidence of state-dependent learning effects; namely that performance is better if the state of the learner is identical both at the time of learning and at subsequent testing; thus performance may be better if the smoker either smokes on both occasions or is abstinent on both occasions, with mixed conditions leading to inferior performance (Kunzendorf and Wigner, 1985).

Ney, Gale and Morris are critical of the memory tasks used in the majority of the studies they review, and claim they bear little relation to memory in everyday life. They also point to the paradox that performance can be worse while smoking yet improved after a delay; if such effects are robust it is hard to reconcile them with smokers' claims that smoking helps them concentrate while performing intellectual tasks. The conditions of testing subjects are seen to be of crucial importance and Ney, Gale and Morris conclude with a series of recommendations for future work, including: the nature of tasks used, the experimental design, the choice of subjects, instructions for abstention and smoking during the task and the necessary controls for aspects of smoking behavior. At the same time, these authors are skeptical about many of the claims made by researchers; typically the statistically significant effects which experiments have yielded are very modest indeed. They express concern that some of the more biological models of smoking may make assumptions which are not fully justified, about the effects of smoking on human performance.

SOCIAL CONTEXT AND THE IMPACT OF SOCIALLY MEDIATED INFLUENCES

Part Four is concerned with the social context of smoking. Roy Shephard reviews the evidence for the negative effects of involuntary or passive smoking, including: health risks for adults, developmental risks for children *in utero*, and the relatively modest demonstrable effects on performance. Shephard applies the Fishbein and Ajzen (1974) theory of reasoned action to explain individuals' attitudes toward passive smoking and the risks it entails. He demonstrates that increasing evidence of the deleterious effects of passive smoking has begun to shift public attitudes. There is controversy as to the extent of health risk caused by passive smoking, and Shephard discusses some of the methodological problems which have fueled controversy and which make it difficult to interpret epidemiological and survey data. He also considers the social and economic costs of creating smoke-free environments.

The Fishbein and Ajzen model is the focus of Stephen Sutton's contribution (Chapter 13). He describes the formal properties of the theory and offers evidence which shows that it can be used to predict a variety of individual behaviors on the basis of measurement of individuals' attitudes. Sutton claims that much of the work on attitudes to smoking behavior has been informal and atheoretical; he suggests that the Fishbein and Ajzen model has considerable power which could be applied in predicting the individual's chances of cessation or response to cessation programs. The model has indeed been used to predict and understand decisions relating to smoking in three areas: beliefs about smoking among smokers and nonsmokers; prediction of intentions relating to smoking; and studies predicting actual behavior. The Fishbein and Ajzen theory has not lacked critics, and Sutton details the grounds upon which the theory has been challenged. Sutton's own criticism of applications in the smoking field is that they have largely been correlational and cross-sectional, lacking appropriate follow-up designs. He ends on a confident note, having demonstrated the value of the theory in his own research.

The problem of intervention is taken up by Howard Leventhal and associates (Chapter 14). Intervention can operate in two contexts: preventing the establishment of the smoking habit (primary prevention) and seeking to establish conditions for cessation and maintenance (secondary). Leventhal et al. argue that prevention programs need to be targeted in very specific ways, taking into account the level of change (for example, whether individual, group or societal), the nature of the actual behavior to be changed (say, quitting or maintenance) and the population in question (pregnant mothers, adolescents, etc.). For the existing smoker intervention must focus not only on motivation to quit but on the coping skills needed to maintain resistance to a variety of pressures for relapse. Again, different strategies are needed both during the withdrawal phase and then subsequently, when more subtle influences are at work. Existing strategies lack specificity or precision. Leventhal et al. consider in great detail the variety of processes involved in quitting, and the range of variables which might influence outcome. They also demonstrate that dynamic changes occur over time both in motives and in the coping skills required. Their detailed review of primary and secondary prevention studies, while it is skeptical of their power to institute long-term change, ends on an optimistic note; for example, unlike earlier reviewers they identify some positive developments in large-scale primary prevention work in schools, particularly since contemporary studies benefit from superior research designs and from the changing social climate in which there is more public awareness of health issues and the dangers of smoking.

Our final chapter, by Robert Coambs, Lynn Kozlowski and Roberta Ferrence, speculates about the future. As smoking prevalence declines and social attitudes change, our conception of the smoker will alter. Once seen as a pleasant habit conveying social status, smoking will progressively acquire the characteristics of an undesirable disease and smokers will become stigmatized. The residual group of smokers will be those who are more addicted and less able to quit. Coambs et al. consider whether it is possible to predict the personality, individual characteristics and personal circumstances of such a group. Suffering from social isolation and limited access to cigarettes, the residual group will come to resemble contemporary drug-dependent deviants, suffering from a number of correlated disadvantages. As a consequence the nature of research will alter, given the reduced availability of smokers as research subjects and the likely confounding with other characteristics and problems. The psychopathological model of smoking will become more prevalent. Public policy will also alter towards the tobacco industry, since what was once a leisure product will be seen as a dependence-producing drug. Civil liberties issues will also arise as progressive restrictions are imposed on smoking in public places and at work. Thus while reductions in smoking by the turn of the century will have many positive consequences, the residual group of smokers will find themselves in an unfavorable situation on several counts.

CONCLUSION

In our introduction to the key issues relating to smoking behavior considered in this volume we have now come full circle to the issues we addressed at the outset. Psychological research into the smoking habit has generated a host of theories and research strategies, in some cases building bridges between disparate areas of the discipline. While our models of smoking behavior have become more sophisticated and subtle so our capacity to offer straightforward explanations of smoking has diminished. The extension of psychological models through increasing their explanatory power and building links between biological and social psychological approaches, represents a considerable achievement. Some of our authors are relatively optimistic about the future potential for psychological research into smoking. But such research will be set against a background of social influence and public policy, which in the last analysis will hold the key to wide-scale cessation. We are entering an exciting period in smoking research because we are able to monitor the social changes and influences which are making an impact both on government and upon individual attitudes towards smoking.

REFERENCES

Ashton, H., and Stepney, R. (1982). *Smoking: Psychology and Pharmacology*. London: Tavistock.

Clark, R. (1976). Cigarette smoking among teenage girls and young women: Summary of the findings of a survey conducted for the American Cancer Society. In: J. Wakefield (ed.), *Public Education About Cancer: recent research and current programmes*. Union Internationale Contre Cancer Technical Report Series, Volume 24, Geneva.

Fishbein, M., and Ajzen, I. (1974). Attitudes towards objects as predictors of single and multiple behavioral criteria. *Psychological Review*, **81**, 59–74.

Gilbert, D.G. (1979). Paradoxical tranquillising and emotion-reducing effects of nicotine. *Psychological Bulletin*, **86**, 643–661.

Gray, J.A. (1982). *The Neuropsychology of Anxiety: an enquiry into the functions of the septo-hippocampal system*. Oxford: Oxford University Press.

Hirayama, T. (1981). Non-smoking wives of heavy smokers have a higher risk of lung cancer: a study from Japan. *British Medical Journal*, **282**, 183–185.

Kunzendorf, R., and Wigner, L. (1985). Smoking and memory: state specific effects. *Perceptual and Motor Skills*, **61**, 558.

Lewit, E.M., and Coate, D. (1982). The potential for using excise taxes to reduce smoking. *Journal of Health Economics*, **1**, 121–145.

McKennell, A.C., and Thomas, R.K. (1967). *Adults' and Adolescents' Smoking Habits and Attitudes*. Government Social Survey. London: Her Majesty's Stationery Office.

O'Connor, K.P. (1986). Motor potentials and motor performance associated with introverted and extraverted smokers. *Neuropsychobiology*, **16**, 109–116.

Office of Population Censuses and Surveys (1981). *Cigarette Smoking: 1972–1980*. OPCS Monitor, General Household Survey 81/2. London: Office of Population Censuses and Surveys.

Peto, J. (1974). Price and consumption of cigarettes: a case for intervention? *British Journal of Social and Preventive Medicine*, **28**, 241–245.

Royal College of Physicians (1977). *Smoking or Health*. London: Pitman Medical.

Russell, M.A.H., Peto, J., and Patel, U.A. (1974). The classification of smoking by factorial structure of motives. *Journal of the Royal Statistical Society*, **137**, 313–346.

Shephard, R.J. (1982). *The Risks of Passive Smoking*. London: Croom Helm.

Shephard, R.J., and LaBarre, R. (1978). Attitudes of the public towards cigarette smoke in public places. *Canadian Journal of Public Health*, **69**, 302–310.

Slater, R. (1984). Ageing. In: A. Gale and A.J. Chapman (eds), *Psychology and Social Problems: an introduction to applied psychology*. Chichester: John Wiley & Sons.

Spielberger, C.D. (1986). Psychological determinants of smoking behaviour. In: R.D. Tollison (ed.), *Smoking and Society: toward a more balanced assessment*. Lexington, MA: Heath & Co.

Sutton, S.R. (1984). Smoking. In: A. Gale and A.J. Chapman (eds), *Psychology and Social Problems: an introduction to applied psychology*. Chichester: John Wiley & Sons.

Szasz, T. (1961). *The Myth of Mental Illness*. New York: Harper & Row.

United States Department of Health and Human Services (1986). *The Health Consequences of Involuntary Smoking. A report of the Surgeon General*. Rockville, Maryland: US DHHS, Publication No. (CDC) 87–8398.

United States Department of Health and Human Services (1987). *High School Senior*

Drug Use: 1975-1986. US DHHS, Public Health Service, Rockville, Maryland: Press Office of the National Institute on Drug Abuse.

United States Surgeon General (1979). *Smoking and Health*. Washington, DC: Department of Health, Education and Welfare.

Wald, N. (1978). Smoking as a cause of disease. In A.E. Bennett (ed.), *Recent Advances in Community Medicine*. London: Churchill-Livingstone.

Walker, E.L. (1958). Action decrement and its relation to learning. *Psychological Review*, **65**, 129-142.

Part One

Motivation and Biological Determinants

2

Smoking: Motivation and Models

HEATHER ASHTON
and
JOHN F. GOLDING

ABSTRACT

Motivation for smoking behavior is analyzed in terms of nicotine's effects on integrated brain systems for reward, arousal and cognition, and the interactions of these systems with constitutional and environmental factors. A neurophysiological synthesis of current smoking models is presented and the implications for smoking cessation are described.

INTRODUCTION

The core of any general theory of smoking must be its ability to explain the *motivation* for smoking at all stages from initiation to maintenance, and the desire to smoke during abstinence. Ideally, such a theory should also suggest strategies for promoting smoking cessation. Since human behavior is complex, and smoking is not unique among drug-taking and pleasure-producing pastimes, the theory must encompass not only the neurophysiological substrates of motivation in general, but also genetic, chemical, pharmacological, psychological and socioeconomic factors which influence it. The universe of discourse is therefore large; its terrain is mapped by Pomerleau and Pomerleau (see Chapter 4), and in this chapter only limited areas are discussed.

Smoking and Human Behavior, Edited by T. Ney and A. Gale
© 1989 John Wiley & Sons Ltd

NEUROPHYSIOLOGICAL SUBSTRATES OF MOTIVATION

Reward/punishment systems

Reward systems

The fundamental mechanism for all motivation, and for goal-seeking and avoidance behavior, appears to reside in the reward/punishment pathways of the brain. Activity in this functional system determines the selection of goals, the initiation and maintenance of behaviors required to achieve them, and signals the attainment or nonattainment of such goals. Such activities are closely integrated with those in the systems for arousal and for cognition, learning and memory. Acting in concert the several systems normally promote the pursuit of reward and the avoidance of punishment. Reward systems form the basis for instinctive drives such as hunger, thirst and sex; they are probably the substrate of more complex emotional/cognitive states such as hope and disappointment, and underlie pleasure-seeking and drug-taking behavior.

Electrical stimulation

Reward systems in the brain can be activated in many different ways. Direct electrical stimulation of reward pathways can reinforce behavior, as demonstrated in animals who will work to obtain repeated stimulation. From intracranial self-stimulation experiments the anatomical pathways of reward and the neurotransmitters involved have been grossly defined in animals, and there is evidence that similar systems exist in man (Heath, 1964; Redgrave and Dean, 1981; Routtenberg, 1978). Most, if not all, of the brain sites which support self-stimulation have anatomical connections with limbic system structures, where the emotional, autonomic and motor responses appropriate to reward may be generated. The neurotransmitters involved appear to include noradrenaline, dopamine, and opioid peptides (enkephalin and beta-endorphin), each subserving slightly different functions in the reward process. Dopaminergic systems appear to be particularly involved in the mobilization of behavior, noradrenergic pathways in selecting and steering particular behaviors, and opioid systems in terminating successful behavior by gratification (Stein, 1978). Furthermore, both intracranial self-stimulation and pharmacological experiments suggest that behaviors leading to reward (for example, pursuit behavior such as the chasing of prey in carnivores) are in themselves rewarding (Wise, 1980).

Reinforcing drugs

Certain drugs can act as reinforcers. Animals will learn to self-inject or inhale these drugs or to self-administer them by intragastric tube, and will work either to continue self-administration or to avoid administration of an antagonist (Woods, 1978). Drugs which are reinforcing also enhance electrical self-stimulation via electrodes implanted in reward pathways and lower the stimulus intensity at which such stimulation becomes rewarding. In all cases, reinforcing drugs can be shown to affect one or more of the neurotransmitters involved in reward systems. Drugs which are reinforcing in animals are the same drugs which are abused by man, and include nicotine in their number.

Punishment systems

Reward systems in the brain are reciprocally connected with punishment systems. Anatomical sites where stimulation is apparently aversive have been located and the neurotransmitters involved appear to include acetylcholine (periventricular system) and serotonin (median forebrain bundle, septohippocampal pathways) (Gray, 1981a; Stein, 1968; Stein and Wise, 1974). Because of the reciprocal arrangements, activation of reward pathways reduces activity in punishment pathways, and vice-versa. Furthermore, relative activation or release of rewarding activity can be achieved indirectly by inhibition of punishment activity or relief from punishment. For example, tranquilizers are thought to act by inhibiting activity in aversive serotonergic systems which generate anxiety (Gray, 1981a,b). Anticholinergic drugs (which are sometimes abused, Pullen, Best and Maguire, 1984) may lead to reward by inhibiting activity in cholinergic punishment pathways. Nicotine too, in appropriate doses, can block nicotinic cholinergic receptors.

Conversely, underactivity of reward systems, with resulting overactivity of punishment systems, may account for the withdrawal syndromes associated with drugs of dependence. Relief from such abstinence effects by administration of the addictive drug may constitute its own reward. The extent to which this mechanism is involved in smoking is discussed further below.

Pain and nociception

A large component of the punishment mechanism must be provided by the systems for signaling pain and nociception (see Thompson, 1984a,b, for reviews). These systems are themselves complex, and incorporate not only central pain-signaling pathways, utilizing excitatory transmitters such as the polypeptide substance P, other nonopioid polypeptides, and possibly glutamate and adenosine triphosphate (ATP), but also powerful pain-suppression pathways in the spinal cord and brain. The inhibitory pathways utilize a number of interacting neurotransmitters including noradrenaline, serotonin, possibly dopamine, gamma-aminobutyric acid (GABA), and acetylcholine, and various opioids including enkephalin, beta-endorphin and dynorphin. While enkephalinergic systems in the spinal cord and elsewhere may be tonically active in pain modulation and contribute to the gate-control of pain, the beta-endorphin system and further enkephalinergic activity appear to be triggered into action by noxious stimuli and other stressors (Thompson, 1984a,b). Under a variety of stressful conditions beta-endorphin may be co-released with ACTH from the pituitary, and enkephalins with adrenaline from the adrenal medulla and noradrenaline from peripheral nerves, as part of the general reaction to stress (Hughes, 1983). All these neurotransmitters and neuromodulators can be released by nicotine and cigarette smoking.

Interactions with other systems

No system of the brain functions in isolation. The machinations of the reward/punishment system are operationally indivisible from those of arousal systems and of cognitive, learning and memory systems. The systems are simultaneously active, utilize the same neurotransmitters and neuromodulators, and share overlapping anatomical pathways. Activity in each system is influenced by, and in turn influences, activity in the others. Thus it is impossible to describe motivation without reference to arousal and cognitive systems.

Arousal systems

Arousal systems in the brain appear to include at least two integrated components (Routtenberg, 1968): a general arousal system, which exerts a tonic background control over central nervous system excitability, and a goal-directed or emotional arousal system, which contributes phasic and affective components of arousal, and is also concerned in selective attention. The main anatomical substrates are the reticular activating system (RAS) for general arousal and the limbic system for goal-directed arousal. The two subsystems interact closely with each other. In many ways they can be thought of as complementary, the general arousal system providing a tonic background of cortical responsiveness while the goal-directed system focuses attention onto factors relevant at the moment. However, Routtenberg (1968) proposes that in certain respects the systems are mutually inhibitory, activity in one tending to suppress activity in the other. It appears that there is a dynamic equilibrium between the two systems, and that maximally efficient behavior under different circumstances requires a shifting optimal balance of activity between general and limbic arousal. Furthermore it seems highly likely that the process of changing arousal levels toward the optimum (like other goal-seeking behaviors) is itself rewarding. Such internal rewards presumably provide motivation for efficient performance in changing environments. Drugs or behaviors which facilitate shifts toward optimal arousal levels may thus indirectly stimulate reward systems. There is much evidence that nicotine can modulate arousal in this manner, providing motivation for continued smoking.

It is clear that reward and arousal are not monotonically related. The excitement of the mountain peak and the drowsy numbness of the fireside can be equally rewarding but are accompanied by quite different levels of arousal. As for punishment, boredom or sensory isolation can be as unpleasant as anxiety or overstimulation. Shifts in arousal level toward the rewarding optimum, for the particular circumstances, can thus consist either of increases or decreases in arousal. Such changes are no doubt mediated by different combinations of neurotransmitter activity in arousal and reward systems, catecholamines being generally stimulant and opioids generally depressant in the central nervous system.

Learning and memory systems

Drug-seeking and drug-taking, like electrical self-stimulation in animals, are examples of operant behavior which depend on the learned consequences of the behaviors (Woods, 1978). Learning and memory systems are therefore vital in forming expectations of reward. Indeed, anticipation of pleasure (derived from remembered previous experience) embodies its own reward. Similarly, avoidance behavior involves learning and memory that certain actions will be punished. However, cognitive factors can be of overriding importance in determining whether an effect is *perceived* as rewarding or punishing. Thus, animals can be trained to accept intrinsically punishing stimuli if the consequence of such punishment is later reward. Such cognitive factors are particularly important in man, and may play a crucial role in smoking initiation and cessation: the neophyte smoker persists despite initial nausea, while the abstinent smoker endures withdrawal symptoms in the expectation of distant rewards to his/her health or pocket.

The basis for learning and memory in the nervous system appears to be a process of selection between a range of genetically possible patterns of neural activity, followed by amplification of the selected paths and shutting down of alternative paths (Changeux and Danchin, 1976; Eccles, 1977; Edelman, 1978; Mark, 1978; Marr, 1969; Young, 1979). Much recent work (reviewed by Ashton, 1987a) indicates that the underlying changes occur at synaptic level. Changes in synaptic efficiency have been linked to various forms of learning in animals, including habituation, sensitization, classical conditioning and hippocampal long-term potentiation. There is also evidence for learning-associated changes in synaptic density, growth of new synapses, activation of previously 'silent' synapses, alterations in dendritic spines, and collateral sprouting of neurons. These changes involve almost all brain areas, but limbic structures, such as the locus coeruleus and amygdala, hippocampus and thalamus, as well as the cerebral cortex, have been shown to make specific contributions.

Many neurotransmitters are involved in this process, but several authors (Deutsch, 1971; Drachman, 1978; Dunn, 1980; Squire and Davis, 1981) have argued that it is in cholinergic synapses that specific alterations related to memory occur. In man, cholinergic antagonists such as scopolamine have profound effects on memory which are reversed by the cholinergic agent physostigmine (Drachman, 1978). More recent work (Lynch and Baudry, 1984) suggests a specific role for glutamate. Biogenic amines and polypeptides, such as ACTH and vasopressin, appear to act as modulators which can influence the development, maintenance and expression of memories, while oxytocin and beta-endorphin may participate in a neurohumoral system which induces forgetting rather than remembering (Izquierdo, 1982). Since nicotine is concentrated in brain areas subserving particular memory functions, and produces effects on nearly all the biochemical mediators (see below), it is not surprising to find that smoking has subtle effects on memory (Mangan and Golding, 1983b).

Constitutional and environmental factors

Susceptibility to reward and punishment, and also intrinsic levels of activity in arousal systems, vary considerably between individuals. Such constitutional variables, perhaps genetically 'hard-wired' in the brain, are among the factors which determine personality characteristics, such as neuroticism, psychoticism and introversion/extraversion (Eysenck, 1983; Eysenck and Eysenck, 1975; Gray, 1972), responsivity to environmental pressures, sensitivity to psychotropic drugs and the ability to develop drug tolerance. All these variables undoubtedly affect an individual's motivation to adopt certain behavior patterns and may crucially influence the initiation, maintenance and cessation of smoking. In this respect they constitute a 'baseline' or 'starting state' of susceptibility to smoking and nicotine.

Smokers as a group are significantly (though only slightly) different from nonsmokers even before taking up the habit (Cherry and Kiernan, 1976, 1978). Two main types at higher risk can be identified: the underaroused 'sensation seeker' (Zuckerman, 1979, 1983) and the emotionally labile 'neurotic' (Mangan and Golding, 1983a). The former, who are relatively insensitive to punishment, may tend to adopt smoking behavior as a stimulating reward; the latter, who are more sensitive to punishment, may tend to fulfill their needs by using smoking as a tranquilizer or 'emotional anesthetic'. The ability of nicotine to exert both stimulant and relaxing effects is discussed further below. There is evidence, derived from other descriptors of personality, that smoking produces different effects on EEG frequency in 'Type A' and 'Type B' personalities (Cinciripini, 1986). However, most individuals occupy the middle ground between personality extremes; for the majority of potential smokers peer-group, family and other sociological and environmental pressures are of crucial importance in both initiation and maintenance of the behavior (Mangan and Golding, 1983a, 1984).

THE IMPORTANCE OF NICOTINE

Smoking is unarguably a drug-taking behavior directed toward the self-administration of nicotine. The evidence that nicotine is the primary reinforcer for smoking is well established and includes the following observations:

(1) Nicotine is absorbed from tobacco smoke in sufficient quantities to produce clear-cut pharmacological effects in the brain.
(2) The most popular form of nicotine self-administration, inhalation of cigarette smoke, is the most rate- and concentration-efficient method for delivering nicotine to the brain.
(3) Nicotine is the main pharmacologically active constituent obtained from all the various forms of tobacco use: inhalation of tobacco smoke, noninhalation of pipe and cigar smoke, tobacco snuffing and tobacco chewing.
(4) Animals will voluntarily self-administer nicotine orally or intravenously and inhale tobacco smoke; certain doses of nicotine reduce electrical self-stimulation thresholds.
(5) Self-administration of nicotine can be altered in both animals and humans by central (but not peripheral) nicotinic cholinergic receptor antagonists.
(6) Smokers down-regulate and up-regulate nicotine intake in the face of variations in tobacco nicotine delivery.
(7) Smoking or snuffing behavior in man is not practised in the absence of known pharmacological reinforcers such as opiates, cannabis, cocaine, organic solvents, or nicotine.

To stress the importance of nicotine is not to deny the contribution of other factors in determining smoking behavior. Countless other, mostly learned or associated, clues add to smoking satisfaction, as discussed below (see also Figure 1). Tar components provide taste and smell, and are responsible for the 'scratch' of inhaled smoke at the back of the throat; these characteristics are used by practised smokers as cues for estimating the nicotine strength of the cigarette (Rose, 1987). Manipulations, lighting-up routines, situational and social pressures all play a part, but these factors lose their motivational power without the reinforcing effect of nicotine. Therefore, in developing a

SMOKING REWARDED   SMOKING PUNISHED

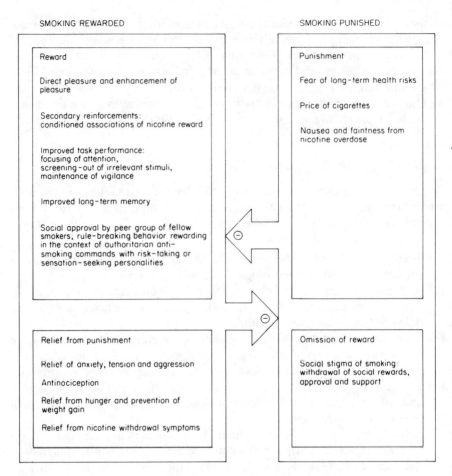

Fig. 1 Rewarding and punishing reinforcers for smoking. Omission of reward is viewed as equivalent to punishment; similarly relief of punishment is viewed as equivalent to reward. These relationships, together with the reciprocally inhibitory reward and punishment systems, are loosely based on Gray's (1972) model of CNS reinforcing systems. ⊖ : Indicates inhibition

general theory of smoking, it is important to inquire how nicotine affects the basic brain systems involved in motivation.

General pharmacology of nicotine

The pharmacology of nicotine has been reviewed by many authors (Ashton and Stepney, 1982; Mangan and Golding, 1984; Russell, 1976). Only features directly relevant to the present discussion are mentioned here. Of pharmacokinetic factors, the delivery of nicotine to the brain from inhalations of tobacco smoke in the form of intermittent, highly concentrated boli appears to be of great importance. The same total dose when delivered at a more constant rate does not produce the same pharmacological effects (Armitage, Hall and Sellers, 1969). Inhaled nicotine reaches the brain within 7–8 seconds, where it is highly concentrated. Areas of high-affinity nicotine binding, according to rat brain studies (Jenner, Kumar, Marsden, Reavill and Stolerman, 1986) are, in decreasing order of magnitude: hypothalamus, thalamus, cortex, striatum, hippocampus, pons medulla, and cerebellum.

Pharmacodynamically, the most important property of nicotine is its interaction with nicotinic cholinergic receptors. Nicotine exerts a biphasic, dose-dependent, stimulant/depressant effect on these receptors at cholinergic synapses (Armitage et al., 1969; Ashton, Marsh, Millman, Rawlins, Telford and Thompson, 1980). The initial combination of nicotine with the receptor stimulates a response, but persistent occupation of the receptors and prolonged effects on the neural membrane may block further responses. In general, small doses of nicotine produce predominantly stimulant effects at synapses and larger doses produce mainly depressant effects. Recent work (reviewed by Karlin, Kao and DiPaola, 1986) demonstrating that the nicotinic acetylcholine receptor exists in four dynamically interchangeable states of sensitivity to agonist effects (and affinity for agonists), may further explain the biphasic effects of nicotine. The permutations of receptor activity include receptive, active, and fast and slow desensitized (inactive) states. It seems likely that different concentrations and rates of delivery of nicotine may have differential effects on the balance between the various functional receptor states, and hence on the consequent pharmacological effects. The effects of smoking may to a large extent depend upon the delivery of rapidly fluctuating concentrations of nicotine at its site of action. In addition, there is evidence that cholinergic receptors in the brain may not all be of the classical muscarinic/nicotinic types (Abood, Lowy and Booth, 1979; Abood, Reynolds, Booth and Bidlack, 1981). The interaction of nicotine with 'nonclassical' cholinergic receptor subtypes is unknown.

The ability of the smoker to achieve fingertip control over his self-administered nicotine dosage has long been recognized (Armitage, 1978) and remains an important feature in smoking behavior. The time/dose relationships of nicotine reaching the brain can be such as to produce either stimulant or depressant effects. Thus, by varying factors such as size of puff and depth of inhalation, a smoker can obtain predominantly inhibitory or predominantly excitatory effects, or a mixture of both, from one cigarette. The ease with which nicotine can produce rapid, reversible, biphasic effects over a small dose range is probably an important factor in determining its subtle effects on many brain functions, and in maintaining smoking motivation.

As mentioned in the previous discussion, cholinergic pathways are involved in many behavioral (as well as somatic) systems. Thus nicotine actions at cholinergic synapses can affect almost every body system. In addition, because of the arrangement of the central nervous system in interlinked multitransmitter pathways, cholinergic stimulation by nicotine leads to the release of many other neurotransmitters and neuromodulators, each of which can produce further effects. There is evidence that nicotine and smoking can provoke the central release of noradrenaline, dopamine, beta-endorphin, ACTH and a number of other substances (Marty, Erwin, Cornell and Zgombick, 1984). Some consequences of such release on reward/punishment, arousal, and learning and memory are discussed further below. In addition, smoking and nicotine produce widespread peripheral effects which affect the autonomic nervous system and include release of noradrenaline and cortisol. The peripheral effects are not discussed in detail here.

Positive reward: direct reinforcement

There is now abundant evidence from animal work (some of which has already been cited) that nicotine and tobacco smoke have direct reinforcing properties (Ando and Yanagita, 1981; Jarvik, 1973; Risner and Goldberg, 1983; Singer, Oei and Wallace, 1982). Such evidence has in practice been difficult to obtain since, unlike humans, animals lack incentives to start smoking, and unlike some other rewarding drugs (amphetamines) nicotine becomes aversive above a critical dose level. A direct rewarding action could account in large measure for the fact that the vast majority of human smokers (including chronic, regular smokers) find smoking pleasurable (*British Medical Journal*, 1968) in a wide variety of circumstances.

Possible mechanisms by which nicotine could stimulate reward pathways in the brain are gradually emerging. In some important studies, Pomerleau and his colleagues (Pomerleau, Fertig, Seyler and Jaffe, 1983; Pomerleau and Pomerleau, 1984) showed that cigarette smoking in man causes an increase in plasma concentrations of beta-endorphin, and that there is a positive correlation between plasma beta-endorphin and nicotine concentrations after smoking. These findings suggest the possibility that the direct reinforcing properties of nicotine result, at least in part, from stimulation of opioid-mediated reward mechanisms.

However, the role of beta-endorphin in the reward process is not clear. This opioid is found in highest concentrations in the pituitary and hypothalamus, and has been regarded as a neurotransmitter mainly for neuroendocrine functions and modulation of nociception. In many limbic reward areas (amygdala, nucleus accumbens, septum, hippocampus and others) the opioid found in highest concentration is metenkephalin rather than beta-endorphin. Nevertheless, hypothalamic areas also support electrical self-stimulation in animals and form part of the reward pathways. Furthermore, beta-endorphin, like the enkephalins, is an agonist of mu and delta opioid receptors, which appear to be involved in the euphoric effects of opiates (Atweh and Kuhar, 1983; Hughes and Kosterlitz, 1983; Koob and Bloom, 1983).

Nor is it clear whether there is a relationship between blood and brain concentrations of opioids. It has been suggested (Pomerleau and Pomerleau, 1984) that direct release of beta-endorphin and perhaps other opioids occurs in the brain in parallel to the peripheral release during smoking. A central cholinergic beta-endorphin releasing pathway has been demonstrated (Risch, Cohen, Janowsky, Kalin and Murphy, 1980; Risch, Kalin, Janowsky, Cohen, Pickar and Murphy, 1983) and it is possible that this pathway is stimulated by nicotine. However, Risch et al. (1980, 1983) found that elevation of plasma beta-endorphin and ACTH induced by the cholinergic agent physostigmine was significantly correlated with negative affect, increase in depression and hostility ratings, and decrease in arousal in normal volunteers. This apparently contradictory finding has not been explained.

A definite relationship between beta-endorphin concentrations during smoking and subjective mood change or smoking satisfaction has yet to be demonstrated. However, the selective opioid receptor antagonist, naloxone, has been reported to decrease the subjective pleasure of smoking (Palmer and Berens, 1983), a finding supported by isolated clinical observations (Stepney, personal communication). Karras and Kane (1980) found that naloxone, compared with a placebo, decreased the desire to smoke and the amount actually smoked in six out of seven subjects, although ratings of satisfaction and mood were not significantly affected. This finding was not supported by Nemeth-Coslett and Griffiths (1986), who found no differences in smoking behavior between placebo conditions and after a range of doses of naloxone in another seven subjects. Naltrexone (a long-acting opiate antagonist) likewise did not change cigarette smoking behavior over a ten day maintenance period in one heroin addict (Mello, Mendelson, Sellers and Kuehnle, 1980a).

On the other hand, the opioid agonists heroin and methodone, and the mixed agonist/antagonist buprenorphine, have been reliably observed to increase cigarette smoking in heroin addicts (Mello, Lukas and Mendelson, 1985). A dose relationship has been demonstrated, an increase in the number of cigarettes smoked occurring at higher opiate dosages and a decrease in the number of cigarettes smoked occurring during detoxification and reduction of opiate dosage.

These data on the effects of opioid agonists and antagonists on smoking behavior are difficult to interpret. Do exogenous opioids increase the pleasure of smoking, or do they merely block aversive effects which would otherwise limit smoking? The apparently enhancing effect of opiates on smoking is reminiscent of the finding that reinforcing drugs increase the rate of (already rewarding) electrical self-stimulation in animals, and the observation that smokers often smoke to enhance the pleasure of an already pleasurable situation. An increase in smoking is also associated with other drugs such as amphetamine (Henningfield and Griffiths, 1981), and alcohol (Mello, Mendelson, Sellers and Kuehnle, 1980b), which have rewarding effects and are unlikely to increase smoking merely by blocking its aversive effects. The evidence concerning opioid antagonists is conflicting. Further studies are needed with more detailed observations of their effects, if any, on smoking behavior, including blood nicotine levels obtained, puffing characteristics such as strength of draw, plasma concentrations of beta-endorphin, and smoking satisfaction in different circumstances. For example, differences in the rate of resting beta-endorphin secretion, or in the manner of smoking under different levels of environmental stress or relaxation, may explain the divergent results on the effect of naloxone on smoking.

In spite of these as yet inconclusive data, the finding that smoking liberates beta-endorphin is important, and it would be surprising if this powerful opioid did not contribute to smoking reward. Nevertheless, although nicotine is clearly a drug of addiction, it must be admitted that its evident effects on reward systems are probably the least understood of its many pharmacological actions.

Other polypeptides released, in a dose-dependent manner, by nicotine and smoking, include arginine vasopressin, its carrier protein neurophysin I and alpha-MSH (Pomerleau, Fertig, Seyler and Jaffe, 1983b). These peptides may have effects on memory and are discussed further below. ACTH, along with growth hormone and prolactin, appear to be released only at aversive nicotine concentrations, when nausea also occurs. Secretion of ACTH and polypeptides, including beta-endorphin, is induced by stress and there is evidence for co-secretion of alpha-MSH and ACTH, and of beta-endorphin and ACTH from the pituitary in a number of conditions. However, smoking can increase peripheral release of beta-endorphin at nicotine concentrations which do not stimulate ACTH release.

It therefore seems unlikely that ACTH is directly involved in the hedonic effects of smoking. Bourne (1985) (see also West, 1985) reported that ACTH injections alleviate smoking withdrawal symptoms and also simulate the pleasurable 'lift' of smoking. This effect may possibly be due to ACTH-induced liberation of cortisol from the adrenal cortex. Smoking and nicotine have been found in several studies to increase plasma cortisol concentrations. This can occur without an increase in ACTH and must therefore result from some mechanism not mediated by ACTH. There is some evidence that cortisol is involved in mood control, and increased concentrations of endogenous and exogenous glucocorticoids can produce euphoria (Haynes and Murad, 1980). However, concentrations of cortisol may be critical for such an effect, and there is no evidence that peripherally released corticosteroids are directly involved in central reward systems or in smoking pleasure (although they may play a part in craving and in withdrawal effects).

Central release of catecholamines by nicotine may contribute to the positive reward of smoking. Nicotine and cigarette smoke release noradrenaline and dopamine from limbic areas and hypothalamus in animals (Hall and Turner, 1972). The exact role of noradrenaline in reward systems is at present not clear, although it is implicated in much of the early work (Stein, 1978). However, it is generally agreed that dopamine is a transmitter in some reward pathways (Redgrave and Dean, 1981; Routtenberg, 1978; Stein, 1978; Wise, 1980). Drugs which inhibit dopamine synthesis or block dopamine receptors disrupt intracranial self-stimulation from a number of sites, including the locus coeruleus, a predominantly noradrenergic structure. When dopamine blockade is limited to one hemisphere, self-stimulation responses are suppressed for that hemisphere but not for the other. Dopamine blockade also increases the threshold for self-stimulation in a dose-dependent manner, while drugs which release dopamine (amphetamine, nicotine) or stimulate dopamine receptors (apomorphine) can increase rates of self-stimulation. Apomorphine is avidly self-administered even after catecholamine depletion, but self-administration is blocked by dopamine receptor antagonists. Wise (1980) concluded that dopamine receptor activation can itself be rewarding, and Royall and Klemm (1981) suggested that dopamine plays a role in the perceived hedonic quality of natural rewards. Furthermore, a dopaminergic link may be involved in opioid reward systems, either by co-release of dopamine and opioids from the same neurons, or by parallel or sequential opioid–dopaminergic pathways (Cooper, 1984; Stein, 1978). Thus the nicotine in cigarette smoke may initiate a cascade of activity in the multiple neurotransmitter systems subserving direct reward in the brain.

The mechanisms of the relationship between smoking and reduced caloric intake and weight are unknown, but may involve effects on hypothalamic appetite and satiety centres (Morley and Levine, 1983), cortisol or catecholamine-mediated effects on blood sugar (Pomerleau and Pomerleau, 1984) and nicotine-induced elevation of metabolic rate. Decreased weight is unlikely to be important as a direct motivator for smoking, but becomes important as a cognitive factor mitigating against giving up smoking (Figure 1).

Negative reward: relief of punishment

Cigarette smoking can relieve a number of aversive emotional states such as anxiety, frustration and aggression. Pomerleau, Turk and Fertig (1984) have recently demonstrated anxiolytic effects of smoking in minimally deprived smokers using an unsolvable anagram test. These results extend previous work showing that smoking increases the amount of slow alpha-activity in the EEG under conditions of mild stress induced by white noise (Golding and Mangan, 1982a), speeds habituation to irrelevant stimuli (Golding and

Mangan, 1982b), reduces muscle tension and spinal reflexes (Domino, 1979; Domino and Von Baumgarten, 1969) and exerts apparent anxiolytic effects in animals (Bättig, 1980; Fleming and Broadhurst, 1975). Anti-aggressive effects of smoking have been demonstrated in deprived smokers (Dunn, 1978; Heimstra, 1973) and in animals (Bernston, Beattie and Walker, 1976; Hutchinson and Emley, 1973). These findings confirm the subjective reports of smokers that they sometimes smoke to calm themselves, and observations that smokers smoke more, and more intensely, in stressful situations including noise, shock or social stress (Dobbs, Strickler and Maxwell, 1981; Golding and Mangan, 1982a; Schachter, Silverstein, Kozlowski, Perlick, Herman and Liebling, 1977). As yet, anxiolytic effects of smoking have not been directly related to plasma nicotine concentrations, but the fact that sham smoking (Golding and Mangan, 1982a) and no-nicotine cigarettes (Pomerleau et al., 1984) were relatively ineffective point to nicotine as the main anxiolytic agent.

Smoking has also been shown to have antinociceptive effects. Nesbitt (1973) and Silverstein (1982) found that smoking increased the pain threshold to electric shocks, and that the increasing threshold was proportional to the nicotine content of the cigarettes. Pomerleau et al. (1984) and Fertig, Pomerleau and Sanders (1986) demonstrated that smoking raised pain aware-ness and pain tolerance thresholds, and also reduced the perception of pain in the McGill Pain Questionnaire, in minimally deprived smokers smoking their usual cigarettes, versus nicotine-free cigarettes. A variety of animal tests have likewise suggested antinociceptive effects of nicotine (Sahley and Bernston, 1979; Tripathi, Martin and Aceto, 1982).

The mechanisms underlying these tranquilizing and antinociceptive effects of smoking are probably multiple. Firstly, certain doses of nicotine, by a depressant effect at cholinergic synapses, may reduce activity in cholinergic punishment pathways such as the periventricular system. Secondly, release of beta-endorphin is probably important for both anxiolytic and analgesic effects and Pomerleau et al. (1984) note that the subject who achieved the greatest pain and anxiety reduction in their experiments was the one with the highest smoking-induced plasma beta-endorphin concentrations in a previous experiment. However, neither plasma beta-endorphin nor nicotine concen-trations have yet been correlated with antinociceptive or tranquilizing effects. Thirdly, nicotine-induced release of catecholamines may contribute to these effects by activating pain suppression systems and stimulating reward systems. It is likely that antinociception itself is a by-product rather than a motivator of smoking in most situations, but the anxiolytic and anti-aggressive effects are almost certainly important in the use of smoking as a coping response to stress.

Withdrawal effects

The effects of smoking described above can all occur in the absence of smoking deprivation. Yet the majority of smokers say that they would stop if they could (National Cancer Institute, 1977). Only a small proportion succeed. One reason that smokers have difficulty in stopping is that smoking cessation can give rise to a definite abstinence syndrome. Abstinence effects in cigarette smokers have recently been measured in a controlled study (Hatsukami, Hughes, Pickens and Svikis, 1984) and found to include the following significant effects compared to continuing smokers: decreased heart rate, increased food intake and weight, craving for tobacco, confusion, depression/dejection, sleep disturbance and poor concentration. Other findings after smoking cessation include nausea, headache, gastrointestinal disturbances, anxiety, restlessness, irritability, sweating, tremor, hypotension, increased noradrenaline secretion, and slowing of EEG activity (for reviews see: Ashton and Stepney, 1982; Mangan and Golding, 1984; Shiffman, 1979). Symptoms and signs start within 24 hours of withdrawal, reach a maximum within a week, and then gradually decline. The syndrome may, however, be prolonged: noradrenaline excretion may be still elevated after fifteen days (Turnbull and Kelvin, 1971) and craving, though intermittent, and often triggered by environmental cues, may still be intense for over a year (Ashton and Stepney, 1982).

Craving

The symptom of craving is common to the abstinence syndromes of many drugs of dependence. Its intensity appears to be directly related to the degree to which the drug activates reward systems in the brain, and (in animals) supports self-administration and lowers the threshold for intracranial electrical self-stimulation. Thus, craving is a marked feature of opiate and alcohol withdrawal, is not severe in benzodiazepine withdrawal in spite of the presence of other widespread withdrawal symptoms (Ashton, 1984), and is absent from drugs such as chlorpromazine which do not support self-stimulation in animals. Craving is usually drug-specific and is clearly an initiator of goal-directed, drug-seeking behavior, involving reward/punishment mechanisms and limbic arousal systems. Decreases in brain and cerebrospinal fluid concentrations of opioids and opioid-like substances have been demonstrated in abstaining alcohol and opiate abusers (Herz, 1981; Sjoquist, Eriksson and Winblad, 1982). It has been suggested that this opioid deficiency underlies the craving. Endogenous opioid concentrations have not yet been explored in tobacco abstinence, although Pomerleau, Scherzer, Grunberg, Pomerleau, Judge, Fertig and Burleson (1987) found a trend toward decreased desire to smoke after acute exercise which considerably elevated plasma beta-endorphin concentrations in smokers. Exercise-induced release of beta-endorphin may partly explain the inverse correlation between smoking in high-risk personalities and physical exercise found in larger surveys (Golding and Cornish, 1987).

Surprisingly, craving for cigarettes in abstaining smokers does not appear to be satisfied by nicotine chewing gum, despite alleviation of other withdrawal symptoms (Henningfield, 1987; Jasinski, 1987; Rose, 1987; West, 1987). Possibly, nicotine from this source does not reach sufficiently high concentrations in the brain, or does not attain sufficient levels rapidly enough. It may be that the hedonic effect of nicotine depends on the intermittent delivery of high-concentration nicotine boli to the brain, as obtained by inhalations of puffs of tobacco smoke. With this mode of administration, brain nicotine concentrations fluctuate, with small 'fronts' of rapidly rising concentration. In this way the cholinergic receptors receiving the leading edge of each bolus might maintain a high-affinity state, whereas steady concentrations of nicotine, as from nicotine chewing gum, might favor the low-affinity receptor state.

Although an uncounted number of individuals apparently stop smoking without difficulty, in others the abstinence syndrome can be severe. In these, the syndrome clearly represents a dysphoric, aversive, 'punishment' condition. It is immediately alleviated by renewed smoking, which in this case provides indirect reward by relief of punishment. The existence of an abstinence syndrome, and its obviation by continued smoking, clearly constitutes a powerful motivator for smoking maintenance. Indeed, the addiction model of smoking (see below) postulates that established smokers continue smoking not for direct rewards but to obtain relief from the punishment of withdrawal effects. Adherents of this model (Schachter, 1978, 1979; Silverstein, Kozlowski and Schachter, 1977) have suggested that the anxiolytic and antinociceptive effects of smoking result indirectly from alleviation of the anxiety and hypersensitivity induced by smoking deprivation. However, a number of investigators (Fertig et al., 1986; Golding and Mangan, 1982a; Pomerleau et al., 1984) (as mentioned above) have shown that smoking can also produce these effects in minimally deprived (one hour) smokers.

Tolerance

The smoking withdrawal syndrome can in general be accounted for by 'rebound' effects resulting from homeostatic adaptations to the biphasic stimulant/depressant actions of nicotine in many systems (Ashton and Stepney, 1982). Such adaptations imply the development of nicotine tolerance. The mechanisms of drug tolerance are complex and as yet somewhat obscure. Pharmacokinetic tolerance (increased rate of metabolism by induction of hepatic drug-metabolizing enzymes) has been well studied for nicotine and other drugs. It probably contributes little to withdrawal effects, apart from determining their rate of onset. Pharmacodynamic tolerance (reviewed by Ashton, 1987a) appears to result from a variety of tissue adaptations which, after chronic administration, decrease the response to a drug at its site of action. These adaptations include receptor modulation, with changes in receptor density and affinity, and changes in transmitter release. Chronic pharmacodynamic tolerance develops unevenly in smokers who become tolerant to the emetic and irritant effects of nicotine (see Figure 2a) but who still exhibit tachycardia, rise in blood pressure, peripheral vasoconstriction, and endocrine and metabolic responses to smoking. Some aspects of tolerance appear to subside rapidly in the absence of nicotine: in chronic smokers the first cigarette of the day elicits greater cardiovascular responses than later cigarettes, and many smokers say that they derive the greatest hedonic effects from the first daily cigarette. The question of how much tolerance develops to the hedonic effects of addictive drugs in general is controversial. Many studies have shown little tolerance to the effects of intracranial self-stimulation (Bush, Bush and Miller, 1976; Kornetsky, Esposito, McLean and Jacobson, 1979; Lorens, 1976; Olds and Travis, 1960; Pert and Hulsebus, 1975). In man, it has been claimed that eventually many opiate addicts take the drugs to avoid withdrawal effects rather than to receive rewarding effects. However, Kornetsky et al. (1979) quote evidence that opiate addicts still experience a 'rush' and a sustained 'high', and that these effects are continued over the entire course of addiction. Reports from chronic smokers suggest that the milder hedonic effects of nicotine can be similarly enduring. Habitual smokers continue to release beta-endorphin on smoking, and it is likely that they derive *both* direct rewards and protection from withdrawal effects.

With many drugs of dependence, the development of tolerance leads to dosage escalation in an attempt to obtain the original drug effect in the face of counteracting body defenses. Thus, narcotics addicts may exceed a dose that would produce fatal respiratory depression in a naive subject, and alcoholics may retain their composure at blood alcohol concentrations that would fell a teetotaller. Such gross escalation of dosage does not occur with smoking. Since the rewarding effects are probably derived from a combination of stimulant and inhibitory actions, and since most smokers seek both these effects, they may be forced into maintaining a medium dosage. Any substantial dosage increase would lead to a predominance of inhibitory and aversive effects (such as nausea) and would simultaneously deprive the smoker of stimulant effects.

Pharmacodynamic changes at the primary site of drug action do not appear to account for all the observed phenomena of tolerance, particularly for drugs of dependence. It has been argued that adaptations in behavior through learning and memory processes (behavioral tolerance) are also involved

(Bierness and Vogel-Sprott, 1984; Demellweek and Goudie, 1983; Goudie and Griffiths, 1986; Siegel, 1975, 1983). For example, rats can learn to overcome the ataxic effects of alcohol if the absence of ataxia is rewarded or its presence punished. Such behavioral modifications may involve several processes, including operant and classical conditioning, habituation and various cognitive processes which compensate for drug-induced disruption of performance. The concept of behavioral tolerance has been particularly applied to drugs such as alcohol and opiates, which severely disrupt performance, but seems less applicable to smoking, since nicotine (almost uniquely amongst addictive drugs) does not seriously disrupt performance, and can even improve it, while still providing reinforcement in nondeprived smokers.

Nevertheless, a smoker must no doubt learn to enjoy smoking, and this process may involve the development of both pharmacodynamic and behavioral tolerance to its aversive effects. Learned cues are almost certainly associated with craving, withdrawal effects, and with smoking behavior in general. The importance of conditioning in human addictive behavior has been clearly demonstrated for heroin and alcohol abuse, and also in obesity (Pomerleau, 1981). No particular neurophysiological mechanisms are assumed to explain behavioral tolerance. It seems likely that many of them are similar to those which underlie learning and memory, involving synaptic changes with receptor modulation and alterations in neurotransmitter release (reviewed by Ashton, 1987a). Thus, drugs may produce adaptive changes not only at their primary sites of action but also in the pathways subserving the particular behaviors and processes which they influence. It could be argued that both these changes are essentially pharmacodynamic tolerance.

Effects on arousal

There is a wealth of evidence that smoking and nicotine affect activity in arousal systems. Animal work, pioneered by Armitage et al. (1969), Domino (1967, 1973), and Hall (1970), showed that small doses of nicotine or cigarette smoke exert powerful alerting effects in many species. Such effects are blocked by mecamylamine and are accompanied by increased output of acetylcholine from the cerebral cortex and by release of noradrenaline from other parts of the brain (Hall and Turner, 1972). Exposure to higher concentrations of nicotine can in certain circumstances cause decrease in electrocortical arousal accompanied by decrease in cortical output of acetylcholine (Armitage et al., 1969). These effects have been interpreted as demonstrating the classical biphasic actions of nicotine in first stimulating and then blocking cholinergic synapses in arousal systems in the brain.

In humans, there is evidence of similar effects from subjective reports, performance studies and electroencephalographic recordings. A large percentage of smokers report that an important motivation for smoking is that it helps them to remain alert in boring situations and to think and concentrate. Objective measurements of performance (reviewed by Mangan and Golding, 1984; Wesnes and Warburton, 1978) in general show that smoking can improve psychomotor performance in a number of tasks, increase speed and accuracy of information processing, facilitate selective attention and sustain vigilance in nondeprived smokers. Investigations of electroencephalographic activity have shown that smoking can increase low-voltage, high-frequency beta activity and increase alpha frequency (Golding, 1988; Lambiase and Serra, 1957; Murphree, Pfeiffer and Price, 1967) and both smoking and intravenous nicotine can increase the amplitude of cortical evoked potentials (Ashton, Millman, Telford and Thompson, 1974; Ashton et al., 1980; Eysenck and O'Connor, 1979). These effects involve activation of both reticular and limbic arousal systems and participation of both cholinergic and noradrenergic mechanisms (Rebert, 1972; Thompson, Ashton, Golding and Marsh, 1986; Timsit-Berthier, 1981).

Many smokers also report that smoking calms them down, especially in stressful situations. In support of this claim, there is evidence that nicotine and smoking can protect against the disruptive effects of stress on performance (Dunn, 1978) and that smokers tend to smoke more in stressful circumstances (Schachter et al., 1977). In EEG studies in man, Mangan and Golding (1978) showed that under mild stress smoking increased EEG alpha activity, indicating a dearousing effect. Ashton et al. (1974) found that in some subjects natural smoking decreased the magnitude of the contingent negative variation (CNV), an evoked potential thought to reflect cortical arousal (Rebert, 1972). Furthermore, in individuals, small intravenous doses of nicotine increased CNV magnitude while larger doses decreased it (both doses were within the range available from ordinary cigarette smoking). These studies provide evidence for dose-related central nervous system stimulant and depressant effects of smoking and nicotine in humans. The mechanism for the depressant effects may be a blocking action by critical doses of nicotine at central cholinergic synapses, and it may also involve release of endogenous opioids.

Since there is a U-shaped relationship between arousal level and performance (Corcoran, 1965) and an optimal level of arousal for maximal efficiency at each level of task difficulty, the ability of nicotine to modulate arousal in either direction confers on it the ability to improve performance under a wide range of conditions. The dosage range of nicotine required to obtain either stimulant or depressant effects is easily available from a cigarette, and there is some indirect evidence that smokers do in fact manipulate their dosage according to task difficulty (Ashton and Watson, 1970). As mentioned above, shifts in arousal level towards the optimum are likely to be rewarding (Figure 2b): reward and arousal are not monotonically related, as illustrated by the fact that two of the most potent reinforcing drugs, cocaine and

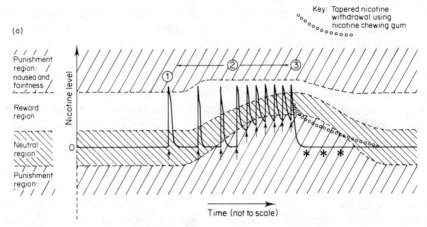

Fig. 2   Neither the nicotine addiction nor the arousal modulation models fully account for all the observations concerning smoking motivation even if combined, e.g., see Figure 1. The processes envisaged by both models doubtless occur simultaneously but with weightings varying with smokers over time and between individual smokers as a function of variation in CNS control systems (perhaps indirectly reflected in personality). See text for more details.

Fig. 2a   Nicotine addiction model of smoking

(1) Novice smoker experiences direct pharmacological reward from nicotine (first arrow) but may also experience transient aversive effects from nicotine overdose, e.g. nausea and faintness. However, some limited tolerance to the aversive effects of nicotine overdose rapidly develops and, more importantly, the novice smoker learns to down-regulate nicotine intake, thus avoiding aversive nicotine overdose.

(2) Smoking continues (arrows). However, tolerance gradually develops to the rewarding effects of nicotine, and receptor(s)/secondarily released neurotransmitter(s) concentration(s) adapt to levels that signal punishment in the *absence* of nicotine. Consequently the smoker receives reduced direct pharmacological reward from nicotine, and smoking behavior becomes increasingly reinforced by the avoidance of, or relief of, nicotine withdrawal symptoms.

(3) Smoker gives up smoking. An aversive nicotine withdrawal syndrome occurs over days or weeks (stars) which may prompt relapse to smoking. However, the target receptor(s)/secondarily released neurotransmitter(s) level(s) readapt to the presmoking state. (Nicotine chewing gum may offer some amelioration of withdrawal symptoms.) Once readaptation has occurred there should be no desire, prompted by nicotine withdrawal, to relapse to smoking, although any subsequent cigarette smoked re-produces the original direct pharmacological reward at full strength and may rapidly reinstate the nicotine addiction state.

morphine, alter arousal levels in opposite directions. The use of nicotine to facilitate arousal shifts may be a potent motivator for smoking, especially since smoking in circumstances requiring particular levels of arousal (e.g. while concentrating, while telephoning, etc.) quickly becomes a learned behavior. Deterioration in performance and concentration is a prominent smoking-withdrawal effect, and is particularly noticeable during activities previously associated with smoking.

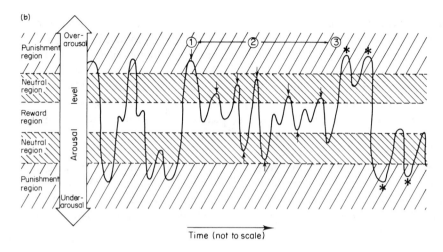

Fig. 2b Arousal modulation model (psychological tool, stimulus filter models) of smoking

(1) Novice smoker learns that nicotine from a cigarette (first arrow) shifts arousal from an aversive level (under- or overarousal) toward an optimal level, signalling CNS reward. Nicotine intake is self-regulated to obtain stimulant (low nicotine dose) or depressant (high nicotine dose) effects, as appropriate to the desired arousal level. Smoking-induced shifts from the 'neutral arousal zones' toward the optimum arousal level are also rewarding.

(2) Smoker continues to smoke using smoking (arrows) as a tool to achieve arousal homeostasis in the face of stress, anxiety, boredom, fatigue, etc. Smoking may occur in response to these states or in anticipation of avoiding them. Smoking in the 'neutral arousal zones' will continue to produce some reward by moving arousal level toward the optimum.

(3) Smoker gives up smoking. Arousal homeostasis is lost and consequently arousal level frequently moves into punishing regions (over- or under-arousal), occasions which may prompt the desire to relapse to smoking (stars). This state continues indefinitely unless alternate strategies of arousal/mood control are learnt by the ex-smoker, e.g. use of yoga, exercise, etc.

Effects on learning and memory

Smoking and nicotine have definite though subtle effects on learning and memory. In animals and humans these effects are complex, dose-related, and biphasic; in general smoking appears to improve selective attention and memory consolidation, while not affecting or slightly impairing initial learning (Andersson, 1975; Andersson and Hockey, 1977; Mangan and Golding, 1978, 1983b; Myrsten and Andersson, 1978; Peeke and Peeke, 1984; Wesnes and Warburton, 1978; Williams, 1980). As with other drugs, these effects may be state-dependent (Lowe, 1986; Warburton, Wesnes, Shergold and James,

1986). Such effects are not surprising in view of the importance of cholinergic mechanisms in learning and memory. In addition, smoking releases arginine vasopressin, which may possibly be involved in memory (Kovacs, Bohus, Vesteeg, Telgedy and deWied, 1982; Pomerleau et al., 1983b), and also releases noradrenaline which appears to modulate memory by affecting selective attention and probably other processes, as discussed above.

The effects of smoking on learning and memory are unlikely in themselves to be important motivators for smoking; indeed most smokers are unaware of them. However, such effects may contribute to the modulation of arousal toward optimal levels and thus indirectly increase smoking rewards. The amnesic effects of beta-endorphin released by smoking may contribute to the tranquilizing effects, since endogenous opioids appear to be involved in a neurohumoral system for forgetting, especially for memories associated with pain (Izquierdo, 1982).

SYNTHESIS OF SMOKING MODELS

The preceding discussion has attempted to show (1) that brain systems are so interlinked that their functions cannot be meaningfully separated, and (2) that nicotine and smoking affect simultaneously all the major functional systems governing behavior—those for reward/punishment, for arousal, and for learning and memory. Viewed from this perspective, the older models of smoking, such as the addiction model and the arousal modulation model, appear somewhat naive. Although it has never been claimed that such models are mutually exclusive, the general thrust of much smoking literature has suggested alternatives for smoking motivation, either in different individuals or at different times in a smoker's career. For example, on the addiction model the initial effect of smoking is direct reward but, once smoking is established, the major incentive for continuing smoking is to ward off withdrawal effects. Higher-order models such as the opponent process theory (Solomon, 1980) and various theories of drug tolerance are further refinements of this model. For the arousal modulation model, the major incentive for smoking is modulation of arousal toward an optimum level required for maximal performance and psychological comfort, the modulation itself providing indirect reward. Other models, such as the psychological tool, stimulus filter, and mood control models, overlap the arousal modulation model and incorporate various other aspects of smoking.

It is a truism in clinical medicine that when there are a large number of explanations or treatments for a disease, then none of them is fully correct. This principle may well apply in the field of smoking, and it is clear that the time has come for a more integrated explanation of the behavior. The multivariate biobehavioral model proposed by Pomerleau and colleagues

(Pomerleau, Fertig and Shanaban, 1983a; Pomerleau and Pomerleau, 1984) is a welcome stride in this direction.

The argument of this chapter is that all the motives discussed in the preceding pages operate together at all times in any smoker, although the weightings between different motivations may vary between and within individuals, over time and in different circumstances. Thus, the addicted smoker, reaching for the next cigarette because he or she feels the onset of withdrawal symptoms, will still derive pleasure from it and will also manipulate the nicotine dosage in accordance with any performance demands or stressors operating at the time. Similarly, the nondeprived smoker may light an extra cigarette to enhance the pleasure of an evening cocktail, while at the same time smoking it in such a way as to maximize its tranquilizing effect or to counteract the depressant effects of the alcohol—depending on what the particular circumstances require.

Learning and cognitive factors are of immense importance throughout the range of smoking behavior. In the above example, anticipation of the early-evening cigarette (and of the accompanying cocktail) provides reward before either have touched the lips. The pairing of the cigarette with the cocktail engenders a type of state-dependent learning so that, should the smoker try abstaining from the cigarette at this time, he or she may develop withdrawal symptoms which would not be experienced after an equal period of smoking abstinence in other circumstances. Such situational-specific tolerance has been described for many drugs (for review see Goudie and Griffiths, 1986). Examples of the intricately woven patterns of motivation for any behavior are endless. Drug reinforcement of behavior by nicotine merely adds another layer of complication.

Implications

Despite the above arguments for smoking as an integrated behavior, is it possible to pinpoint particular features applicable at different stages and to develop practical strategies for smoking cessation?

Smoking recruitment

Smoking recruitment should be a relatively straightforward problem to tackle, since it is at least not complicated by the presence of nicotine. As discussed above, individuals with particular characteristics (mainly genetically determined) appear to be especially vulnerable, and are most likely to succumb to smoking when exposed to certain sociocultural pressures. These pressures must provide motivation largely through cognitive channels such as expectation of reward and the perception of smoking as a desirable goal. An important strategy would therefore utilize cognitive methods to downgrade the image of smoking, while at the same time offering healthier alternatives which can be perceived as more desirable. Educational methods must therefore be devised.

A problem arises from the fact that there appear to be two types of individuals at risk: the risk-taking sensation-seeker and the more emotionally labile individual with a high neuroticism score. Tailoring educational programs to cater for these two types presents difficulties, although these need not be insuperable. Stress on the health risks may encourage smoking in the sensation-seekers (who are inherently less sensitive to punishment). On the other hand, fostering a general attitude that smoking is an unimportant and not particularly exciting activity may be aided by placing less emphasis on smoking itself and more on alternative activities. A program of active encouragement, both at school and in the community, of a wide variety of activities for children and adolescents, seems necessary (especially in the lower socioeconomic groups). Such activities could include competitive and 'adventure' sports, games, and social activities to provide excitement for the sensation-seekers, and more relaxing sports, yoga, meditation and more intellectual games for the more sensitive.

Disinterest in smoking amongst children and adolescents could be further encouraged by reduction in the numbers of smoking adults, restriction of smoking in public places (especially those associated with enjoyment) and the dissociation of smoking and sport by restrictions on advertising and sport-sponsorship by tobacco companies.

Prevention of recruitment to smoking is worthy of much public effort, since there is no doubt that the easiest way to be a nonsmoker is never to have started smoking.

Smoking cessation

Encouragement of smoking cessation in established smokers presents further problems. Motivations for smoking are many and diverse (Figure 1); the majority of them apply, in various but multiple combinations, to each smoker. Withdrawal symptoms, arousal and mood modulation, weight control and many other factors conspire to militate against smoking cessation. The factors reinforcing smoking (Reward side of Figure 1) appear to outweigh the relatively few factors favouring cessation (Punishment side of Figure 1).

Yet a human being is both a social and a thinking animal, and social and cognitive factors are very powerful influences on behavior. Such influences can be of overriding importance in changing attitudes toward behaviors, including drug-reinforced behavior. Clinical experience with tranquilizers, alcohol and other drugs of abuse has shown that people can and do give up these drugs, despite withdrawal effects and loss of drug-related rewards, once they become sufficiently motivated to do so. The greater the conscious motivation, the less important the physical and psychological factors become. For example, in the 'permissive society' of the 1960s it became socially acceptable to take a tranquilizer for minor worries. Later experience revealed the dangers of long-term tranquilizer use, and there was a reaction against permissiveness in general. Attitudes changed, and now many tranquilizer users are positively anxious to stop these drugs, and are often successful in doing so, despite the physical and psychological difficulties involved (Ashton, 1984, 1987b).

Public attitudes to smoking

With regard to smoking, a wind of change in social attitudes is already blowing. Smoking motivation is clearly susceptible to modification, as evidenced by the fact that millions of smokers successfully give up every year, and that smokers have become a minority group (about 30 percent) in many countries (Ramprakash and Morris, 1986; Thornberry, Wilson and Golden, 1986). This wind of change must be nurtured and encouraged so that nonsmoking comes to be perceived as the accepted norm in all social groups. Educational methods and social pressures by the nonsmoking majority are as relevant for adults as for schoolchildren, and should include restriction of smoking in public places and work environments, and decreased tobacco advertising. Encouragement of healthier alternatives such as sports and leisure pursuits may require public education and increased availability. In adults, awareness of the health risks of smoking assumes greater import-ance than in children. There is evidence that health information in other fields is already making some impact on the incidence of cardiovascular disease and (in some socioeconomic groups) on diet (Pomerleau, 1981).

Smoking cessation clinics

Such general measures are likely in the long run to influence the largest number of smokers, and also, by providing continuous pressure, to be most effective in preventing relapse. However, the effects may be only gradual, and may eventually reach a limit. 'Nicotine dependence implies a pattern of heavy smoking which is resistant to change' (Pomerleau et al., 1983a, p. 291). For such resistant smokers there is a place for more specialized techniques including smoking cessation clinics and use of drugs as aids to smoking withdrawal.

Drugs

No drugs have yet been found to be universally successful for smoking withdrawal. Nicotine chewing gum has achieved the highest success rates

(Stolerman, 1986; West and Belcher, 1986). If properly used it can alleviate many of the withdrawal symptoms and also prevent weight gain on smoking cessation. However, it does not appear completely to satisfy craving (West, Jarvis, Russell, Carruthers and Feyerabend, 1984; West and Belcher, 1986; West, 1987) which can be prolonged after cessation and is an important cause of relapse. As discussed above, this lack of effect may result from failure to supply rapidly fluctuating blood nicotine concentrations to central cholinergic receptors. Inhalation of smoke-free nicotine (as in Favor cigarettes) may be more efficacious in this respect, but such administration may merely maintain nicotine dependence. It is difficult to escape the conclusion that at some point the abstaining smoker must undergo some discomfort. Inhalation of small quantities of tar extracts has been claimed to decrease craving (Rose, 1987) but requires further investigation. The possibilities of cholinergic antagonists (Stolerman, 1986), opioid antagonists (Karras and Kane, 1980) and ACTH (Bourne, 1985) are interesting but also require further exploration. Acupuncture, which can release endogenous opioids (Clement-Jones and Besser, 1983), and hypnosis have so far produced limited results. At present, the failure and relapse rates of smoking cessation clinics are disappointingly high, only about 10–30 percent of attenders still abstaining after one year (British Thoracic Society Research Committee, 1983; Jarvis, Raw, Russell and Feyerabend, 1982; Raw, 1978).

Behavioral techniques

Meanwhile, further developments in the use of behavioral and cognitive techniques are urgently needed, not only for smokers but for drug-abusers in general. Individual strategies may have to be taught and learnt (for example, how to concentrate without a cigarette; how to relax without smoking; what alternative behavior can be utilized when the desire to smoke is strong?). There is a large field for psychologists, paramedicals and lay counselors in discovering and teaching alternate coping strategies for the demands of everyday living, and in helping individuals to find rewards from safer sources than smoking.

Safer cigarettes

Fears have been expressed that a proportion of those who give up smoking substitute the habit with some other equally damaging behavior, including alcohol or even suicide (Lee, 1979). In exploring all avenues for decreasing the health toll of smoking, the question must arise as to whether there is a middle way. Is there any possibility of being a moderate, occasional smoker analogous to the socially accepted moderate drinker? Such a possibility requires the development of safer cigarettes. The use of filters and lower tar delivery have possibly already decreased the death rate from smoking (Wynder, 1980) although the health risks remain unacceptably high. Perhaps for a hard core of smokers who cannot or will not stop, safer cigarettes may be a partial solution. In this context both nicotine aerosol cigarettes (e.g. Favors) (Russell, 1987) and low-dose tar extracts (Rose, 1987) merit consideration. Both are smoke-free and present no known dangers of passive smoking. Although nicotine carries health hazards, these are smaller than those of whole tobacco smoke. Social restraints, as discussed above, might still serve to restrict such smoking to limited environments, and it should not be impossible to add financial discouragement by suitable pricing policies.

Development of safer cigarettes may present both ethical and logical dilemmas. Yet in view of the primacy of nicotine as a rewarding drug, it may be unrealistic to view anything more than a partial elimination of smoking as an attainable goal. In developing countries, where smoking is still increasing (Pobee, 1983; Taha and Ball, 1980) the introduction of safer cigarettes could prevent literally millions of deaths within the next half-century.

THE FUTURE

Strategies for smoking cessation are inherently flawed by imperfections in the state of knowledge of the smoking phenomenon. There are some encouraging signs that this knowledge is increasing. Greater understanding of the central actions of nicotine is provided by rapid advances in the field of receptor structure and function (Brown, 1986; Karlin et al., 1986). Equally swift developments are occurring in the area of opioid receptors and the functions of endogenous opioid systems in the brain (*British Medical Bulletin*, 1983). New insights on drug tolerance, including behavioral tolerance (Goudie and Griffiths, 1986; Siegel and MacRae, 1984) and dispositional tolerance (Melchior and Tabakoff, 1985) and distinctions between drug tolerance and withdrawal effects (Bachy, Biziere, Keane, Morre and Simiand, 1987) continue to emerge from animal work. Novel techniques such as positron emission tomography (PET) and nuclear magnetic resonance (NMR) scanning are coming into use for examining the dynamic effects of psychotropic drugs on the human brain. These and more refined EEG techniques are suggesting important differences in hemispheric function (Itil, Shapiro, Eralp, Akman, Itil and Garbizu, 1985).

All these advances are of great scientific interest, and may in time yield ideas of practical value. Unfortunately, the most urgent problem in the present context is also the most difficult. It involves sociological, environmental, political, economic and ethical issues affecting whole populations. Such issues are difficult to grasp and largely unamenable to scientific analysis. How to persuade countless millions of smokers and incipient smokers throughout the world to renounce the habit may remain an enigma. For scientists, the immediate task must be to chip away at the foundations in the hope that eventually the bastion may crumble, leaving only a hardcore of acceptable dimensions.

REFERENCES

Abood, L.G., Lowy, K., and Booth, H. (1979). Acute and chronic effects of nicotine in rats and evidence for a noncholinergic site of action. *National Institute on Drug Abuse Research Monographs Series*, **23**, 136–149.

Abood, L.G., Reynolds, D.T., Booth, H., and Bidlack, J.M. (1981). Sites and mechanisms for nicotine's action in the brain. *Neurosciences and Biobehavioural Review*, **5**, 479–486.

Andersson, K. (1975). Effects of cigarette smoking on learning and retention. *Psychopharmacologia*, **41**, 1–5.

Andersson, K., and Hockey, G.R.J. (1977). Effects of cigarette smoking on incidental memory. *Psychopharmacology*, **52**, 223–226.

Ando, K., and Yanagita, T. (1981). Cigarette smoking in rhesus monkeys. *Psychopharmacology*, **72**, 117–127.

Armitage, A.K. (1978). The role of nicotine in the tobacco smoking habit. In: R.E. Thornton (ed.), *Smoking Behaviour: Physiological and Psychological Influences*. Edinburgh: Churchill Livingstone.

Armitage, A.K., Hall, G.H., and Sellers, C.M. (1969). Effects of nicotine on electrocortical activity and acetylcholine release from the cat cerebral cortex. *British Journal of Pharmacology*, **35**, 152–160.

Ashton, H. (1984). Benzodiazepine withdrawal: an unfinished story. *British Medical Journal*, **288**, 1135–1140.

Ashton, H. (1987a). *Brain Systems, Disorders, and Psychotropic Drugs*. Oxford: Oxford University Press.

Ashton, H. (1987b). Benzodiazepine withdrawal: outcome in 50 patients. *British Journal of Addiction*, **82**, 665–671.

Ashton, H., and Stepney, R. (1982). *Smoking, Psychology and Pharmacology*. London: Tavistock.

Ashton, H., and Watson, D.W. (1970). Puffing frequency and nicotine intake in cigarette smokers. *British Medical Journal*, **3**, 679–681.

Ashton, H., Marsh, V.R., Millman, J.E., Rawlins, M.D., Telford, R., and Thompson, J.W. (1980). Biphasic dose-related responses of the CNV (contingent negative variation) to I.V. nicotine in man. *British Journal of Clinical Pharmacology*, **10**, 579–589.

Ashton, H., Millman, J.E., Telford, R., and Thompson, J.W. (1974). The effects of caffeine, nitrazepam and cigarette smoking on the contingent negative variation in man. *Electroencephalography and Clinical Neurophysiology*, **37**, 59–71.

Atweh, S.F., and Kuhar, M.J. (1983). Distribution and function of opioid receptors. *British Medical Bulletin*, **39**, 47–52.

Bachy, A., Biziere, K., Keane, P., Morre, M., and Simiand, J. (1987). Effects of chronic diazepam and tetrazepam on tolerance and dependence in mice. *British Journal of Pharmacology*, Proceedings Suppl., **90**, 262P.

Bättig, K. (1980). The smoking habit and psychopharmacological effects of nicotine. *Activitas Nervosa Superior*, **22**, 274–288.

Berntson, G.G., Beattie, M.S., and Walker, J.M. (1976). Effects of nicotine and muscarinic compounds on biting attack in the cat. *Pharmacology, Biochemistry and Behavior*, **5**, 235–239.

Bierness, D., and Vogel-Sprott, M. (1984). Alcohol tolerance in social drinkers: operant and classical conditioning effects. *Psychopharmacology*, **84**, 393–397.

Bourne, S. (1985). Treatment of cigarette smoking with short-term high-dosage corticotrophin therapy: a preliminary communication. *Journal of the Royal Society of Medicine*, **78**, 649–650.

British Medical Bulletin (1983). Opioid peptides. In: J. Hughes (Ed.) *British Medical Bulletin* **39**, 1–100.

British Medical Journal (1968). Leading article. *British Medical Journal*, **1**, 73.

British Thoracic Society Research Committee (1983). Comparison of four methods of smoking withdrawal in patients with smoking related disease. *British Medical Journal*, **286**, 595–597.

Brown, D.A. (1986). Voltage-sensitive ion channels mediating modulatory effects of acetylcholine, amines, and peptides. In: L.L. Iverson and E. Goodman (eds), *Fast and Slow Chemical Signalling in the Nervous System*. Oxford: Oxford University Press.

Bush, H.D., Bush, M.F., and Miller, M.A. (1976). Addictive agents and intracranial self-stimulation: daily morphine and lateral hypothalamic self-stimulation. *Physiological Psychology*, **14**, 79–85.

Changeux, J.-P., and Danchin, A. (1976). Selective stabilisation of developing synapses as a mechanism for the specification of neuronal networks. *Nature*, **264**, 705–712.

Cherry, N., and Kiernan, K. E. (1976). Personality scores and smoking behaviour. A longitudinal study. *British Journal of Preventive and Social Medicine*, **30**, 123–131.

Cherry, N., and Kiernan, K.E. (1978). A longitudinal study of smoking and personality. In: R.E. Thornton (ed.), *Smoking Behaviour: Physiological and Psychological Influences*. Edinburgh: Churchill Livingstone.

Cinciripini, P.M. (1986). The effects of smoking on electrocortical arousal in coronary prone (Type A) and non-coronary prone (Type B) subjects. *Psychopharmacology*, **90**, 522–527.

Clement-Jones, V., and Besser, G.M. (1983). Clinical perspectives in opioid peptides. *British Medical Bulletin*, **39**, 95–100.

Cooper, S.J. (1984). Neural substrates for opiate-produced reward: solving the dependency puzzle. *Trends in Pharmacological Science*, **5**, 49–50.

Corcoran, D.W.J. (1965). Personality and the inverted-U relation. *British Journal of Psychology*, **56**, 267–273.

Demellweek, C., and Goudie, A.J. (1983). Behavioural tolerance to amphetamine and other psychostimulants: the case for considering behavioural mechanisms. *Psychopharmacology*, **80**, 287–307.

Deutsch, J.A. (1971). The cholinergic synapse and the site of memory. *Science*, **174**, 788–794.

Dobbs, S.D., Strickler, D.P., and Maxwell, W.E. (1981). The effects of stress and relaxation in the presence of stress in urinary pH and smoking behavior. *Addictive Behaviors*, **6**, 345–353.

Domino, E.F. (1967). Electroencephalographic and behavioural arousal effects of small doses of nicotine: a neuropsychopharmacological study. *Annals of the New York Academy of Sciences*, **142**, 216–244.

Domino, E.F. (1973). Neuropsychopharmacology of nicotine and tobacco smoking. In: W.L. Dunn (ed.), *Smoking Behavior: Motives and Incentives*. Washington, DC: Winston.

Domino, E.F. (1979). Behavioural, electrophysiological, endocrine, and skeletal muscle actions of nicotine and tobacco smoking. In: A. Remond and C. Izard (eds), *Electrophysiological Effects of Nicotine*. Proceedings of the International Symposium on the Electrophysiological Effects of Nicotine, 19–20 Oct. 1978, Paris (France). Amsterdam: Elsevier North-Holland Biomedical Press.

Domino, E.F., and von Baumgarten, A.M. (1969). Tobacco cigarette smoking and patellar reflex depression. *Clinical Pharmacology and Therapeutics*, **10**, 72–79.

Drachman, D.A. (1978). Central cholinergic system and memory. In: M.A. Lipton, A. DiMascio and K.F. Killam (eds), *Psychopharmacology: A Generation of Progress*. New York: Raven Press.

Dunn, A.J. (1980). Neurochemistry of learning and memory: an evaluation of recent data. *Annual Review of Psychology*, **31**, 343–390.

Dunn, W.L. (1978). Smoking as a possible inhibitor of arousal. In: K. Bättig (ed.), *Behavioral Effects of Nicotine* (International Workshop on Behavioral Effects of Nicotine, Zurich, 15–17 Sept. 1976). Basel, New York: S. Karger.

Eccles, J.C. (1977). An instruction–selection theory of learning in the cerebellar cortex. *Brain Research*, **127**, 327–352.

Edelman, G.M. (1978). Group selection and phasic re-entrant signalling: a theory of higher brain function. In: G.M. Edelman and V.B. Mountcastle (eds), *The Mindful Brain*. Cambridge, Mass: MIT Press.

Eysenck, H.J. (1983). Psychophysiology and personality: extraversion, neuroticism and psychoticism. In: A. Gale and J.A. Edwards (eds), *Physiological Correlates of Human Behaviour*, vol. 3: *Individual Differences and Psychopathology*. London: Academic Press.

Eysenck, H.J., and Eysenck, S.B.G. (1975). *Manual of the Eysenck Personality Questionnaire (Junior and Adult)*. London: Hodder & Stoughton.

Eysenck, H.J., and O'Connor, K. (1979). Smoking, arousal and personality. In: A. Remond and C. Izard (eds), *Electrophysiological Effects of Nicotine*. Proceedings of the International Symposium on the Electrophysiological Effects of Nicotine, Paris (France), 19–20 Oct. 1978. Amsterdam: Elsevier North-Holland Biomedical Press.

Fertig, J.B., Pomerleau, O.F., and Sanders, B. (1986). Nicotine-produced antinociception in minimally deprived smokers and ex-smokers. *Addictive Behaviors*, **11**, 239–248.

Fleming, J., and Broadhurst, P. (1975). The effects of nicotine on two-way avoidance conditioning in bidirectionally selected strains of rats. *Psychopharmacologia*, **42**, 147–152.

Golding, J.F. (1988). Effects of cigarette smoking on resting EEG, visual evoked potentials and photic driving. *Pharmacology, Biochemistry and Behavior*, **29**, 23–32.

Golding, J.F., and Cornish, A.M. (1987). Personality and lifestyle in medical students: psychopharmacological aspects. *Psychology and Health*, **1**, 287–301.

Golding, J.F., and Mangan, G.L. (1982a). Arousing and de-arousing effects of cigarette smoking under conditions of stress and mild sensory isolation. *Psychophysiology*, **19**, 449–456.

Golding, J.F., and Mangan, G.L. (1982b). Effects of cigarette smoking on measures of arousal, response suppression and excitation/inhibition balance. *International Journal of Addiction*, **17**, 793–804.

Goudie, A.J., and Griffiths, J.W. (1986). Behavioural factors in drug tolerance. *Trends in Pharmacological Sciences*, **7**, 192–196.

Gray, J.A. (1972). The psycho-physiological nature of introversion–extraversion: a modification of Eysenck's theory. In: V.D. Nebylitsyn and S.A. Gray (eds), *Biological Bases of Individual Behaviour*. London: Academic Press.

Gray, J.A. (1981a). Anxiety as a paradigm case of emotion. *British Medical Bulletin*, **37**, 193–197.

Gray, J.A. (1981b). A critique of Eysenck's theory of personality. In: H.J. Eysenck (ed.), *A Model for Personality*. Berlin: Springer-Verlag.

Hall, G.H. (1970). Effects of nicotine and tobacco smoke on the electrical activity of the cerebral cortex and olfactory bulb. *British Journal of Pharmacology*, **38**, 271–286.

Hall, G.H., and Turner, D.M. (1972). Effects of nicotine on the release of 3H-noradrenaline from the hypothalamus. *Biochemical Pharmacology*, **21**, 1829–1838.

Hatsukami, D.K., Hughes, J.R., Pickens, R.W., and Svikis, D. (1984). Tobacco withdrawal symptoms: an experimental analysis. *Psychopharmacology*, **84**, 231–236.

Haynes, R.C., and Murad, F. (1980). Adrenocorticotropic hormone, adrenocortical steroids and their synthetic analogs; inhibitors of adrenocortical steroid biosynthesis. In: A.G. Gilman, L.S. Goodman and A. Gilman (eds), *The Pharmacological Basis of Therapeutics*. New York: Macmillan.

Heath, R.G. (1964). Pleasure responses of human subjects to direct stimulation of the brain: physiological and psychodynamic considerations. In: R.G. Heath (ed.), *The Role of Pleasure in Behavior*. New York: Harper & Row.

Heimstra, N.W. (1973). The effects of smoking on mood change. In: W.L. Dunn (ed.), *Smoking Behavior: Motives and Incentives*. Washington, DC: Winston.

Henningfield, J.E. (1987). Pharmacologic basis for nicotine replacement. Paper given at symposium on Nicotine Replacement in the Treatment of Smoking: A Critical Evaluation, 21–22 Jan. 1987, Bethesda, Maryland.

Henningfield, J.E., and Griffiths, R.R. (1981). Cigarette smoking and subjective response: effects of d-amphetamine. *Clinical Pharmacology and Therapeutics*, **30**, 497–505.

Herz, A. (1981). Role of endorphins in addiction. *Modern Problems in Pharmacopsychiatry*, **17**, 175–180.

Hughes, J. (1983). Biogenesis, release and inactivation of enkephalins and dynorphins. *British Medical Bulletin*, **39**, 17–24.

Hughes, J., and Kosterlitz, W.H. (1983). Opioid peptides: introduction. *British Medical Bulletin*, **39**, 1–3.

Hutchinson, R.R., and Emley, G.S. (1973). Effects of nicotine on avoidance, conditioned suppression and aggression response measures in animals and man. In: W.L. Dunn (ed.), *Smoking Behavior: Motives and Incentives*. Washington, DC: Winston.

Itil, T.M., Shapiro, D.M., Eralp, E., Akman, A., Itil, K.Z., and Garbizu, C. (1985). A new brain function diagnostic unit, including the dynamic brain mapping of computer analyzed EEG, evoked potential and sleep (a new hardware/software system and its application in psychiatry and psychopharmacology). *New Trends in Experimental Clinical Psychiatry*, **1**, 107–177.

Izquierdo, I. (1982). Beta-endorphin and forgetting. *Trends in Pharmacological Sciences*, **3**, 455–457.

Jarvik, M.E. (1973). Further observations on nicotine as the reinforcing agent in smoking. In: W.L. Dunn (ed.), *Smoking Behavior: Motives and Incentives*. Washington, DC: Winston.

Jarvis, M.J., Raw, M., Russell, M.A.H., and Feyerabend, C. (1982). Randomised controlled trial of nicotine chewing gum. *British Medical Journal*, **285**, 537–540.

Jasinski, D.R. (1987). Conceptual basis for substance replacement strategies. Paper given at Symposium on Nicotine Replacement in the Treatment of Smoking: A Critical Evaluation, 21–22 Jan. 1987, Bethesda, Maryland.

Jenner, P.G., Kumar, R., Marsden, C.D., Reavill, C., and Stolerman, I.P. (1986). Characteristics of [3H]-(−)-nicotine binding in rat brain. *British Journal of Pharmacology*, **88**, 297P.

Karlin, A., Kao, P.N., and DiPaola, M. (1986). Molecular pharmacology of the nicotinic receptor. *Trends in Pharmacological Sciences*, **7**, 304–308.

Karras, A., and Kane, J.M. (1980). Naloxone reduces cigarette smoking. *Life Sciences*, **27**, 1541–1545.

Koob, G.F., and Bloom, F.E. (1983). Behavioural effects of opioid peptides. *British Medical Bulletin*, **39**, 89–94.

Kornetsky, C., Esposito, R.U., McLean, S., and Jacobson, O. (1979). Intracranial self-stimulation threshold. *Archives of General Psychiatry*, **36**, 289–292.

Kovacs, G.L., Bohus, B.E., Vesteeg, D.H.G., Telgedy, G., and deWied, D. (1982). Neurohypophyseal hormones and memory. In: H. Yoshida, Y. Hagihara and S. Ebashi (eds), *Advances in Pharmacology and Therapeutics II*, vol. 1: *CNS Pharmacology–Neuropeptides*. Oxford: Pergamon Press.

Lambiase, M., and Serra, C. (1957). Fume a sistema nervoso. I. Modificazioni dell'attivita elettrica corticale da fumo. *Acta Neurologica (Napoli)*, **12**, 475–493.

Lee, P.N. (1979). Has the mortality of male doctors improved with the reductions in their cigarette smoking? *British Medical Journal*, **2**, 1538–1540.

Lorens, S.A. (1976). Comparison of the effects of morphine on hypothalamic and medial frontal cortex self-stimulation in the rat. *Psychopharmacology*, **48**, 217–224.

Lowe, G. (1986). State-dependent learning effects with a combination of alcohol and nicotine. *Psychopharmacology*, **89**, 105–107.

Lynch, G., and Baudry, M. (1984). The biochemistry of memory: a new and specific hypothesis. *Science*, **224**, 1057–1063.

Mangan, G.L., and Golding, J. (1978). An enhancement model of smoking maintenance? In: R.E. Thornton (ed.), *Smoking Behaviour: Physiological and Psychological Influences*. Edinburgh: Churchill Livingstone.

Mangan, G.L., and Golding, J.F. (1983a). Factors underlying smoking recruitment and maintenance amongst adolescents. *Advances in Behaviour Research and Therapy*, **4**, 225–272.

Mangan, G.L., and Golding, J.F. (1983b). The effects of smoking on memory consolidation. *Journal of Psychology*, **115**, 65–77.

Mangan, G.L., and Golding, J.F. (1984). *The Psychopharmacology of Smoking*. Cambridge: Cambridge University Press.

Mark, R.F. (1978). The developmental view of memory. In: R. Porter (ed.), *Studies in Neurophysiology*. Cambridge: Cambridge University Press.

Marr, D. (1969). A theory of cerebellar cortex. *Journal of Physiology (London)*, **202**, 437–470.

Marty, M.A., Erwin, V.G., Cornell, K., and Zgombick, J.M. (1984). Effects of nicotine on beta-endorphin, alpha-MSH and ACTH secretion by isolated perfused mouse brains and pituitary glands, in vitro. *Pharmacology, Biochemistry and Behavior*, **22**, 317–325.

Melchior, C.L., and Tabakoff, B. (1985). Features of environment-dependent tolerance to ethanol. *Psychopharmacology*, **87**, 94–100.

Mello, N.K., Lukas, S.E., and Mendelson, J.H. (1985). Buprenorphine effects on cigarette smoking. *Psychopharmacology*, **86**, 417–425.

Mello, N.K., Mendelson, J.H., Sellers, M.L., and Kuehnle, J.C. (1980a). Effects of heroin self-administration on cigarette smoking. *Psychopharmacology*, **67**, 45–52.

Mello, N.K., Mendelson, J.H., Sellers, M.L., and Kuehnle, J.C. (1980b). Effects of alcohol and marihuana on tobacco smoking. *Clinical Pharmacology and Therapeutics*, **27**, 202–209.

Morley, J.E., and Levine, A.S. (1983). The central control of appetite. *Lancet*, i, 398–401.

Murphree, H.B., Pfeiffer, C.C., and Price, L.M. (1967). EEG changes in man following smoking. *Annals of the New York Academy of Sciences*, **142**, 245–260.

Myrsten, A.-L., and Andersson, K. (1978). Effects of cigarette smoking on human performance. In: R.E. Thornton (ed.), *Smoking Behaviour: Physiological and Psychological Influences*. Edinburgh: Churchill Livingstone.

National Cancer Institute (1977). *The Smoking Digest: Progress Report on a Nation Kicking the Habit*. Washington, DC: US Public Health Service.

Nemeth-Coslett, R., and Griffiths, R.R. (1986). Naloxone does not affect cigarette smoking. *Psychopharmacology*, **89**, 261–264.

Nesbitt, P.D. (1973). Smoking, physiological arousal, and emotional response. *Journal of Personality and Social Psychology*, **25**, 137–145.

Olds, J., and Travis, R.P. (1960). Effects of chlorpromazine, meprobamate, pentobarbital and morphine on self-stimulation. *Journal of Pharmacology and Experimental Therapeutics*, **128**, 397–404.

Palmer, R.F., and Berens, A. (1983). Double blind study of the effects of naloxone on the pleasure of cigarette smoking. *Federation Proceedings*, **42**, 654.

Peeke, S.C., and Peeke, H.V.S. (1984). Attention, memory and cigarette smoking. *Psychopharmacology*, **84**, 205–216.

Pert, A., and Hulsebus, R. (1975). Effect of morphine on intracranial self-stimulation behaviour following brain amine depletion. *Life Sciences*, **17**, 19–20.

Pobee, J.O.M. (1983). Will the African escape the ravages of tobacco smoke? In: W.F. Forbes, R.C. Frecker and D. Nostbakken (eds), *Proceedings of the 5th World Conference on Smoking and Health*, Winnipeg, Canada, 1983, vol. 2. Canadian Council on Smoking and Health.

Pomerleau, O.F. (1981). Underlying mechanisms of substance abuse: examples from research on smoking. *Addictive Behaviors*, **6**, 187–196.

Pomerleau, O.F., and Pomerleau, C.S. (1984). Neuroregulators and the reinforcement of smoking: Towards a biobehavioral explanation. *Neuroscience Biobehavioural Review*, **8**, 503–513.

Pomerleau, O.F., Fertig, J.B., and Shanaban, S.O. (1983a). Nicotine dependence in cigarette smoking: An empirically-based, multivariate model. *Pharmacology, Biochemistry and Behavior*, **19**, 291–299.

Pomerleau, O.F., Fertig, J.B., Seyler, L.E., and Jaffe, J. (1983b). Neuroendocrine reactivity to nicotine in smokers. *Psychopharmacology*, **81**, 61–67.

Pomerleau, O.F., Turk, D.C., and Fertig, J.B. (1984). The effects of cigarette smoking on pain and anxiety. *Addictive Behaviors*, **9**, 265–271.

Pomerleau, O.F., Scherzer, H.H., Grunberg, N.E., Pomerleau, C.S., Judge, J., Fertig, J.B., and Burleson, J. (1988). The effects of acute exercise on subsequent cigarette smoking. *Journal of Behavioural Medicine*, **10**, 117–127.

Pullen, G.P., Best, N.R., and Maguire, J. (1984). Anticholinergic drug abuse: a common problem? *British Medical Journal*, **289**, 612–613.

Ramprakash, D., and Morris, J. (eds) (1986). *Social Trends*, No. 16, 1986 edition. London: Her Majesty's Stationery Office.

Raw, M. (1978). The treatment of cigarette dependence. In: Y. Israel, F.B. Glaser,

H. Kalant, R.E. Popham, W. Schmidt and R.G. Smart (eds), *Research Advances in Alcohol and Drug Problems*. New York: Plenum Press.

Rebert, C.S. (1972). Cortical and subcortical slow potentials in the monkeys brain during a preparatory interval. *Electroencephalography and Clinical Neurophysiology*, **33**, 389–402.

Redgrave, P., and Dean, P. (1981). Intracranial self-stimulation. *British Medical Bulletin*, **37**, 141–146.

Risch, S.C., Cohen, R.M., Janowsky, D.S., Kalin, N.H., and Murphy, D.L. (1980). Mood and behavioural effects of physostigmine on humans are accompanied by elevations in plasma beta-endorphin and cortisol. *Science*, **209**, 1545–1546.

Risch, S.C., Kalin, N.H., Janowsky, D.S., Cohen, R.M., Pickar, D., and Murphy, D.L. (1983). Co-release of ACTH and beta-endorphin: immunoreactivity in human subjects in response to central cholinergic stimulation. *Science*, **222**, 77.

Risner, M.E., and Goldberg, S.R. (1983). A comparison of nicotine self-administration in the dog: fixed-ratio and progressive-ratio schedules of intravenous drug infusion. *Journal of Pharmacology and Experimental Therapeutics*, **224**, 319–326.

Rose, J.E. (1987). The role of upper airway stimulation in smoking. Paper given at Symposium on Nicotine Replacement in the Treatment of Smoking: A Critical Evaluation, 21–22 Jn. 1987, Bethesda, Maryland.

Routtenberg, A. (1968). The two-arousal hypothesis: reticular formation and limbic system. *Psychological Review*, **75**, 51–80.

Routtenberg, A. (1978). Reward systems of the brain. *Scientific American*, **239**, 125–131.

Royall, D.R., and Klemm, W.R. (1981). Dopaminergic mediation of reward: evidence gained using a natural reinforcer in a behavioural contrast paradigm. *Neurosciences Letter*, **21**, 223 229.

Russell, M.A.H. (1976). Tobacco smoking and nicotine dependence. In: R.J. Gibbins, Y. Israel, H. Kalant, R.E. Popham, W. Schmidt and R.G. Smart (eds), *Research Advances in Alcohol and Drug Problems*, vol. III. New York: John Wiley & Sons.

Russell, M.A.H. (1987). Smoking and nicotine replacement: the role of blood nicotine levels, their rate of change and nicotine tolerance. Paper given at Symposium on Nicotine Replacement in the Treatment of Smoking: A Critical Evaluation, 21–22 Jan. 1987, Bethesda, Maryland.

Sahley, T., and Bernston, G. (1979). Antinociceptive effects of central and systemic administrations of nicotine in the rat. *Psychopharmacology*, **65**, 279–283.

Schachter, S. (1978). Pharmacological and psychological determinants of smoking. In: R.E. Thornton (ed.), *Smoking Behaviour: Physiological and Psychological Influences*. Edinburgh: Churchill Livingstone.

Schachter, S. (1979). Regulation, withdrawal and nicotine addiction. *National Institute on Drug Abuse (NIDA) Research Monograph Series*, **23**, 123–133.

Schachter, S., Silverstein, B., Kozlowski, L.T., Perlick, D., Herman, C.P., and Liebling, B. (1977). Studies of the interaction of psychological and pharmacological determinants of smoking. *Journal of Experimental Psychology (Gen.)*, **106**, 3–40.

Shiffman, S.M. (1979). The tobacco withdrawal syndrome. *National Institute on Drug Abuse (NIDA) Research Monograph Series*, **23**, 158–184.

Siegel, S. (1975). Evidence from rats that morphine tolerance is a learned response. *Journal of Comparative and Physiological Psychology*, **89**, 498–506.

Siegel, S. (1983). Classical conditioning, drug tolerance and drug dependence. In: Y. Israel, F.B. Glaser, H. Kalant, R.E. Popham, W. Schmidt and R.G. Smart (eds),

Research Advances in Alcohol and Drug Problems, vol. 7. New York: Plenum Press.

Siegel, S., and MacRae, J. (1984). Environmental specificity of tolerance. *Trends in Neurosciences*, **7**, 140–143.

Silverstein, B. (1982). Cigarette smoking, nicotine addiction and relaxation. *Journal of Personality and Social Psychology*, **42**, 946–950.

Silverstein, B., Kozlowski, L.T., and Schachter, S. (1977). Social life, cigarette smoking and urinary pH. *Journal of Experimental Psychology (General)*, **106**, 20–23.

Singer, G., Oei, T.P.S., and Wallace, M. (1982). Schedule-induced self-injection of drugs. *Neuroscience Biobehavioural Review*, **6**, 77–83.

Sjoquist, B., Eriksson, A., and Winblad, B. (1982). Brain salsolinol levels in alcoholism. *Lancet*, **i**, 675–676.

Solomon, R.L. (1980). The opponent-process theory of acquired motivation: the cost of pleasure and the benefit of pain. *American Psychologist*, **35**, 691–712.

Squire, L.R., and Davis, H.P. (1981). The pharmacology of memory: a neurobiological perspective. *Annual Review of Pharmacology and Toxicology*, **21**, 323–356.

Stein, L. (1968). Chemistry of reward and punishment. In: D.H. Efron (ed.), *Psychopharmacology: A Review of Progress*. Publ. No. 1836, Washington, DC: US Government Printing Office.

Stein L. (1978). Reward transmitters: catecholamines and opioid peptides. In: M.A. Lipton, A. DiMascio and K.F. Killam (eds), *Psychopharmacology: A Generation of Progress*. New York: Raven Press.

Stein, L., and Wise, C.D. (1974). Serotonin and behavioural inhibition. *Advances in Biochemical Psychopharmacology*, **11**, 281–291.

Stolerman, I.P. (1986). Could nicotine antagonists be used in smoking cessation? *British Journal of Addiction*, **81**, 47–53.

Taha, A., and Ball, K. (1980). Smoking and Africa: the coming epidemic. *British Medical Journal*, **280**, 991–993.

Thompson, J.W. (1984a). Pain: mechanisms and principles of management. In: J. Grimley Evans and F.I. Caird (eds), *Advanced Geriatric Medicine*, vol. 4. London: Pitman.

Thompson, J.W. (1984b). Opioid peptides. *British Medical Journal*, **288**, 259–261.

Thompson, J.W., Ashton, C.H., Golding, J.F., and Marsh, V.R. (1986). Pharmacology of event-related potentials in humans. In: W.C. McCallum, R. Zappoli and F. Denoth (eds), *Cerebral Psychophysiology: Studies in Event-Related Potentials (EEG Suppl. 28)*, Amsterdam: Elsevier.

Thornberry, O.T., Wilson, R.W., and Golden, P. (1986). Health promotion and disease prevention provisional data from the National Health Interview Survey: United States, Jan.–June, 1985. In: *Advance Data From Vital and Health Statistics*, No. 119, US Department of Health and Human Services, Public Health Services, DHSS Publication No. PHS 86-1250, May 1986.

Timsit-Berthier, M. (1981). A propos de l'interprétation de la variation contingente négative en psychiatrie. *Revue de l'Electroencephalographie et de Neurophysiologie*, **11**, 236–244.

Tripathi, H., Martin, B., and Aceto, H. (1982). Nicotine-induced antinociception in rats and mice: correlations with nicotine brain levels. *Journal of Pharmacology and Experimental Therapeutics*, **221**, 91–96.

Turnbull, M.J., and Kelvin, A.S. (1971). Cigarette dependence. *British Medical Journal*, **3**, 115–117.

Warburton, D.M., Wesnes, K., Shergold, K., and James, M. (1986). Facilitation of learning and state dependency with nicotine. *Psychopharmacology*, **89**, 55–59.

Wesnes, K., and Warburton, D.M. (1978). The effects of cigarette smoking and nicotine tablets upon human attention. In: R.E. Thornton (ed.), *Smoking Behaviour: Physiological and Psychological Influences*. Edinburgh: Churchill Livingstone.

West, R. (1985). Corticotrophin injections to treat cigarette withdrawal symptoms. *Journal of the Royal Society of Medicine*, **78**, 1065–1066.

West, R.J. (1987). Nicotine as a dependence-producing substance. Paper given at Symposium on Nicotine Replacement in the Treatment of Smoking: A Critical Evaluation, 21–22 Jan. 1987, Bethesda, Maryland.

West, R.J., and Belcher, M. (1986). Which smokers report most relief from craving when using nicotine chewing gum? *Psychopharmacology*, **89**, 189–191.

West, R.J., Jarvis, M., Russell, M., Carruthers, M., and Feyerabend, C. (1984). Effects of nicotine replacement on cigarette withdrawal syndrome. *British Journal of Addiction*, **79**, 215–219.

Williams, D.G. (1980). Effects of cigarette smoking on immediate memory and performance in different kinds of smoker. *British Journal of Psychology*, **71**, 83–90.

Wise, R.A. (1980). The dopamine synapse and the notion of pleasure centres in the brain. *Trends in Neurosciences*, **3**, 91–95.

Woods, J.H. (1978). Behavioural pharmacology of drug self-administration. In: M.A. Lipton, A. DiMascio and K.F. Killam (eds), *Psychopharmacology: A Generation of Progress*. New York: Raven Press.

Wynder, E.L. (1980). Some concepts of the less harmful cigarettes. In: G.B. Gori and F.G. Bock (eds), *Banbury Report 3: A Safe Cigarette?* New York: Cold Spring Harbor Laboratory.

Young, J.Z. (1979). Learning as a process of selection and amplification. *Journal of the Royal Society of Medicine*, **72**, 801–814.

Zuckerman, M. (1979). *Sensation Seeking: Beyond the Optimal Level of Arousal*. New Jersey: Lawrence Erlbaum.

Zuckerman, M. (1983). Sensation Seeking: a biosocial dimension of personality. In: A. Gale and J.A. Edwards (eds), *Physiological Correlates of Human Behavior*, vol. 3: *Individual Differences and Psychopathology*. London: Academic Press.

3
Tobacco Dependence

MURRAY E. JARVIK
and
DOROTHY K. HATSUKAMI

ABSTRACT

Controversy concerning the dependence-producing effects of tobacco is diminishing. This chapter reviews the evidence of their extent and strength, and compares dependence on tobacco with dependence on other types of drugs affecting behavior or acting peripherally. The roles of tolerance and positive reinforcement are discussed.

INTRODUCTION

There is growing consensus throughout the world that regular tobacco use is a form of drug dependence. Anecdotal evidence supports the great strength of this dependence. For example, to illustrate the hold of tobacco, Charles Lamb once wrote, 'For thy sake, Tobacco, I would do anything but die' (Lamb, in Bartlett, 1980, page 442). Mark Twain's famous quip about his quitting smoking ('To cease smoking is the easiest thing I ever did; I ought to know for I have done it a thousand times') certainly implied a dependence upon tobacco (in his case, cigar smoking). A similar illustration of the possible strength of dependence upon tobacco was shown in the early part of this century when a tobacco company advertised: 'I'd walk a mile for a Camel.' In the 1940s, approximately 70 percent of young American men smoked (United States Department of Health and Human Services, 1980), and there

Smoking and Human Behavior, Edited by T. Ney and A. Gale

was little social pressure to stop; in the 1960s and 1970s some of the same men found it difficult to stop.

Until the mid-1960s smoking was generally considered a habit or a form of 'habituation', but not really a chemical dependency (United States Department of Health, Education and Welfare, 1964). A withdrawal syndrome comparable to that seen with alcohol or opioids was not recognized until fairly recently (Jaffe and Jarvik, 1978) and finally in 1980 the *Diagnostic and Statistical Manual of Mental Disorders of the American Psychiatric Association* (DSM III, third edition, 1980) recognized a tobacco dependence disorder. This does not go as far as to assert that all smoking is a form of dependence or a disorder; rather it is a liberal interpretation of the definition which encompasses most instances of smoking. The purpose of this chapter is to describe drug dependence in general, and to discuss whether regular tobacco use can be considered as a drug dependence, with particular emphasis on physical dependence on tobacco.

GENERAL CONCEPT OF DEPENDENCE

A working definition of drug dependence is: 'a repetitive self-administration of a chemical substance characterized by an overwhelming involvement with the use of the substance, difficulty in refraining from its use and producing potentially adverse consequences.' We are primarily concerned with tobacco cigarette smoking, as a form of drug dependence, and with its major determinant for use, nicotine.

Let us interpret the above definition. 'Repetitive' is the regular use of a chemical substance over a sustained period of time. 'Self-administration' may also include the ready acceptance of a substance even when given by another; however, the major method of administering the chemical would be by the individual him/herself. A chemical substance is any drug administered for a desired effect and not normally present in the body. 'Overwhelming involvement' is an arbitrary concept and such involvement may become apparent only when deprivation occurs (e.g. cigarettes, caffeine or alcohol).

'Difficulty in refraining' means that the user will overcome obstacles to obtain the substance, even self-imposed restraint. This may be measured by the effort expended or the punishment one will endure to obtain the substance. Difficulty in refraining from the use of a substance implies a high probability of subsequent drug-seeking behavior.

'Adverse consequences' may refer to two different sets of events. The first includes the unpleasant consequences of withdrawal and constitutes a barrier to cessation. The second includes social disapproval, impaired functioning, or impaired health (immediate or delayed), and constitutes an incentive for cessation.

Cigarette smokers have clearly met the above criteria for dependency on a drug. The high relapse rates and continued smoking in spite of the potentially adverse health and, more recently, social consequences attest to this dependency on tobacco. The definition of dependence on a drug, as described above, does not explicitly include the necessity for physical dependence on the drug (that is, the occurrence of tolerance and/or withdrawal signs and symptoms of tolerance). However, physical dependence on a drug, particularly the experience of withdrawal signs and symptoms, may be an important determinant for continued use of drugs. The rest of the chapter will discuss the occurrence of physical dependence on tobacco and its importance on becoming dependent on the drug.

TOLERANCE TO TOBACCO

Tolerance is manifested by a decreasing effectiveness of a drug and the need to increase the dose to obtain the same effect with successive doses. It is not clear whether tolerance is necessary for the formation of dependence upon a drug. It certainly is not sufficient, since tolerance occurs to many drugs such as antipsychotics or antihypertensives which do not produce dependence.

Tolerance to the effects of tobacco was reviewed by one of us in 1979 (Jarvik, 1979). Three kinds of tolerance were discussed: (1) drug dispositional or metabolic tolerance, (2) pharmacodynamic or tissue tolerance, and (3) behavioral tolerance. All three occur in smoking. While tolerance to components of tar and to carbon monoxide has been demonstrated, our major interest is in the tolerance to nicotine. Cigarette smoking induces microsomal enzyme formation, primarily in the liver, and thereby increases *metabolic* tolerance to a wide variety of drugs and poisons, including the hydrocarbons in cigarette tar and to nicotine. *Pharmacodynamic* or tissue tolerance to a drug such as nicotine is probably due to up or down regulation of receptors (e.g. nicotinic cholinergic receptors as well as others involved in the nicotine-initiated cascade). Anecdotal evidence suggests that adolescents overcome the nausea and dizziness produced by the first few cigarettes. Beckett, Gorrod and Jenner (1971) found that intravenous injection of nicotine induced nausea and dizziness in all nonsmokers tested, whereas the same dose did not induce nausea in any smokers. *Behavioral* tolerance is an adaptive and reduced response to a given dose of a drug, and may occur even when it is difficult to demonstrate physiological tolerance (MacRae, Scoles and Siegel, 1987). Tolerance to behavioral as well as physiological effects of nicotine has been shown in animals (Jarvik, 1973; Morrison and Stephenson, 1972; Stolerman, Goldfarb, Fink and Jarvik, 1973).

An example of behavioral tolerance to smoking is the change in sensory responses to the irritation of the respiratory tract by cigarette smoke. While the novice finds it aversive, and may attempt to avoid it, the chronic smoker learns to tolerate this sensation and may even grow to like it (Rose, Zinser, Tashkin, Newcomb and Ertle, 1984).

Other data providing evidence of behavioral tolerance as demonstrated by the subjective effects of nicotine use in humans are less clear. Nicotine gum is considered more unpleasant by nonsmokers than by smokers. Jones, Farrell and Herning (1978) not only showed that smokers could tolerate higher doses of intravenous nicotine than nonsmokers but also reported more pleasant effects from higher doses than nonsmokers. Additionally, they were able to demonstrate acute tolerance. Successive hourly injections of nicotine evoked decreased responses. This resembles, and may involve, tachyphylaxis, a rapid development of tolerance to substances such as catecholamines. Tachyphylaxis has been demonstrated in a number of animal preparations and is presumably due to temporary occupation of the receptors by the ligand itself.

TOBACCO WITHDRAWAL SYNDROME

As with tolerance, it is not clear to what extent tobacco withdrawal is necessary for the occurrence of general dependence upon the drug. If dependence upon a substance requires the potential for a withdrawal syndrome, then an empirical demonstration of such a syndrome must be made. The first successful attempt to quantify a withdrawal syndrome was by Himmelsbach (1942), who developed a widely used scale of opioid dependence. This scale included both objective signs and subjective symptoms. These classical studies, as well as others, have demonstrated that in order for signs and symptoms to be classified as a true drug withdrawal syndrome, they must meet the following criteria: (1) a change in physiological, subjective and/or behavioral functioning as a result of deprivation from the drugs; (2) time course of signs and symptoms that show overshoot or rebound phenomena; (3) alleviation of withdrawal symptoms when the drug is reinstated.

There are a number of studies which show a change in physical, subjective, and behavioral functioning during deprivation from cigarettes (Hatsukami, Hughes and Pickens, 1985a; Grabowski and Hall, 1985; Shiffman, 1979). The major signs and symptoms include: craving for nicotine; irritability, frustration or anger, anxiety, difficulty concentrating, restlessness, decreased heart rate, and increased appetite or weight gain (DSM III-R, p. 150; see Table 1). Other signs and symptoms include insomnia, decreased cortical arousal and increased reaction time (Surgeon General Report, 1988). More recently, there is evidence that there are changes in similar areas of functioning after withdrawal from smokeless tobacco (Hatsukami, Gust and Keenan, 1987) and nicotine gum (Hughes, Hatsukami and Skoog, 1986; West and Russell, 1985b; West, Russell, Jarvis, Pizzey and Kadam, 1984). The signs and symptoms found resulting from acute cessation of nicotine gum intake indicate that the tobacco withdrawal syndrome may be a direct result of nicotine deprivation as opposed to other components of cigarettes. Studies have also shown that some of the signs and symptoms of tobacco withdrawal, although not all, have been found to be alleviated by nicotine gum (Schneider, Jarvik and Forsythe, 1984; Hughes and Hatsukami, 1986). This finding again indicates that some of these signs and symptoms may be directly due to nicotine rather than other constituents of tobacco. Smokeless tobacco thus would have the same type of withdrawal syndrome, as evidenced by the data, since it is deprivation of nicotine which is primarily responsible for these signs and symptoms. The occurrence of withdrawal signs and symptoms may reflect lowering of blood or brain levels of nicotine with consequent release of overdeveloped compensatory mechanisms. That is, an adaptation to certain nicotine levels has occurred, and sudden withdrawal lowers the nicotine levels, allowing compensatory mechanisms which have developed to take over. This is a general phenomenon seen with all forms of drug dependence and withdrawal.

Table 1 Diagnostic criteria for nicotine withdrawal (DSM-IIIR)

A: Daily use of nicotine for at least several weeks; and
B: Abrupt cessation of nicotine use, or reduction in the amount of nicotine use followed within 24 hours by at least four of the following signs:
  (1) craving for nicotine
  (2) irritability, frustration or anger
  (3) anxiety
  (4) difficulty concentrating
  (5) restlessness
  (6) decreased heart rate
  (7) increased appetite or weight gain

A true withdrawal sign or symptom should therefore be indicated by a rebound or overshoot caused by the drug resulting from the release of the compensatory mechanisms, and not merely a return to normal or baseline levels of functioning. For example, decreases in heart rate, increases in weight, or changes in electrocortical activity may not be nicotine withdrawal manifestations but rather merely a return to no-smoking levels. Heart rate has been found to decrease to levels found among nonsmokers (Weybrew and Stark, 1967). Weight gain has persisted for long periods of time (Blitzer, Rimm and Giefer, 1977) and has also been reported to approach levels of nonsmokers (Khosla and Lowe, 1971; Lincoln, 1969; Wack and Rodin, 1982). The dominant alpha-frequency of the EEG has been found to be similar for smokers and nonsmokers, thereby leading to the speculation that the decreased alpha-frequency found after tobacco deprivation is the actual baseline state of the smoker (Knott and Venables, 1978, 1979). Unfortunately, few studies have plotted the course of signs and symptoms of withdrawal over prolonged periods of time. More recent studies show that the signs and symptoms of withdrawal demonstrating an overshoot phenomenon following four to five days of cigarette deprivation include increased craving for tobacco, anxiety, problems with concentration, caloric intake, problems with sleep, and general subjective distress (Hatsukami et al., 1985a; Hughes and Hatuskami, 1986; Schneider and Jarvik, 1985). Hutchinson and Emley (1973) found a clear overshoot phenomenon for masseter contractions examined over the course of a month for some of their human subjects. When examining squirrel monkeys, they also found that when nicotine was withdrawn after chronic administration the subjects showed large increases in post-shock biting attack behavior which then returned to pre-drug biting level. West et al. (1984) found the occurrence of a rebound phenomenon in urinary adrenaline concentrations which dropped significantly in the first three days of cigarette withdrawal followed by a significant rise. The majority of these studies show that the onset of withdrawal effects is rapid and peaks at the end of 24–72 hours.

There are several studies which have demonstrated that the signs and symptoms resulting from cigarette deprivation are alleviated by the resumption of cigarette smoking. The study which most clearly depicts this is one conducted by Hughes, Hatsukami, Pickens, Krahn, Malin and Luknic (1984). In this study the consistency of tobacco withdrawal syndrome across repeated periods of abstinence was measured using a modified A–B–A–B design. They found that the changes in functioning occurred during cigarette deprivation, returned to levels prior to cigarette deprivation upon resumption of cigarette smoking, and then recurred during a second deprivation period. The symptoms which showed consistent changes in all subjects were: supine heart rate, insomnia, reduced caloric intake, irritability, restlessness, drowsiness, general mood disturbance (measured by the profile of mood states), and withdrawal discomfort (a composite score based on the Shiffman–Jarvik questionnaire). Furthermore, the intensity of the withdrawal discomfort experienced within subjects across the two deprivation periods was similar.

Thus, it appears that there is good evidence to support the existence of a tobacco withdrawal syndrome. There is clear evidence: (1) that there are changes in subjective, behavioral and physiological functioning which occur after tobacco and nicotine deprivation; (2) that some of these withdrawal signs and symptoms demonstrate either an overshoot or rebound phenomenon; and (3) that these signs and symptoms are alleviated with the reinstitution of tobacco (or nicotine). Furthermore, we have evidence that the severity of withdrawal may be dose-dependent (Pomerleau, Fertig and Shanahan, 1983; Hatsukami, Hughes and Pickens, 1985b; Zeidenberg, Jaffe, Kanzler, Levitt, Langone and Van Vunakis, 1977; West and Russell, 1985a). For example, West and Russell (1985b) found that pre-abstinence plasma nicotine concentration significantly predicted craving, hunger, restlessness, inability to concentrate and overall withdrawal severity. Finally, most of these symptoms have been demonstrated to be specifically due to the pharmacological effects of nicotine.

Now the question is how important is this withdrawal syndrome for the occurrence of dependence on a drug such as nicotine? One way to address this question is to examine the extent to which people who manifest all the behaviors ascribed to the aforementioned definition of drug dependence also exhibit symptoms of withdrawal. In a study conducted by Hughes, Gust and Pechacek (1987), only 21 percent of the subjects who were classified as experiencing a tobacco dependence disorder showed the tobacco withdrawal syndrome according to DSM III criteria (see Table 2). The results could indicate that either the DSM III classification of tobacco dependence disorder and/or tobacco withdrawal syndrome is not valid, or the withdrawal syndrome is not an important feature for the occurrence of general dependence on a drug. Hughes and his associates also examined a classification system of tobacco withdrawal which they developed. They considered it to have more validity than the DSM III definition and to be more in line with the recently revised DSM III-R criteria (see Table 2). They found that, when using their criteria, 46 percent of cigarette quitters experienced a tobacco withdrawal syndrome. Thus, 54 percent of these cigarette quitters did not experience a withdrawal syndrome.

Table 2 Diagnostic criteria for tobacco withdrawal

DSM-III criteria
A: Use tobacco for at least several weeks at a level equivalent to more than 20
    cigarettes/day with each cigarette containing at least 0.5 mg of nicotine.
and
B: At least four of the following within 24 hours of stopping:
    (1) craving for tobacco
    (2) irritability
    (3) anxiety
    (4) difficulty concentrating
    (5) restlessness
    (6) headache
    (7) drowsiness
    (8) gastrointestinal disturbances

Hughes et al. (1987) criteria
At least four of the following when stopping for 24 hours:
(1–5) symptoms 1–5 of the DSM-III criteria
    (6) increased appetite
    (7) impatience
    (8) somatic complaints (headache, dizziness, tremor, stomach or bowel problems)
    (9) insomnia

Another way to examine this question is to determine to what extent smokers relapse or continue to smoke due to signs and symptoms of withdrawal. Both retrospective and prospective studies have shown contradictory findings in the importance of withdrawal symptoms in relapse to smoking. Some studies have shown that smokers who are unsuccessful in quitting report more withdrawal symptoms than successful quitters (Shiffman, 1979), and that withdrawal symptoms can predict relapse (Gunn, 1986; Manley and Boland, 1983). Other studies have shown withdrawal symptoms rarely account for the occurrence of relapse (Schachter, 1982; Hughes and Hatsukami, 1986). Most relapses occur long after obvious signs of physiological abstinence have disappeared. A prolonged physiological withdrawal syndrome to opioids has been demonstrated (Martin and Kay, 1977) and a similar situation might occur with smokers, but this has not yet been demonstrated. In addition, withdrawal symptoms may become conditioned to external or internal stimuli which may take several months to extinguish.

In summary, there is clear evidence that both tolerance and dependence to tobacco develop with chronic use, as in cigarette smoking. Acute withdrawal from nicotine, while causing mild to severe distress, unlike opioids or sedative-hypnotics, is almost never accompanied by debilitating illness. At this point there is no universally accepted classification system of withdrawal similar to that of Himmelsbach's scale of opiate withdrawal (1942). However, the DSM III-R criteria perhaps provide the best classification scheme at this time. The individual differences observed in the occurrence of withdrawal signs and symptoms or tolerance among those classified as 'dependent' on tobacco have not yet been extensively studied. Furthermore, the effects of withdrawal signs and symptoms to relapse require explanation. It appears that the urge to smoke is prompted in varying degrees both by withdrawal relief and by positive reinforcement.

CONCLUSIONS

(1) Dependence upon tobacco implies repetitive drug-seeking behavior in spite of experience of knowledge of possible adverse consequences.
(2) Nicotine-seeking behavior may in part be due to physical dependence.
(3) Tobacco use may be due to positive reinforcement from nicotine.
(4) Not all individuals who use tobacco regularly appear to be physically dependent on, or tolerant to, the drug. Perhaps this is in part due to the fact that we have not been able to measure subtle physiological and psychological changes which may occur due to deprivation from the drug. Research with more sensitive measures is clearly needed.

ACKNOWLEDGEMENTS

This work was supported in part by National Institute of Drug Abuse Research Grants Nos. DA 02988, DA 03848 and DA 05013, and by the Medical Research Service of the Veterans Administration.

REFERENCES

Beckett, A.H., Gorrod, J.W., and Jenner, P. (1971). The effect of smoking on nicotine metabolism in vivo in Man. *Journal of Pharmacy and Pharmacology*, Suppl., **23**, 625–627.

Blitzer, P.H., Rimm, A.A., and Giefer, E.E. (1977). The effect of smoking cessation on body weight in 57,032 women: cross-sectional and longitudinal analyses. *Journal of Chronic Diseases*, **30**, 415–429.

Grabowski, J., and Hall, S.M. (eds) (1985). *Pharmacological Adjuncts in Smoking Cessation*. National Institute on Drug Abuse Monograph 53. Washington, DC: Department of Health and Human Services.

Gunn, R.C. (1986). Reactions to withdrawal symptoms and success in smoking cessation clinics. *Addictive Behaviors*, **11**, 49–53.

Hatsukami, D.K., Gust, S.W., and Keenan, R.M. (1987). Physiologic and subjective changes from smokeless tobacco withdrawal. *Clinical Pharmacology and Therapeutics*, **41**, 103–107.

Hatsukami, D.K., Hughes, J.R., and Pickens, R.W. (1985a). Characteristics of tobacco abstinence: physiological and subjective effects. In: J. Grabowski and S.M. Hall (eds), *Pharmacological Adjuncts in Smoking Cessation*. National Institute on Drug Abuse Monograph Series 53. Washington, DC: US Department of Health and Human Services.

Hatsukami, D.K., Hughes, J.R., and Pickens, R.W. (1985b). Blood nicotine, smoke exposure and tobacco withdrawal symptoms. *Addictive Behaviors*, **10**, 413–417.

Himmelsbach, C.K. (1942). Clinical studies of drug addiction. Physical dependence, withdrawal and recovery. *Archives of Internal Medicine*, **69**, 766–772.

Hughes, J.R., and Hatsukami, D.K. (1986). Signs and symptoms of tobacco withdrawal. *Archives of General Psychiatry*, **43**, 289–294.

Hughes, J.R., Gust, S.W., and Pechacek, T.F. (1987). Prevalence of tobacco dependence and withdrawal. *American Journal of Psychiatry*, **144**, 205–208.

Hughes, J.R., Hatsukami, D.K., Pickens, R.W., Krahn, D., Malin, S., and Luknic, A. (1984). Effect of nicotine on the tobacco withdrawal syndrome. *Psychopharmacology*, **83**, 82–87.

Hughes, J.R., Hatsukami, D.K., and Skoog, K.P. (1986). Physical dependence on nicotine gum: a placebo substitution trial. *Journal of the American Medical Association*, **255**, 3277–3279.

Hutchinson, R.R., and Emley, G.S. (1973). Effects of nicotine on avoidance, conditioned suppression, and aggression response measures in animals and man. In: W.L. Dunn, Jr (ed.), *Smoking Behavior: Motives and Incentives*. Washington, DC: Winston, pp. 171–188.

Jaffe, J.H., and Jarvik, M.E. (1978). Tobacco use and tobacco use disorder. In: M.A. Lipton, A. Di Mascio and K.F. Killam (eds), *Psychopharmacology: A Generation of Progress*. New York: Raven Press, pp. 1665–1676.

Jarvik, M.E. (1973). Further observations on nicotine as the reinforcing agent in smoking. In: W.L. Dunn, Jr (ed.), *Smoking Behavior: Motives and Incentives*. Washington, DC: Winston, pp. 33–49.

Jarvik, M.E. (with the assistance of Maxwell, K., Pearlman, P., and Fowler, J.) (1979). Biological influences on cigarette smoking. In: N.A. Krasnegor (ed.), *The Behavioral Aspects of Smoking*. National Institute on Drug Abuse Research Monograph 27. Washington, DC: US Department of Health, Education and Welfare, pp. 268–274.

Jones, R.T., Farrell, T.R., and Herning, R.I. (1978). Tobacco smoking and nicotine tolerance. In: N.A. Krasnegor (ed.), *Self-Administration of Abused Substances: Methods for Study*. National Institute on Drug Abuse Research Monograph 20. Washington, DC: US Department of Health, Education and Welfare.

Khosla, T., and Lowe, C.R. (1971). Obesity and smoking habits. *British Medical Journal*, **4**, 10–13.

Knott, V.J., and Venables, P.H. (1977). EEG alpha correlates of non-smokers, smokers, smoking, and smoking deprivation. *Psychophysiology*, **14**, 150–156.

Knott, V.J., and Venables, P.H. (1978). Stimulus intensity control and the cortical evoked response in smokers and nonsmokers. *Psychophysiology*, **15**(3), 186–192.

Knott, V.J., and Venables, P.H. (1979). EEG alpha correlates of alcohol consumption in smokers and nonsmokers. *Journal of Studies on Alcohol*, **40**, 247–257.

Lamb, C. (In: Bartlett, J., 1980). A farewell to tobacco. *Familiar Quotations*, 15th edn. E.M. Beck (ed.). Boston: Little, Brown, p. 442.

Lincoln, J.E. (1969). Weight gain after cessation of smoking. *Journal of the American Medical Association*, **210**, 1765.

MacRae, J.R., Scoles, M.T., and Siegel, S. (1987). The contribution of Pavlovian conditioning to drug tolerance and dependence. *British Journal of Addiction*, **82**, 371–380.

Manley, R., and Boland, F. (1983). Side-effects and weight gain following a smoking cessation program. *Addictive Behaviors*, **8**, 375–380.

Martin, W.R., and Kay, D.C. (1977). Effects of opioid analgesics and antagonists on the EEG. In: V.G. Longo (ed.), *Handbook of Electroencephalography and Clinical Neurophysiology*, vol. 7, Part C. Amsterdam: Elsevier, pp. 97–109.

Morrison, C.F., and Stephenson, J.A. (1972). The occurrence of tolerance to a central depressant effect of nicotine. *British Journal of Pharmacology*, **46**, 151–156.

Pomerleau, O., Fertig, J., and Shanahan, S. (1983). Nicotine dependence in cigarette smoking. An empirically based, multivariate model. *Pharmacology, Biochemistry and Behavior*, **19**, 291–299.

Rose, J.E., Zinser, M.C., Tashkin, D.P., Newcomb, R., and Ertle, A. (1984). Subjective response to cigarette smoking following airway anesthetization. *Addictive Behaviors*, **9**, 211–215.

Schachter, S. (1982). Recidivism and self-cure of smoking and obesity. *American Psychologist*, **37**, 436–444.

Schneider, N.G., and Jarvik, M.E. (1985). Nicotine vs placebo gum: comparisons of withdrawal symptoms and success rates. In: J. Grabowski and S.M. Hall (eds), *Pharmacological Adjuncts in Smoking Cessation*. National Institute on Drug Abuse Monograph 53. Washington, DC: US Department of Health and Human Services, pp. 83–101.

Schneider, N.G., Jarvik, M.E., and Forsythe, A.B. (1984). Nicotine vs placebo gum in the alleviation of withdrawal during smoking cessation. *Addictive Behaviors*, **8**, 256–261.

Shiffman, S.M. (1979). The tobacco withdrawal syndrome. In: N.A. Krasnegor (ed.), *Cigarette Smoking as a Dependence Process*. National Institute on Drug Abuse Research Monograph 23. Washington, DC: US Department of Health, Education and Welfare, pp. 158–184.

Stolerman, I.P., Goldfarb, T., Fink, R., and Jarvik, M.E. (1973). Influencing cigarette smoking with nicotine antagonists. *Psychopharmacologia*, **28**, 247–259.

United States Department of Health, Education and Welfare (1964). *A Report to the Surgeon General*. Public Health Service. Washington, DC: US Government Printing Office.

United States Department of Health and Human Services (1988). *A Report to the Surgeon General*. Public Health Service. Washington, DC: US Government Printing Office.

Wack, J.T., and Rodin, J. (1982). Smoking and its effects on body weight and the systems of caloric regulation. *American Journal of Clinical Nutrition*, **35**, 366–380.

West, R.J., and Russell, M.A.H. (1985a). Effects of withdrawal from long-term nicotine gum use. *Psychological Medicine*, **15**, 891–893.

West, R.J., and Russell, M.A.H. (1985b). Pre-abstinence smoke intake and smoking motivation as predictors of cigarette withdrawal symptoms. *Psychopharmacology*, **87**, 334–336.

West, R.J., Russell, M.A.H., Jarvis, M.J., Pizzey, T., and Kadam, B. (1984). Urinary adrenaline concentrations during 10 days of smoking abstinence. *Psychopharmacology*, **84**, 141–142.

Weybrew, B.B., and Stark, J.E. (1967). *Psychological and Physiological Changes Associated with Deprivation From Smoking*. US Naval Submarine Medical Center Report No. 490.

Zeidenberg, P., Jaffe, J.H., Kanzler, M., Levitt, M.D., Langone, J.J., and Van Vunakis, H. (1977). Nicotine: cotinine levels in blood during cessation of smoking. *Comprehensive Psychiatry*, **18**, 93–101.

4

A Biobehavioral Perspective on Smoking

OVIDE F. POMERLEAU
and
CYNTHIA S. POMERLEAU

ABSTRACT

Formulations of smoking stressing physiological addiction or behavioral factors do not adequately explain its tenacity. This chapter reviews evidence that nicotine alters the bioavailability of behaviorally active neuroregulators; thus, it can be used as a pharmacological 'coping response', promoting temporary improvements in affect or performance. An understanding of these processes may lead to more effective therapies.

INTRODUCTION

The long litany of pathological conditions associated with cigarette smoking and tobacco use has been frequently rehearsed (Clee and Clark, 1984). The most devastating of these involve the cardiovascular and pulmonary systems, with epidemiological studies documenting the role of smoking as a contributor to acute myocardial infarction and sudden cardiac death (Auerbach, Carter, Garfinkel and Hammond, 1976). The pathological processes whereby smoking causes or enhances the risk of coronary heart disease seem to involve carbon monoxide, which compromises myocardial oxygen supply by elevating carboxyhemoglobin levels (Koch, Hoffman, Steck, Horsch, Hengen and Morl, 1980). This effect is exacerbated by the cardiovascular effects of nicotine, which include stimulation of sympathetic neurons and

Smoking and Human Behavior, Edited by T. Ney and A. Gale
© 1989 John Wiley & Sons Ltd

release of adrenal medullary catecholamines, resulting in increased blood pressure, cardiac rate, and myocardial oxygen demand (Cryer, Haymond, Santiago and Shah, 1976; Trap-Jensen, Carlsen, Svendsen and Christensen, 1979).

Manifestations of smoking-related pulmonary pathology include chest and respiratory tract infections (Bewley, Halil and Snaith, 1973; Colley, Douglas and Reid, 1973; Crowdy and Sowden, 1975), chronic bronchitis and emphysema (Doll and Peto, 1976), and bronchial carcinoma (Califano, 1979; Doll and Peto, 1976). Smokers' chances of dying from lung cancer are ten times those of nonsmokers (Brett and Benjamin, 1968), with early onset of smoking (Doll and Hill, 1964; Hammond, 1966), inhaling (Royal College of Physicians, 1977), relighting half-smoked cigarettes (Dark, O'Connor, Pemberton and Russell, 1963), and holding the cigarette in the mouth between puffs (Brett and Benjamin, 1968) associated with higher risk.

THEORIES OF SMOKING

The persistence of smoking in the face of these well-publicized statistics defies simple explanation. A number of theorists in the late 1970s conceptualized smoking as primarily an escape-avoidance response to the aversive consequences of nicotine withdrawal (Jarvik, 1977; Russell, 1977; Schachter, 1978). This formulation is essentially an addiction model, implying regulation to achieve a minimal level of nicotine intake, tolerance to nicotine, and a defined symptomatology in the absence of the drug. By implication, pleasurable or other reinforcing aspects of the drug are discretionary or incidental, as can be seen in the widely used definition of tobacco dependence in the *Diagnostic and Statistical Manual* (DSM III) of the American Psychiatric Association (Spitzer, 1980; see Chapter 3 in this volume). The addiction model is supported by demonstrations of both regulation and tolerance in humans and infrahumans (Gritz, 1980; Jarvik, 1979; McMorrow and Foxx, 1983; Pomerleau, Fertig and Shanahan, 1983c). Tobacco withdrawal symptoms, however, have been somewhat more difficult to document and have generally been found to vary from smoker to smoker as well as from environment to environment (Hatsukami, Hughes and Pickens, 1985); they are relatively mild, even at their peak (Hatsukami, Hughes, Pickens and Svikis, 1984; Shiffman and Jarvik, 1976). Indeed, as several investigators (Ashton and Stepney, 1982; Schachter, Silverstein, Kozlowski, Perlick, Herman and Liebling, 1977) have observed, smokers are able to undergo extended periods of deprivation under certain conditions without experiencing much discomfort. Only recently have investigators been satisfied that the scientific criteria for physiological addiction to nicotine have been fully met at both the human and animal level (Henningfield, Miyasato and Jasinski, 1985; Henningfield and Jasinski, 1987).

The opponent process theory of acquired motivation proposed by Solomon (Solomon, 1977; Solomon and Corbit, 1974) exerted considerable influence upon psychological thinking about drug abuse in general in the 1970s and represented an attempt to incorporate behavioral as well as physiological factors into an integrated model of substance abuse. It postulates central mechanisms operating homeostatically to reduce significant departures, either positive or negative, from affective equilibrium. According to this analysis, an initial drug-induced euphoria is followed, after a delay, by a compensatory decrease in pleasure as the drug effect decays and a neutral state is restored. With repeated use the euphoria weakens, and the compensatory response becomes dominant, causing the user to seek larger drug doses in an effort to offset dysphoria (perceived as craving or withdrawal). Like the addiction model, then, it ultimately explains addiction in terms of withdrawal. The theory has been applied to smoking (Solomon and Corbitt, 1973; Ternes, 1977), as described in some detail by Pomerleau (1980); its implications are still largely untested, however, and physiological and biochemical manifestations of euphoria, dysphoria and craving have not been identified.

Although 'addiction' is clearly a factor in the maintenance of smoking, neither of the above theories seems adequate as a comprehensive explanation, nor do they satisfactorily account for the difficulties most smokers experience in quitting (Karras, 1982; Shiffman, 1982). Investigation of situations that cue smoking (Best and Hakstian, 1978; Epstein and Collins, 1977), retrospective examination of factors associated with craving (Myrsten, Elgerot and Edgren, 1977), and analysis of the circumstances surrounding recidivism (Pomerleau, Adkins and Pertschuk, 1978; Shiffman, 1982) indicate that stimuli independent of the nicotine-addiction cycle (i.e. unrelated to the time since the last cigarette) reliably increase the probability of smoking. Such stimuli include termination of a meal, coffee drinking, dysphoric states, and cognitive and intellectual demands. Consistent with these observations are reports that many cigarettes are smoked because of perceived improvement in performance, enhancement of pleasure or relaxation, and relief of anxiety (Mausner and Platt, 1971; Pomerleau, 1986). Thus, with the exception of the first cigarette of the day, or after an extended period of deprivation, many cigarettes smoked have no clear connection with nicotine deprivation or time since the last cigarette.

Schachter, a prominent proponent of the addiction model, attempted to resolve this apparent difficulty. He and his colleagues (Schachter et al., 1977) demonstrated that smokers smoke more when anxious or when subjected to painful stimulation (for example, before giving a lecture, during doctoral examinations, after receiving electric shocks, etc.); they also found that these stressors decreased urinary pH, which led them to hypothesize that acidification of the urine (known to increase the excretion of nicotine; Goodman and Gilman, 1958) by stress caused nicotine withdrawal. Schachter (1978) concluded from these and related studies that the principal consequence of smoking is simply relief from the painful and anxiety-provoking state of nicotine withdrawal. Schachter's data were not based on direct measurement of changes in plasma nicotine or of nicotine withdrawal during stress, however, and the conclusions may not be warranted. For instance, Rosenberg, Benowitz, Jacob and Wilson (1980) administered intravenous nicotine boli to smokers at widely differing urinary pH and found only small differences in peak and trough plasma nicotine at low pH, with no differences in subjective or physiological responses during the time period in which stress-induced smoking occurs. It is equally plausible, therefore, that nicotine may produce *direct* physiological and biochemical changes that, in addition to relieving withdrawal, provide pleasurable sensations, enhance performance or alleviate anxiety in stressful situations.

These observations argue the need for a broader-based conceptualization of dependence that includes reinforcement value (generally using self-administration as an index; for example, Henningfield et al., 1985) among the criteria for dependence, along with the associated phenomena of discriminability and conditionability (Iversen and Iversen, 1981). The rationale is that these properties, while not exclusive to 'addictive' substances, are shared by virtually all and could be said to constitute a profile of such drugs. This formulation is buttressed by demonstrations that laboratory animals will maintain drug intake at doses below those necessary to induce physical dependence (Deneau, Yanagita and Seevers, 1969; van Ree, Slangen and de Wied, 1975) and that they will persistently self-administer such drugs, even in the absence of clearcut withdrawal symptoms (Pickens, 1968). At the human level, recent research by Rose and his colleagues (Rose, 1988; Rose, Tashkin, Ertle, Zinser and Lafer, 1985), in which sensory blockade of the upper bronchi reduced smoking satisfaction independently of nicotine level or withdrawal status, lends support for a hedonic, pleasure-potentiating factor involving the upper airways in smoking.

There is now considerable evidence to suggest that the tenacity of the cigarette smoking habit is based upon different reinforcing effects appropriate to a variety of circumstances (Pomerleau and Pomerleau, 1984). In fact, most behavioral strategies for treating smoking have been based on the assumption that both escape from withdrawal and the other reinforcing consequences of smoking must be disrupted if stimulus control of the habit is to be effectively terminated (Pomerleau, 1979). This perspective is derived from behavior modification theory, and ultimately from operant conditioning concepts that emphasize the contribution of antecedent and consequent environmental stimuli in determining behavior (Pomerleau, 1981). Implicitly or explicitly, however, these formulations ascribe the rewarding aspects of smoking to 'conditioning' and have little to say about the biological substrate for the reinforcement of smoking or the mediation of environment–behavior interactions. What is called for at this juncture is an integrated formulation of smoking that takes into account the complexity of the pharmacological actions of nicotine and the contribution of both behavioral and biological factors.

A BIOBEHAVIORAL EXPLANATION OF SMOKING

A review of the pharmacological effects of inhaled nicotine makes clear that the drug exerts direct and indirect effects upon several neuroregulatory systems. It acts initially upon nicotinic cholinergic receptors, mimicking the effects of acetylcholine at low doses but blocking transmission after initial agonist activity at higher doses (Volle and Koelle, 1975). It readily penetrates into the brain, where it has been shown to act upon central nicotinic cholinergic receptors (Clarke, 1987; Romano, Goldstein and Jewell, 1981; Roth, McIntyre and Barchas, 1982); a biphasic response paralleling the peripheral pattern of activation superseded by blockade has been inferred (Ashton and Stepney, 1982; Gritz, 1980). Though the drug influences both sympathetic and parasympathetic activity, its most striking peripheral effects are sympathomimetic (Volle and Koelle, 1975), involving release of norepinephrine (noradrenaline) from postganglionic sites and epinephrine (adrenaline) from the adrenal medulla (Kershbaum, Pappajohn, Bellet, Hirabayashi and Shafiiha, 1968; Westfall and Watts, 1964).

Centrally, nicotine has been shown to increase rates of release and turnover of acetylcholine and the catecholamines, norepinephrine, epinephrine and dopamine (Andersson, Fuxe, Eneroth and Agnati, 1982; Balfour, 1982; Cryer et al., 1976; Goodman, 1974; Hall and Turner, 1972; Westfall, 1974). Nicotine also alters and stimulates the release of a variety of neuromodulatory peptides, including arginine vasopressin (Husain, Frantz, Ciarochi and Robinson, 1975; Pomerleau, Fertig, Seyler and Jaffe, 1983b), growth hormone (Wilkins, Carlson, van Vunakis, Hill, Gritz and Jarvik, 1982), prolactin (Wilkins et al., 1982), and endogenous opioids (Kamerling, Wettstein, Sloan, Su and Martin, 1982; Marty, Erwin, Cornell and Zgombick, 1984; Rosecrans, Hendry and Hong, 1985; Novack and Allen-Rowlands, 1985; Pomerleau et al., 1983b; Seyler, Pomerleau, Fertig, Hunt and Parker, 1986; Yao, Narita, Baba, Kudo, Kudo and Oyama, 1985). Serotonin (5-hydroxytryptamine) is apparently affected by nicotine as well, but the nature of the relationship is not well understood, with reports of decreased turnover in some brain locations (Benwell and Balfour, 1982; Fuxe, Everitt and Hokfelt, 1979) and of increased activity at other sites (e.g. Bhargana, Salamy and Shah, 1981; Lee, 1985). The neuroendocrinological effects of nicotine have been reviewed at some length in a recent report of the Surgeon General of the United States (USDHHS, 1988).

Many of the endogenous substances whose synthesis, release and turnover in the central nervous system are affected by nicotine have been shown, independently of nicotine, to influence behavior and subjective state. Cholinergic mechanisms, for example, seem to play a role in learning and memory (Davis and Yamamura, 1978; Wesnes and Revell, 1984), alertness (electrocortical arousal; Kawamura and Domino, 1969), and pain inhibition (Green and Kitchen, 1986; Kaakola and Ahtee, 1977; Pert and Maxey, 1975). Noradrenergic pathways are associated with modulation of arousal level (Robbins, 1984; Mason, 1980; Redmond, 1979; Carruthers, 1976), and stimulation of central pathways such as those in the locus coeruleus is associated with improvements in selective attention, increased alertness, enhanced vigilance and facilitation of rapid information processing (Olpe, Jones and Steinmann, 1983; Svensson, 1987; Svensson and Engberg, 1980). A number of studies have identified dopaminergic neurons as a critical part of the brain reward mechanism (Wise, 1983; Wise and Bozarth, 1982). Though its behavioral effects are still not well understood, administration of vasopressin has been shown to promote memory consolidation and retrieval in both normal and memory-deficient populations (Legros, Gilot, Seron, Claessen, Adam, Moeglen, Audibert and Berchier, 1978; Weingartner, Gold, Ballenger, Smallberg, Summers, Rubinow, Post and Goodwin, 1981). Finally, endogenous opioids have been linked to pain reduction (Green and Kitchen, 1986; Tripathi, Martin and Aceto, 1982) and alleviation of anxiety (Hill, 1981; Millan and Emrich, 1981); they may have a direct rewarding effect as well (van Ree and de Wied, 1981).

These endogenous neuroregulators, as noted, can exert their behavioral effects independently of nicotine administration. But because nicotine alters the bioavailability of such substances, it is reasonable to suppose that smokers learn to 'use' the drug to regulate or fine-tune the body's normal adaptive mechanisms. Table 1 gives an idea of the range and diversity of the subjective and behavioral consequences that have been reported or demonstrated for smoking. The congruence of these consequences with the psychological effects of the endogenous neuroregulators known to be stimulated by nicotine is striking. Table 2, based on a recently promulgated biobehavioral theory of smoking (Pomerleau and Pomerleau, 1984), suggests possible links between the reinforcing consequences of smoking and putative neuroregulatory mechanisms. (In those situations in which the pre-smoking context is neutral or positive and does not involve deprivation or aversive stimulation, the reinforcing consequences have been classified as positive reinforcers. Alternatively, in those situations in which an aversive state or behavioral deficiency can be identified as part of the presmoking context, the reinforcing consequences have been classified as negative reinforcers.)

Table 1   Commonly reported behavioral and subjective effects of smoking

---

Consequences of smoking in habitual smokers
↑ concentration/ ↑ ability to tune out irrelevant stimuli
↑ memory (recall)
↑ psychomotor performance
↑ alertness/ ↑ arousal
↓ anxiety/ ↓ tension
↑ pleasure/ ↑ facilitation of pleasure
↓ body weight (↓ consumption of sweet-tasting substances?)

Consequences of not smoking in habitual smokers
↓ concentration/ ↓ ability to tune out irrelevant stimuli
memory impairment
impaired psychomotor performance
dullness/anhedonia
↑ anxiety/ ↑ tension
↑ irritability/ ↑ dysphoria
↑ craving for cigarettes
↑ body weight (↑ consumption of sweet-tasting substances?)

Adapted from Pomerleau and Pomerleau, 1984.

Table 2   Reinforcement consequences of smoking and putative neuroregulatory mechanisms

Positive reinforcement	Negative reinforcement
Pleasure/enhancement of pleasure	Reduction of anxiety and tension
↑ dopamine	↑ acetylcholine
↑ norepinephrine	↑ beta-endorphin
↑ beta-endorphin	Antinociception
Facilitation of task performance	↑ acetylcholine
↑ acetylcholine	↑ beta-endorphin
↑ norepinephrine	Avoidance of weight gain
Improvement of memory	↑ dopamine
↑ acetylcholine	↑ norepinephrine
↑ norepinephrine	Relief from nicotine withdrawal
↑ vasopressin (?)	↑ acetylcholine
	(↑ noncholinergic
	nicotinic activity?)

Adapted from Pomerleau and Pomerleau, 1984.

In accordance with the above conceptualization, dysphoric states such as anxiety may prompt smoking because such distress has previously been alleviated by the anxiolytic effects of nicotine-stimulated beta-endorphin release and/or cholinergic activity. Similarly, work or performance demand may trigger smoking because sustained psychomotor performance and alertness have been enhanced in the past by increased cholinergic and/or noradrenergic activity. Though these effects of nicotine may be associated with parallel changes in the neuroregulatory substrates for nicotine withdrawal, a series of studies in our laboratory (Fertig, Pomerleau and Sanders, 1986; Pomerleau, Turk and Fertig, 1984) suggests that favorable or adaptive drug effects unrelated to the addiction/withdrawal cycle can be produced by nicotine (Pomerleau, 1986). These studies clearly demonstrated nicotine-produced antinociception using a mode of nicotine administration (intranasal snuff) unfamiliar to minimally deprived cigarette smokers as well as to ex-smokers (who were no longer nicotine-dependent and thus not susceptible to relief of nicotine withdrawal).

The number of affective states or performance demands (and associated stimuli) that might cue smoking independently of nicotine withdrawal is potentially very large, providing a plausible explanation for the thorough interweaving of the smoking habit into the fabric of daily life (Pomerleau and Pomerleau, 1984). The fact that nicotine does not produce a dramatic intoxication or withdrawal may even add to its reinforcing value, in that the 'benefits' of smoking may be achieved without disrupting ongoing activity.

Because nicotine exerts its actions upon several neuroregulatory systems, smoking may provide a variety of temporary but potentially useful effects applicable to different situations. Nicotine can produce both arousing and calming effects. The mechanisms underlying this biphasic response are not yet well understood (USDHHS, 1988; Russell, 1987). Among the possibilities is that in low doses nicotine from smoking enhances arousal by stimulating both cholinergic and catecholaminergic activity (Jarvik, 1979; Lee, 1985; Wesnes and Warburton, 1983), whereas in higher doses the initial phase of cholinergic activation is followed by sedation or relaxation resulting from cholinergic blockade (Ashton and Stepney, 1982); such a pattern would parallel the peripheral actions of nicotine (Volle and Koelle, 1975). Alternatively, it may be that at lower doses the cholinergic–catecholaminergic response predominates, producing arousal; but at higher doses (centrally) the initial response is superseded or swamped by a slower and longer-lasting endogenous opioid response (Pomerleau and Pomerleau, 1984). This interpretation is strengthened by the demonstration of a significant dose–response relationship between nicotine from smoking research cigarettes and beta-endorphin in plasma (Pomerleau et al., 1983b) and of significant decreases in plasma beta-endorphin levels after a few hours of abstinence and significant increases upon resumption of smoking using commercial cigarettes (Yao et al., 1985). Additional support comes from the finding that mean inspiratory flow rate increases during smoking but is depressed shortly after smoking; naloxone administration does not affect the initial stimulation of respiration in response to smoking but blunts the subsequent depression (Tobin, Jenouri and Sackner, 1982).

Regardless of the mechanism, considerable evidence has been accumulated suggesting that smokers readily learn to adjust nicotine intake—in effect, 'sculpting' neuroregulatory responses to achieve selective enhancement of one component or the other of the biphasic response (Ashton and Stepney, 1982). Thus, they may take in lower doses to obtain stimulation or higher doses to obtain sedative effects, depending on environmental demands (Ashton, Millman, Rawlins, Telford and Thompson, 1978; Gilbert, 1979; Golding and Mangan, 1982; Mangan and Golding, 1984; Rose, Ananda and Jarvik, 1983; Warburton and Wesnes, 1978). Personality factors such as predisposition to underarousal or to anxiety may also contribute to the individual differences observed in nicotine self-administration (Eysenck, 1967; Myrsten, Andersson, Frankenhauser and Elgerot, 1975; Spielberger, 1986).

IMPLICATIONS FOR RESEARCH

The biobehavioral formulation described above is an attempt to explain how smoking, once initiated, is so tenaciously maintained. Figure 1 makes explicit some formal elements and identifies critical areas for investigation. Among the major components are (a) conditions that predispose or modulate smoking behavior or nicotine reinforcement unconditionally, (b) internal and external environmental factors that provide the stimulus context for smoking and set the occasion for reinforcement, (c) smoking and nicotine administration, along with the neuroregulatory effects that define the biobehavioral response, and finally, (d) the reinforcing consequences (favorable changes in performance and/or affect as well as relief of withdrawal) that maintain smoking behavior.

Some of the links represented in Figure 1 are more firmly established than others. Though not all of the findings are unequivocal, there is a large body of research on the behavioral and subjective effects of smoking and nicotine intake (see Ashton and Stepney, 1982). Nicotine's effects on key neuroregulators have also been documented (Balfour, 1982). Whether such neuroregulatory changes are indeed a controlling (causal) factor in the reinforcement of smoking, and not simply an epiphenomenon, however, remains unproven. Experiments using cholinergic, noradrenergic and endogenous opioid agonists and antagonists (see reviews by Jarvik, 1979; Karras, 1982; Pomerleau and Pomerleau, 1984) tend to support such an inference, but much more research is needed (USDHHS, 1988), particularly on the specification of the neural pathways involved (Kamerling et al., 1982; Wu and Martin, 1983).

Most of the research presented thus far has focused on factors maintaining the habit in regular smokers. Much less is known about how nonsmokers become smokers (Kozlowski and Harford, 1976). Although nicotine addiction is obviously not a factor, knowledge of the contribution of other setting conditions (predisposing variables such as personality or environmental factors that elicit intense emotion) may be critical to understanding the

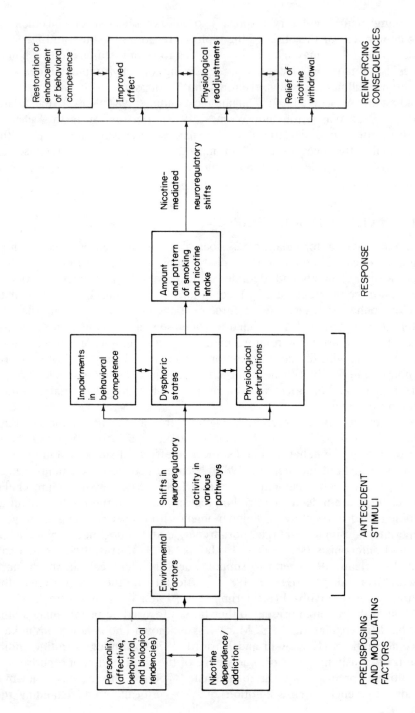

Fig. 1 Biobehavioral factors in smoking

initiation of smoking. Most previous research has involved the use of questionnaires to examine, retrospectively, the effects of personality traits (Eysenck, 1967) or of environmental stressors (Spielberger, 1986) on smoking. Recent work on animal behavior, however, may provide a way of examining these difficult problems prospectively, using experimental methods. Events occurring in daily life on an intermittent basis, particularly events eliciting dysphoric or euphoric states (which have been shown to be associated with shifts in central neurogulator levels; Wallace and Singer, 1976) may constitute a sensitization condition that increases the probability of initiation of certain directed, 'adjunctive' behaviors (for example, behaviors such as chewing, sipping, inhaling and even injecting) that constitute the ingestive vehicle for drug taking (Falk, Dews and Schuster, 1983; Jeffreys, Oei and Singer, 1979; Singer, Oei and Wallace, 1982; Wetherington, 1982). Once started, the use of certain drugs may persist because these substances produce alterations in the internal neurochemical milieu that have reinforcement value in that particular setting (Singer et al., 1982; Weisz and Thompson, 1983). Schedule induction has been used to produce oral, intravenous and inhaled nicotine self-administration in animals (Slifer, 1983) as well as to enhance ongoing cigarette smoking in humans (Cherek, 1982; Wallace and Singer, 1976). The use of schedule-induction procedures may make possible for the first time the dissection of interactions between environmental and pharmacological factors involved in drug-seeking behavior (Jeffreys et al., 1979).

Research on the role of the physical and social environment in controlling smoking may also enhance our understanding of smoking recidivism. The delineation of exteroceptive and interoceptive stimuli in Figure 1 is based on an analysis of stimulus control in substance abuse (Pomerleau, 1981) in which both external and internal stimuli are believed to serve as discriminative stimuli, setting the occasion for the reinforced behavior—smoking. Stimulus control concepts have been used for some time to explain relapse to opiate use following protracted abstinence (O'Brien, Testa, O'Brien and Greenstein, 1976; Schuster, 1986; Wikler, 1965) and, more recently, craving in alcoholics (Pomerleau, Fertig, Baker and Cooney, 1983a), but research on smoking has lagged behind. A few investigators have examined the stimulus conditions that cue smoking (Epstein and Collins, 1977) as well as some of the factors associated with craving (Myrsten et al., 1977). Similarly, there have been occasional reports on the contribution of environmental factors (physical setting, cigarette availability, stressors, etc.) to smoking recidivism (e.g. Pomerleau et al., 1978; Shiffman, 1982). In only one study, however, have these variables been manipulated experimentally (Abrams, Monti, Pinto, Elder, Brown and Jacobus, 1987).

The relationship between nicotine addiction and relapse also needs to be specified more clearly. Because nicotine plays a critical role in maintaining smoking behavior, and because smoking cessation is associated with with-drawal symptoms, it is generally assumed that nicotine addiction influences smoking cessation and relapse. Partial support for this assumption is provided by several studies that used cotinine as a marker of nicotine intake to show that the greater the nicotine intake, the poorer the prognosis for quitting (Zeidenberg, Jaffe, Kanzler, Levitt, Langone and Van Vunakis, 1977; Hall, Herning, Jones, Benowitz and Jacob, 1984). The mechanisms are unclear, but the phenomenon may result from cues for smoking exerting a more intense response (conditioned craving; see Pomerleau, 1979) in highly dependent smokers. The lack of controlled experimentation on the stimulus conditions that elicit craving/withdrawal or of systematic information about biochemical or physiological changes that might underlie a protracted nicotine abstinence 'syndrome' (Kissin, Schenker and Schenker, 1959) is unfortunate in view of the fact that prevention of relapse is a major weakness in the current smoking-cessation effort (Brownell, Marlatt, Lichtenstein and Wilson, 1986).

CLINICAL IMPLICATIONS

Responsible researchers and therapists have tended to shy away from the topic of potential benefits of smoking because of an understandable reluc-tance to appear to be touting the virtues of a highly hazardous product. The fear that manufacturing interests or scurrilous media elements may try to turn such findings to their own advantage is not altogether unfounded. Yet if tobacco use and its associated pathology are to be eradicated, such issues need to be confronted directly.

A clear implication of the formulation described above is that smoking is maintained by a number of critical variables, involving changes in exterocep-tive and interoceptive stimuli as well as reinforcement provided by nicotine and its putative neuroregulatory effects. Disruption of a habit that is as overdetermined as smoking will, of necessity, require a multifactorial approach. Three broad categories of intervention suggest themselves. The first involves changing the environment to modify the stimulus context for smoking and to decrease motivation to smoke. These techniques have been in use for some time as part of behavior modification therapy for smoking and include stimulus control/contingency management procedures that seek to rearrange the environment so as to minimize temptation and decrease the reinforcement value of smoking by delaying gratification (see, for example, Pomerleau, 1979).

A second category involves modulation of the neuroregulatory patterns that seem to be involved in the reinforcement of smoking. For the most part these approaches have not been examined in formal clinical trials, but they are readily testable. One strategy, for example, would be to use a nicotinic cholinergic blocker. Mecamylamine has been suggested as a possibility (see Stolerman, 1986), and although it has recently been demonstrated in an experimental context that the immediate effect of mecamylamine pretreatment is an apparent compensatory increase in nicotine intake (Pomerleau, Pomerleau and Majchrzak, 1987), it is logical to expect that self-administration would extinguish within a short time once the rewarding effects of the drug were eliminated. Mecamylamine has fairly powerful side-effects, however, which may limit its clinical acceptability. Reduction of smoking might also be facilitated by short-term administration of naloxone to block calming and anxiety relief from nicotine-stimulated endogenous opioid release (Karras, 1982; Karras and Kane, 1980). Small doses of clonidine, a drug that acts to reduce central noradrenergic activity, have recently been used to relieve nicotine craving/withdrawal (Glassman, Jackson, Walsh, Roose and Rosenfeld, 1984); a similar approach might be used to interfere with the noradrenergic arousing and alerting effects of nicotine, thereby decreasing the reinforcement value of smoking (Carruthers, 1976).

A third class of interventions involves the identification of pharmacological and behavioral substitutes for smoking. For instance, the use of nicotine in chewing gum (see Pomerleau and Pomerleau, 1988) has been shown to be helpful in relieving nicotine withdrawal symptoms (Hughes, Hatsukami, Pickens, Krahn, Malin and Lucknic, 1984) and, in the context of a habit change program, in reducing recidivism (Hall, Tunstall, Rugg, Jones and Benowitz, 1985; Schneider, Jarvik, Forsythe, Read, Elliott and Schweiger, 1983). While tested only in case studies to date, behavioral substitutes for the calming or relaxing effects of smoking, such as deep muscle relaxation (Pechacek, 1976) or aerobic exercise (Morgan, Gildiner and Wright, 1976), show potential. In particular, physical exercise has powerful effects on neuro-regulatory activity, including that of the endogenous opioids (Carr and Fishman, 1985; Pomerleau, Scherzer, Grunberg, Pomerleau, Judge, Fertig and Burleson, 1987), and numerous reports indicate favorable affective changes with regular exercise (Hughes, 1984; Stern and Cleary, 1982). Dietary precursors of neuroregulators (Wurtman and Wurtman, 1986) stimulated by nicotine might provide an alternative method of enhancing their effects (McCarty, 1982). These procedures are relatively safe and sustainable over extended periods of time, and their use should be investigated more systematically.

No discussion of nicotine abuse from a clinical point of view would be complete without the observation that prevention is the best treatment. Although public education campaigns have made impressive inroads into the habit among certain segments of the population, young people, for whom the threat of the ultimate aversive consequences of smoking seems remote, are still taking up smoking and other forms of tobacco use in discouragingly large numbers. Research on the mechanisms by which nicotine intake is regulated and smoking behavior reinforced may help in the identification of individuals who are particularly vulnerable to the blandishments of nicotine. For example, the onset of nausea following the first smoking experience may be an important factor in discouraging some people from habitual smoking (Kozlowski and Harford, 1976); therefore, lack of susceptibility to nausea induced by nicotine or by other substances that stimulate the emetic center may provide an index of receptivity to smoking, and the resulting hormonal response may constitute an objective indicator of these subjective effects (Seyler, Pomerleau, Fertig, Hunt and Parker, 1986). Similarly, it may be possible to identify potential responders to the arousing or anxiolytic effects of the drug (Pomerleau and Pomerleau, 1987). Such an approach would permit targeting of subpopulations of presmokers who could be exposed to specialized educational efforts or taught alternative coping skills.

CONCLUSION

The biobehavioral analysis of smoking propounded herein suggests a general strategy for research on substance abuse and for integrating findings from fields as diverse as psychology, pharmacology, neuroendocrinology and physiology. Such a broad overview may be particularly useful in advancing our knowledge of smoking, for not only are the pharmacological properties of nicotine highly complex, but its effects seem peculiarly well suited as a response for coping with the exigencies of modern life. The public health problems posed by the smoking habit are extensive, and have resisted our best efforts to date. The major challenge at present is to increase our scientific understanding of smoking to provide the basis for rational and more effective therapies.

ACKNOWLEDGEMENT

Preparation of this chapter was facilitated by a grant from the United States National Cancer Institute (CA 42730).

REFERENCES

Abrams, D.B., Monti, P.M., Pinto, R.P., Elder, J.P., Brown, R.A., and Jacobus, S.I. (1987). Psychosocial stress and coping in smokers who relapse or quit. *Health Psychology*, **6**, 289–303.

Andersson, K., Fuxe, K., Eneroth, D., and Agnati, L.F. (1982). Effects of acute central and peripheral administration of nicotine on hypothalamic catecholamine nerve terminal systems and on the secretion of adenohypophyseal hormones in the male rat. *Medical Biology*, **60**, 98–111.

Ashton, H., Millman, J.E., Rawlins, M.D., Telford, R., and Thompson, J.W. (1978). The use of event-related slow potentials of the brain in the analysis of the effects of cigarette smoking and nicotine in humans. In: K. Bättig (ed.), *Behavioral Effects of Nicotine*. Basel: S. Karger, pp. 26–37.

Ashton, H., and Stepney, R. (1982). *Smoking: Psychology and Pharmacology*. London: Tavistock Publications.

Auerbach, O., Carter, H.W., Garfinkel, L., and Hammond, E.C. (1976). Cigarette smoking and coronary artery disease. *Chest*, **70**, 697–705.

Balfour, D.J.K. (1982). The effects of nicotine on brain neurotransmitter systems. *Pharmacological Therapeutics*, **16**, 269–282.

Benwell, M.E.M., and Balfour, D.J.K. (1982). The effects of nicotine administration on 5-HT uptake and biosynthesis in rat brain. *European Journal of Pharmacology*, **84**, 71–77.

Best, J.A., and Hakstian, A.R. (1978). A situation specific model of smoking behavior. *Addictive Behaviors*, **3**, 79–82.

Bewley, B.R., Halil, T., and Snaith, A.H. (1973). Smoking by primary school children. Prevalence and associated symptoms. *British Journal of Preventive and Social Medicine*, **27**, 150–153.

Bhargana, V., Salamy, A., and Shah, S. (1981). Role of serotonin in the nicotine-induced depression of brainstem auditory evoked response. *Pharmacology, Biochemistry, and Behavior*, **15**, 587–589.

Brett, G.Z., and Benjamin, B. (1968). Smoking habits of men employed in industry, and mortality. *British Medical Journal*, **iii**, 82–85.

Brownell, K.D., Marlatt, G.A., Lichtenstein, E., and Wilson, G.T. (1986). Understanding and preventing relapse. *American Psychologist*, **41**, 765–782.

Califano, J.A. (1979). *Smoking and Health: A Report of the Surgeon General*. Washington, DC: Department of Health, Education and Welfare (DHEW Publication No. PHS 79-50066).

Carr, D.B., and Fishman, S.M. (1985). Exercise and the endogenous opioids. In: K. Fotherby and S. Pal (eds), *Exercise Endocrinology*. New York: De Gruyter, pp. 157–182.

Carruthers, M. (1976). Modification of the noradrenalin related effects of smoking by beta-blockade. *Psychological Medicine*, **6**, 251–256.

Cherek, D.R. (1982). Schedule-induced cigarette self-administration. *Pharmacology, Biochemistry and Behavior*, **17**, 523–527.

Clarke, P.B.S. (1987). Nicotine and smoking: a perspective from animal studies. *Psychopharmacology*, **92**, 135–143.

Clee, M.D., and Clark, R.A. (1984). Tobacco smoking: the medical sequelae. In: D.J.K. Balfour (ed.), *Nicotine and the Tobacco Smoking Habit*. Oxford: Pergamon Press, pp. 177–198.

Colley, J.R.T., Douglas, J.W.B., and Reid, D.D. (1973). Respiratory disease in young adults: influence of early childhood lower respiratory tract illness, social class, air pollution and smoking. *British Medical Journal*, **iii**, 195–198.

Crowdy, J.P., and Sowden, R.R. (1975). Cigarette smoking and respiratory ill-health in the British Army. *Lancet*, **i**, 1232–1234.

Cryer, P.E., Haymond, M.W., Santiago, J.V., and Shah, S.D. (1976). Norepinephrine and epinephrine release and adrenergic mediation of smoking-associated hemodynamic and metabolic events. *New England Journal of Medicine*, **295**, 573–577.

Dark, J., O'Connor, M., Pemberton, M., and Russell, M.H. (1963). Relighting of cigarettes and lung cancer. *British Medical Journal*, **ii**, 1164–1166.

Davis, K.L., and Yamamura, H.I. (1978). Cholinergic underactivity in human memory disorders. *Life Sciences*, **23**, 1729–1734.

Deneau, G.A., Yanagita, T., and Seevers, M.H. (1969). Self-administration of psychoactive substances by the monkey. *Psychopharmacologia*, **16**, 30–48.

Doll, R., and Hill, A.B. (1964). Mortality in relation to smoking: ten years' observations of British doctors. *British Medical Journal*, **i**, 1399–1410, 1460–1462.

Doll, R., and Peto, R. (1976). Mortality in relation to smoking: 20 years' observation on male British doctors. *British Medical Journal*, **ii**, 1525–1536.

Epstein, L., and Collins, F. (1977). The measurement of situational influences of smoking. *Addictive Behaviors*, **2**, 47–54.

Eysenck, H.J. (1967). *The Biological Basis of Personality*. Springfield, IL: Charles C. Thomas.

Falk, J.L., Dews, B., and Schuster, C.R. (1983). Commonalities in the environmental control of behavior. In: P.K. Levison, D.R. Gerstein and D.R. Maloff (eds), *Commonalities in Substance Abuse and Addictive Behavior*. Lexington, MA: D.C. Heath, pp. 47–110.

Fertig, J.B., Pomerleau, O.F., and Sanders, B. (1986). Nicotine-produced antinociception in minimally deprived smokers and ex-smokers. *Addictive Behaviors*, **11**, 239–248.

Fuxe, K., Everitt, B.J., and Hokfelt, T. (1979). On the action of nicotine and cotinine on central 5-hydroxytryptamine neurons. *Pharmacology, Biochemistry and Behavior*, **10**, 671–677.

Gilbert, D.G. (1979). Parodoxical tranquilizing and emotion-reducing effects of nicotine. *Psychological Bulletin*, **86**, 643–661.

Glassman, A.H., Jackson, W.K., Walsh, B.T., Roose, S.P., and Rosenfeld, B. (1984). Cigarette craving, smoking withdrawal, and clonidine. *Science*, **226**, 864–866.

Golding, J., and Mangan, G.L. (1982). Arousing and de-arousing effects of cigarette smoking under conditions of stress and mild sensory isolation. *Psychophysiology*, **19**, 449–456.

Goodman, F.R. (1974). Effects of nicotine on distribution and release of ^{14}C-norepinephrine and ^{14}C-dopamine in rat brain striatum and hypothalamic slices. *Neuropharmacology*, **13**, 1025–1032.

Goodman, L.S., and Gilman, A. (1958). *The Pharmacological Basis of Therapeutics*. New York: Macmillan, p. 622.

Green, P.G., and Kitchen, I. (1986). Antinociception, opioids, and the cholinergic system. *Progress in Neurobiology*, **26**, 119–146.

Gritz, E.R. (1980). Smoking behavior and tobacco abuse. In: N.K. Mello (ed.), *Advances in Substance Abuse*, vol. 1. Greenwich, CT: JAI Press, pp. 127–158.

Hall, G.H., and Turner, D.M. (1972). Effects of nicotine on the release of ^{3}H-noradrenalin from the hypothalamus. *Biochemistry and Pharmacology*, **21**, 1829–1838.

Hall, S.M., Herning, R.I., Jones, R.T., Benowitz, N.L., and Jacob, P. (1984). Blood cotinine levels as indicators of smoking treatment outcome. *Clinical Pharmacology and Therapeutics*, **35**, 810–814.

Hall, S.M., Tunstall, C., Rugg, D., Jones, R.T., and Benowitz, N. (1985). Nicotine gum and behavioral treatment in smoking cessation. *Journal of Consulting and Clinical Psychology*, **532**, 256–258.

Hammond, E.C. (1966). Smoking in relation to the death rate of one million men and women. *National Cancer Institute Monographs*, **19**, 167–182.

Hatsukami, D.K., Hughes, J.R., and Pickens, R.W. (1985). Characterization of tobacco withdrawal: physiological and subjective effects. In: J. Grabowski and

S. Hall (eds), *Pharmacological Adjuncts in Smoking Cessation* (NIDA Research Monograph 53). Rockville, MD: National Institute on Drug Abuse, pp. 56–67.

Hatsukami, D.K., Hughes, J.H., Pickens, R.W., and Svikis, D. (1984). Tobacco withdrawal symptoms: an experimental analysis. *Psychopharmacology*, **84**, 2331–2336.

Henningfield, J.E., and Jasinski, D.R. (1987). Pharmacological basis for nicotine replacement. In: O.F. Pomerleau and C.S. Pomerleau (eds), *Nicotine Replacement in the Treatment of Smoking: A Critical Evaluation*. New York: Alan R. Liss, pp. 35–61.

Henningfield, J.E., Miyasato, K., and Jasinski, D.R. (1985). Abuse liability and pharmacodynamic characteristics of intravenous and inhaled nicotine. *Journal of Pharmacological and Experimental Therapeutics*, **234**, 1–12.

Hill, R.G. (1981). The status of naloxone in the identification of pain control mechanisms operated by endogenous opioids. *Neuroscience Letters*, **2**, 217–222.

Hughes, J.R. (1984). Psychological effects of habitual aerobic exercise: a critical review. *Preventive Medicine*, **13**, 66–78.

Hughes, J.R., Hatsukami, D.K., Pickens, R.W., Krahn, D., Malin, S., and Lucknic, A. (1984). Effect of nicotine on the tobacco withdrawal syndrome. *Psychopharmacology*, **83**, 82–87.

Husain, M.K., Frantz, A.C., Ciarochi, F., and Robinson, A.G. (1975). Nicotine-stimulated release of neurophysin and vasopressin in humans. *Journal of Clinical Endocrinology and Metabolism*, **41**, 1113–1117.

Iversen, S.D., and Iversen, L.L. (1981). *Behavioral Pharmacology*, 2nd edn. New York: Oxford University Press.

Jarvik, M. (1977). Biological factors underlying the smoking habit. In: M. Jarvik, J. Cullen, E. Gritz, T. Vogt and L. West (eds), *Research on Smoking Behavior* (NIDA Research Monograph 17). Rockville, MD: National Institute on Drug Abuse, pp. 122–146.

Jarvik, M. (1979). Biological influences on cigarette smoking. In: N. Krasnegor (ed.), *Behavioral Aspects of Smoking* (NIDA Research Monograph 26). Rockville, MD: National Institute on Drug Abuse, pp. 7–45.

Jeffreys, D., Oei, T.P.S., and Singer, G. (1979). A reconsideration of the concept of drug dependence. *Neuroscience and Biobehavioral Reviews*, **3**, 149–153.

Kaakola, S., and Ahtee, L. (1977). Effect of muscarinic cholinergic drugs on morphine-induced catalepsy, antinociception and changes in brain dopamine metabolism. *Psychopharmacology*, **52**, 7–15.

Kamerling, S.G., Wettstein, J.W., Sloan, J.W., Su, F.P., and Martin, W.R. (1982). Interaction between nicotine and endogenous opioid mechanisms in the unanesthetized dog. *Pharmacology, Biochemistry and Behavior*, **17**, 733–740.

Karras, A. (1982). Neurotransmitter and neuropeptide correlates of cigarette smoking. In: W.B. Essman and L. Valzelli (eds), *Neuropharmacology: Clinical Applications*. New York: Spectrum, pp. 41–67.

Karras, A., and Kane, J. (1980). Naloxone reduces cigarette smoking. *Life Sciences*, **27**, 1541–1545.

Kawamura, M., and Domino, E.F. (1969). Differential actions of *m* and *n* cholinergic agonists on the brainstem activating system. *International Journal of Neuropharmacology*, **8**, 105–115.

Kerschbaum, A., Pappajohn, D.J., Bellet, S., Hirabayashi, M., and Shafiiha, H. (1968). Effect of smoking and nicotine on adrenocortical secretion. *Journal of the American Medical Association*, **203**, 113–116.

Kissin, B., Schenker, V., and Schenker, A. (1959). The acute effects of ethyl alcohol and chlorpromazine on certain physiological functions in alcoholics. *Quarterly Journal of Studies on Alcohol*, **20**, 480–492.

Koch, A., Hoffman, K., Steck, W., Horsch, A., Hengen, N., and Morl, H. (1980). Acute cardiovascular reactions after cigarette smoking. *Atherosclerosis*, **35**, 67–75.

Kozlowski, L.T., and Harford, M.A. (1976). On the significance of never using a drug: an example from cigarette smoking. *Journal of Abnormal Psychology*, **85**, 433–434.

Lee, E.H.Y. (1985). Effects of nicotine on exploratory behavior in rats: correlation with regional brain monoamine levels. *Behavioral Brain Research*, **17**, 59–66.

Legros, J.J., Gilot, P., Seron, X., Claessen, J., Adam, A., Moeglen, J.M., Audibert, A., and Berchier, P. (1978). Influence of vasopressin on learning and memory. *Lancet*, **i**, 41–42.

Mangan, A.L., and Golding, J.F. (1984). *The Psychopharmacology of Smoking*. London: Cambridge University Press, pp. 128–129.

Marty, M.A., Erwin, V.G., Cornell, K., and Zgombick, J.M. (1984). Effect of nicotine on beta-endorphin, alpha-MSH, and ACTH secretion by isolated perfused mouse brains and pituitary glands, *in vitro*. *Pharmacology, Biochemistry and Behavior*, **22**, 317–325.

Mason, S.T. (1980). Noradrenaline and selective attention: a review of the model and the evidence. *Life Sciences*, **27**, 617–631.

Mausner, B., and Platt, E.S. (1971). *Smoking: A Behavioral Analysis*. New York: Pergamon Press.

McCarty, M.F. (1982). Nutritional support of central catecholaminergic tone may aid smoking withdrawal. *Medical Hypotheses*, **8**, 95–102.

McMorrow, M.J., and Foxx, R.M. (1983). Nicotine's role in smoking: an analysis of nicotine regulation. *Psychological Bulletin*, **93**, 302–327.

Millan, M., and Emrich, H. (1981). Endorphinergic systems and the response to stress. *Psychotherapy and Psychosomatics*, **36**, 43–56.

Morgan, R., Gildiner, M., and Wright, G. (1976). Smoking reduction in adults who take up exercise: a survey of a running club for adults. *Journal of the Canadian Association for Health, Physical Education, and Recreation*, **52**, 39–43.

Myrsten, A.L., Andersson, K., Frankenhauser, M., and Elgerot, A. (1975). Immediate effects of cigarette smoking as related to different smoking habits. *Perceptual and Motor Skills*, **40**, 515–523.

Myrsten, A.L., Elgerot, A., and Edgren, B. (1977). Effects of abstinence from tobacco smoking on physiological and psychological arousal levels in habitual smokers. *Psychosomatic Medicine*, **39**, 25–38.

Novack, D.H., and Allen-Rowlands, C.F. (1985). Pituitary–adrenal response to cigarette smoking (abstract). *Psychosomatic Medicine*, **47**, 78.

O'Brien, C., Testa, T., O'Brien, T., and Greenstein, R. (1976). Conditioning in human opiate addicts. *Pavlovian Journal of Biological Sciences*, **11**, 195–202.

Olpe, H.R., Jones, R.S.G., and Steinmann, M.W. (1983). The locus coeruleus: actions of psychoactive drugs. *Experientia*, **34**, 242–249.

Pechacek, T. (1976). Specialized treatment for high anxious smokers. Paper presented at the Annual Meeting of the Association for the Advancement of Behavior Therapy (December), New York.

Pert, A., and Maxey, G. (1975). Asymmetrical cross-tolerance between morphine and scopolamine induced antinociception in the primate: differential sites of action. *Psychopharmacologia*, **44**, 139–145.

Pickens, R. (1968). Self-administration of stimulants by rats. *International Journal of the Addictions*, **3**, 215–221.

Pomerleau, C.S., and Pomerleau, O.F. (1987). The effects of a psychological stressor on cigarette smoking and subsequent behavioral and physiological response. *Psychophysiology*, **24**, 278–285.

Pomerleau, C.S., Pomerleau, O.F. and Majchrzak, M.I. (1988). Mecamylamine pretreatment increases subsequent nicotine self-administration as indicated by changes in plasma nicotine level. *Psychopharmacology*, **91**, 391–393.

Pomerleau, O.F. (1979). Commonalities in the treatment and understanding of smoking and other self-management disorders. In: N. Krasnegor (ed.), *Behavioral Analysis and Treatment of Substance Abuse* (NIDA Research Monograph 25). Rockville, MD: National Institute on Drug Abuse, pp. 140–156.

Pomerleau, O.F. (1980). Why people smoke: current psychobiological theories. In: P. Davidson (ed.), *Behavioral Medicine: Changing Health Lifestyles*. New York: Brunner/Mazel, pp. 94–115.

Pomerleau, O.F. (1981). Underlying mechanisms in substance abuse: examples from research on smoking. *Addictive Behaviors*, **6**, 187–196.

Pomerleau, O.F. (1986). Nicotine as a psychoactive drug: anxiety and pain reduction. *Psychopharmacology Bulletin*, **22**, 863–883.

Pomerleau, O.F., Adkins, D., and Pertschuk, M. (1978). Predictors of outcome and recidivism in smoking cessation treatment. *Addictive Behaviors*, **3**, 65–70.

Pomerleau, O.F., Fertig, J., Baker, L., and Cooney, N. (1983a). Reactivity to alcohol cues in alcoholics and non-alcoholics: Implications for a stimulus control analysis of drinking. *Addictive Behaviors*, **8**, 1–10.

Pomerleau, O.F., Fertig, J.B., Seyler, L.E., and Jaffe, J. (1983b). Neuroendocrine reactivity to nicotine in smokers. *Psychopharmacology*, **83**, 61–67.

Pomerleau, O.F., Fertig, J.B., and Shanahan, S.O. (1983c). Nicotine dependence in cigarette smoking: an empirically-based, multivariate model. *Pharmacology, Biochemistry and Behavior*, **19**, 291–299.

Pomerleau, O.F., and Pomerleau, C.S. (1984). Neuroregulators and the reinforcement of smoking: towards a biobehavioral explanation. *Neuroscience and Biobehavioral Reviews*, **8**, 503–513.

Pomerleau, O.F., and Pomerleau, C.S. (1988). Nicotine replacement: an overview. In: O.F. Pomerleau and C.S. Pomerleau (eds), *Nicotine Replacement in the Treatment of Smoking: A Critical Evaluation*. New York: Alan R. Liss, pp. 279–295.

Pomerleau, O.F., Scherzer, H.H., Grunberg, N.E., Pomerleau, C.S., Judge, J., Fertig, J., and Burleson, J. (1986). The effects of acute exercise on subsequent cigarette smoking. *Journal of Behavioral Medicine*, **10**, 117–127.

Pomerleau, O.F., Turk, D., and Fertig, J.B. (1984). The effects of cigarette smoking on pain and anxiety. *Addictive Behaviors*, **9**, 265–271.

Redmond, D.E. (1979). New and old evidence for the involvement of a brain norepinephrine system in anxiety. In: W.E. Fann, I. Karacan, A.D. Pokorney and R.L. Williams (eds), *Phenomenology and Treatment of Anxiety*. New York: S.P. Medical and Scientific, pp. 153–203.

Robbins, T.W. (1984). Cortical noradrenaline, attention, and arousal. *Psychological Medicine*, **14**, 13–21.

Romano, C., Goldstein, A., and Jewell, N.P. (1981). Characterization of the receptor mediating the nicotine discriminative stimulus. *Psychopharmacology*, **74**, 310–315.

Rose, J.E. (1988). The role of upper airway stimulation in smoking. In: O.F. Pomerleau and C.S. Pomerleau (eds), *Nicotine Replacement in the Treatment of Smoking: A Critical Evaluation*. New York: Alan R. Liss, pp. 95–106.

Rose, J.E., Ananda, S., and Jarvik, M.E. (1983). Cigarette smoking during anxiety-provoking and monotonous tasks. *Addictive Behaviors*, **8**, 353–359.

Rose, J.E., Tashkin, D.P., Ertle, A., Zinser, M.C., and Lafer, R. (1985). Sensory blockade of smoking satisfaction. *Pharmacology, Biochemistry and Behavior*, 23, 289–293.

Rosecrans, J.A., Hendry, J.S., and Hong, J.S. (1985). Biphasic effects of chronic nicotine treatment on hypothalamic immunoreactive beta-endorphin in the mouse. *Pharmacology, Biochemistry and Behavior*, 23, 141–143.

Rosenberg, J., Benowitz, N.L., Jacob, D., and Wilson, K.M. (1980). Disposition kinetics and effects of intravenous nicotine. *Clinical Pharmacology*, 28, 517–522.

Roth, K., McIntyre, S.L., and Barchas, J.D. (1982). Nicotinic–catecholaminergic interactions in the rat brain: Evidence for cholinergic nicotinic and muscarinic interactions with hypothalamic epinephrine. *Pharmacology and Experimental Therapeutics*, 221, 416–420.

Royal College of Physicians (1977). *Smoking or Health*. Tunbridge Wells. Pitman:

Russell, M.A.H. (1977). Smoking problems: an overview. In: M. Jarvik, J. Cullen, E. Gritz, T. Vogt and L. West (eds), *Research on Smoking Behavior* (NIDA Research Monograph 17). Rockville, MD: National Institute on Drug Abuse, pp. 13–34.

Russell, M.A.H. (1988). Nicotine replacement: the role of blood nicotine levels, their rate of change, and nicotine tolerance. In: O.F. Pomerleau and C.S. Pomerleau (eds), *Nicotine Replacement in the Treatment of Smoking: A Critical Evaluation*. New York: Alan R. Liss, pp. 63–94.

Schachter, S. (1978). Pharmacological and psychological determinants of smoking. *Annals of Internal Medicine*, 88, 104–114.

Schachter, S., Silverstein, B., Kozlowski, L.T., Perlick, D., Herman, C.P., and Liebling, B. (1977). Studies of the interaction of psychological and pharmacological determinants of smoking. *Journal of Experimental Psychology*, 106, 3–40.

Schneider, N.G., Jarvik, M.E., Forsythe, A.B., Read, L.L., Elliott, M.L., and Schweiger, A. (1983). Nicotine gum in smoking cessation: a placebo-controlled double-blind trial. *Addictive Behaviors*, 8, 253–261.

Schuster, C.R. (1986). Implications of laboratory research for the treatment of drug dependence. In: S.R. Goldberg and I.P. Stolerman (eds), *Behavioral Analysis of Drug Dependence*. New York: Academic Press, pp. 357–385.

Seyler, L.E., Pomerleau, O.F., Fertig, J., Hunt, D., and Parker, K. (1986). Pituitary hormone response to cigarette smoking. *Pharmacology, Biochemistry and Behavior*, 24, 159–162.

Shiffman, S. (1982). Relapse following smoking cessation: a situational analysis. *Journal of Consulting and Clinical Psychology*, 50, 71–86.

Shiffman, S., and Jarvik, M. (1976). Smoking withdrawal symptoms in two weeks of abstinence. *Psychopharmacologia*, 50, 35–39.

Singer, G., Oei, T.P.S., and Wallace, M. (1982). Schedule-induced self-injection of drugs. *Neuroscience and Biobehavioral Reviews*, 6, 77–83.

Slifer, B.L. (1983). Schedule-induction of nicotine self-administration. *Pharmacology, Biochemistry and Behavior*, 19, 1005–1009.

Solomon, R. (1977). An opponent-process theory of acquired motivation: IV. The affective dynamics of addiction. In: J. Maser and M. Seligman (eds), *Psychopathology: Experimental Models*. San Francisco: W.H. Freeman, pp. 66–103.

Solomon, R., and Corbit, J. (1973). An opponent-process theory of motivation: II. Cigarette addiction. *Journal of Abnormal Psychology*, 81, 158–171.

Solomon, R., and Corbit, J. (1974). An opponent-process theory of motivation: I. Temporal dynamics. *Psychological Review*, 81, 119–145.

Spielberger, C.D. (1986). Psychological determinants of smoking behavior. In: R.D.

Tollison (ed.), *Smoking and Society: Toward a More Balanced Assessment*. Lexington, MA: D.C. Heath, pp. 89–134.

Spitzer, R.L. (1980). *Diagnostic and Statistical Manual*, 3rd edn. Washington, D.C.: American Psychiatric Association.

Stern, M.J., and Cleary, P. (1982). The National Exercise and Heart Disease Project: long-term psychosocial outcome. *Archives of Internal Medicine*, **142**, 1093–1097.

Stolerman, I.P. (1986). Could nicotine antagonists be used in smoking cessation? *British Journal of Addiction*, **81**, 47–53.

Svensson, T.H. (1987). Peripheral autonomic regulation of locus coeruleus noradrenergic neurons in brain: putative implications for psychiatry and psychopharmacology. *Psychopharmacology*, **92**, 1–7.

Svensson, T.H., and Engberg, G. (1980). Effect of nicotine on single cell activity in the noradrenergic nucleus *locus coeruleus*. *Acta Physiologica Scandinavica*, **479**, 31–34.

Ternes, J.W. (1977). An opponent-process theory of habitual behavior, with special reference to smoking. In: M.E. Jarvik, J. Cullen, E. Gritz, T. Vogt and L. West (eds), *Research on Smoking Behavior*, (NIDA Research Monograph 17). Rockville, MD: National Institute on Drug Abuse, pp. 157–182.

Tobin, M.J., Jenouri, G., and Sackner, M.A. (1982). Effects of naloxone on change in breathing pattern with smoking. *Chest*, **82**, 530–537.

Trap-Jensen, J., Carlsen, J.E., Svendsen, T.L., and Christensen, N.J. (1979). Cardiovascular and adrenergic effects of cigarette smoking during immediate non-selective and selective beta-adrenergic blockade in humans. *European Journal of Clinical Investigation*, **9**, 181–183.

Tripathi, J., Martin, B., and Aceto, M. (1982). Nicotine-induced antinociception in rats and mice: correlation with nicotine brain levels. *Journal of Pharmacology and Experimental Therapeutics*, **221**, 91–96.

US Department of Health and Human Service (1988). Nicotine: sites and mechanisms of action. In: *The Health Consequences of Smoking: Nicotine Addiction*, Report of the Surgeon General. DHHS 88-84-06. Washington DC: US Government Printing Office, pp. 75–143.

van Ree, J.M., and de Wied, D. (1981). Brain peptides and psychoactive drug effects. In: Y. Israel, F. Glaser, H. Kalant, R. Popham, W. Schmidt and R. Smart (eds), *Research Advances in Alcohol and Drug Problems*. New York: Plenum, pp. 67–105.

van Ree, J.M., Slangen, J.L., and de Wied, D. (1975). Self-administration of narcotic drugs in rats. Dose response studies. *Excerpta Medica International Congress Series*, No. 359.

Volle, R.L., and Koelle, G.B. (1975). Ganglionic stimulating and blocking agents. In: L.S. Goodman and A. Gilman (eds), *The Pharmacological Basis of Therapeutics*, 5th edn. New York: Macmillan, pp. 565–574.

Wallace, M., and Singer, G. (1976). Adjunctive behavior and smoking induced by a maze solving schedule in humans. *Physiology and Behavior*, **17**, 849–852.

Warburton, D.M., and Wesnes, K. (1978). Individual differences in smoking and attentional performance. In: R.E. Thornton (ed.), *Smoking Behavior: Physiological and Psychological Influences*. Edinburgh: Churchill Livingstone, pp. 19–43.

Weingartner, H., Gold, P., Ballenger, J., Smallberg, S., Summers, R., Rubinow, D., Post, R., and Goodwin, F. (1981). Effects of vasopressin on human memory functions. *Science*, **211**, 601–603.

Weisz, D.J., and Thompson, R.F. (1983). Endogenous opioids: brain behavior relations. In: P.K. Levison, D.R. Gerstein and D.R. Maloff (eds), *Commonalities in Substance Abuse and Addictive Behavior*. Lexington, MA: D.C. Heath, pp. 297–321.

Wesnes, K., and Revell, A. (1984). The separate and combined effects of scopolamine and nicotine on human information processing. *Psychopharmacology*, **84**, 5–11.

Wesnes, K., and Warburton, D.M. (1983). Smoking, nicotine, and human performance. *Pharmacological Therapeutics*, **21**, 189–208.

Westfall, T.C. (1974). Effect of nicotine and other drugs on the release of ³H-norepinephrine and ³H-dopamine from rat brain slices. *Neuropharmacology*, **13**, 693–700.

Westfall, T.C., and Watts, D.T. (1964). Catecholamine excretion in smokers and nonsmokers. *Journal of Applied Physiology*, **19**, 40–42.

Wetherington, C.L. (1982). Is adjunctive behavior a third class of behavior? *Neuroscience and Biobehavioral Reviews*, **6**, 329–350.

Wikler, A. (1965). Conditioning factors in opiate addiction and relapse. In: D. Wilner and G. Kassenbaum (eds), *Narcotics*. New York: McGraw Hill, pp. 85–100.

Wilkins, J., Carlson, H., Van Vunakis, H., Hill, M., Gritz, E., and Jarvik, M. (1982). Nicotine from smoking increases the circulating levels of cortisol, growth hormone, and prolactin in male chronic smokers. *Psychopharmacology*, **78**, 305–308.

Wise, R.A. (1983). Brain neuronal systems mediating reward processes. In: J.E. Smith and J.D. Lane (eds), *The Neurobiology of Opiate Reward Processes*. New York: Elsevier, pp. 405–438.

Wise, R.A., and Bozarth, M.A. (1982). Action of drugs of abuse on brain reward systems: an update with specific attention to opiates. *Pharmacology, Biochemistry, and Behavior*, **17**, 239–243.

Wu, K.M., and Martin, W.R. (1983). An analysis of nicotinic and opioid processes in the medulla oblongata and nucleus ambiguus of the dog. *Journal of Pharmacology and Experimental Therapeutics*, **227**, 302–307.

Wurtman, R.J., and Wurtman, J.J. (1986). *Nutrition and the Brain*. New York: Raven Press.

Yao, M., Narita, M., Baba, S., Kudo, M., Kudo, T., and Oyama, T. (1985). Effects of cigarette smoking on endocrine function in man. *Masui*, **34**, 1105–1114.

Zeidenberg, P., Jaffe, J.H., Kanzler, M., Levitt, M.D., Langone, J.J., and Van Vunakis, H. (1977). Nicotine: cotinine levels in blood during cessation of smoking. *Comprehensive Psychiatry*, **18**, 93–101.

Part Two

Psychophysiology, Emotion and Individual Differences

5

Brain Event-related Potentials (ERPs) in Smoking Performance Research

Verner J. Knott

ABSTRACT

Facilitation of mental, cognitive efficiency is one of the most frequently reported motives for cigarette smoking. This chapter examines the evidence supporting such claims by reviewing the effects of smoking on scalp recordings of event-related potentials (ERPs) which are considered manifestations of intracranial cognitive functions. A specific focus is directed at the relationship between brain potentials and arousal–attentional processes. The review systematically examines the effects of smoking, subject and task variables on ERP components tapping such processes. The present status of smoking–ERPs as it relates to performance is summarized, and conclusions regarding the future of such research are discussed.

INTRODUCTION TO SMOKING, PERFORMANCE AND ERPs

Interpretations of smoking-enhanced task performance have been and continue to be couched within neurophysiological arousal theory and, inevitably, the predominant hypothesis of smoking-related performance changes has strongly implicated nicotine-induced shifts in brain-state arousal (Wesnes and Warburton, 1983). Major support for this theory has evolved from brain electrical potential studies (Edwards and Warburton, 1983) which have reported smoke- and nicotine-induced electroencephalographic (EEG)

Smoking and Human Behavior, Edited by T. Ney and A. Gale
© 1989 John Wiley & Sons Ltd

desynchronization patterns similar to those observed following electrical stimulation of the ascending reticular activating brain stem (ARAS) circuitry regulating cortical and behavioral arousal states (Hobson and Brazier, 1980). Although these brain potential studies provide convincing evidence for arousal theory, the relevance of this body of data can be questioned on the basis that electrocortical recordings were collected under non-task conditions without assessment of perceptual, cognitive or behavioral performance. Similarly, the vast majority of human performance studies have employed the brain arousal concept to explain smoking-related changes but have not attempted its measurement. In short, cortical arousal has been widely used as an explanatory construct, but simultaneous measurement of brain-behavior indices is rarely contemplated or attempted. When smoking/nicotine-related electrocortical measures are recorded during task conditions, EEG effects are found to be negligible relative to those observed in non-task conditions (Pickworth, Herning and Henningfield, 1986) and they do not appear to be consistent with pharmaco-EEG profiles observed with classic psychostimulants (Fink, 1980).

A number of additional arguments may be levelled against the usefulness of this theory in explaining smoking-performance data, but these critiques do not necessarily imply that the ubiquitous arousal concept be abandoned for lack of precision and explanatory power. Gale and Edwards (1986) have rightly argued that arousal performance relationships are extremely complex: rigorous definitions of these relations await systematic, empirical trials in which the functional significance of arousal indices are assessed with proven information-processing theories and paradigms. These attempt to identify and describe the nature and interaction of component processes yielding behavioral outcomes. Within this framework, smoking-induced cortical arousal may directly or indirectly alter performance efficiency by shifting the balance, speed and effectiveness of different perceptual–cognitive processes. This is, however, as far as a theoretical analysis of arousal effects can go without assessing the specific underlying brain processes involved during human performance.

Human perceptual–cognitive functions are typically examined with the traditional behavioral measures of reaction time (RT) and frequency and type of response errors. However, these behavioral measurements are seriously limited in that they represent a single output measure which is determined by numerous intervening brain processes and their interactions (Pachella, 1974). A number of investigators have argued that the averaging and extraction of minute brain potentials related to transient sensory and task-relevant cognitive and/or motor events (event-related potentials or ERPs) provide a much more versatile and powerful point of entry into the analysis of perceptual–cognitive processes (Desmedt, 1981; Donchin, 1979, 1984; Donchin, Karis, Bashore, Coles and Gratton, 1986).

In typical auditory RT paradigms, information from stimulus transients travels from the peripheral sensory receptors to the brain in 15–30 milliseconds (ms) (depending on modality) and overt motor responses occur relatively later at approximately 150–500 ms, or longer (depending on task requirements). Current evidence suggests that all decision-making processes necessary to produce the RT may be completed up to 100 ms before overt behavioral responses are measurable, and probably even before electromyographical (EMG) events (occurring 30–80 ms prior to RT) can be recorded (Rabbitt, 1979). As shown in the upper panel of Figure 1, the transient ERPs to such critical stimuli consist of a series of well-defined positive (P) and negative (N) electrical potential oscillations lasting up to 500 ms, roughly the same time duration as the perceptual–cognitive response to the stimulus. Donald (1979) has commented on the temporal overlap of ERPs and processing stages (as evidenced in Figure 1) to stimulus transients in RT paradigms. Very early ERPs, occurring primarily in the sensory projection systems and sensory cortex, are said to parallel the automatic, data-driven, sensory-analysis processes. Further, they are determined by 'exogenous' (physical stimulus attributes) factors and are apparently insensitive to fluctuation in state as induced by attention, sleep and anesthesia. The intermediate ERP compound potentials, centering on sensory cortical regions and secondary sensory regions, are considered 'mesogenous' in nature (Picton, 1980), being sensitive to exogenous-stimulus related factors (e.g. intensity) and endogenous factors (e.g. attentional and cognitive states and individual differences). Late ERP potentials, whose amplitudes are greatest over posterior–central scalp regions, are like the later controlled- or limited-resource-driven processes, almost entirely 'endogenous' in nature, reflecting not the stimulus attributes, but the subject's processing response to the stimulus.

In view of this parallel, it is not surprising that a great deal of time and effort has been expended on the attempt to examine the specific functional and temporal relationship of ERPs to hypothetical central processes. A good proportion of this energy has been spent examining ERP correlates of attentional states, particularly selective–attentional processes. Such processes enable perceptual or motor responses to be made selectively to one (relevant) stimulus category or dimension in preference to other (irrelevant) stimuli which are either partially or completely rejected from perception, experience and entry into long-term memory and control over behavior (Hillyard and Picton, 1979). This focus on selective–attentional processes in relation to smoking–performance data appears warranted in view of the frequent association of attention with arousal—the hypothetical mediator of smoking-induced performance increments, and by the frequent suggestion by a number of investigators that improved central-selective processing, mediated by arousal increments, is the critical vehicle by which smoking facilitates human performance (Dyer, 1986; Wesnes and Warburton, 1983).

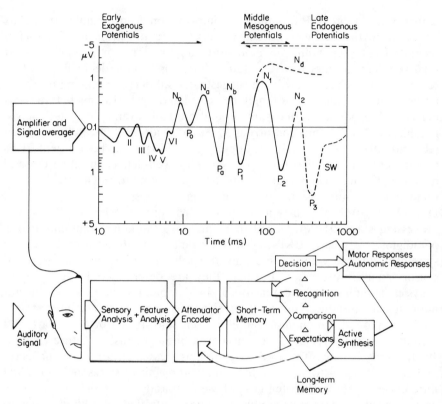

Fig. 1   The two domains of ERP research. In the upper panel an auditory stimulus elicits synchronous neural activity in widespread regions of the brain, which appears as a sequence of potential oscillations occurring at characteristic time delays as indicated on the abscissa. The same stimulus elicits selective perceptual and motor responses, from which one may infer hypothetical processing stages or operations (lower panel). (After Hillyard, Picton and Rozan, 1978)

Auditory ERPs are a frequently employed investigative modality within the context of current, selective–attention research (Hillyard and Hansen, 1986), and a number of components have been linked, one way or another, to early and late selective processes. Although initial studies failed to observe any attentional-induced alterations in cochlear nerve responses or brain stem potentials, a recent report by Lukas (1980) supports the action of a peripheral gating mechanism. Here, instructions to ignore acoustic stimuli while simultaneously engaging in a visual task resulted in significant amplitude reductions and longer latencies of brain stem peaks I (auditory nerve) and V (midbrain). During certain sensory or attentional states then, this early, precortical 'passive' filter, which is modulated by higher-order corticofugal paths, is said to modify the impulse conduction capacity of the sensory fibers prior to the arrival of the sensory stimuli and, as such, functions to inhibit background, irrelevant and potentially distracting stimuli, thus allowing maximal utilization of processing capacity for relevant sensory input.

The N_1 (or N_1–P_2) peak has been the most extensively explored aspect of the cortical potentials in selective attention research. Hillyard, Hink, Schwent and Picton (1973) were the first to demonstrate a selective attention effect on N_1 over and above any influences of nonselective arousal or alertness factors, and they interpreted this enhanced 'N_1 effect' to attended input as a sign of an early Broadbentian (1970) 'stimulus-set' attentional filter. Such a filter is tonically maintained in that it does not involve active discrimination: it passively rejects irrelevant unattended channel stimuli on the basis of simple physical/sensory attributes (without accessing memory and decisional stages), and accepts all incoming channel stimuli for subsequent processing.

Unlike N_1, which appears to be tapping automatic selective processes during voluntary attentional states, the N_2 component appears to reflect an involuntary attentional switch by any kind of physical stimulus deviations (Ford, Roth and Kopell, 1976) regardless of whether subjects are attending or not (Snyder and Hillyard, 1976). As such it is said to reflect only stimulus 'deviance' *per se*, and not stimulus 'relevance'. Although this exogenous N_2 (otherwise termed 'mismatch negativity'—MMN) is said to be generated by a preperceptual, automatic cerebral mismatch process occurring when the input does not match the existing 'sensory' neuronal trace, and although it is a necessary operation, it is apparently not sufficient for conscious detection of stimulus change (Näätänen and Gaillard, 1983). The underlying generating process may, however, serve as a signal for further higher-order conscious, perceptual processing and discrimination of auditory input.

P_{300} may reflect this higher-level processing as it is commonly elicited in task paradigms which require two or more stimuli to be cognitively categorized (Donchin et al., 1986). In contrast to the enhanced N_1, which was said to reflect a 'stimulus-set' selective filter, discriminating between channel inputs on the basis of rapidly discriminable physical cues, P_{300} is said to reflect a subsequent higher-order Broadbentian (1970) type 'response-set' selection process. Here, the selection process classifies stimuli according to acquired categories of meaning, rather than by simple physical attributes (Hillyard and Hansen, 1986). It has been suggested that the occurrence/latency of P_{300} reflects a shift from pre-attentive, automated processing to controlled attentional processing within a limited central capacity system and that P_{300} amplitude together with P_{300} latency, which is considered an index of 'stimulus evaluation time', reflect the perceptual capacity demands which are placed upon this limited central processor (Rösler, 1983).

Last, but by no means least, the early 'O' and late 'E' components of the contingent negative variation (CNV), indexing stimulus-related (S_1) processes and response-related (to S_2) processes, respectively, have been intimately linked to selective processes (Rockstroh, Elbert, Birbaumer and Lutzenberger, 1982). Both CNV (in particular motor-preparatory aspects) development and its associated RT have been repeatedly shown to be disrupted by distraction processes, presumably via their effects on attentional–arousal coupling processes (Syndulko and Lindsley, 1977; Tecce, Savignano-Bowman and Meinbresse, 1976).

KEY FINDINGS OF SMOKING—ERP STUDIES

Unfortunately, a good proportion (approximately 40 percent) of ERP research on smoking resists facile interpretive arousal–attentional formulations as they are in essence, merely 'sensory' ERP studies which have examined the effects of smoking and smoking deprivation in the passive, static subject, under quiescent, nonbehaving states. Human subjects in a laboratory, however, rarely sit and do or think about nothing, and interpretations of the functional significance of ERPs assessed in such contrived, simplistic laboratory environments, without assessment of task-related behavioral anchors with which to assess cognitive/performance efficiency, are seriously impaired.

Although, relative to task-based ERP paradigms, data from nontask, sensory ERPS contribute less weight to an overall smoking-performance assessment, they are not completely without merit, and indeed they can, if properly couched within well-defined methodology, provide informative insight into basic brain activational and sensory processing mechanisms which may be relevant to smoking maintenance and cessation. This section will briefly review the major findings of these two separate empirical approaches, namely nontask and task ERPs. Although the majority of studies focus on acute smoking/nicotine effects, their results vary depending on smoking variables, stimulus conditions, individual differences, etc. As such this review will be sectioned into seven foci including the effects of dose/time factors, acute vs chronic effects, the role of nicotine, cessation/deprivation effects, stimulus/task factors, initial state effects, and individual differences. Following a review of these two approaches, a brief summary will be formulated as to the relevance of the findings to smoking-performance research.

Non-task ERPs

Dose/time factors

Evidence from infrahuman studies have reported quantitative differences in electrocortical activity with varying smoking doses of nicotine, sequential biphasic (initial desynchronization followed by synchronization) effects with single doses, and biphasic dose–effect relationships with different doses of nicotine producing qualitatively different (stimulant vs depressant) effects.

Yet not a single human study has examined dose– or time–response relationships on sensory ERPs. Implementation of such studies would provide informative data on absolute thresholds (i.e. minimal effective dose required for producing ERP changes), terminal thresholds (i.e. dose level which produced qualitative changes), peak effect times, and duration of effects across varying types of cigarettes and routes of nicotine administration.

Acute vs. chronic effects

Attempts to compare acute effects of single cigarettes with chronic multiple cigarette consumption over a period of time have also been sparse and, to date, only two studies have examined such acute–chronic differences. Vasquez and Toman (1967), in a brief descriptive report, compared visual ERPs of three chronic smokers immediately after smoking one cigarette (following 36 hours (h) of abstinence) and some (?) hours after resumption of their habitual smoking pattern. Significant reductions of late negative (N_{140}) and positive (P_{170}) waves were observed immediately after the cigarette, and these effects persisted during the subjects' habitual smoking pattern. Hall, Rappaport, Hopkins and Griffin (1973) also compared the acute effects of one cigarette (following 36 h of abstinence) with satiated, nonabstinence states, and found equivalent effects for acute and chronic smoking states. However, in contrast to the Vasquez and Toman ERP reduction effects, and relative to the 36-h abstinent state, both acute and chronic smoking resulted in overall increases in the mean amplitude envelopes of visual ERPs across four stimulus intensities. These later findings were said to be convergent with independent EEG and subjective data, indicating a general alerting effect on brain function as a result of smoking.

Role of nicotine

Both Friedman, Goldberg, Horvath and Meares (1974) and Woodson, Bättig, Etkin, Kallman, Harry, Kallman and Rosecrans (1982) attempted to separate out the effects of nicotine on sensory ERPs from those due to other elements in cigarette smoke. In Friedman et al.'s study the effects of smoking two real cigarettes (nicotine and tar yield unknown) were compared with smoking two placebo cigarettes made of roasted chicory leaves. Following 12 h of smoking abstinence, placebo cigarettes produced no significant ERP changes, whereas real cigarettes increased both the maximum peak-to-peak amplitudes and the late positive (VI)–negative (VII) complex (125–300 ms) of visual ERPs. These results were suggested to be reflective of enhanced sensory–attentional processing of visual input. Woodson and colleagues also examined visual ERPs across five stimulus intensities but controlled more precisely the non-nicotine substances of control (0.14 mg nicotine; 19.4 mg tar) and experimental (1.3 mg nicotine; 19.4 mg tar) cigarettes by equating total particulate matter, H_2O content, and number of machine puffs. Relative to low nicotine yield cigarettes, high nicotine cigarettes, smoked after 2 h of abstinence, were found to enhance, across intensities, the peak-to-peak amplitude of the middle negative (III)–positive (IV) complex (50–140 ms). This effect was considered to be due to nicotine's enhancement/restorative effect on visual–attentive processes.

Cessation/deprivation effects

A few studies have examined the short-term (hours-to-several-days) effects of cigarette deprivation, but not one study has focused on the long-term (days-to-years), prolonged effects of cessation on ERPs. The effects of imposed cigarette deprivation have typically been examined by comparing sensory ERPs in smoke-satiated, nonabstaining smokers arriving at the laboratory, with smokers arriving at the laboratory following an overnight abstinence period ranging from 12 to 36 h. Hall et al. (1973) examined visual ERPs, across four stimulus intensities, during nonabstinence periods and following 12 and 36 h of overnight deprivation. Significant decreases in the mean amplitude envelope (for all intensities) was found after both 12 and 36 h abstinence and, in addition, a selective 35-h induced amplitude decrement was observed with the middle latency positive (IV)–negative (V) complex evoked by the lowest intensity stimulus (resulting in steeper, positive amplitude-intensity edges). Friedman et al. (1974) compared ERPs of smokers during no interruption of smoking patterns and following 12 h of overnight abstinence. Relative to nondeprived states, deprivation resulted in decreased peak-to-peak amplitudes of the middle positive (IV)–negative (V) complex (75–165 ms) evoked by visual stimuli while the maximum peak-to-peak amplitudes of the auditory ERPs were increased following deprivation. In a second follow-up study, Friedman and Meares (1980) compared the effects of 1 and 12 h of deprivation on sensory ERPs evoked by four intensities of visual and auditory stimuli. Relative to 1 h, 12 h of deprivation significantly decreased the middle positive (IV)–negative (V) complex of visually evoked ERPs (across all intensities), and in contrast, increased the late positive (P_2)–negative (N_2) complex (180–300 ms) of auditory ERPs across all intensities. The authors again suggested that these results reflected a differential effect of smoking on sensory input regulation, with smoking seemingly acting (a) to enhance input into the visual system, thereby increasing efficiency of visual vigilance tasks; and (b) to dampen down or reduce auditory sensation, thereby reducing efficiency of primary auditory vigilance tasks, but at the same time acting to filter out distractive, irrelevant and aversive auditory input, which has been shown to induce performance decrements on primary visual tasks.

Knott and Venables (1978) also examined deprivation effects on visual

ERPs (across four stimulus intensities) by comparing non-abstinent smokers and abstinent (15–18 h of deprivation) smokers with an additional group of nonsmoker subjects. Deprived smokers evidenced faster peak IV latencies (across all stimulus intensities) and larger peak-to-peak amplitudes (at the two lowest intensities) of the middle positive (IV)–negative (V) complex compared to nondeprived smokers and nonsmokers who exhibited comparable responsiveness on both latency and amplitude parameters. These authors suggested that smoking had a 'normalizing' effect on brain hypersensitivity observed in deprived smokers, and that this smoking-induced filtering protected consciousness (i.e. memory and decision stages) from being overloaded with irrelevant or unwanted information.

Stimulus/task factors

Sensory ERP studies have indicated that acute and chronic smoking effects vary as a function of stimulus modality and stimulus intensity. In two separate studies, Friedman and colleagues (1974, 1980) reported that the immediate acute effect of smoking two cigarettes (after 2–12 h of deprivation) was to increase peak-to-peak amplitudes of middle negative (V)–positive (VI) and late positive (VI)–negative (VII) complexes of visual ERPs and to either decrease (Friedman and Meares, 1980) or have no effect (Friedman et al., 1974) on late positive (P_2)–negative (N_2) complexes evoked by auditory stimuli. As mentioned earlier, this was taken as evidence against a general arousing effect of smoking and, instead, was considered to be supportive of a selective sensory processing effect induced by smoking.

With respect to stimulus intensity, Hall et al. (1973) reported a selective, deprivation-induced depressant effect on middle peak-to-peak (IV–V) amplitudes elicited by low-intensity visual stimuli, but not with high-intensity stimuli. Smoking two cigarettes resulted in nonsignificant increments of these same amplitudes. Knott and Venables (1978) observed contrasting effects with deprived smokers exhibiting larger middle-latency peak-to-peak amplitudes (IV–V) to low-intensity stimuli compared to nondeprived smokers. Friedman and Meares (1980) also examined stimulus intensity effects on both auditory and visual modalities, and although their data graphs indicated selective smoking-induced amplitude enhancement (of visual ERPs) and amplitude attenuation (of auditory ERPs) to high-intensity stimuli, no significant smoking × intensity interactions were reported.

Initial state effects

The acute effects of cigarette smoking on sensory ERPs appear to be partially dependent on presmoking states and, specifically, differential smoke-induced effects have been related to the smokers' abstinence state, with a greater frequency of significant smoking effects being observed following deprived than nondeprived states. After 12 h of deprivation, Friedman et al. (1974) reported that two cigarettes increased maximum peak-to-peak amplitudes, late positive (VI)–negative (VII) complexes and amplitude ratios (VII/VI) of visual ERPs, but the effects of two cigarettes in the same nondeprived subjects were restricted to increased amplitude ratios (VII/VI). Similarly, Friedman and Meares (1980) observed significant smoke-induced (two cigarettes) increases in visual peak-to-peak (VI–VII) amplitude–intensity slopes following 12 h of abstinence, but no such changes in slopes were induced by smoking after 1 h of abstinence.

Individual differences

Emphasis on individual variations in response to cigarette smoking has been reflected in two separate approaches: the first has examined sensory ERP differences between smokers and nonsmokers, and the second has focused on the perception–personality dimension of augmentation–reduction by measuring peak-to-peak (P_1–N_1 for auditory ERPs and IV–V for visual ERPs) amplitude–intensity slopes. Knott and Venables (1978) combined both of these procedures by examining visual ERPs to varying stimulus intensities in nonsmokers and deprived smokers. Deprived smokers, as mentioned earlier, were found to exhibit faster peak IV latencies and larger peak-to-peak (IV–V) amplitudes to low stimulus intensities. These results were suggested to be indicative of constitutional differences between the two groups, and this trait-based hypersensitivity in deprived smokers was considered a significant predispositional motive for seeking smoking's attenuating effect which was observed in nondeprived smokers. The frequency of positive (indicating a stimulus-augmenting style) and negative (indicating a stimulus-reducing style) amplitude–intensity slopes was not found to be different across the three groups.

Hall et al. (1973) examined the effects of deprivation and acute smoking on visual ERP amplitude–intensity slopes and found that 36 hours of deprivation resulted in significant slope reduction effects. This reducing was not, however, due to attenuation of responsivity to high-intensity stimuli, i.e. a smoking-induced protective reaction against aversive stimuli, but was due to enhanced amplitudes to low-intensity stimuli. Hall et al. suggested that this selective enhancement of weak stimuli may be an attractive perception-related psychophysiological factor to smokers. Friedman and Meares (1980) did not observe any slope changes with ERP peaks typically associated with auditory (P_1–N_1) and visual (IV–V) augmenting–reducing patterns. Differences in slope were only evident in the late component (VI–VII) of visual

ERPs, with 12 h of deprivation resulting in reduced slopes and acute smoking of cigarettes resulting in augmentation.

Remond, Izard, Martinerie and Grab (1979) presented a somewhat vague and brief description of the acute effects of smoking (two cigarettes, 1.6 mg nicotine) on patterned evoked ERPs. Smoking was said to reduce latencies of the P_1 positive (100 ms) peak and, although in general it increased its amplitude, it tended to be reduced in nervous heavy smokers and nervous nonsmokers.

Task ERPs

Dose/time factors

A number of studies have examined, either directly or indirectly, dose–response and time effects of smoking/nicotine on task-related ERPs. Ashton, Marsh, Millman, Rawlins, Telford and Thompson (1980) examined the effects of intravenous injections of nicotine, given in intermittent smoking-dose 'shots' ranging from 12.5 to 800 μg on the magnitude (area) of the CNV (S_1–S_2=1.25 s). Relative to saline injections, individual and mean dose–response curves were found to be biphasic with smaller doses producing an increase in CNV magnitude and larger doses producing a decrease in CNV. The total intravenous dosages producing CNV increments were typically found to be under 100 μg. These results were said to reflect nicotine's ability to produce both stimulant and depressant effects on brain function, possibly via dose-specific selective effects on two mutually inhibitory systems: the nonspecific ARAS and the specific goal-directed limbic system (Routtenberg, 1968).

Herning and Pickworth (1985) examined the effect of 0, 4 and 8 mg doses of nicotine gum (following 12 h of deprivation) on stimulus evaluation time as indexed by P_{300} latency. P_{300} was elicited by auditory (60 dB) signals in an 'oddball' task assessed under low-intensity (40 dB) and high-intensity (60 dB) white noise conditions. Here, high-intensity noise tended to prolong N_1 and P_{300} latencies of relevant signal stimuli. This P_{300} effect was found to be blocked by the 8 mg nicotine dose and, as such, was suggested to be reflective of improved processing in distracting environments. P_{300} amplitude was also affected by nicotine dose and was dependent on noise condition and mecamylamine (10 mg) treatment. P_{300} amplitudes were increased by 4 mg gum in low noise and decreased by 4 and 8 mg gum in high noise, while these effects were reversed by mecamylamine.

P_{300} latency was also examined by Edwards, Wesnes, Warburton and Gale (1985), who studied the effects (after 12 h of deprivation) of two levels (0.9 mg and 1.5 mg) of nicotine delivery cigarettes within a rapid visual information processing task (RVIP), assessed during a 10-min presmoking and a 20-min postsmoking period. Although both cigarettes improved target detections equally, only the high-nicotine cigarette was found to shorten P_{300} latency and response speed. These effects were viewed as being consistent with the 'psychological tool' model of smoking, with performance enhancement being mediated by changes in higher-order cognitive brain function. However, the effects were restricted to the initial 10-min postsmoke period, and as such were said to parallel nicotine blood levels which have been shown to rise rapidly during smoking, reaching a peak immediately after the last puff, and then declining rapidly, often by less than 50 percent in 10 min (Armitage, 1973).

A number of studies have indirectly examined dose effects by correlating ERPs with smoke exposure measures estimated via carboxyhemoglobin (COHb) levels, butt nicotine analysis and smoking behavior indices, including puff volume and puff frequency. Although Ashton, Millman, Telford and Thompson (1973) failed to observe any significant relationship between smoke intake (COHb) and CNV changes, they subsequently reported that nicotine intake was negatively correlated with both extraversion personality scores and CNV changes (Ashton et al., 1980). Further, the slower nicotine intake of extraverts was found to be associated with the production of larger CNVs, while faster nicotine intake was followed by smaller CNVs in the introverts. RT, which was improved by smoking, was not related to nicotine intake estimates. Binnie and Comer (1978) also reported smoke intensity to be positively correlated with CNV change (direction ignored), but contrary to Ashton et al. (1973), CNV increases were associated with greater smoking intensity than CNV decreases, and no relationship was observed between smoking intensity and personality.

O'Connor's (1980a, 1986) CNV findings did support a personality–smoke exposure relationship, but here extraverts were reported to puff more intensely than introverts who, in turn, puffed more frequently than extraverts. This was taken as support for the notion that extraverts (low-activity smokers) rely more on pharmacological effects from smoking to achieve desired effects while introverts (high-activity smokers) may rely more on the motor aspects of smoking (O'Connor, 1980b). In general, high-intensity smokers (regardless of personality) exhibited significant reductions in early 'O' waves and increases in later 'E' waves with smoking, while low-intensity smokers showed no significant CNV effects. As such, the results suggest that the pharmacological effects of smoking principally affect the negative CNV components, which are specifically achieved by extraverts. In signal detection tasks, higher puff frequencies in extraverts were related to postwarning (S_1) positivity (SPW) and a more negative post-S_2 baseline. In introverts, higher puff frequency related to lower frontal (F_z) M-wave (between O and E wave) negativity and lower response cautiousness (B). Higher puff intensities in extraverts were also associated with increased signal sensitivity.

Acute vs. chronic effects

Task-related ERPs have not been systematically examined within designs comparing smoking effects over varying number of cigarettes. Knott and Venables (1980) did, however, compare CNVs in nondeprived smokers, 12–15 h deprived smokers, and nonsmokers, but failed to observe any significant differences.

Role of nicotine

The results of Edwards et al. (1985), previously cited, regarding the differential effects of high and low nicotine delivery cigarettes on P_{300} latency, provide supportive evidence for a smoke-related nicotine effect on brain processes. Ashton et al. (1980) have provided additional support for the role of nicotine underlying smoking-related effects. Here, in each of the subjects tested ($n=$ 5), the direction and magnitude of the changes produced by smoking a single standard cigarette were identical to that produced by intravenous nicotine. Similarly, the CNV effects of smoking a single cigarette of their own brand, and that of an equivalent dose of intravenous nicotine (estimated from butt analysis), were comparable both in magnitude and direction. The authors concluded that the effects of cigarette smoking on the CNV were due largely, if not entirely, to nicotine absorbed from tobacco smoke.

Cessation/deprivation effects

Although Knott and Venables (1980) failed to observe any significant deprivation effects on CNV amplitudes, Herning, Pickworth and Cone (1986) reported significant effects with both sensory ERPs and P_{300} elicited in an auditory information processing task which was monitored over a 5-day smoking period and 10 days of nonsmoking. Data were also collected on subjects who chose to return to smoking after 10 days of abstinence. No significant effects were observed with BSEP latencies but auditory N_1 elicited during the processing task was reduced during the entire cessation period and remained attenuated even in subjects who returned to smoking after the 10-day cessation trial. In contrast, the P_{300} amplitude was reduced early in the nonsmoking period and returned to pre-cessation baseline when subjects resumed smoking. It was argued that the data provided evidence for a selective directional effect of cessation on sensory and higher-order cognitive processes involving a transient impairment in stimulus evaluation (P_{300} reduction) and a prolonged alteration of N_{100}, perhaps reflecting a constitutional characteristic of smokers.

Stimulus/task factors

The Herning and Pickworth (1985) study, cited earlier, illustrates that nicotine effects interact with task variables as nicotine's facilitating effect on ERPs was only observed during high background noise, and in this case it appeared to protect stimulus evaluation from noise-induced disruption. Knott (1985a) also examined the effects of smoking on ERPs to irrelevant, low-intensity (60 dB SPL) and high-intensity (100 dB SPL) auditory stimuli presented during nontask and dual-task conditions. Although P_1 and N_1 were significantly increased by smoking (depending on task and intensity), P_2 was significantly reduced in response to high-intensity stimuli. As P_2 had been related to habituation processes (Rust, 1977), this was interpreted as being reflective of more efficient filtering of aversive stimuli. In a subsequent study, Knott (1985b) examined smoking effects on a primary CNV–RT task (S_1–S_2= 1.5 s) and associated N_1 and P_2 potentials to the auditory warning (S_1) and visual imperative (S_2) signals under nondistraction and secondary-task distraction conditions: smoking again reduced positive potentials (S_1–P_2) and increased CNV amplitudes in both distraction conditions (depending on pre-experimental carbon monoxide levels). Similar findings were observed in a third study in which ERPs to S_1 and S_2 stimuli were examined under varying levels of task complexity (single vs. four choice) and task distraction (Knott, 1986). Here, increased N_1 and reduced P_2 amplitudes to S_1 were said to reflect enhancement of two sequential cognitive operations—an initial attentional focus to S_1 and a subsequent attentional disengagement on switching to future-oriented, perceptual/cognitive/motor processing of S_2.

In a series of elegantly designed studies, O'Connor (1980a, 1982, 1986) examined smoking effects on topographical (P_z, C_z, F_z) CNVs (S_1–S_2=1.5 and 4.0 s) and associated ERPs to S_1 and S_2 signals in RT and signal detection tasks manipulating attentional demand (single vs. choice RT) as well as response motivation in introverted and extraverted subjects. In general, smoking tended to produce increases in negativity in extraverts, as evidenced by enhanced E-wave amplitudes, and decreases in positivity in introverts as indicated by reductions in SPW and pre-S_2 baseline positivity (i.e. baseline became more negative). These results varied as a function of recording site (F_z vs P_z) and task demands. Reductions in E-wave amplitude in introverts, for example, were observed in both simple and choice RT conditions at C_z but only during simple RT at F_z. Extraverts, on the other hand, exhibited increased E-wave amplitudes in both RT conditions at C_z and F_z sites. These results were interpreted within an hypothesized motor-sensory model of attentional strategies in which extraverted smokers aim to relieve boredom and enhance readiness to react, whereas introverts smoke to inhibit distraction and maintain a complex attentional set (see Chapter 7, by O'Connor, in this volume).

Initial state effects

Aside from studies on individual differences mentioned earlier (and to be discussed below), very few attempts have been made to examine variations in presmoking state on the acute effects of smoking. Knott and Venables (1980) examined the acute effects of smoking on CNV amplitudes in groups of deprived (12-15 h) and nondeprived smokers who were administered four cigarettes and/or 0.65 g/kg of ethyl alcohol. Although smoking alone did not alter CNVs, nondeprived smokers who received alcohol, or alcohol and cigarettes, exhibited significant CNV attenuation relative to deprived smokers and a group of nonsmokers. Enhanced sedation via combined usage of tobacco and alcohol was considered to be of motivational significance to certain populations.

As discussed previously, Knott (1985b) also reported that the acute effects of smoking on CNV and ERPs to S_1–S_2 signals vary as a function of pre-experimental CO levels (in 12–15 h deprived subjects). High resting CO levels were associated with S_1–P_2 reductions and CNV increases in distraction conditions, while low resting CO levels were associated with similar changes but on nondistraction conditions.

Individual differences

Ashton et al. (1980) have shown that, in normal circumstances, a biphasic CNV pattern varying with nicotine dosage is characteristic for all subjects. O'Connor (1980a) justifiably points out, however, that the contribution of individual differences is marked in their data, and this is reflected in the precise shape of the dose–response curve effects on the CNV, which differ for each subject. Despite this intersubject variability, intrasubject stability in response to smoking/nicotine is pointed out in the Ashton et al. report (1980), which showed that an individual's CNV response to smoking, be it stimulant or depressant, is reproducible over 2–3-week periods.

Whereas Ashton et al. emphasize dose as the primary variable influencing electrocortical responsivity, O'Connor (1980a, 1982, 1986) focuses on personality, specifically the introversion–extraversion dimension, and draws from neurophysiological and neurochemical literature to formulate a personality-based, sensory-motor model of smoking. Here, high arousal introverts, hypothesized to be more under limbic inhibitory control than reticular control, are characterized by greater electrocortical positivity (i.e. SPW–S_1, and pre-S_1 baseline positivity) which is reflective of a state of increased inhibition of response selection that favors focal concentration of response preparation and speed (as evidenced in their faster RTs and larger E-waves) at the expense of efficient reception of environmental stimuli. In this sample, small doses of nicotine or the motor activity associated with shallow, frequent puffing, serve to stimulate the noradrenergic system sufficiently to release the limbic system from inhibition (reflected in reduced surface positivity) and allow enhanced accuracy of signal reception and detection needed in choice conditions and distracting environments. Extraverts, on the other hand, who are more under reticular control, are characterized by low cortical arousal and increased distractibility due to poor selective attentional processes (evidenced by larger O-waves), regulate their smoking behavior (particularly in nonstimulating, boring environments) for high nicotine intake so as to boost arousal (via acetylcholine stimulation of noradrenergic activity) and channel sustained attention to the response preparation (as evidenced in increased E-wave amplitudes) needed to enhance response speed (as evidenced by faster RTs).

SUMMARY AND CONCLUSIONS OF SMOKING–ERP RESEARCH

The scarcity of ERP data in each of the preceding smoking sections makes any summaries and conclusions presumptuous and clearly tentative. This uncertainty is significantly enhanced by our lack of knowledge of brain–behavior systems and their interactions with brain-activating compounds. One can no longer conclude, for example, that depression of afferent elicited scalp ERPs by smoking necessarily reflects depression of brain neuronal systems. Nevertheless, cautionary summary statements may be tolerably exercised if one is fully aware of the fragile nature of the data base that supports them.

With respect to smoking and brain state activation, one might generally conclude that deprivation reduces the intensity of brain responsivity to sensory input while acute smoking increases such responsivity. An exception arises from Vasquez and Toman (1967), but due to their small sample size ($n=3$) and uncontrolled design, this cannot justifiably negate the general conclusion. The Knott and Venables (1978) data also contradict this claim. However, comparison groups were nonsmokers and deprived smokers, while smoking comparisons were 'between-group' with smoking being chronic and satiated. Work by Friedman and colleagues (1974, 1980) also resists this general arousal interpretation, as they argue that it does not explain their findings of differential effects of smoking on visual and auditory ERPs. However, significant modality differences were only observed in their latter (1980) study and the smoking-induced reduction of the auditory P_2–N_2 complex is not necessarily at odds with smoking enhancement of visual ERPs. In fact, the existing ERP literature would suggest that smoking-related auditory P_2–N_2 ERP changes are supportive of a general arousal interpretation. Early studies by Picton and colleagues (Picton and Hillyard, 1974; Picton, Hillyard, Krausz and Galambos, 1974) have indicated that the auditory N_2 peak exhibits an inverse relationship with behavioral arousal, being significantly enhanced during sleep states. In addition, these authors have argued for a functional separation of auditory N_1-P_2 and P_2-N_2 complexes, suggesting that the former reflects more closely attentive processes which can be increased during behavioral–attentional tasks without concomitant significant increases in N_2. Similar evidence was forwarded by Maclean, Öhman and Lader (1975), who, in reviewing their own work and work of others, reported N_1-P_2 to be directly related to both attentional and activational manipulations, whereas P_2-N_2 was related inversely to the latter variable only, being significantly smaller during high activation states. Smaller N_2 amplitudes have also been associated with slower RTs (Öhman and Lader, 1977). These arguments then suggest that the Friedman et al. data do not provide evidence for an opposite effect in auditory and visual systems, but instead argue for a general activational effect of smoking on brain sensory systems.

This arousal thrust is further supported by Knott's (1987) recent investigation, which examined the acute effects (one cigarette) on human brain stem auditory evoked potentials (BSEPs). Relative to sham smoking, real smoking was found to increase the amplitude of peak V, a precortical peak reflecting activity from upper pontine–lower midbrain sites. This finding is supportive of the neurophysiological arousal hypothesis, which suggests that smoking enhances cortical arousal via nicotine's action on the midbrain tegmental–neocortical cholinergic pathway.

Insofar as ERPs have been proven sensitive to attentional, perceptual and cognitive processes, one might comfortably summarize that the task-related ERPs reviewed in this section demonstrate that smoking influences performance outcome via its effect on the underlying brain mechanisms subserving these functions. This was indicated by smoking's ability to enhance: processing of stimulus attributes (P_1); attentional selectivity and stimulus filtering (N_1, P_2, O-wave); stimulus evaluation (P_3); and response preparation (E-wave). One might further add that studies on nicotine manipulation provide convincing evidence that these performance-related central effects are mediated primarily by nicotine's action on brain structures. Data from Ashton et al. (1973, 1974, 1980) and O'Connor (1980a, 1982, 1986) provided additional evidence that endogenous ERP components, tapping cognitive processes, are differentially affected depending on dose and individual differences in arousal–attentional style, and as such they seem to illustrate that smoking can potentially alter higher-level brain processes under varying demand conditions. This emphasis on higher-level benefit, accrued by smoking, does not imply, however, that enhanced cognitive processes exceed in importance the more basic smoking-induced, nonspecific brain state activational effects observed in sensory, nontask ERP studies. Smoking appears to affect both processes—nonspecific activation and cognitive process—and their interrelationship, in some complex fashion, in determining response outcome in task performance.

Our seemingly 'definitive' summary relating smoking to enhanced brain functioning does not by any means suggest that the smoking–ERP data base is flawless, or that it requires no further additional support. This sectional review adopted an 'accept at face value' stance, and made no attempt to document the endless methodological shortcomings which cut across smoking–ERP findings. Disappointingly, a number of studies have been conducted without reference to acceptable standards of stimulating/recording techniques (Donchin, Callaway, Cooper, Desmedt, Goff, Hillyard and Sutton, 1977) and a good proportion have not approached the sophisticated level of design/control manipulation or data analysis observed in the current major body of human ERP research (e.g. McCarthy and Donchin, 1983).

Although ERPs can never give more than an incomplete picture of what is going on in the brain (Donald, 1979; Picton, 1980), they can serve as a powerful, unintrusive technique for studying different aspects of cognitive–behavioral processes which may be altered by smoke intake. The successful application of this technique depends to a great extent, however, on the future experimenter's creativity and diligence in couching ERP measures within astute designs and control procedures which allow one to isolate and probe the effects of smoking on specific targeted processes under investigation (Rösler, 1983). If smoking does function as a psychopharmacologically based coping tool (Pomerleau and Pomerleau, 1984), then there is a pressing need to determine its range of efficacy over a wide variety of performance paradigms and acute and chronic smoking conditions. To this end, smoking designs should cast their nets beyond the narrow scope of 'arousal–attentional' processes and examine additional perceptual–cognitive functions. Such functions may be tapped by the complex proliferation of ERP component processes which overlap in time and space, and in a complex fashion at the scalp (Picton and Stuss, 1980). It is, of course, essential that these designs incorporate a control group of nonsmokers in order to determine whether smoke-induced alterations on brain–behavior processing systems are reflective of an absolute improvement in brain–behavior processing operations or a relief from the unpleasant and debilitating effects of smoking deprivation (Knott, 1978; Knott and Venables, 1977, 1978). In this light, nicotine manipulation via smoke or via routes which mimic smoke uptake (West, Jarvis, Russell and Feyerabend, 1984) may be added to our design armamentarium for isolating the mechanisms underlying smoke-induced brain-performance changes. To this repertoire, cessation—either experimentally induced or spontaneously occurring—may also be added as the nature and extent of brain-performance alterations resulting from deprived states may be as informative as smoke-induced effects themselves in terms of their potential to yield critical factors underlying smoking motivation. These directions are by no means new or enlightening, but active pursuit of such avenues with noninvasive ERP scalpels will enable us to explore the depth and breadth of brain–behavior relationships and the psychological processes which subserve the smoking act.

REFERENCES

Armitage, A. (1973). Some recent observations relating to the absorption of nicotine from tobacco smoke. In: W. Dunn (ed.), *Smoking Behavior: Motives and Incentives*. New York: John Wiley & Sons.

Ashton, H., Marsh, V., Millman, J., Rawlins, M., Telford, R., and Thompson, J. (1980). Biphasic dose-related responses of the CNV (contingent negative variation) to I.V. nicotine in man. *British Journal of Pharmacology*, **10**, 579–589.

Ashton, H., Millman, J., Telford, R., and Thompson, J. (1973). Stimulant and depressant effects of cigarette smoking on brain activity in man. *British Journal of Pharmacology*, **48**, 715–717.

Ashton, H., Millman, J., Telford, R., and Thompson, J. (1974). The effect of caffeine, nitrazepam and cigarette smoking on the contingent negative variation in man. *Electroencephalography and Clinical Neurophysiology*, **37**, 59–71.

Binnie, A., and Comer, K. (1978). The effect of cigarette smoking on the contingent negative variation and eye movement. In: R. Thornton (ed.), *Smoking Behaviour. Physiological and Psychological Influences*. Edinburgh: Churchill Livingstone.

Broadbent, D. (1970). Stimulus set and response set: two kinds of selective attention. In: D. Mostofsky (ed.), *Attention: Contemporary Theory and Analysis*. New York: Appleton-Century Crofts.

Desmedt, J. (1981). Scalp-recorded cerebral event-related potentials in man as a point of entry into the analysis of cognitive processing. In: F. Schmitt, F. Morden, G. Adelman and S. Dennis (eds), *The Organization of the Cerebral Cortex*. Cambridge, MA: MIT Press.

Donald, M. (1979). Limits on current theories of transient evoked potentials. In: J. Desmedt (ed.), *Cognitive Components in Cerebral Event-related Potentials and Selective Attention*. Vol. 6 of *Progress in Clinical Neurophysiology*. Basel: Karger.

Donchin, E. (1979). Event-related brain potentials: a tool in the study of human information processing. In: H. Begleiter (ed.), *Evoked Potentials and Behavior*. New York: Plenum.

Donchin, E. (1984). *Cognitive Psychophysiology: Event-related Potentials and the Study of Cognition*. Hillsdale, NJ: Erlbaum.

Donchin, E., Callaway, E., Cooper, R., Desmedt, J., Goff, W., Hillyard, S., and Sutton, S. (1977). Publication criteria for studies of evoked potentials (EP) in man. *Progress in Clinical Neurophysiology*, 1–11.

Donchin, E., Karis, D., Bashore, T., Coles, M., and Gratton, G. (1986). Cognitive psychophysiology and human information processing. In: M. Coles, E. Donchin and S. Porges (eds), *Psychophysiology: Systems, Processes and Applications*. New York: Guilford.

Dyer, F. (1986). *Smoking and Soldier Performance*. US Army Aeromedical Research Laboratory, Report No. 86–13. FT. Rucker, Alabama.

Edwards, J., and Warburton, D. (1983). Smoking, nicotine and electrocortical activity. *Pharmacology and Therapeutics*, **19**, 147–164.

Edwards, J., Wesnes, K., Warburton, D., and Gale, A. (1985). Evidence of more rapid stimulus evaluation following cigarette smoking. *Addictive Behaviors*, **10**, 113–126.

Fink, M. (1980). An objective classification of psychoactive drugs. *Progress in Neuro-Psychopharmacology*, **4**, 495–502.

Ford, J., Roth, W., and Kopell, B. (1976). Auditory evoked potentials to unpredictable shifts in pitch. *Psychophysiology*, **13**, 32–39.

Friedman, J., and Meares, R. (1980). Tobacco smoking and cortical evoked potentials: an opposite effect on auditory and visual systems. *Clinical and Experimental Pharmacology and Physiology*, **7**, 609–615.

Friedman, J., Goldberg, H., Horvath, T., and Meares, R. (1974). The effect of tobacco smoking on evoked potentials. *Clinical and Experimental Pharmacology*, **1**, 249–258.

Gale, A., and Edwards, J. (1986). Individual differences. In: M. Coles, E. Donchin and S. Porges (eds), *Psychophysiology: Systems, Processes and Applications*. New York: Guilford.

Hall, R., Rappaport, M., Hopkins, H., and Griffin, R. (1973). Tobacco and evoked potential. *Science*, **180**, 212–214.

Herning, R., and Pickworth, W. (1985). Nicotine gum improved stimulus processing during tobacco withdrawal. *Psychophysiology*, **22**, 595.

Herning, R., Pickworth, W., and Cone, E. (1986). Impaired information processing in heavy smokers undergoing withdrawal from tobacco. Paper presented to the American Psychological Association, Washington, DC.

Hillyard, S., and Hansen, J. (1986). Attention: electrophysiological approaches. In: M. Coles, E. Donchin and S. Porges (eds), *Psychophysiology: Systems, Processes and Applications*. New York: Guilford.

Hillyard, S., and Picton, T. (1979). Event-related brain potentials and selective information processing in man. In: J. Desmedt (ed.), *Cognitive Components in Cerebral Event-related Potentials and Selective Attention*. Vol. 6 of *Progress in Clinical Neurophysiology*, Basel: Karger.

Hillyard, S., Hink, R., Schwent, V., and Picton, T. (1973). Electrical signs of selective attention in the human brain. *Science*, **182**, 177–180.

Hillyard, S., Picton, T., and Rozan, D. (1978). Sensation, perception and attention: analysis using ERPs. In: E. Callaway, P. Tueting and S. Koslow (eds), *Event-related Brain Potentials in Man*. New York: Academic Press.

Hobson, J., and Brazier, M. (1980). *The Reticular Formation Revisited*. New York: Raven Press.

Knott, V. (1978). Smoking, EEG and input regulation in smokers and non-smokers. In: R. Thornton (ed.), *Smoking Behaviour: Physiological and Psychological Influences*. Edinburgh: Churchill Livingstone.

Knott, V. (1985a). Tobacco effects on cortical evoked potentials to distracting stimuli. *Neuropsychobiology*, **13**, 74–80.

Knott, V. (1985b). Effects of tobacco and distraction on sensory and slow cortical evoked potentials during task performance. *Neuropsychobiology*, **13**, 136–140.

Knott, V. (1986). Tobacco effects on cortical evoked potentials to task stimuli. *Addictive Behaviors*, **11**, 219–223.

Knott, V. (1987). Acute effects of tobacco on human brain stem evoked potentials. *Addictive Behaviors*, **12**, 375–379.

Knott, V., and Venables, P. (1977). EEG alpha correlates of non-smokers, smokers, smoking and smoking deprivation. *Psychophysiology*, **14**, 150–156.

Knott, V., and Venables, P. (1978). Stimulus intensity control and the cortical evoked response in smokers and non-smokers. *Psychophysiology*, **15**, 186–192.

Knott, V., and Venables, P. (1980). Separate and combined effects of alcohol and tobacco on the amplitude of the contingent negative variation. *Psychopharmacology*, **70**, 167–172.

Lukas, J. (1980). Human attention: the olivo-cochlear bundle may function as a peripheral filter. *Psychophysiology*, **17**, 193–201.

Maclean, V., Öhman, A., and Lader, M. (1975). Effects of attention, activation and stimulus regularity on short-term habituation of the averaged evoked response. *Biological Psychology*, **3**, 57–69.

McCarthy, G., and Donchin, E. (1983). Chronometric analysis of human information processing. In: A. Gaillard and W. Ritter (eds), *Tutorials in ERP Research: Endogenous Components*. Amsterdam: North-Holland.

Näätänen, R., and Gaillard, A. (1983). The orienting reflex and the N_2 deflection of the event-related potential (ERP). In: A. Gaillard and W. Ritter (eds), *Tutorials in ERP Research: Endogenous Components*. Amsterdam: North-Holland.

O'Connor, K. (1980a). The CNV and individual differences in smoking and behaviour. *Personality and Individual Differences*, **1**, 37–72.

O'Connor, K. (1980b). Individual differences in situational preferences amongst smokers. *Personality and Individual Differences*, **1**, 249–257.

O'Connor, K. (1982). Individual differences in the effect of smoking on the frontal–central distribution of the CNV: some observations on smokers' control of attentional behaviour. *Personality and Individual Differences*, **3**, 271–285.

O'Connor, K. (1986). The effects of smoking and personality on slow cortical potentials recorded within a signal detection paradigm. *Physiological Psychology*, **14**, 49–62.

Öhman, A., and Lader, M. (1977). Short-term changes of the human auditory evoked potentials during repetitive stimulation. In: J. Desmedt (ed.), *Auditory Evoked Potentials in Man: Psychopharmacology Correlates of Evoked Potentials*, Vol. 2 of *Progress in Clinical Neurophysiology*. Basel: Karger.

Pachella, R. (1974). The interpretation of reaction time in information processing research. In: B. Kantowitz (ed.), *Human Information Processing: Tutorials in Performance and Cognition*. Hillsdale, NJ: Erlbaum.

Pickworth, W., Herning, R., and Henningfield, J. (1986). Electroencephalographic effects of nicotine chewing gum in humans. *Biochemistry and Behavior*, **25**, 879–882.

Picton, T. (1980). The use of human event-related potentials in psychology. In: I. Martin and P. Venables (eds), *Techniques in Psychophysiology*. Chichester: John Wiley & Sons.

Picton, T., and Hillyard, S. (1974). Human auditory evoked potentials: II. Effects of attention. *Electroencephalography and Clinical Neurophysiology*, **36**, 191–200.

Picton, T., and Stuss, D. (1980). The component structure of the human event-related potentials. In: H. Kornhuber and L. Deecke (eds), *Motivation, Motor and Sensory Processes of the Brain: Electrical Potentials, Behavior and Clinical Use*. Amsterdam: Elsevier.

Picton, T., Hillyard, A., Krausz, H., and Galambos, R. (1974). Human auditory evoked potentials, I: Evaluation of components. *Electroencephalography and Clinical Neurophysiology*, **36**, 179–190.

Pomerleau, O., and Pomerleau, C. (1984). Neuroregulators and the reinforcement of smoking: towards a biobehavioural explanation. *Neuroscience and Biobehavioral Reviews*, **8**, 503–513.

Rabbitt, P. (1979). Current paradigms and models in human information processing.

In: V. Hamilton and D. Warburton (eds), *Human Stress and Cognition: An Information Processing Approach*. Chichester: John Wiley & Sons.

Remond, A., Izard, C., Martinerie, J., and Grab, R. (1979). The action of smoking on visual evoked potentials, biofeedback EEG changes and autonomous responses. In: A. Remond and C. Izard (eds), *Electrophysiological Effects of Nicotine*. Amsterdam: Elsevier.

Rockstroh, B., Elbert, T., Birbaumer, N., and Lutzenberger, W. (1982). *Slow Brain Potentials and Behavior*. Baltimore: Urban & Schwarzenberg.

Rösler, F. (1983). Endogenous ERPs and cognition: Probes, prospects and pitfalls in matching pieces of the mind-body puzzle. In: A. Gaillard and W. Ritter (eds), *Tutorials in ERP Research: Endogenous Components*. Amsterdam: North-Holland.

Routtenberg, A. (1968). The two arousal hypothesis: reticular formation and limbic system. *Psychological Review*, **75**, 51–80.

Rust, J. (1977). Habituation and the orienting response in the auditory cortical evoked potential. *Psychophysiology*, **14**, 123–126.

Snyder, E., and Hillyard, S. (1976). Long latency evoked potentials to irrelevant deviant stimuli. *Behavioral Biology*, **16**, 319–331.

Syndulko, K., and Lindsley, D. (1977). Motor and sensory determinants of cortical slow potential shifts in man. In: J. Desmedt (ed.), *Attention, Voluntary Control and Event-related Cerebral Potentials*. Basel: Karger.

Tecce, J., Savignano-Bowman, J., and Meinbresse, D. (1976). Contingent negative variation and the distraction–arousal hypothesis. *Electroencephalography and Clinical Neurophysiology*, **41**, 277–286.

Vasquez, A., and Toman, J. (1967). Some interactions of nicotine with other drugs upon central nervous function. *Annals of the New York Academy of Sciences*, **142**, 201–215.

Wesnes, K., and Warburton, D. (1983). Smoking, nicotine and human performance. *Pharmacology and Therapeutics*, **21**, 189–208.

West, R., Jarvis, M., Russell, M., and Feyerabend, C. (1984). Plasma nicotine concentrations from repeated doses of nasal nicotine solution. *British Journal of Addiction*, **79**, 443–445.

Woodson, P., Bättig, K., Etkin, M., Kallman, W., Harry, G., Kallman, M., and Rosecrans, J. (1982). Effects of nicotine on the visual evoked response. *Pharmacology, Biochemistry and Behavior*, **17**, 915–920.

6

Smoking and the Human EEG

ROBERT E. CHURCH

ABSTRACT

Many papers report the use of the electroencephalogram (EEG) as a tool to investigate the effects of cigarette smoking on the central nervous system. This literature is critically reviewed and cautious conclusions are presented. An increase in our understanding of the functional significance of smoking-induced EEG shifts is contingent upon two fundamental changes in research strategy. First, the circumstances under which smokers smoke in laboratory studies must come to reflect more closely those associated with naturally occurring smoking behavior. Second, the existing simple-minded collection of physiological data must give way to an integrated approach involving the concurrent sampling of physiological *and* performance data (including smoking behavior itself); moreover, it is to be preferred that this occurs within paradigms designed to manipulate subject state in order that the possibility of interactions can be explored.

THE ELECTROENCEPHALOGRAM

Introduction

Electrocortical measurement is a blanket term used to refer to all those physiological recording techniques which employ scalp electrodes to record the electrical activity of the brain. The techniques covered by this term can be divided into two discrete areas of research on the basis of the type of analysis undertaken. One approach entails the measurement of changes in

Smoking and Human Behavior, Edited by T. Ney and A. Gale
© 1989 John Wiley & Sons Ltd

the electrical activity of the brain which occur in response to the presentation of simple physical stimuli, in conjunction with information processing, and during the preparation for motor outputs. Such recordings are referred to as evoked, or event-related, potentials (ERPs). ERP measures have been widely used in smoking research, and that body of literature is reviewed elsewhere in this volume (see Chapter 5 by Knott). The other approach involves the recording of the spontaneous, ongoing, background electrical activity of the brain, and the resolution of the resulting waveform into its component frequencies. It is recordings of this type which are termed the electroencephalogram (EEG), and EEG analysis provides the focus of the present discussion.

The attention of the reader is also drawn to general sources on the topics of EEG–behavior relations (Andreassi, 1980; Brown and Klug, 1973; Empson, 1986) and issues of biological origin, measurement and recording (Spehlmann, 1981).

Overview and history

The human EEG was first reported by Berger (1929). He discovered the alpha rhythm and went on to demonstrate that it disappeared with mental effort and on exposure to unpleasant or painful stimuli. However, it was only when Adrian and Matthews (1934) replicated Berger's work and, a year later, gave a working demonstration at a meeting of the Physiological Society, that widespread attention was given to the phenomenon.

The raw EEG signal is a complex waveform comprising many frequencies, mostly in the range of 1–25 Hz. The bioelectric potential differences available between two scalp electrodes, which make up the EEG, are very small, being in the range of 2–200 μV. Therefore the raw signal is amplified to a voltage sufficient to drive pen recorders, or be stored on magnetic tape or in computer memory. The amplified signal is typically then passed through a series of narrow bandpass or tuned filters to resolve it into the frequency bands of interest. Historically, and in much of the smoking research, most attention has been paid to those frequencies in the 8–13 Hz range, which are termed the *alpha* waveband. However, valuable information may be lost by ignoring the other frequencies. This may be especially true when the EEG is used as an index of arousal. A reduction in alpha is commonly interpreted as a sign of increased fast activity, and so as evidence of an upward shift in arousal. However, alpha activity can give way to lower-frequency *theta* waves (i.e. a shift toward drowsiness) or to faster *beta* components (i.e. a shift toward alertness). Thus, when just the alpha frequencies are attended to, claims about cortical activation sometimes go beyond the evidence.

Early investigators relied almost entirely on the visual analysis of pen recorder write-outs or photographs of oscilloscope displays. Subsequently quantitative methods of analysis have been developed, and the past two or three decades have seen an explosion of analysis techniques. Such progress has been made possible and encouraged by the widespread availability of small laboratory computers and the provision in the mathematical field of efficient algorithms such as the fast Fourier transform (Cooley and Tukey, 1967). However, the range of choices for conditioning, quantifying and analysing the EEG signal come as a mixed blessing. This multitude of possibilities, combined with the lack of consensus as to the best approach, and even as to the definitions and terminology to be employed, places a stumbling block in the way of those wishing to make straightforward comparisons between studies.

Psychological significance

For a long time it was held that the EEG was useful only for distinguishing changes in tonic activity. That is, activity which is relatively unchanging across time. Hence the EEG was used primarily for identifying differences between individuals. The obvious example is in the field of medicine, where the EEG has proven a valuable diagnostic tool for distinguishing clinical populations. However, later research confirmed that the EEG is responsive to changes in phasic activity—that is, to relatively short-term changes in physiological activity most commonly occurring in response to identifiable stimuli or events. For example, the EEG has been shown to be a sensitive index of such things as cognitive effort, stimulus complexity, sustained attention and the cue value of stimuli. A further important application of the EEG was in the explosion of sleep research which occurred in the 1960s. Here the EEG was found to be a reliable correlate of sleep stage, and shown to be an invaluable tool which greatly assisted in the important discoveries made at that time about the neurophysiological substrates of sleep and wakefulness.

The concept of arousal

Probably the major application of the EEG within psychophysiology has been as an index of arousal or behavioral alertness. This possibility was implicit in Berger's original discoveries, where the alpha wave was shown to be sensitive to events which might be expected to influence organismic arousal. Lindsley (1952) presented an unambiguous tabulation of the relation of EEG components to behavioral alertness and efficiency, which has avoided direct challenge for over three decades. Lindsley plotted parallel EEG, state of awareness and behavioral efficiency correlates, divided into eight categories running from strong excited emotion through relaxed wakefulness to coma and death. However, the notion that the EEG can be mapped directly onto behavioral and experiential states in this way is not without problems.

As with psychophysiologists working in other areas, those engaged in smoking research have shown no reticence in using the term arousal, whether as an explanation or a description. There are good reasons why cortical arousal should be of interest to workers in this field. Smoking-induced shifts in cortical arousal provide the cornerstone of the popular arousal modulation or psychological tool model of smoker motivation (e.g. Eysenck, 1973, 1983; Pomerleau and Pomerleau, 1984; Stepney, 1979). Moreover, despite the criticisms of arousal interpretations in the field of vigilance (e.g. Parasuraman and Davies, 1977), others still favor the view that nicotine-induced shifts in cortical arousal underpin the observed benefits to performance in sustained attention that have been repeatedly shown to accompany smoking (e.g. Wesnes and Warburton, 1983b). However, the usefulness of the construct of arousal has been repeatedly brought into question. This has been in part because of limitations stemming from its overapplication (see, e.g., Gale, 1987), and also because of the problems found in reconciling its use with the empirical evidence. Lacey (e.g. 1959, 1967) stands out as the most persistent and prolific critic of the arousal concept. Largely due to his efforts it is now widely accepted that the empirical evidence does not support the notion of arousal as a unitary construct.

Central and autonomic measures do not always exhibit positive covariation. Moreover, within each of these subsystems fractionation of response is often observed. For example, electrodermal and cardiac measures frequently reveal dissociations. Importantly, even when dealing with central measures alone, concluding that a shift in arousal has occurred is not straightforward. When recording the EEG from more than one site on the scalp it is not uncommon to record changes at one location which are absent, or different in nature, at another. Indeed, in EEG studies of hemispheral function, evidence of differential activation is the key goal of research. Clearly, when such topographical differences occur, the *subject* cannot be simultaneously in two different states. Hence it is going beyond the evidence to talk about shifts in arousal, used in the conceptual sense, on the basis of EEG data alone.

Such problems are especially relevant in electrocortical studies of smoking. Often in the literature researchers talk as if EEG activation (generally an increase in frequency and reduction in amplitude) *is* arousal in the conceptual sense. This is clearly not the case. EEG signs of activation are just one index of arousal, albeit a particularly important one. Insufficient is known about the relationships between physiology, behavior and experience for it to be sensible to draw general conclusions when studying just physiology. This is an important issue which is taken up again in a subsequent section.

A REVIEW OF THE EXISTING EEG STUDIES

Introduction

For convenience, the EEG studies of cigarette smoking can be organized under three headings. The results of the studies where the EEG has been used as a simple measure of cortical activity in the search for relatively enduring differences between smokers and nonsmokers will be summarized first. This will be followed by a summary of the findings from the bulk of the EEG–smoking studies. In these, cortical measures have been used in much the same way, but to examine the acute effects of smoking and/or smoking deprivation. Under a final heading can be placed studies where contrasts between smokers and nonsmokers, or between those deprived and nondeprived, have been combined with some additional factor or manipulation. A summary of all smoking and EEG studies and their outcomes is presented in Table 1.

Differences between smokers and nonsmokers

Brown (1968, 1973) compared the resting EEGs of nonsmokers with those of various categories of smokers. In her 1973 study she was able to replicate most of the findings of her first study. Nevertheless, there is need for caution in accepting these findings. In the 1968 study nine of the twelve heavy-smoker subjects (50–100/day) experienced a twelve-hour period of deprivation and then smoked to satiation. No EEG effect of deprivation was found. Hence, deprivation was ignored as a factor and the data from the deprived and nondeprived states were combined. This failure of the EEG to discriminate deprivation is very surprising when such effects have been regularly demonstrated in most other studies (e.g. Knott and Venables, 1977, 1979; Philips, 1971).

The second reason for caution rests upon the nature of the group effect found. The conclusion offered most support was that, relative to nonsmokers, heavy smokers possessed EEGs showing some of the features associated with activation. This result is consistent with the work of Comer, Binnie, Lewis, Lloyd, Oldman and Thornton (1979), who found one-hour deprived smokers to have less EEG power than nonsmokers. Remond, Martierie and Baillon (1979) also found the EEGs of deprived smokers to be more activated than those of nonsmokers, and this difference was emphasized by smoking. In contrast, however, in two carefully designed experiments conducted by Knott and Venables (1977, 1979), exactly the opposite outcome occurred; the EEGs

Table 1 Summary details of all published EEG-smoking studies

Hypothesis	n	Subjects	1. Depriv. 2. Design 3. Experiment	Activity/recording situation	Control for nicotine	Smoking/nicotine treatment	Electrode montage	Aspect of EEG analyzed	Conclusions
Brown (1968): Will EEG measures distinguish smokers from nonsmokers?	15 13 8 6	NS 50–100/day 10–20/day Ex-smokers	1. N/A 2. Between 3. 3 h	Eyes open and closed. Only eyes closed data analyzed.	N/A	N/A	Bilateral, bipolar temporo-parietal, parietal-occipital, and occipital.	Frequency analysis, using an interval histogram technique. Concentrated on 8–12 and 13–25 Hz activity.	Relative to nonsmokers, nondeprived heavy smokers possessed EEGs characterized by some of the features usually associated with cortical arousal.
Brown (1973): Will EEG measures distinguish smokers from nonsmokers and/or between different smoker categories?	26 13 13 13 13	NS 15–25/day 40–60/day >60/day Ex-smokers	1. N/A 2. Between 3. 1½ h	?	N/A	N/A	Bipolar parieto-occipital.	Frequency analysis, using an interval histogram approach for 3.5–7.5, 8.5–13 and 13–28 Hz activity. Also dominant frequency and amplitude analyzed.	Relative to nonsmokers, nondeprived very heavy smokers possessed activated EEGs. A linear trend relating daily consumption to the degree of deviation from the pattern shown by nonsmokers is claimed.
Cinciripini (1986): Will EEG smoking effects reveal interactions with Type A and B personality?	57	10–20/day	1. 4 h 2. Mixed 3. 45 min	Seated in a reclining chair, eyes open.	None	One 1.1 mg cigarette, 3 s puffs every 30 s to within 1 mm of overwrap.	Monopolar, P$_z$ referred to linked earlobes.	Rectified, integrated values for 4–7, 8–13 and 14–30 Hz activity.	Personality by smoking effects were found in the patterning, rather than the direction, of EEG change with smoking.
Comer et al. (1979): Will the EEG reveal sex, hemisphere, personality, age or smoker–nonsmoker effects?	30 30	NS Smokers	1. 1 h 2. Between 3. ?	Seated, eyes open and closed.	N/A	N/A	Twenty-four bipolar derivations were employed.	Power spectral analysis divided into 1–4, 4–8, 8–13 and 13–24 Hz bands.	Various correlations were found between the EEG and age, sex, neuroticism and smoker status. Smokers, relative to nonsmokers, exhibited signs of activation.

Hypothesis	n	Subjects	1. Depriv. 2. Design 3. Experiment	Activity/ recording situation	Control for nicotine	Smoking/ nicotine treatment	Electrode montage	Aspect of EEG analyzed	Conclusions
DeGood and Valle (1978): Smokers will be less able to regulate EEG activity in a biofeedback task.	40 40	>15/day NS	1. 4 h 2. Between 3. 4×40 min	Seated in a quiet, dark room, eyes closed.	N/A	N/A	Monopolar, midline occipital referred to left earlobe.	All 1 s epochs of 8–13 Hz activity which exceeded 10 μV (subject input) were summed.	Smokers were less able than nonsmokers to regulate their EEG alpha activity in a biofeedback task.
Friedman et al. (1974): Smoking will speed EEG orienting habituation.	10	>20/day	1. 12 h 2. Within 3. ?	Soundproof room.	Roast chicory cigarettes.	Two cigarettes, own brand or chicory.	Monopolar, C_z referred to the left mastoid.	'Alpha desynchronization' to tone presentation was assessed.	EEG habituation to a tone was speeded by smoking in deprived and nondeprived smokers.
Golding and Mangan (1982a,b): Will the EEG effect of smoking interact with a 'stress' manipulation?	24	8–15/day	1. ? 2. Mixed 3. 45 min	On a bed in a quiet room or seated and exposed to white noise.	Sham smoking.	One 1.3 mg cigarette over 5 min.	Bipolar, F_z-01, mastoid as ground (reversed for left-handed subjects).	Visual detection of alpha activity from the polygraph record.	Real (and less so sham) smoking was associated with EEG signs of arousal under sensory isolation, and sedation under exposure to white noise.
Hauser et al. (1958): Will there be EEG effects of smoking?	?		1. ? 2. Within 3. ?	Seated, eyes closed.	Sham smoking.	?	?	Limited information, all analyses based on dominant alpha frequency.	Smoking produced EEG arousal; however, similar effects were found with sham smoking.
Herning et al. (1983): Exp. I Exp. II Both to examine the EEG effects of smoking.	7 11	>30/day >30/day	1. 8 h 2. Within 3. Under observation for 7 and 48 h.	Seated with eyes fixed on a mark 3 m in front of subjects.	Non-tobacco cigarettes.	Cigarettes, similar delivery to own brand, or nicotine-free, at 30 min intervals.	Monopolar, F_z, C_z and P_z referred to linked ear tips.	Power spectral analysis of 0–3, 4–7, 8–14 and 15–25 Hz activity.	EEG signs of sedation followed deprivation. Signs of arousal followed real smoking, but only in the records taken from the central and parietal sites.

(*Continued*)

Table 1 (*Continued*)

Hypothesis	n	Subjects	1. Depriv. 2. Design 3. Experiment	Activity/ recording situation	Control for nicotine	Smoking/ nicotine treatment,	Electrode montage	Aspect of EEG analyzed	Conclusions
Itil et al. (1971): Will there be EEG effects of smoking and deprivation?	32	>30/day	1. 24 h 2. Within 3. 6×25 min	Eyes closed, resting and RT task.	None	Three unspecified cigarettes in 10 min.	Monopolar, O₂ referred to right ear and bipolar O₂ to anterior vertex.	Power spectral analysis.	Deprivation was accompanied by EEG signs of sedation, which were eliminated by the signs of central arousal following smoking.
Kenig and Murphree (1973): Will i.v. nicotine elicit similar EEG changes in smokers and nonsmokers?	8 6	>10/day Nonsmokers	1. O/night 2. Mixed 3. ?	Soundproof room.	i.v. saline.	Saline infusion with nicotine (6 µg/s) to max of 3 mg or 15 bpm rise in heart rate.	?	Spectral analysis.	i.v. nicotine produced similar EEG changes in both smokers and nonsmokers alike. However, due to poor reporting it is not clear what these changes were.
Knott and Venables (1977): Smoking will shift the EEGs of deprived smokers such as to make them like those of nonsmokers.	30 10	>10/day Nonsmokers	1. 13–15 h 2. Mixed 3. 30 min	Both experiments: seated, eyes closed. To maintain alertness, smokers were required to keep a key depressed.	Sham smoking.	Two 1.6 mg cigarettes in 10 min, puffs every 30 s.	Monopolar, O₂ referred to the right earlobe, left earlobe as ground.	Fast fourier transform, 'amount' of voltage in the 8–12 Hz range and dominant alpha frequency.	The EEGs of deprived smokers were less activated than those of nonsmokers. However, with smoking their EEGs changed to become more like those of nonsmokers.
Knott and Venables (1979): Will EEG measures suggest a central antagonism between alcohol and tobacco?	26 9	>10/day Nonsmokers	1. 15–18 h 2. Mixed 3. 55 min		Sham smoking.	Four 1.6 mg cigarettes equally spaced throughout a 35 min period.	Ditto	Ditto	Alcohol and tobacco were shown to have opposite effects on the EEG and when combined acted to cancel each other's effects.

Hypothesis	n	Subjects	1. Depriv. 2. Design 3. Experiment	Activity/ recording situation	Control for nicotine	Smoking/ nicotine treatment	Electrode montage	Aspect of EEG analyzed	Conclusions
Kumar et al. (1977, 1978): Will smoking and/or i.v. nicotine reveal dose-dependent effects?	12	25–60/day	1. None 2. Within 3. 2×3½ h	Seated in an isolated test room.	Herbal cigarettes and distilled water.	Twelve puffs on 1.3 mg or herbal cigarette or alternate on each. Or i.v. water, or 0.035, or 0.7 mg/kg nicotine.	Vertex and left parietotemporal sites (not clear if monopolar or bipolar).	Rectified and integrated values for 2.3–4, 4–7.5, 7.5–13 and 13.5–26 Hz bands collected for each 1 s epoch.	In nondeprived smokers, smoking resulted in an insignificant, and i.v. nicotine a significant, EEG change that resembled activation.
Murphree (1979): Will deprivation reveal EEG effects; will such effects be blocked by meprobamate?	8	>20/day	1. 6 h 2. Within 3. 2×6 h	Reclined on a N/A couch in a dark room.		Placebo or 800 mg of the anxiolytic meprobamate.	Monopolar, left occipital referred to linked ears, ground to forehead.	Spectral analysis.	Deprivation was accompanied by a qualitative EEG shift toward sedation which was unaffected by meprobamate.
Murphree et al. (1967): Will smoking reveal EEG effects?	? ?	'Smokers' Nonsmokers	1. ? 2. Mixed 3. ?	Supine, eyes closed in a dark room.	Sham smoking.	?	Monopolar, left occipital referred to linked earlobes.	Rectified and integrated area measures over unspecified bandwidths.	Smoking was followed by EEG signs of arousal.
Philips (1971): Will smoking produce EEG signs of activation in 2 h deprived smokers?	6	'Moderate smokers'	1. 2 h 2. Within 3. 2×33 min	Eyes closed and visual task.	Conversation control period.	One unspecified cigarette in 5 min.	Bipolar, O_2–C_4.	Mean alpha amplitude, and dominant frequency.	Smoking produced EEG signs of activation not seen after the 'conversation' control period.

(Continued)

Table 1 (*Continued*)

Hypothesis	n	Subjects	1. Depriv. 2. Design 3. Experiment	Activity/ recording situation	Control for nicotine	Smoking/ nicotine treatment	Electrode montage	Aspect of EEG analyzed	Conclusions
Pickworth et al. (1986): Will nicotine chewing gum elicit EEG changes?	3	16–30/day	1. 12 h 2. Within 3. 25 min	Reclining, eyes closed resting and mental task.	Placebo gum.	Chewed for 10 min gum containing 0, 2 or 4 mg of nicotine.	Bipolar, C_z-T6, C_z-T5, C_z-F7 and C_z-F8.	Power spectral analysis to locate the power and peak frequency for 4–7, 7.25–14 and 14.25–25 Hz.	Nicotine gum produced EEG signs of stimulation which were most apparent during the nontask period.
Remond et al. (1979): To examine EEG smoking effects in smokers and nonsmokers, and the differences between categories of smokers.	4 4 4 8	Nonsmokers >10/day 10–20/day >20/day	1. 12 h 2. Mixed 3. 2 h	Exposure to a range of stimuli; all analyses on eyes closed, rest data.	Sham smoking.	Two Gauloise 1.6 mg cigarettes in 10 min (smokers and nonsmokers alike).	Bipolar, left and right parietal sites referred to a common frontal electrode.	Frequency and amplitude measures, also 'mimetic analysis', although most of the report is concerned with alpha (7–14 Hz) activity.	Smoking in deprived smokers and nonsmokers produced marked variations in individual response. Some subjects showed signs of sedation, others increases in arousal.
Roos (1977): Will smoker status and consumption level covary with EEG 'reactivity'?	12 12 12	Nonsmokers <12/day >12/day	1. ? 2. Between 3. ?	Reclining on bed, exposed to auditory stimuli.	N/A	N/A	Bipolar, occipital–temporal.	Faraday waveform analyzer used to sample 10 s epochs of 8–13 Hz and to output histograms.	Limited support found for the view that the tonic level of arousal is positively related to daily cigarette consumption.
Szalai et al. (1986): Will smoker/deprivation status interact with the ability to self-regulate EEG activity, or with alpha suppression in a task?	12 10 20	Nonsmokers Ex-smokers >12/day	1. O/night 2. Between 3. ?	Reclining, eyes closed, exposed to auditory stimuli and biofeedback task.	N/A	N/A	Bipolar, O_1-O_2.	'Alpha amplitude integration'.	No differences were found between groups in their ability to regulate EEG alpha activity. Nondeprived smokers revealed less alpha suppression in a backward recall task than deprived smokers and nonsmokers.

Hypothesis	n	Subjects	1. Depriv. 2. Design 3. Experiment	Activity/ recording situation	Control for nicotine	Smoking/ nicotine treatment	Electrode montage	Aspect of EEG analyzed	Conclusions
Ulett and Itil (1969): Will deprivation and smoking produce EEG changes?	10	>20/day	1. 24 h 2. Within 3. 4×?	Reclining, eyes closed. 'Checking' used to keep subjects alert.	None	Two unspecified cigarettes in 5 min.	Monopolar, right occipital referred to the right ear.	Rectified and integrated for 24 frequency bands over 3–33 Hz per 10 s epoch, also used 'period analysis'.	Deprivation produced EEG signs of sedation, smoking signs of arousal.
Vogel et al. (1977, 1979): Will EEG photic driving responses distinguish smokers from nonsmokers, and the effects of smoking in both groups?	20 16	Nonsmokers >20/day	1. 3 h 2. Mixed 3. ?	Information absent, but the task requires open eyes.	None	One unspecified cigarette smoked with inhalation by both smokers and nonsmokers.	Bipolar, left and right occipital.	Detection of EEG driving responses (i.e. waves of the frequency of the photic stimulation of one full second with no other EEG wave present).	Deprived smokers revealed a greater incidence of driving responses than nonsmokers. Smoking reduced photic driving in both groups, but less so for nonsmokers, so removing the group differences.
Warburton and Wesnes (1979): Will smoking produce EEG changes which relate to performance on a vigilance task?	?		1. ? 2. Within 3. >30 min	Engaged in a visual vigilance task.	?	?	Bipolar, O1–P3 and O2–P4, with ground to the mastoid.	Rectified and integrated values for 4.5–6.5, 7.5–9.5, 9.5–11.5, 11.5–13.5 and 13.5–20 Hz bands over 6 min epochs.	During a vigilance task smoking prevented both the performance decrements and the EEG depression found in the nonsmoking condition.
Wechsler (1958): Smoking will produce EEG changes.	10	?	1. ? 2. ? 3. ?	?	Nicotine-free cigarettes.	Three 'regular' cigarettes in 10 min.	?	?	Smoking was accompanied by EEG signs of activation.

?: Information not provided or unclear.
N/A: Not applicable.
bpm: Beats per minute.

The electrode montage information refers to the Internation 10–20 System where its use is claimed by authors.

of nonsmokers were more activated than those of deprived smokers. Moreover, Knott and Venables found that the difference between groups was eliminated after the smokers had smoked.

Thus between-subject studies have yielded inconsistent results and provide no firm basis for choosing between outcomes. However, had the few studies conducted produced similar outcomes, the task of interpretation would remain. Do group differences exist as causes or effects? Does the possession of some correlate of high-frequency EEG activity predispose one to become a heavy smoker, or is such an EEG pattern a consequence of heavy smoking? Brown favors the conclusion that EEG measures are tapping some enduring characteristic of smokers which predisposes them to smoke. Clearly only a prospective longitudinal study would resolve this issue.

The acute effects of smoking and deprivation

One straightforward application of EEG measurement has been as a means of externally validating the self-reports of smokers. Questionnaire data have led to the conclusion that at least some individuals can be classified as 'high' or 'low' arousal smokers. Such a conclusion, combined with some animal work (e.g. Armitage, Hall and Sellers, 1969), has led some researchers to draw the inference that smoking has the potential to produce both central stimulant and sedative effects. It follows that, if the EEG is assumed to be tapping central arousal, EEG studies might be expected to reveal bidirectional effects of smoking. Few if any of the EEG studies have been conceived explicitly to test the bidirectional hypothesis. However, as the majority of the existing studies have been concerned with the phasic consequences of smoking and deprivation, the question has been directly, if unintentionally, addressed. As will be seen, the EEG studies give little support to the biphasic hypothesis.

The within-subject studies differ greatly in terms of sophistication of design and reporting, smoker definitions, periods of deprivation, magnitude of smoking treatments, and so on. However, this variation does not require that choices be made between studies and outcomes, because the results from most studies point to the same conclusion. A wide range of periods of deprivation, with just two exceptions (discussed later), have been consistently associated with a reduction in cortical activation (Herning, Jones and Bachman, 1983; Itil, Ulett, Hsu, Klingenberg and Ulett, 1971; Murphree, 1979; Ulett and Itil, 1969). Such shifts are usually taken to indicate central sedation. Corresponding between-subject differences have also been demonstrated by Knott and Venables (1977, 1979). The EEGs of their deprived smoker subjects were characterized by signs of sedation relative to those of nondeprived smokers. Thus it would appear that smoking deprivation is reliably accompanied by EEG signs of central nervous system sedation.

Smoking, on the other hand, has been consistently followed by signs of EEG activation in deprived smokers (Itil et al., 1971; Knott and Venables, 1977, 1979; Philips, 1971; Ulett and Itil, 1969), in nondeprived smokers (Knott and Venables, 1979; Kumar, Cooke, Lader and Russell, 1977, 1978; Wesnes and Warburton, 1978) and in smokers in an unspecified state of deprivation (Hauser, Schwarz, Roth and Bickford, 1958; Murphree, Pfeiffer and Price, 1967). Similar arousing effects have been found with intravenous nicotine in nondeprived smokers (Kumar et al., 1978), deprived smokers and nonsmokers (Kenig and Murphree, 1973; Kumar, 1979), and with nicotine chewing gum in deprived smokers (Pickworth, Herning and Henningfield, 1986).

So for the most part EEG studies of smoking have failed to reveal sedative effects of smoking, let alone dose-, or subject-related bidirectional effects. In summary, smoking deprivation has been followed by EEG signs of sedation, smoking by EEG signs of arousal. In some cases there are problems with such conclusions. For example, a few of these 'effects' have been below the level conventionally ascribed to chance, and in many of the studies the EEG changes revealed some, but not all, of the hallmarks of shifts in cortical arousal. There are also other problems with both internal and external validity. Some studies failed to control for the motoric aspects of smoking through, for example, the use of sham smoking (e.g. Itil et al., 1971; Ulett and Itil, 1969). Thus strictly speaking it is going beyond the evidence to attribute the changes observed to smoking; they might just as well be explained as an effect of repeated testing. However, the bulk of the evidence favors the conclusion that smoking, or more precisely nicotine, is the crucial variable which accounts for the observed shifts in cortical arousal.

Miscellaneous studies

Vogel, Broverman and Klaiber (1977, 1979) found that three-hour deprived smokers revealed a greater incidence of photic driving responses (i.e. the tendency of EEG rhythms to mimic the frequency of a bright flashing light) than nonsmokers. The difference disappeared after both the smokers and the nonsmokers smoked one cigarette. These authors review evidence which could be seen as supporting the conclusion that relatively high photic driving responses are associated with a central adrenergic insufficiency which has in turn been implicated in anxiety and depression. They suggest that the higher driving responses of deprived smokers may be evidence of such an insufficiency. The anxiolytic tricyclic drugs, they claim, reduce anxiety by virtue of their adrenergic stimulant properties. Hence, they argue, despite the apparent central stimulant effect of nicotine, it may work through a mechanism similar to the tricyclic drugs to produce similar reductions in anxiety.

Studies employing autonomic measures have pointed to the general conclusion that the speed of habituation of the orienting response is inversely related to the level of anxiety. The majority of such studies have employed electrodermal measures, and fairly clear relationships have been demonstrated between skin conductance response habituation speed and anxiety, and with the action of sedative drugs (e.g. Lader, 1967; Sartory, 1983). Following up such findings, Friedman, Horvath and Meares (1974) examined the effect of smoking on the speed of habituation of EEG orienting responses (alpha desynchronization). Smoking increased the speed of habituation to the repeated presentation of a tone in both deprived and nondeprived smokers, while no such effect was found with 'nicotine-free' chicory cigarettes. The authors interpret this result in terms of tobacco smoke acting centrally as a 'stimulus barrier' which functions to block out irrelevant environmental inputs. If one is prepared to draw an analogy with the electrodermal findings, then one would conclude that their study supports the view that smoking has a sedative effect. The notion that smoking may act as a stimulus input filter is shared by Knott (e.g. 1979, 1985), who has suggested that the reinforcing properties of nicotine may stem from its ability to act as a 'chemical stimulus filter'. This is an interesting suggestion, because it can go some way toward reconciling the subjective data pointing to the calming effects reported by smokers with most of the available direct evidence which points to smoking acting as a central stimulant.

Both of the foregoing studies are attractive in that they go beyond simply reporting the EEG consequences of smoking, to suggest how the observed effects might be functionally implicated in the maintenance of the habit. In similar fashion, DeGood and Valle (1978) produced evidence of a smoking-related electrocortical difference which provides a competing explanation. They found that in a biofeedback situation smokers who had undergone a four-hour deprivation period were less able to regulate their EEG alpha activity than nonsmokers. However, because of the rather long deprivation period used, smoker status was confounded with withdrawal. Hence the difference obtained might reflect a withdrawal-induced motivational decrement rather than the type of enduring difference claimed by the authors. Moreover, if the authors' interpretation was shown to be correct, one is still left with two equally plausible explanations: such differences may be the cause of, or be caused by, chronic tobacco use.

A more recent study, conducted by Szalai, Allon, Doyle and Zamel (1986), failed to replicate the findings of DeGood and Valle. No differences were found between nonsmokers and overnight-deprived smokers in terms of their ability to control EEG alpha activity in a biofeedback paradigm. However, the failure to uncover differences is not entirely surprising, given that only six minutes was devoted to biofeedback training.

The final study falling into this category was reported by Cinciripini (1986). Here interactions between the EEG effects of smoking, and the coronary-prone (Type A) and noncoronary-prone (Type B) personality traits, were investigated. Both groups of subjects revealed clear EEG signs of arousal (i.e. alpha suppression, and an increase in fast activity) upon smoking one cigarette after a three- to four-hour period of deprivation. However, the two groups of subjects revealed different patterns of change, as well as different patterns of recovery. These findings are discussed in terms of possible underlying neurophysiological differences in the control of arousal between Type A and B subjects.

Before closing this section a few words must be devoted to the topic of hemispheric specialization. In Chapter 8 in this volume, on anxiety and emotion, Gilbert and Welser make reference to a series of soon-to-be published studies concerned with lateralized EEG effects of smoking. In these studies EEG recordings taken from the right hemisphere were found to be more changed by smoking than those taken from the left hemisphere, with the pattern of change a function of stress manipulations. Other evidence exists (see, e.g., Davidson, 1983) to suggest that the left hemisphere is more concerned with cognitive processing than with affective processes, while the reverse is true for the right hemisphere. Against such a background, Gilbert and Welser interpret their findings in terms of stress level interacting with the effect of smoking to influence either cognitive or affective processes. This is an interesting proposition, and one which deserves extension and exploration. However, it is too early to draw clear conclusions. In our own laboratory we have found exactly the opposite outcome, with smoking producing bigger EEG effects in the left, than in the right, hemisphere. Quite how this discrepancy between the two sets of data is to be explained is not clear. What is clear is that this type of work is not well advanced; moreover, the general area of laterality and emotion is itself not well worked out. Nevertheless, Gilbert's data, along with those produced in our own laboratory, do suggest that further research effort is justified and may produce rewards, since it could enable us to distinguish the differential effects of nicotine on cognitive and emotional processes.

CONCLUSIONS AND RECOMMENDATIONS

Introduction

Nearly all the EEG studies share a number of methodological weaknesses which limit the extent to which the results obtained can be held to tell us anything about naturally occurring smoking behavior. In addition, there are two key questions thrown up by the existing research. The first of these is also concerned with external validity, but has a specific focus. That is, are the general findings of EEG activation following smoking merely an artefact of the circumstances under which recordings have been completed? The second question is one of interpretation. What do the observed EEG effects of smoking mean? What, if any, functional significance can be ascribed to the EEG changes which have been shown to accompany smoking?

Questions of validity

The existing studies are characterized by many limitations and weaknesses (e.g. nonrepresentative subject samples; lack of operational definitions of smoker groups; failure to control for sex, time of day, or nicotine; failure to consider individual differences; or the time course of effects). All the studies harbor some of these weaknesses; a few embrace them all. Such problems go to make between-study comparisons difficult, and reduce the credibility of claims for internal and external validity. However, there are two issues which stand out as of particular importance. The first is the period of deprivation employed; the second, the nature of the smoking treatment given.

The deprivation times employed in existing studies have ranged from one (Comer et al., 1979), to six (Murphree, 1979), to even 24 hours (Itil et al., 1971). An alternative approach has been to request overnight abstention (e.g. Kenig and Murphree, 1973). Smokers do not habitually deprive themselves for hours at a time. Thus if external validity is a goal, prolonged abstention periods are inappropriate. Moreover, requiring subjects to undergo long periods of deprivation raises the possibility that those smokers prepared to participate as subjects will be atypical along relevant dimensions. Overnight deprivation with early-morning testing provides a compromise solution, in that one is sampling something more closely approximating naturally occurring behavior. This approach also has the attraction that it controls for circadian influences. However, it is likely that the first cigarette of the day carries greater consequences (physiological, behavioral and experiential) than, say, the second or fifth. Therefore, while overnight abstentions may permit the sampling of realistic behavior, it may be a rather special instance of realistic behavior. The deprivation period employed should, it seems, be entirely determined by the nature of the question under examination, and the rationale for the selection of a particular period should be made explicit. In none of the existing studies has this been done. For most purposes it would seem to be difficult to justify an abstention period of more than one hour. Moreover, it would greatly assist between-study comparisons if such a period were adopted as a standard.

After exposure to these unnaturally long deprivation periods subjects have often been exposed to equally exaggerated doses of cigarette smoke. Wide variations exist in terms of the smoking treatment employed, and in terms of how clearly the issue has been reported. Information on the type of cigarette used has also been lacking. Despite the limitations of machine-smoked estimates, reporting such information should be routine. On the question of dose, nearly all researchers have used cigarettes rather than individual puffs as the unit of treatment. Moreover, the doses used have tended to bear little relationship to naturally occurring patterns. For example, Itil et al. (1971) required subjects to smoke three unspecified cigarettes in ten minutes. Knott and Venables (1979) increased this already high figure, and had subjects smoke four 1.6 mg cigarettes on a fixed inhalation schedule during a 35-minute period. It may be the case that the effects of smoking reach some asymptote after one cigarette. However, it would seem safer to assume that the scarcity of chain-smokers points to the conclusion that there are important pharmacological and sensory consequences of such behavior.

In short, there seems to be no justification for going above one cigarette as the unit of treatment. Moreover, if we have faith in both the resolution of the measures we employ, and the sensitivity of smokers who partition their smoking behavior into discrete puffs, then there is no reason to constrain analysis to the level of the cigarette. Presumably smokers take individual puffs because of the specific consequences of such behavior. If we also assume, which we surely must to engage in such research, that EEG measures are sufficiently sensitive to tap important aspects of the behavior, then it is reasonable to look for EEG consequences of individual puffs. Work in our own laboratory is proceeding along these lines, with encouraging results. It would seem that ultimately progress in this area will depend upon a marriage between the methodologies developed in the nicotine regulation, or titration, studies and more traditional EEG work. It is just possible that, in titration studies, EEG measures will be sufficiently sensitive to provide some evidence of regulation of bodily exposure to nicotine when compensatory puffing behaviors have been observed.

Smoking as a central stimulant: fact or artefact?

The experiential self-reports of smokers, together with inferences drawn from the information given by smokers about the circumstances under which they find smoking particularly attractive (e.g. Frith, 1971; Ikard, Green and Horn, 1969; O'Connor, 1980, 1985; Russell, Peto and Patel, 1974; Stanaway and Watson, 1980; Tomkins, 1966, 1968) have produced two distinct and opposed beliefs about the motivational basis of the habit. One entails the view that smoking aids attention and boosts concentration; the other that smoking has some calming effect in situations perceived by the smoker as stressful. While evidence has been produced to support the notion that smoking may aid concentration and sustained attention (for example, Heimstra, Bancroft and DeKock, 1967; Wesnes and Warburton, 1983a,b, 1984), the physiological evidence for sedation is limited in quantity, and where it does exist it is less than totally convincing. Indeed, as should be clear from the foregoing review, the bulk of the EEG studies lend support to the opposite conclusion, that smoking augments, rather than reduces, central arousal. Nesbitt's paradox (Schachter, 1973) has its origin in this failure to uncover the anticipated physiological evidence of sedation. However, the argument which is to be developed here is that Nesbitt's paradox may well be a pseudoproblem, merely an artefact of the way in which studies have been designed, executed and analyzed.

One possibility is that all of the existing EEG evidence of central stimulation simply reflects a Law of Initial Values effect. Wilder (1950) observed that the ability of a particular physiological measure to exhibit change is to some extent constrained by, and therefore a function of, the initial level of the system being measured. In nearly all the smoking studies subjects have been maintained at rest, often with their eyes closed to boost alpha activity and reduce eye movement artefacts, and this over long periods of time. Such conditions are likely to induce boredom and drowsiness. It may simply be the case that the uniformly boring conditions under which recordings have been completed have ensured that the mean response to smoking has been an increase in cortical arousal. Under similar circumstances a similar EEG shift might be anticipated in response to any activity, regardless of any pharmacological consequences. Just such a conclusion was implicit in the findings of one of the very first EEG smoking studies. Hauser et al. (1958) found that smoking, and sham smoking on a glass tube, were both accompanied by similar signs of EEG activation. They drew the reasonable conclusion that these effects were more to do with activity *per se* than to the central action of nicotine.

The treatment of physiological data may also serve to obscure sedative effects. The mean response to smoking, especially in bored or drowsy subjects, may well be a shift toward activation. However, the probability of drawing such a conclusion will be increased by the convention with electrophysiological data of only analyzing averaged data collapsed across all subjects. This may be an inappropriate way of looking at smoking data. It is conceivable that individual differences in direction of response have regularly occurred, only to be swamped by a mean trend toward activation. The only study in the literature to report individual data (Remond et al., 1979), uncovered marked individual differences in direction and magnitude of response. Their study also demonstrated how such differences can be lost in averaged data. Here subjects were not given a task to perform, but they were kept occupied. Hence they may have been more alert prior to smoking, and because of initial level more likely to reveal sedative effects which, because individual responses were analyzed, were less likely to be lost in the mass of the data.

There is yet a third candidate which may help to account for the existing findings. High-arousal smokers (i.e. those who claim to smoke to achieve sedative effects) may well need to be in high-arousal situations to reveal such effects. Two suggestions have been forwarded as to the mechanism which might make this possible (cf. Eysenck and O'Connor, 1979; Ashton, Millman, Telford and Thompson, 1973). However, in the present context it is only the possibility of such an effect which is important, not the process underlying its realization. To return to the argument, EEG recordings have not been completed with smokers reporting concurrent sedation. Neither has such measurement been adequately completed under those circumstances where it would be reasonable to predict that a sedative effect would be attractive to the smoker. The reports and conclusions about the sedative effects of smoking specifically relate to situations perceived by smokers as stressful. On the other hand, the bulk of the physiological evidence has been collected in laboratory environments, where it might be predicted that boredom and drowsiness would prevail.

The only study to address this problem was conducted by Golding and Mangan (1982a,b). They found that smoking was associated with EEG signs of stimulation under conditions of sensory isolation, and with what appeared to be a sedative effect under the relatively stressful conditions associated with exposure to bursts of white noise. Sham smoking produced qualitatively similar, but nonsignificant, results. Because of the way in which the data were collected (i.e. visual inspection of the polygraph record), and because of the time course of the effects observed, their findings are not entirely convincing. However, the paradigm employed is excellent and deserves exploration and extension. If sedative effects do occur there is clearly a higher probability that they will be revealed in studies which attempt to reproduce the circumstances under which such effects would be attractive to the smoker.

In conclusion, if there really is a paradox it has still to be adequately demonstrated. It may be the case that the consistent EEG findings of activation are merely an artefact of the experimental protocols and paradigms employed, and/or of the way in which physiological data have been analyzed. However, as the suggestions put here can be framed as unambiguous empirical questions, the hope is that future studies will shed new light upon these issues.

The functional significance of electrocortical measures

Whether or not signs of central activation are ultimately shown to be the genuine and unique EEG effects of smoking, the interpretation of EEG data will continue to present difficulties unless further changes in experimental design occur. Despite the earlier call for caution when using the term arousal, it featured largely in the preceding sections. How can such use be justified? Indeed, why use the EEG in smoking research at all? The following premises appear reasonable: (i) there exist lawful relationships between behavioral state, psychological state and brain state (i.e. some form of materialism); (ii) the action of nicotine on the central nervous system is implicated as a causal factor in the maintenance of the smoking habit; and (iii) of all available techniques, electrocortical measures hold out the firmest promise of mapping onto brain state changes and processes. If these three premises are accepted, then the EEG could be seen as having at least the potential to provide direct and objective evidence of the effect of nicotine on the central nervous system. The possibility of drawing this conclusion might be seen to provide sufficient justification for the employment of EEG measures in smoking research.

However, optimistic acceptance of the foregoing conclusion must be tempered by recognition of the inherent limitations of electrocortical measures. At best the EEG provides only a statistical representation of the underlying neural activity. In addition, this representation is certain to be incomplete in that many brain state changes and processes will fail to give rise to electrical fields of adequate size, duration or synchrony to appear in the EEG record. Moreover, any electrocortical changes found to accompany smoking may be mere epiphenomena, reflections of nothing of functional significance to the smoker. Thus, while it might be concluded that there are at least some reasons to use the EEG in smoking research, there remain problems of interpretation. How are such problems to be overcome? To attempt to answer this question it seems that we need to go back and look at the *raison d'être* for the bridge discipline of psychophysiology itself.

Psychophysiologists attempt to integrate psychological and physiological information in the hope that the addition of the latter will improve the understanding of the former. Rarely, in smoking research or elsewhere, is the rationale for the adoption of a particular physiological measure made explicit. However, for many applications, and certainly in relation to arousal, the rationale must be something like the following. Over a broad range of instances of some behavioral or experiential trait, the physiological measure in question has been shown to be a reliable covariate. The observed correlation is then taken to imply a more or less linear relationship between the two. This in turn is taken as grounds for transferring attention from the original experiential or behavioral variable to the physiological measure, which thereafter acts as the index of the former. Clearly, there is potentially a problem of circularity and redundancy here. However, this is only the case if the second measure fails to make available something not attainable with the first. If nothing is added, an unnecessary encumbrance will have been gained which, because of its secondhand nature, will probably tend to inflate the measurement error term. Moreover, by virtue of the 'scientific' appearance of the technology used in recording, the data produced may tend to be surrounded by a misleading, spurious air of credibility.

This, of course, is a rather jaundiced view of psychophysiology. Something commonly added with the use of physiological measurement is objectivity and access to data, which are both continuous and firmly quantitative in nature. However, it must always be remembered that the usefulness of the data obtained will be directly proportional to the extent to which the assumptions about the relationship between the physiological variable and the variable of real interest hold. It is precisely in relation to this assumption that the EEG studies of smoking are found to be wanting. In the past the EEG has been shown to be a useful and sensitive covariate of behavioral alertness and subjective feelings of arousal. However, it has also been shown to be sensitive to a host of other psychological phenomena. Thus, while a great deal is known about EEG–behavior relationships, many mysteries and uncertainties remain. The simple fact is that too little is known about the relationships between physiology, behavior and experience for it to be sensible to study just physiology alone. In the smoking studies there has been a consistent failure to integrate electrocortical measurement with the collection of concurrently sampled data from the behavioral and experiential domains. A genuinely psychophysiological analysis must replace what, so far, has been simple, if not to say simple-minded, physiological measurement. In the absence of concurrently gathered information about smoking's effect on performance or subjective experience it is difficult, if not impossible, to gain insight into the functional significance for the smoker of any electrocortical changes observed.

A prescription

Electrocortical effects of smoking have been observed. Then, by analogy with similar EEG changes uncovered in separate studies, where concurrent behavioral/psychological changes have been recorded, behavioral interpretations have been made. Against the current state of our knowledge such inferential leaps cannot be justified. These *post hoc* attempts to integrate behavioral and physiological data from different samples in separate studies must give way to a more integrated approach if our understanding is to be increased.

Relations between concurrently sampled physiological, behavioral and experiential data must be studied if the elucidation of the functional significance of electrocortical changes is to be a goal. The exploration of relationships between the EEG and behavioral efficiency can be commenced by incorporating performance tasks into EEG–smoking studies. This integration will be facilitated if the tasks chosen have a well-charted history within experimental psychology. Moreover, requiring subjects to perform tasks will have the beneficial effect of reducing the probability that they will become bored or drowsy, thereby avoiding the attendant problems already discussed. On a cautionary note, it is unrealistic to anticipate that the relationships between central measures and performance will be simple (see for example,

Gale and Edwards, 1983). However, real progress should be possible if such potential complexity is given due consideration when research is still at the design stage.

A move toward the collection of simultaneously sampled experiential data is not quite so straightforward. Due to the combined efforts of behaviorists, social psychologists and workers in the field of cognitive science, it is fashionable to eschew the notion that it is worthwhile asking subjects to report on moment-to-moment changes in affective state. The belief is that people will be either unwilling or, more likely, unable to provide useful information. If this position is accepted, it may be more sensible to approach the problem from the opposite direction, using an affect manipulation paradigm similar to that used by Golding and Mangan (1982a,b). The electrocortical consequences of exposure to manipulations designed to induce changes in affective state could be examined. If such manipulations appear to be successful, the possibility of interactions with smoking can then be explored. Importantly this approach is free from the need to solicit, or rely upon, subjective reports.

Conclusion

Some 25 EEG–smoking studies have been conducted, and a few of the relationships between smoking and the EEG have started to emerge. However, there exists the strong possibility that in the main these findings only apply to bored subjects who have undergone periods of deprivation far in excess of any they would ever choose to expose themselves to, and who have then smoked more intensely than they normally would. Hence, much is still to be learned about EEG–smoking relationships under more natural circumstances. Moreover, the relationships between electrocortical indices and behavior and experience are themselves poorly understood. Consequently, studies concerned only with the collection of electrocortical data fail to confront the fundamental question: are the electrocortical changes associated with smoking of functional significance to the smoker?

However, cautious optimism is justified in that most of the barriers to understanding are logistical rather than logical. With more attention and imagination applied at the design stage fundamental questions can be framed such that they· should elicit unequivocal answers. The EEG holds out the promise of providing direct, objective and firmly quantitative information about the effects of nicotine on the central nervous system of intact human subjects. Important discoveries may be made. Alternatively it may ultimately be demonstrated that EEG effects of smoking are absent or minimal under more natural conditions and/or show no relationship with other variables of interest. The key point is that after over two decades of research there are still hypotheses awaiting testing. Hopefully the next decade will see answers to most of the relevant questions. With such answers, the role of electrocortical measurement in smoking research, if any, will be decided.

REFERENCES

Adrian, E.D., and Matthews, B.H.C. (1934). The Berger rhythm: potential changes from the occipital lobes of man. *Brain*, **57**, 355.

Andreassi, J.L. (1980). *Psychophysiology: Human Behaviour and Physiological Response.* New York: Oxford University Press.

Armitage, A.K., Hall, G.H., and Sellers, C.M. (1969). Effects of nicotine on electrocortical activity and acetylcholine release from the cat cerebral cortex. *British Journal of Pharmacology*, **35**, 152–160.

Ashton, H., Millman, J.E., Telford, R., and Thompson, J.W. (1973). Stimulant and depressant effects of cigarette smoking on brain activity in man. *British Journal of Pharmacology*, **48**, 715–717.

Berger, H. (1929). Uber das Elektrenkephalogram des Menschen (On the electroencephalogram of man). *Archiv fuer Psychiatrie und Nervenkrankheiten*, **87**, 511–570.

Brown, B.B. (1968). Some characteristic EEG differences between heavy smoker and nonsmoker subjects. *Neuropsychologia*, **6**, 381–388.

Brown, B.B. (1973). Additional characteristic EEG differences between heavy smokers and non-smokers. In: W.L. Dunn (ed.), *Smoking Behaviour: Motives and Incentives.* Washington, DC: Winston.

Brown, B.B., and Klug, J.W. (1973). *The Alpha Syllabus: A Handbook of Human EEG Alpha Activity.* Springfield, IL: Charles C. Thomas.

Cinciripini, P. (1986). The effects of smoking on electrocortical arousal in coronary prone (type A) and non-coronary prone (type B) subjects. *Psychopharmacology*, **90**, 522–527.

Comer, A.K., Binnie, C.D., Lewis, P.H., Lloyd, D.S.L., Oldman, M., and Thornton, R.E. (1979). An electroencephalographic study of smokers and non-smokers with reference to age, sex and personality. In: A. Remond and C. Izard (eds), *Electrophysiological Effects of Nicotine.* Amsterdam: Elsevier.

Cooley, J.W., and Tukey, J.W. (1967). An algorithm for machine calculations of complex Fourier series. *Mathematical Computations*, **19**, 197–301.

Davidson, R.J. (1983). Hemispheric specialization for cognition and affect. In: A. Gale and J. Edwards (eds), *Physiological Correlates of Human Behaviour*, vol. 2: *Attention and Performance.* London: Academic Press.

DeGood, D.E., and Valle, R.S. (1978). Self-reported alcohol and nicotine use and the ability to control occipital EEG in a bio-feedback situation. *Addictive Behaviors*, **3**, 13–18.

Empson, J. (1986). *Human Brainwaves: The Psychological Significance of the Electroencephalogram.* London: Macmillan.

Eysenck, H.J. (1973). Personality and the maintenance of the smoking habit. In: W.L. Dunn (ed.), *Smoking Behaviour: Motives and Incentives.* Washington, DC: Winston.

Eysenck, H.J. (1983). A note on 'smoking, personality and reasons for smoking'. *Psychological Medicine*, **13**, 447–448.

Eysenck, H.J., and O'Connor, K. (1979). Smoking, arousal and personality. In: A. Remond and C. Izard (eds), *Electrophysiological Effects of Nicotine.* Amsterdam: Elsevier.

Friedman, J., Horvarth, T., and Meares, R. (1974). Tobacco smoking and a 'stimulus barrier'. *Nature*, **248**, 455–456.

Frith, C.D. (1971). Smoking behaviour and its relation to the smoker's immediate experience. *British Journal of Social and Clinical Psychology*, **10**, 73–78.

Gale, A. (1987). Arousal, control, energetics and values: an attempt at review and appraisal. In: J. Strelau and H.J. Eysenck (eds), *Personality Dimensions and Arousal*. New York: Plenum.

Gale, A., and Edwards, J. (1983). The EEG and human behaviour. In: A. Gale and J. Edwards (eds), *Physiological Correlates of Human Behaviour*, vol. 2: *Attention and Performance*. London: Academic Press.

Golding, J., and Mangan, G. (1982a). Arousing and de-arousing effects of cigarette smoking under conditions of stress and mild sensory isolation. *Psychophysiology*, **19**, 449–456.

Golding, J., and Mangan, G. (1982b). Effects of cigarette smoking on measures of arousal, response suppression and excitation/inhibition balance. *International Journal of Addiction*, **17**, 793–804.

Hauser, H., Schwarz, B.E., Roth, G., and Bickford, R. (1958). Electroencephalographic changes related to smoking. *Electroencephalography and Clinical Neurophysiology*, **10**, 576 (abstract).

Heimstra, N.W., Bancroft, N.R., and DeKock, A.R. (1967). Effects of smoking upon sustained performance in a simulated driving task. *Annals of the New York Academy of Sciences*, **142**, 295–307.

Herning, R.I., Jones, R.T., and Bachman, J. (1983). EEG changes during tobacco withdrawal. *Psychophysiology*, **20**, 507–512.

Ikard, F.F., Green, D.E., and Horn, D. (1969). A scale to differentiate between types of smoking as related to the management of affect. *International Journal of the Addictions*, **4**, 649–659.

Itil, T.M., Ulett, G.A., Hsu, W., Klingenberg, H., and Ulett, J.A. (1971). The effects of smoking withdrawal on quantitatively analysed EEG. *Clinical Electroencephalography*, **2**, 44–51.

Kenig, L.P., and Murphree, H.B. (1973). Effects of intravenous nicotine in smokers and non-smokers. *Federation Proceedings*, **32**, 805 (abstract).

Knott, V.J. (1979). Personality, arousal and individual differences in cigarette smoking. *Psychological Reports*, **45**, 423–428.

Knott, V.J. (1985). Effects of tobacco and distraction on sensory and slow cortical evoked potentials during task performance. *Neuropsychology*, **13**, 136–140.

Knott, V.J., and Venables, P.H. (1977). EEG alpha correlates of nonsmokers, smokers smoking, and smoking deprivation. *Psychophysiology*, **14**, 150–156.

Knott, V.J., and Venables, P.H. (1979). EEG alpha correlates of alcohol consumption in smokers and nonsmokers. *Journal of Studies on Alcohol*, **40**, 247–257.

Kumar, R. (1979). Tobacco smoking: tests of the nicotine dependence hypothesis. In: A. Remond and C. Izard (eds), *Electrophysiological Effects of Nicotine*. Amsterdam: Elsevier.

Kumar, R., Cooke, E.C., Lader, M.H., and Russell, M.A.H. (1977). Is nicotine important in tobacco smoking? *Clinical Pharmacology and Therapeutics*, **21**, 520–529.

Kumar, R., Cooke, E.C., Lader, M.H., and Russell, M.A.H. (1978). Is tobacco smoking a form of nicotine dependence? In: R.E. Thornton (ed.), *Smoking Behaviour: Physiological and Psychological Influences*. London: Churchill Livingstone.

Lacey, J.I. (1959). Psychophysiological approaches to the evaluation of psychotherapeutic process and outcome. In: E.A. Rubinstein and M.B. Parloff (eds), *Research in Psychotherapy*. Washington, DC: American Psychological Association.

Lacey, J.I. (1967). Somatic response patterning and stress: some revisions of activation theory. In: M.H. Appley and R. Trumbull (eds), *Psychological Stress: Issues in Research*. New York: Appleton Century Crofts.

Lader, M.H. (1967). Palmar skin conductance measures in anxiety and phobic states. *Journal of Psychosomatic Research*, **11**, 271–281.

Lindsley, D.B. (1952). Psychological phenomena and the electroencephalogram. *Electroencephalography and Clinical Neurophysiology*, **4**, 443–456.

Murphree, H.B. (1979). EEG effects in humans of nicotine, tobacco smoking, withdrawal from smoking and possible surrogates. In: A. Remond and C. Izard (eds), *Electrophysiological Effects of Nicotine*. Amsterdam: Elsevier.

Murphree, H.B., Pfeiffer, C.C., and Price, L.M. (1967). Electroencephalographic changes in man following smoking. *Annals of the New York Academy of Sciences*, **142**, 245–260.

O'Connor, K. (1980). Individual differences in situational preference amongst smokers. *Personality and Individual Differences*, **1**, 249–258.

O'Connor, K. (1985). A model of situational preference among smokers. *Personality and Individual Differences*, **6**, 151–160.

Parasuraman, R., and Davies, D.R. (1977). A taxonomic analysis of vigilance performance. In: R.R. Mackie (ed.), *Vigilance: Theory, Operational Performance and Physiological Correlates*. New York: Plenum.

Philips, C. (1971). The EEG changes associated with smoking. *Psychophysiology*, **8**, 64–67.

Pickworth, W., Herning, R., and Henningfield, J. (1986). Electroencephalographic effects of nicotine chewing gum in humans. *Biochemistry and Behaviour*, **25**, 879–882.

Pomerleau, O.F., and Pomerleau, C.S. (1984). Neuroregulators and the reinforcement of smoking: towards a biobehavioural explanation. *Neuroscience and Biobehavioural Reviews*, **8**, 503–513.

Remond, A., Martinerie, J., and Baillon, J. (1979). Nicotine intake compared with other psychophysiological situations through quantitative EEG analysis. In: A. Remond and C. Izard (eds), *Electrophysiological Effects of Nicotine*. Amsterdam: Elsevier.

Roos, S.S. (1977). A psychophysiological re-evaluation of Eysenck's theory concerning cigarette smoking. *South African Medical Journal*, **52**, 237–240.

Russell, M.A.H., Peto, J., and Patel, U.A. (1974). The classification of smoking by factorial structure of motives. *Journal of the Royal Statistical Society*, **137**, 313–346.

Sartory, G. (1983). The orienting response and psychopathology: anxiety and phobias. In: D. Siddle (ed.), *Orienting and Habituation: Perspectives in Human Research*. Chichester: John Wiley & Sons.

Schachter, S. (1973). Nesbitt's paradox. In: W. Dunn (ed.), *Smoking Behaviour: Motives and Incentives*. Washington, DC: Winston.

Spehlmann, R. (1981). *EEG Primer*. Amsterdam: Elsevier.

Stanaway, R.G., and Watson, D.W. (1980). Smoking motivation: a factor analytical study. *Individual Differences*, **1**, 371–380.

Stepney, R.E.G. (1979). Smoking as a psychological tool. *Bulletin of the British Psychological Society*, **32**, 341–345.

Szalai, J.P., Allon, R., Doyle, J., and Zamel, N. (1986). EEG alpha reactivity and self-regulation, correlates of smoking and smoking deprivation. *Psychosomatic Medicine*, **48**, 67–72.

Tomkins, S.S. (1966). Psychological model for smoking behaviour. *American Journal of Public Health*, **56**, 17–20.
Tomkins, S.S. (1968). A modified model of smoking behaviour. In: E.F. Borgatta and R.R. Evans (eds), *Smoking, Health and Behaviour*. Chicago, IL: Aldine.
Ulett, J.A., and Itil, T.M. (1969). Quantitative electroencephalogram in smoking and smoking deprivation. *Science*, **164**, 969–970.
Vogel, W., Broverman, D., and Klaiber, E.L. (1977). Electroencephalographic responses to photic stimulation in habitual smokers and non-smokers. *Journal of Comparative and Physiological Psychology*, **91**, 418–422.
Vogel, W., Broverman, D.M., and Klaiber, E.L. (1979). Gonadal, behavioural and electroencephalographic correlates of smoking. In: A. Remond and C. Izard (eds), *Electrophysiological Effects of Nicotine*. Amsterdam: Elsevier.
Wechsler, R.L. (1958). Effects of cigarette smoking and intravenous nicotine on the human brain. *Federation Proceedings*, **17**, 169 (abstract).
Wesnes, K., and Warburton, D.M. (1978). The effects of cigarette smoking and nicotine tablets upon human attention. In: R.E. Thornton (ed.), *Smoking Behaviour: Physiological and Psychological Influences*. London: Churchill Livingstone.
Wesnes, K., and Warburton, D.M. (1983a). Smoking, nicotine and human performance. *Pharmacology and Therapeutics*, **21**, 189–208.
Wesnes, K., and Warburton, D.M. (1983b). The effects of smoking on rapid information processing performance. *Neuropsychobiology*, **9**, 223–229.
Wesnes, K., and Warburton, D.M. (1984). The effects of cigarettes of varying yield on rapid information processing performance. *Psychopharmacology*, **82**, 338–342.
Wilder, J. (1950). The law of initial values. *Psychosomatic Medicine*, **12**, 392.

7

Individual Differences and Motor Systems in Smoker Motivation

KIERON O'CONNOR

ABSTRACT

The nicotine motivation model of smoking is challenged by a motor-sensory model of smoking. Both behavioral and pharmacological aspects of the smoking act are considered complementary in their purpose of transforming motor set. Smoking stimulates the motor system centrally and proprioceptively, so creating energy, improving task motivation and gating out stress and distraction. The type of motor action mimicked by smoking varies according to situational smoking preference and personality.

INTRODUCTION

Current models of smoker motivation view smoking solely as a convenient mean for ingesting nicotine. The smoking habit is seen as a form of nicotine dependence and the physiological effects of smoking are attributed to the isolated action of nicotine on central mechanisms controlling mood, arousal and/or sensory processes.

It is indisputable both that nicotine is the dominant psychoactive agent in tobacco smoke and that nicotine has direct and powerful neurochemical effects on the CNS. Yet, curiously, attempts to establish equivalence between the effects of smoking and the effects of nicotine, or even a general uniformity between these effects, have remained inconclusive. Many researchers would

Smoking and Human Behavior, Edited by T. Ney and A. Gale
© 1989 John Wiley & Sons Ltd

concur with Ashton, Millman, Rawlins, Telford and Thompson (1978, page 327) that 'the thesis that cigarette smoking is used essentially as a peculiarly effective form of nicotine self-administration has been singularly difficult to prove experimentally'; or with Domino (1973, page 6) that 'there is more to tobacco smoking than the intake of nicotine'.

It is common to cite sensory-motor factors or the 'fidget factor' as an important nonpharmacological concomitant of smoking. Indeed, every study of smoking motives to date has revealed at least one sensory-motor component to craving. But motor aspects have been dismissed as secondary peripheral factors tangential both to the maintenance of the habit and its physiological effects. Typical is the comment by Russell, Peto and Patel (1974, page 315) that 'there is little doubt that if it were not for the nicotine in tobacco smoke, people would be little more inclined to smoke cigarettes than they are to blow bubbles or light sparklers'.

An alternative to ascribing a separate minor psychological role to motor factors is to propose that sensory-motor acts are in part a form of *motor-sensory-regulation* which operates via both central and peripheral mechanism. Smoking can then be viewed as a motor behavioral act. Both pharmacological and nonpharmacological aspects of smoking can be seen as complementary operants. Thus nicotine ingestion is not *the* motive for smoking, but *part* of smoking with the same aim of regulating motor action. Implicit in this model is that there is a desire on the part of the smoker to transform motor activity in some way.

Before outlining the motor model, some problems with the conventional nicotine dependence model of smoke motivation will be discussed.

THE FIXED-EFFECT NICOTINE DEPENDENCE MODEL

The molecular similarity of nicotine to the neurotransmitter acetylcholine (ACh), established by Dale (1914), enables nicotine to combine with ACh receptors and to mimic the action of ACh. ACh receptors are widely distributed in autonomic ganglia, neuromuscular junctions and subcortical structures, and as Armitage (1979) notes, the resemblance of nicotine to ACh means that it can basically have effects, both direct and indirect, on the cholinergic system; thus neurochemical evidence makes a nicotine dependence model of smoking highly plausible. If such a model were valid, it would seem reasonable to expect, firstly, that the physiological effects of nicotine and smoking are comparable and, secondly, that smoking can be satisfactorily substituted with other forms of nicotine administration. The nicotine dependence model remains, however, largely unsubstantiated.

The physiological effects of nicotine

Since the work of Paton and Perry (1953) which established the biphasic actions of nicotine on cell membranes, the effects of nicotine have been considered as dosage-linked, small doses producing excitation and large doses producing inhibition. Smoking has also been reported to have a biphasic stimulant/sedative action, and a biphasic model is widely accepted as an explanation of many experimental effects in smoking research, so endorsing the pharmacological view of a nicotine dependence model (Eysenck, 1967; Nesbitt, 1973).

But generalization of the biphasic nicotine model to smoking effects is undoubtedly premature. Firstly, the biphasic model of nicotine itself needs to be treated with caution. Certainly the evidence indicates that nicotine in a variety of doses activates or energizes human physiological responses, but the relation between high doses and inhibition is less certain. Most studies demonstrating the inhibitory physiological effects of nicotine have directly administered nicotine to animals (e.g. Manser, 1972; Rosencrans, Spencer, Krynock and Chance, 1978) and these effects have anyway been inconsistent (Clarke, 1982). Frequently, behavioral inhibition was produced by an initial dose, with the same dose producing activation following the priming dose.

A study by Ashton et al. (1978), however, did claim to establish a biphasic dose–response curve in human subjects using electrocortical responses as the dependent measure. After administering five intravenous doses of nicotine covering a range from 10 to 800 mg over a period of five minutes, the authors reported a tendency for the electrocortical responses to increase at small doses and decrease in amplitude at larger doses, thus indicating a biphasic dose–response action on cortical arousal.

But in both the Ashton et al. study (1978) and the animal studies, dosages used were high and in excess of normal doses achieved from smoking. Possibly the inhibitory effects reported were due less to a unitary process of inhibition and more to general disruption. As Armitage (1973) points out, chronic ingestion will stretch the tolerance of the system and produce general incapacity. This view is particularly pertinent to the Ashton et al. study, since similar decreases in their electrocortical measure have been reported by other researchers as a consequence of distractibility due to hyper-, rather than hypo-arousal (Tecce, 1972). The more general finding, where physiological activity has been monitored during intermittent administration of nicotine, is that nicotine *activates*, and often this activation bears a linear relation to dosage.

Jarvik (1973), Kumar (1979) and Wesnes and Warburton (1978) have all reported that nicotine tablets produce a dose-dependent effect on heart rate (HR), larger doses producing a greater increase. Nicotine induces vasoconstriction as a direct function of dosage, shifts in EEG frequency toward greater activation, increases in blood pressure, electrodermal responsivity and muscle tension. Such findings have all been reported at widely different dosage levels (Gilbert, 1979).

Thus the main neurochemical actions of nicotine at autonomic and central sites shown in studies involving ingestion, would support a monophasic activation model; a simple dose-related activation hypothesis of nicotine's action seems the most tenable within the range of doses equivalent to smoking doses.

Physiological effects of smoking

However, when we look for a similar dose-related effect of smoking itself on physiological responses, no clearcut picture emerges. The magnitude of the physiological response bears no consistent relationship to the amount of nicotine in the cigarettes. For example, Woodson, Buzzi and Bättig (1983) reported that smoking increases HR only when accompanied by deep inhalation, whilst Roos (1977) reported that HR increased in moderate but not heavy smokers and with low- but not high-nicotine cigarettes. Mangan and Golding (1978) reported that HR increased in subjects smoking middle-range cigarettes. Similar variability in results and lack of dose relationships have been reported for other ANS measures such as circulation effects, skin conductance, body temperature and muscle tension, as well as for electrocortical responses (O'Connor, 1984). Remond, Martinerie and Baillon (1979) computed EEG spectra over a range of tasks during smoking, and concluded that the effects of smoking are complex, appearing in a variety of forms and depending on the quantity consumed by the smoker, the subject's psychological involvement in the task, the situation he or she is experiencing and the individual's personality.

Two mediating factors consistently emerge from the smoking–physiology literature. These are the influence of the state of the smoker and individual differences amongst smokers. Unfortunately, we have little systematic knowledge on the forms that either factor may take. Suter (1981), for example, found that smoking increased HR only when subjects were in a state of rest. Erwin (1971) found that task engagement mitigated the effects of smoking on HR. Friedman, Goldberg, Horvath and Meares (1974) likewise found that the effects of smoking on evoked potentials were a function of task demand. Mangan and Golding (1978) reported that the task stress mediated the excitatory effects of smoking on sensory performance. This influence of prior degree of activation is coupled with wide individual differences which themselves interact with task effects. For example, Armitage (1973) found that HR increased in only half his subjects, though all smoked in identical conditions. Kumar, Cooke, Lader and Russell (1978) found little effect on HR in most of their subjects after smoking under rest conditions. Ashton,

Millman, Telford and Thompson (1974), and O'Connor (1983), found increases in cortical arousal in some subjects and decreases in others under identical activities, but these authors systematized the differences in terms of degree of extraversion of the smoker. Wesnes and Warburton (1978) accounted for some of their variable effects in terms of neuroticism.

The clear influence of mediating behavioral variables in the regulation of smoking effects poses severe problems for a simple nicotine dependence model, and the problems are reflected in methodological difficulties met by researchers in attempts to derive equivalent measures of nicotine and smoking effects.

Psychological mediation of physiological effects

Armitage (1973) states rather despairingly that the conclusive experiment to demonstrate equivalence between smoking and nicotine effects has not yet been performed. The question is, can it ever be done?

The peculiar self-paced bolus-like intake of nicotine through smoking cannot in practice be mimicked by the artificial administration of nicotine. There is the obvious problem of dose matching. How does one approximate a single injection to a normal, intermittent puff dosage? But more importantly there is the problem of effect matching, since individual differences in puff styles and state may dictate that, even with a large equivalent dose of nicotine in a cigarette, the absorption rate may not be adequate to elicit any noticeable equivalent effect among the smokers (Armitage, 1965). The problem of dose equivalence is compounded by a divergence between the distribution and metabolism of nicotine in the blood, as a function of whether the nicotine is inhaled or injected.

These problems indicate clearly that the most pertinent characteristic of human cigarette smoking is that it is an exercise in continuous behavioral self-regulation, meeting the demands of a continually adapting and functioning system. The influence of individual differences over more general state factors in such self-regulation is shown in the idiosyncratic nature of smokers' puff profiles.

SMOKERS' CONTROL OF MEDIATING EFFECTS

Smokers may vary the depth, the duration or the frequency of their puffing, but in particular, the profile of a smoker's puff volume yields what might be called a 'puff-print' of an individual smoker (Ashton and Stepney, 1982). There is the possibility that variations in smoking style are attempts to lower or raise the amount of nicotine inhaled, and represent titration or compensation strategies.

Titration studies

Studies have produced conflicting evidence of compensation amongst smokers and have examined puff responses under conditions of: differing cigarette nicotine content (Ashton and Watson, 1970; Ashton, Marsh, Millman, Rawlins, Stepney, Telford and Thompson, 1979; Creighton and Lewis, 1978); shortened cigarettes (Ashton et al., 1979; Goldfarb and Jarvik, 1972; Russell, Sutton, Feyerabend and Cole, 1978; Sutton, Russell, Feyerabend and Saloojee, 1978) and substitution of smoking for other means of nicotine ingestion (Jarvik, Glick and Nakaruma, 1970; Kumar et al., 1978; Raw, Jarvis and Russell, 1980). Russell, Raw and Jarvis (1980), for example, report that nicotine chewing gum and smoking, rather than compensating for each other, could be combined by the smoker to form a peak plasma nicotine level. Furthermore, in titration studies compensation downward to avoid high nicotine levels is far more common than compensation upwards (Russell, 1978) whereas the nicotine-dependence model would predict the converse.

In general, the association between nicotine content and smoking behavior has proved weak. Friedman and Fletcher (1976) suggest that it is more accurate to speak of *adaptations* of smoking behavior to variations in nicotine content rather than compensation. Ashton et al. (1978) conclude that changes in smoking patterns to accommodate variations in cigarette nicotine content are generally not large enough to prove convincingly that the self-administration of nicotine is the major factor in the maintenance of the smoking habit. McMorrow and Foxx (1983) echo this sentiment and state that even when changes in behavior do correspond to changes in a direct nicotine measure, this relation remains correlational (page 323).

One of the outcomes of titration research has been the recognition that there may be a mixture of types of smokers who have been confounded within titration studies; in particular, that there may be a group of smokers who take in little or no nicotine and show few withdrawal symptoms when deprived of nicotine cigarettes. Russell (1978) concludes that perhaps less than 50 percent of smokers smoke principally to obtain nicotine. Bättig and Schlatter (1978) and Domino (1973) admit that the possibility that smokers who smoke milder cigarettes do so for their nicotine content is negligible.

The titration hypothesis as a blanket explanation of smoker differences thus seems untenable. Clearly some smokers do compensate, others do not, but smoker strategies cannot easily be quantified along a dimension of nicotine dependence. The failure of most titration studies to control for individual differences, and even in some cases to specify on control for type of smoker, has not helped to sort out the methodological confusion. (See Chapter 9, by Nil and Bättig, in this volume.)

THE BIPHASIC AROUSAL MODEL OF SMOKER REGULATION

One popular approach to explaining the effects of state-situation and individual differences on variation in smoker styles and effects is the arousal model. The original notion of the arousal model was that different types of smoker strategy might reflect the desire of the smoker to increase or decrease arousal. This arousal theory was largely influenced by Eysenck's (1967, 1973, 1980) theory of personality which views differences in the behavior of introverts and extraverts as reflections of their respectively high and low CNS arousal level. The most straightforward test of the role of arousal mechanisms, as hypothesized by Eysenck, is an examination of the relationships between high/low arousal smoking and personality, and personality differences in smoking under high–low arousal situations. Unfortunately, much confusion has resulted from authors differing not only on how to measure arousal, but on how to define and manipulate it. For example, Frith (1971), Fuller and Forrest (1973), Hultberger (1974), Myrsten, Andersson, Frankenhaeuser and Elgerot (1975), and Waller (1975) all constructed high/low arousal smoker divisions on the assumption that nicotine would be a stimulant for some smokers (those who would be most likely to smoke during undesirably low levels of arousal) but would be a sedative for other smokers (those who would smoke during high levels of arousal). Unfortunately, these authors' definitions of high and low arousal conflicted with each other and, consequently, left their various attempts at cross-validation in jeopardy. Gale (1981) notes that the term 'arousal' is often confused by being employed in different senses, as a source of stimulation, an endogenous variation, a correlate, a consequence, a drive and/or a motivation, all of which are clearly different processes.

The general consensus from studies which have used comparable definitions of arousal derived from experimental manipulations is that low-arousal preference smokers take in more nicotine than high-arousal smokers, not less as the biphasic arousal model would predict. The studies by Fuller and Forrest (1973), Mangan and Golding (1978) and Williams (1980) have all noted this high-arousal–low-arousal distinction in habit.

Extraverts (who have low cortical arousal and thus require a stimulant effect) should take in less nicotine than introverts, but are generally reported to take in more nicotine and be more nicotine-dependent than introverts and neurotics. Conversely, several studies have commented on the importance of nonpharmacological factors in high stress smokers (e.g. Williams, 1980).

Frith (1967), Mangan and Golding (1978), Warburton and Wesnes (1978) and Williams (1980) all prefer to cite *attentional* rather than *arousal mechanisms* in their attempts to explain smoking-related performance effects. For example, Mangan and Golding (1978) found conflicting effects of nicotine on autonomic arousal, and they suggested the direction of these effects interacted with attentional not arousal demands. In a subsequent study of vigilance performance, Mangan (1982) found that middle-nicotine cigarettes increased sensitivity and detection proper (as measured by increases in accuracy), but high-nicotine cigarettes increased false positives (responding to nonwanted signals). These results are not consistent with any standard arousal predictions, which propose more uniform performance differences as a function of dose response.

Friedman and Meares (1980), studying the effects of smoking and personality on evoked potentials (ERPs), found a differential effect of smoking on auditory and visual ERPs and a differential effect on early and late components. They suggest that their findings are difficult to explain in terms of an arousal theory, and propose that the effects of smoking and personality are mediated through attentional regulation. O'Connor (1983), in a study designed to replicate the biphasic arousal theory of smoking as applied to cortical arousal (Ashton et al., 1974), also found an attentional explanation of slow potential differences to be the most parsimonious. Of course, level of attention and arousal do interact, but these attentional explanations focus the effects of smoking onto qualitatively different attentional strategies rather than simply biphasic changes in level.

A further curious anomaly for the biphasic model is that no study has reported clearcut behavioral evidence for the sedating effects of smoking. Some studies of learning and memory, reviewed by Ney and Gale (1984) and by Ney, Gale and Morris in this volume, have indicated that smokers as a group perform worse than nonsmokers, but these studies are confounded by the deleterious effects of deprivation. All studies exploring attention, sensory, motor or cognitive function only report different degrees of enhanced performance postsmoking. There is also no evidence that nicotine smoking interacts with the effects of sedative drugs (Ashton, Millman, Telford and Thompson, 1976). In fact, evidence of the sedative effect of smoking comes not from single-measure studies, but from studies noting incongruence across measures, and in particular those that have explored Nesbitt's (1973) paradox of subjective evaluations of calming and tranquilizing effects on mood coupled with physiological and performance measures of alertness.

The effects of smoking on mood

The effects of smoking on mood are reported by the arousal theorists to be calming, but by the pleasure–reward theorists as being reinforcingly pleasurable or pleasurable by virtue of being reinforcing. In fact, most studies do not show an elevation of mood following smoking. Rather they more often show negative reinforcement by virtue of a decrease in negative and aggressive affect, which is not synonymous with achieving pleasure, or positive reinforcement. Bernston (1971) showed that nicotine in appropriate doses produces a selective decrease in predatory behavior in the cat. Hutchinson and Emley (1973) showed that, for both monkeys and men, intake of small quantities of nicotine produced a differential reduction in behavior patterns associated with aggressiveness, hostility and irritability. Hall and Morrison (1973) reported that rats given nicotine exhibited less distress when exposed to electric shock. Dunn (1978) found that in aggressive situations smokers appeared able to protect themselves from the disruptive effects of anger.

Schachter (1973) also found that subjects tolerated more shock the greater the nicotine delivery of their cigarettes. Friedman et al. (1974) found an increase in habituation to noxious tones under smoking conditions. Heimstra (1973) found, during performance of a driving simulator and other stressful tests, that ratings of aggression and urgency were attenuated in smokers, and smokers showed overall flattened fluctuations in mood variation. Heimstra (1973), as other authors, emphasized the importance of stress in eliciting mood differences in smokers. Easy tasks produced no group differences in mood, and intermediate stress produced less change than very difficult tasks. There is, in addition, some evidence suggesting that chronic smokers are in fact *more* likely than nonsmokers to experience negative emotions such as anxiety and anger. McKennell (1970) identifies nervous irritation as a motive for smoking, and Nelsen (1978) reports evidence that smokers may be predisposed to emotional disturbance.

An important point to note in these studies of the interaction between smoking and mood is that there is little in the way of dose-dependent relationships. Basically smokers of any type, and smoking any strength of cigarette, show reduced irritability. This, of course, runs counter to the sedation part of the nicotine–arousal model. Furthermore, it is clear that the emotion-reducing aspects of smoking are hardly sedative as predicted by the arousal model, and are not incompatible either with enhanced pleasure or positive reinforcement effects from smoking. Indeed, the nicotine–reward model of smoking, which is inspired by the pleasurable affect reported from smoking, views psychological dependence as a consequence of the stimulant, not sedative, action of nicotine on brain reward systems. But more importantly, decrease in negative affect in the studies cited above is more often *accompanied by* enhanced performance and attention. Enhanced performance and sedation are not mutually exclusive as the biphasic inhibition–excitation arousal model proposes. In the studies of self-reported motives for smoking, arousal control factors do not support a biphasic classification of smokers, or the expected relationship between arousal and nicotine consumption.

Questionnaire studies of smoker motivation

A number of factor analytic studies of smoker motivation show that, if there is an affective motive, it covers both reduction of negative affect and enhancement of pleasurable affect, which merge in one type of affect–control smoker. Both Stanaway and Watson (1980) and Coan (1973) report that high- and low-affect items load on the same factor, and O'Connor (1984, 1985) similarly found that preference to smoke under pleasurable excitement and unpleasant anxiety were part of the same motivational complex. But even so this arousal factor accounts on average for little more than 10 percent of the variance. There is no evidence to suggest that even this common affect factor correlates with other more objective aspects of smoker habit, and in particular with pharmacological indices of the habit. Studies conflict on the means by which smoking influences affect.

Russell, Peto and Patel (1974) suggest that stimulation smoking, to keep awake, loads on a pharmacological addiction factor. McKennel (1970) and Tomkins (1966) suggest that affect smoking is a sensory-motor factor, and relies on a range of indulgent, taste and somatic accompaniment factors. Stanaway and Watson (1980) also note that the stimulation effects of smoking have a strong sensory component. Coan (1973) suggests that reduction of negative affect is an addictive factor, whilst Russell et al (1974) suggest that it is an indulgent–oral–manipulative factor.

The addictive or pharmacological dependence factor itself fails to emerge as a clear smoking motive, and Russell et al. (1974), who attempted to construct a pharmacological dependence continuum ranging from addiction to indulgent smoking, admit that their typology offers a profile of smoking rather than a typing of smokers. In fact, addictive factors tend to emerge as artefacts of numbers of cigarettes smoked, and when this factor is controlled, other puff factors fail to relate systematically to general affect motives.

But though pharmacological addiction fails to emerge as a consistent motive, sensory-motor and, in particular, activity accompaniment factors do relate consistently to aspects of the habit and other motivational factors. For example, Stanaway and Watson (1980) note that smoking, as an activity accompaniment, is a motive that relates to a large number of items, and that psychosocial and sensory motives may be more important for a larger number of smokers than is usually accredited. Studies of sham smoking illustrate the psychophysiological effects of nonpharmacological motives.

Psychophysiological correlates of sham smoking

Sham smoking is, of course, habitually used by researchers as a control or baseline condition from which to gauge the effects of real smoking. The sham smoking condition is generally identical in every way to the real smoking condition, save that a lit cigarette is replaced by either an unlit cigarette or a dummy filter, and the smokers mimic smoking at equivalent periods to the real smoking condition. In general it has been noted that the effects of sham smoking on the CNS and ANS mimic those induced by nicotine cigarette smoking. For example, Woodson et al. (1983) found that in some smokers an anticipatory sham smoking period under a noise stress condition elicited stress-dampening effects on both subjective and autonomic measures that equalled those observed during real smoking. Mangan and Golding (1978) examined the psychophysiology of smoking during a vigilance task and reported that the sham smoking condition accounted for a percentage of the increase in heart rate and skin response increase elicited during real smoking. Suter (1981), using a very low-nicotine cigarette as a control, noted that both the sham smoking and real smoking condition produced similar changes in respiration pattern, skin response and EEG during Stroop test performance. (See Chapter 10 in this volume, by Warburton and Walters, for an account of the Stroop test.)

Fuller and Forrest (1973) found that simulated smoking induced both equivalent tension reduction to real smoking (when smokers viewed an aversive stress film) and equivalent arousal (when subjects were relaxed doing nothing). Fuller and Forrest (1973) are unequivocal in their view that more attention be paid to individual differences between smokers and to the motor act of smoking *per se* rather than simply to the pharmacological properties of nicotine. O'Connor (1984) also found that the electrocortical changes associated with real smoking could be induced by motor activity alone in some smokers.

Since the effects of sham smoking are in the same, not the opposite, direction to smoking effects, they cannot easily be explained as a form of conditioned anticipation in line with the opponent process priming model applied to opiate use (Segal, 1979). The current state of research into smoker motivation is dominated by attempts to render some account of nicotine dependence plausible. As a consequence of this concern with attributing primacy to a fixed pharmacological effect, there has been little appreciation of smoking as a self-regulated behavioral activity, and functional components of both the motor actions of smoking and the motor behavioral background activity of the smoker have been neglected. Although motor activity levels have occasionally been noted as mediators of smoking effects, the *idée fixe* that pharmacological effects act via sensory arousal processes has prevented consideration of the motor system as a regulator of smoking. A shift in thinking toward a motor-behavioral approach to smoking may resolve some of the paradoxes thrown up by the pharmacological approach.

THE MOTOR APPROACH VS THE SENSORY APPROACH TO SMOKER MOTIVATION

The essence of the sensory viewpoint is that the behavior or motor processes are an endpoint, resulting from sensory effects of a physiological nature (for example, arousal) or a psychological nature (attention) or a pharmacological nature. Inherent in the sensory model is a unidirectional temporally ordered sequence of events, leading from sensory state (an induced internal event, either exteroceptively or pharmacologically) to motor action and behavioral adjustment.

On both theoretical and empirical grounds it seems reasonable to propose a closed-loop systems model of function, where motor and sensory processes mutually interact and reciprocate with one another. In other words, motor activity may, by itself, perform a regulatory function controlling central state and information flow, and hence may be an operant in its own right for controlling central mood, cognition or pharmacological effects.

Several challenges have been made recently to the sensory model both at a physiological and psychological level. In particular the division of neurophysiological function into sensory and motor areas may be inappropriate. It is by no means certain at what level efferent processes meet afferent processes, or whether, from a functional point of view, the two can be usefully distinguished (Wiemer, 1977). For example, emotional experience and muscular activity can be seen as part of the same action system (Lang, Kozak, Miller, Levin and McLean, 1980).

The essential difference between a sensory and a motor approach to explaining behavior is the emphasis placed by the motor model on the *behavioral* activity of the person prior to any stimulus intervention in determining future response. The motor view is that activity generates relationships between organism and environment which leads both to different sensations and behavior patterns.

The next section outlines ways in which motor activity could exert a significant influence on the motivation to smoke. The outline begins with some general observations on the role of nicotine and the motor system. Readers who wish to skip the detailed arguments relating smoking to the motor system will find a summary on page 156.

Nicotine and the motor system

The main action of nicotine is on ACh, and this means that the central site of nicotine lies in the noradrenergic brain stem region. The central site of action of the noradrenergic system is the reticular formation (RF) and the hypothalamus, which has connections primarily with the prefrontal cortex. Activation of dorsal or ventral noradrenergic pathways causes massive release

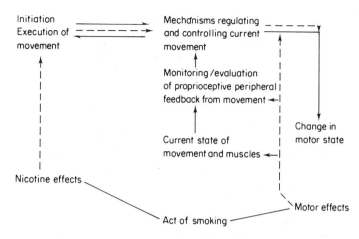

Fig. 1   Block diagram of possible smoking effects on the motor system

of noradrenaline in many forebrain structures causing a high rate of non-selective motor activity. Ascending cholinergic pathways feed into the limbic system. The limbic system contains a number of structures which are important in the activation and suppression of movement (McCleary, 1966).

The reticular formation exerts an ascending influence on the hippocampus via the hypothalamus and septal nuclei. This ascending activity acts as a general trigger or initiator of movement, since similar frequency shifts in this activity accompany a number of quite distinct motor patterns. One may thus see the hippocampus as controlling execution of movement. However, both limbic–cholinergic and brain stem noradrenergic systems rely on activation of ACh to initiate movement controlling mechanisms.

This release of ACh may be activated pharmacologically, or mimicked pharmacologically, e.g. by nicotine. It may be inhibited directly by cholinergic mechanisms acting on parietal–limbic feedback of information, *or* importantly, it may be inhibited by adenosine triphosphate (ATP) at muscular prejunctional levels. ATP is the energy-producing hormone, formed during muscle movement to regulate energy processing. It is coreleased with ACh at times of activity and may have a neuromodulation effect on ACh and on cholinergic receptors, so inhibiting ACh release. Levels of ATP reflect very closely the type and extent of current movement in peripheral musculature.

Motor system regulation of motor demand

Muscle coordination, and hence motor skill, is a fundamental aspect of energy regulation at molecular, cellular and organic levels. Different types of movement induce different rates of energy regulation, and different methods of metabolization. The energy demands during exertion are met by adrenaline and oxygen. Adrenal secretion by the adrenal medulla is enhanced by behavioral conditions of exercise, excitement, anxiety, exertion and stress, and smoking. The oxygen, however, is supplied by increased respiration. Respiration, as has been emphasized by Smith (1973), is an extremely important body tracking mechanism which regulates energy supply.

Smith and Putz (1970) applied behavioral tracking methods to the study of respiration, and demonstrated respiratory tracking of peripheral movement. Respiratory behavior is closely allied with other body movements, such as those of speech, head movement, arm movement and lower limb movement. According to Smith (1973) the motor system is not simply a dependent variable of physiological drive and regulation; rather the skeletal motor system is the dominant dynamic center for the control of energy production.

Both adrenergic and cholinergic systems are then intricately involved in the energy–movement–physiologic–regulation system of motor commands. When movement is localized and ATP production is specific, ATP and ACh are jointly released, and they modulate jointly the neurotransmitter release of energy demands toward the brain. Where energy demands are more drastic a more centrally coordinated release of ACh takes place which gears the organism for action. Rates of respiration largely play a feedforward role here, and are themselves tied to movement exertion. Hence efferent modulation may occur peripherally in terms of sliding muscle fiber generation of ATP, or at the central midbrain level with cholinergic inhibition of nor-adrenergic activity. Clearly these two will interact depending on the motor state of the organism. In particular they will vary depending on type of movement undertaken.

Freeman's (1948) empirical observations on the relationship of focal to nonfocal actions, and the way in which activity interacts within the organism as a whole, are of relevance to the present argument. In particular, Freeman noted that it is the patterning of activity, rather than the gross sum of activity, which determines the efficient use of energy.

The limbic–pyramidal system is linked with the parietal region which essentially controls action programs *already formulated*. This system is responsible for the regulation of minor articulated expressive movements, e.g. facial and finger movements. These movements will in turn, of course, provide a proprioceptive input evaluated by the limbic system as an index of current motor states. The limbic system is principally affected by *small* doses of nicotine through their influence on cholinergic–muscarinic receptors (Nelsen, 1978). So we see that the actions of both heavy and light smokers can affect different parts of the motor system. Furthermore, there is an important link between tobacco smoking's effect on the motor system and its stress-reduction properties.

Nicotine as a stressor

One consistent finding amongst the diversity of reported smoking effects is that nicotine attenuates the effects of severe stress. However, the pharmacological effects of nicotine are precisely those of a *mild* stressor. The distinction between smoking as a mild stressor and anxiety as a severe stressor should be emphasized. A mild, short-lasting stressor is likely to increase regional 5HT concentration, accelerate glial metabolism, stimulate hippocampal activity through limbic–cholinergic connections, and increase central motivation to act (Murray, 1958). A chronic, severe stressor, however, is likely to lead to excessively high ACh secretion. Corticosteroid hypersecretion concomitant with stress-inducing anxiety may lead to noradrenaline, dopamine and eventually serotonin depletion in the limbic areas. This may in turn lead to an increasing ratio of acetylcholine to catechol/serotonin in the CNS, which could overstimulate the reticular formation and lead to a catatonic depressive state of inactivity or 'behavioral silence' (Nicolis, 1978). The differential control of ACh secretion under high- and low-stress conditions has led some researchers to postulate the operation of two separate hippocampal and hypothalamic mechanisms controlling low-stress and high-stress reactions respectively (Balfour, 1978).

A mild stressor, then, has the opposite effect to a severe stressor. The function of mild stress would appear to be to prepare or motivate the organism to adapt to further stress, and produce a 'what-is-to-be-done' reaction. If smoking normally has a mild stressor effect on the CNS it may motivate the smoker to prepare for greater stress, and in a sense act as a stress inoculation. Froehlich (1978) points to the interesting observation that under mildly stressful attentional conditions there is an 'effort-after-stress' effect, which results in increased attentional effort. Tecce (1980) has reported a rebound effect of cortical arousal after stress. After exposure to choice RT conditions, arousal increases when the subject is exposed again to simple RT conditions. Mild stressors do enhance electrocortical indices of motor preparation as measured by electrocortical motor potentials, particularly in subjects with high action preparedness (Janssen, Mattie, Plooij Van Gorsen and Werre, 1978) and in smoking this increase relates to high nicotine intake (O'Connor, 1986). The stress-reducing effects of nicotine are thus compatible with a mild stressor effect of increasing specific motor preparation.

Equivalence in speed and tolerance of nicotine and motor action

Because of their similar neurochemical effects on the energy regulation system both nicotine and motor actions have two further characteristics in common. They both achieve central effects quickly (in a matter of seconds) and the CNS, though it may develop short-term habituation to either nicotine or repetitive motor action, can never develop long-term tolerance to either. This must be so since a system cannot survive and develop resistance to the neurochemicals controlling its own regulation. These observations on speed of nicotine action and tolerance are often quoted to explain the unique attraction and persistence of nicotine smoking and the inability of other nicotine-free (e.g. herbal) cigarettes to act as substitutes (Jarvik, 1977).

Summary of motor effects

The foregoing sections on the differential effects of smoking on the motor system and the mechanisms involved do not contradict the argument that smoking is intricately linked with motor activity demands. The main elements of the argument are now summarized.

Nicotine can affect the motor system both at a central and at a peripheral level as a function of dosage. Large doses of nicotine are likely to activate generalized motor preparation and increase metabolic rate in preparation for gross action via the RF and hypothalamus ('gross' meaning a group or groups of muscles). Small doses are likely to induce a mild activation effect on limbic structures controlling the future planning of fine motor coordination ('fine' here meaning minor adjustment within a functional muscle group already activated). This is the top-down aspect of motor control, but there is also a bottom-up input to the system. Proprioceptive feedback to the midbrain and limbic system, coupled with direct neurochemical feedback about energy from the muscles can exert control over central motor programming. The skeletal musculature is intimately involved in monitoring demand for energy, and respiration closely tracks body movement. When energy demands are high, a hormone released in the muscles can trigger secretion of adrenaline and subsequently lead to increased central neurotransmitter activity involved in muscular preparation. But large doses of nicotine can also cause a release of this neurotransmitter and hence mimic the same sense of initiating motor preparation. When there is only minor motor action, but no drastic change in motor state, proprioceptive feedback is likely to be via limbic structures modifying action already in progress. There is evidence that small doses of nicotine tend to affect the centers involved in finer motor control. So small or negligible doses of nicotine are coupled with minor motor adjustment within an existing motor program.

Whatever the nicotine dosage level taken in, smoking can produce an effect on the motor system which is equivalent to the effect produced when the person acts in response to a mild external stressor. The behavioral equivalence of smoking and motor action is supported by a comparison of the inoculation effect of both on severe stress, and by evidence matching speed and tolerance of both nicotine's action and motor actions. The next section extrapolates from the above evidence and speculates on how a motor model might explain the motivation to smoke.

Motor model of smoker motivation

The essence of the motor model of smoker motivation is that smoking acts as a behavioral substitute for whatever form of coordinated motor action is necessary to alleviate stress-induced motor conflict. The utility of smoking is that it allows the smoker to experience the benefits of action without benefiting from the experience of such action. The subjective effects of this may be to introduce a feeling of decisive action where none is possible, or at least a feeling of having achieved more than has actually been done.

A key aspect of the model is that the use by different smokers of pharmacological and nonpharmacological operants may be integrated within a unitary dimension of motor processing, with both operants producing changes in motor state. A motor dimension is envisaged which ties the central actions of nicotine on gross motor preparation at one end and the peripheral limbically mediated fine motor movement influenced by low nicotine dosage at the other end. According to the motor theory a small amount of nicotine has an equivalent effect to a minor motor movement in adjusting peripheral motor set. There may thus be a point at which the smoker who smokes because of minor motor discomfort may rely *either* on a low dose of nicotine *or* the overt motor actions of the smoking act itself to resolve motor conflict.

What then are the mechanisms by which smoking alleviates this motor conflict in both groups of smokers? The stress inoculation effects of nicotine as a mild stressor amongst high-inhaling smokers have already been detailed. Smoking here has an energizing role, normally performed by feedback from respiratory-muscular systems, and which steers the central action system toward greater preparation. This leads to more 'active coping,' increased mood, and improvement in certain grosser types of motor performance.

Amongst the group of low-inhaling–high-activity smokers, the motor aspects of smoking may alleviate minor motor conflict in two ways. Firstly, the purposeful peripheral movement involved in smoking will generate energy and associated ACh release as a direct consequence of the movement. Thus the movement will have some effect on motor activation. Since this activation effect will come largely through proprioceptive impulses it is more likely to affect the feedback control receptors at the cholinergic–limbic sites and hence, principally, reduce their inhibitory influence. Nevertheless, this activation will increase available effort and mobilize attentional resources. At the peripheral level, energy available at the muscles involved in smoking will increase, and if these muscles happen also to be involved in the primary activity alongside which smoking takes place, then this increase in local muscle energy will aid perseverance of task-relevant action.

However, the importance of the general increase in effort available as a consequence of the secondary activity of smoking is that this will increase information processing capacity available for the main task (against which smoking takes place), through the capacity of a secondary task to gate cues for other possible movements. In a conflict situation the smoker's general lack of motor coordination may give rise to a variety of peripheral cues for action, which will lead to a prolonged evaluation of movement possibilities, and will impede continuation of a course of action. Engagement in a minor goal-oriented secondary activity will gate other diverse peripheral, isolated sources of movement, and this gating effect will carry over postsmoking and focus evaluation of motor possibilities on the main action 'set' adopted. Kahneman (1973) has noted that dual-task performance can increase rather than decrease attentional resources under conditions of multiple distraction. Sabat (1979) has demonstrated, in the context of dual auditory task performance, that this division of attention and management of attentional effort can be refined through skill.

Wine (1971) has suggested that heightened self-awareness accompanies inability to attend. This is manifested in lack of coordination and a postural uneasiness. Knott (1979) noted that in high-arousal smokers internally generated distractors are more potent impediments to performance than externally generated ones. According to the motor model, smoking alleviates this attentional conflict to allow resumption of the smooth operation of preselected intentions.

Predictions of the model about smoker behavior

The general predictions of the motor model are that motor activity regulates the effects of smoking. This means, if the model is a sufficient account of smoker motivation, that different degrees of smoker inhalation should bring about different changes in motor state. Conversely, changes in motor states should be the prime movers in changing smoker regulation.

In terms of the motor theory, smokers who inhale a lot should represent a different group of smokers from those who inhale little and/or rely on sensory-motor rituals. These groups should be distinct types of smokers, differing in habit and in typical motor activity levels and achieving different types of effects on motor performance.

The clinical predictions of the model are equally important in its validation. Craving should arise as a function of identifiable motor conflict. The type of conflict would depend on type of smoker. The desire to smoke should thus be reduced primarily with the aid of individually tailored motor strategies which preempt the build-up of conflict.

ACTIVITY CLASSIFICATION OF SMOKERS

O'Connor (1984, 1985) conducted two separate principal-component analysis studies on 140 smokers designed to examine the craving profiles in smokers over a range of 25 background situations. A main bipolar factor which was related to an *active–inactive* dimension emerged from both studies and accounted for approximately 35 percent of the total item variance. Two other factors indicated that this active–inactive preference dimension could be subdivided according to whether the activity or inactivity had high or low emotional content and high or low attentional demand. The validity of typing preference according to different activity accompaniments emerged when the relationships between habit, personality and smoking preference were examined.

Extraverts and introverts, for example, expressed no marked difference in their preference to smoke under generally active or inactive conditions, but introverts showed higher cravings on attentionally active items involving concentration (for example, making a telephone call), and extraverts showed higher cravings on low attentional items relating to boring situations. Emotional items differentiated high and low neuroticism scorers, and females reported higher cravings than males under emotional stress.

Aspects of the smoker's habit differed amongst the activity subtypes. Reported amount of inhalation correlated positively with extraversion, inversely with the L-scale, and inversely with age, and age of starting smoking. Within the extraverted group, inhalation correlated positively on all items relating to stress. This finding can be linked to previously cited studies of smoking and arousal.

The arousal studies reviewed earlier reported that subjects who smoked under high attentional activity were more likely to rely on 'sensory-motor' factors rather than pharmacological factors. Low-activity smokers were likely to inhale deeply. It was particularly pertinent that the attentional activity dimension differentiated between introverts and extraverts. Introverts and

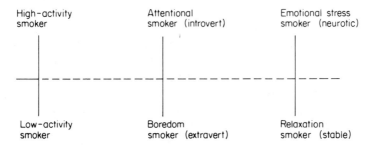

Fig. 2   Factor analytic division of activity situations

extraverts differ not only in smoking habits, but also in styles of information processing, and more especially in motor organization.

Personality and motor organization

There is evidence suggesting that introverts and extraverts differ intrinsically in the way their action plans are formulated and executed (Barratt, 1983; Strelau, 1983). Introverts are more motorically differentiated and more able to exert fine control over complex tasks than extraverts. Extraverts, on the other hand, exhibit a greater central unity of action. They are more certain about engaging totally in action, are quicker to respond, better prepared and more efficient in responses of a grosser nature (Eysenck, Nias and Cox, 1982).

Both Brebner and Cooper (1978) and Paisey and Mangan (1982) note the response-oriented nature of extraverts. Strelau (1983) noted extraverts (low reactives) spend less time on auxiliary incidental actions than do high reactive introverts. The extraverts are more concerned with primary goal-directed action. Pivik, Stelmack and Bylsma (1988) suggest that high disinhibition and stimulus-seeking behavior is distinguished not by a need for stimulation but by reduced motor neuronal excitability.

Introverts in general may be more cautious in decision-making than extraverts, since the motor coordination required to effect action may be more involved. Introverts, especially neurotic introverts, are more inclined to experience stress in apparently trivial tasks (Eysenck, 1971). A vigilance situation typically requires the sustained coordination and occasional highly selective adjustment of motor interaction, which might produce stress in introverts.

The extravert is not likely to find difficulty in formulating decision action programs, and is more likely to increase responding rather than become absorbed in small decision adapting conflicts (Venables, 1955). The extravert is more likely to find stress in situations where she/he is prohibited from acting or where she/he is in conflict as to when to respond. Such situations involve frustration, impatience and boredom.

The activity classification of smokers previously noted that introverts tend to smoke in attentional stress situations and inhale little. Extraverts crave more in boredom situations and inhale a lot. Furthermore, there is evidence that smoking tends to enhance performance selectively amongst personality groups in their preferred smoking situation.

Mangan (1982) noted that low nicotine intake enhanced attentional sensitivity whilst high nicotine intake increased false positive rate (increased indiscriminate response rate). Both Kucek (1975) and Warburton and Wesnes (1978), using a restricted range of extraversion scorers, showed that attention was enhanced by smoking only in a highly neurotic subgroup.

Williams (1980) reported improved motor performance (cancellation speed) in a low-arousal group of smokers and increased cognitive performance (memory) in a high-arousal group postsmoking. Williams also reported that high-arousal smokers were less influenced by pharmacological factors. Williams's definition of high arousal would include O'Connor's high-activity smokers.

Smoking, personality and motor activity

There has been no direct investigation of the effect of smoking on motor coordination and personality, but Suter (1981) noted wide variations and individual differences in the direction of smoking effects on EMG activity. Domino (1979) found a patterning effect on muscle action, and reported that head and neck EMG increased after smoking, whilst leg and arm EMG decreased. This was with the subject at rest. Domino also noted that small doses of nicotine were likely to inhibit motor activity through their action on inhibitory spinal neurons called Renshaw cells, and that this inhibition could reduce central output or have a peripheral effect. Interestingly, Hughes, Crow, Jacobs, Mittlemark and Leon (1984) reported that smoking induced muscle fatigue only in some smokers, which impaired subsequent exercise, but no personality measures were taken.

O'Connor (1984, 1986), found improved skillful performance in introverts after smoking, and that smoking reduced an early electrocortical positive component related to selective motor inhibition. O'Connor (1986) also reported electrocortical evidence that smoking increased extraverts' level of motor readiness, whereas introverts showed greater involvement than extraverts in motor processing prior to and during the act of smoking. However, smoking puff parameters were not found to differ as a function of motor activity level, which is contrary to the motor model, though nicotine cigarette content was low. Some of the links between personality, smoking and motor organization are encouraging for the motor model, but firm conclusions must await independent replication.

Clinical implications of the motor model

If smokers use smoking as a portable stationary activity generator, to produce the effects of required action under conditions where the opportunity for such action is lacking, then appropriate motor action could theoretically displace the need to smoke. The low-activity smoker, for example, who smokes when she/he is about to act in order to increase motor preparation, could achieve a similar activating effect through preparatory exercises if the opportunity for such exercise were presented. Similarly, the attentional smoker, for whom smoking provides a secondary motor task to aid selective

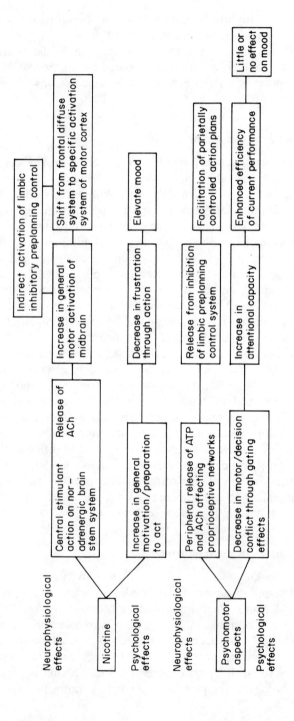

Fig. 3   Outline of the motor model showing proposed psychomotor and pharmacological effects on motor activity.

inhibition, could substitute smoking, if an equivalent socially convenient substitute minor motor movement were available. Exploring and evaluating the effectiveness of such substitutions would seem an essential test of the motor model.

In a study attempting to validate a model similar to the current one, O'Connor and Stravynski (1982) found behavioral substitution easier for the high-activity attentional group of smokers than for other low-activity groups. In this group the substitution strategy employed was other minor movements, such as tapping, twiddling clips, or fidgeting with other objects. In a sense this high-activity group is likely to be the easiest group with whom to substitute action, since smoking for this group probably functions most at a psychomotor activity level.

High-stress social smokers are another group for whom substitution of minor motor adjustments should obviate the need to smoke. However, in this group the muscle groups involved in smoking may also play a direct functional role in the social activity against which smoking takes place. Smoking involves principally forearm, facial and oral muscles. Facial and oral muscles in particular are directly involved in social communication.

An increase in peri-oral and tongue muscle activity is associated with conditions of demanding processing and stress (Cacioppo and Petty, 1981). Tongue and peri-oral muscles are, of course, involved in speech preparation. Under situations of semantic and interpersonal stress, as would be present during social stress situations, smoking might well mimic some of the muscular actions of linguistic processing and verbal preparatory activity, and hence reduce conflict. Interestingly, chewing gum would appear to be one viable substitute for the oral effects of smoking. Chewing non-nicotine chewing gum might therefore be beneficial as a cessation strategy in this group. Raw et al. (1980), in their evaluation of nicotine chewing gum, have reported that a few smokers showed a favorable response to placebo chewing gum.

Boredom/frustration smokers (extraverts) and low-activity stress smokers are clearly the most difficult groups in which to substitute behavioral strategies, since these groups require a fuller physical substitute for the pharmacological actions of nicotine in motivating motor action. However, engaging in physical exertion is likely to be difficult to fit into everyday activities. Imagery techniques may be of use with this group, since Lang et al. (1980) have shown that response-oriented imagery may often produce similar physiological effects to actual response behavior.

CONCLUSION

The motor behavioral model emphasizes the integration of peripheral proprioceptive motor aspects of the smoking act with the central pharmaco-

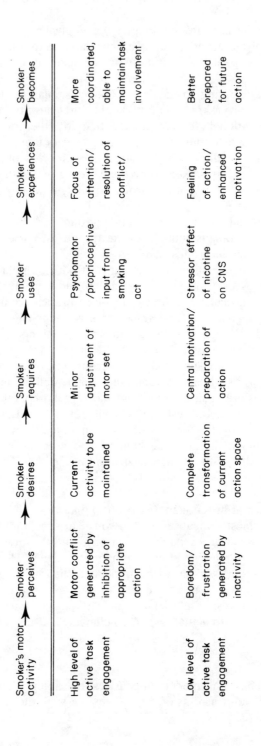

Fig. 4   Stages in resolving motor conflict through smoking.

logical motor effects, and explains the so-called 'paradoxical' sensory effects of smoking on the CNS, ANS and subjective mood. The resolution of conflicting action induces improved mood and feelings of 'togetherness' in the smoker.

The motor behavioral model highlights the importance of studying the ongoing *processes* of the smoking act itself, rather than simply looking for isolated *effects* of smoking on aspects of behavior.

Clark (1978), who has adopted a process approach to social psychological aspects of smoking, reports that smoking is a flowing process which coincides with the shifting flow of social interaction. Such a view is difficult to accommodate within the conventional fixed pharmacological effect model of smoking. The effects achieved from smoking are part of a skilled behavioral regulation of the situation, and smoking, rather than being simply an acquired response, is an acquired coping skill. Extinction of the habit comes not only from extinction of learned associations but also from acquiring an alternative motor skill. Motor skills concepts might therefore in future provide the most apt vocabulary in which to address issues in smoker behavior.

REFERENCES

Armitage, A.K. (1965). Effects of nicotine and tobacco smoke on blood pressure and release of catecholamines from the adrenal glands. *British Journal of Pharmacology and Chemotherapy*, **25**, 515–526.

Armitage, A.K. (1973). Some recent observations relating to the absorption of nicotine from tobacco smoke. In: W.L. Dunn (ed.), *Smoking Behaviour: Motives and Incentives*, Washington, DC: Winston, pp. 83–92.

Armitage, A.K. (1979). An action of nicotine on transmission to the superior cervical ganglion of the cat. In: A. Remond and C. Izard (eds), *Electrophysiological Effects of Nicotine*. Amsterdam: North-Holland.

Ashton, H., and Stepney, R. (1982). *Smoking: Psychology and Pharmacology*. London: Tavistock.

Ashton, H., and Watson, D.W. (1970). Puffing frequency and nicotine intake in cigarette smokers. *British Medical Journal*, **3**, 679–681.

Ashton, H., Marsh, V.R., Millman, J.E., Rawlins, M.D., Stepney, R., Telford, R., and Thompson, J.W. (1979). Patterns of behavioural, autonomic, and electrophysiological response to cigarette smoking and nicotine in man. In: A. Remond and C. Izard (eds), *Electrophysiological Effects of Nicotine*, Amsterdam: North-Holland, pp. 159–182.

Ashton, H., Millman, J.E., Telford, R., and Thompson, J.W. (1974). The effects of caffeine, nitrazepam and cigarette smoking on the contingent negative variation in man. *Electroencephalography and Clinical Neurophysiology*, **37**, 59–71.

Ashton, H., Millman, J.E., Telford, R., and Thompson, J.W. (1976). A comparison of some physiological and psychological effects of propanolol and diazepam in normal subjects. *British Journal of Clinical Pharmacology*, **3**, 551–559.

Ashton, H., Millman, J.E., Rawlins, M.D., Telford, R., and Thompson, J.W. (1978). The use of event related slow potentials of the brain in the analysis of effects of cigarette smoking and nicotine in humans. In: K. Bättig (ed.), *Behavioural Effects of Nicotine*. Basel: Karger.

Balfour, D.J.K. (1978). Biochemical approach to the study of nicotine in rats. In: K. Bättig (ed.), *Behavioural Effects of Nicotine*. Basel: Karger.

Bättig, K., and Schlatter, J. (1978). Effects of nicotine and amphetamine on maze exploration and on spatial memory by roman high avoidance and roman low avoidance rats. In: K. Bättig (ed.), *Behavioural Effects of Nicotine*. Basel: Karger.

Barratt, E.S. (1983). The biological basis of impulsiveness: the significance of timing and rhythm disorders. *Personality and Individual Differences*, **4**, 387–392.

Bernston, G.G. (1971). Blockade and release of hypothalamically and naturally elicited aggressive behaviors in cats following midbrain lesions. Unpublished doctoral dissertation, University of Minnesota.

Brebner, J., and Cooper, C. (1978). Stimulus- or response-induced excitation. A comparison of the behavior of introverts and extraverts. *Journal of Research in Personality*, **12**, 306–311.

Cacioppo, J.T., and Petty, R.E. (1981). Electromyographic specificity during covert information processing. *Psychophysiology*, **18**, 518–523.

Clark, R.R. (1978). Cigarette smoking in social interaction. *International Journal of the Addictions*, **13**, 257–269.

Clarke, P. (1982). Responding for electrical stimulation of the brain in rats treated with nicotine. Unpublished doctoral thesis, University of London.

Coan, R.W. (1973). Personality variables associated with cigarette smoking. *Journal of Personality and Social Psychology*, **26**, 86–104.

Creighton, D.E., and Lewis, P.H. (1978). The effect of different cigarettes on human smoking patterns. In: R.E. Thornton (ed.), *Smoking Behaviour: Physiological and Psychological Influences*, Edinburgh: Churchill Livingstone, pp. 289–300.

Dale, H.H. (1914). The action of certain esters and ethers of choline, and their relation to muscarine. *Journal of Pharmacology and Experimental Therapeutics*, **6**, 147–190.

Domino, E.F. (1973). Neuropsychopharmacology of nicotine and tobacco smoking. In: W.L. Dunn (ed.), *Smoking Behaviour: Motives and Incentives*, Washington, DC: Winston, pp. 5–32.

Domino, E.F. (1979). Behavioural, electrophysiological, endocrine and skeletal muscle actions of nicotine and tobacco smoking. In: A. Remond and C. Izard (eds), *Electrophysiological Effects of Nicotine*, Amsterdam: North-Holland, pp. 136–146.

Dunn, W.L. (1978). Smoking as a possible inhibitor of arousal. In: K. Bättig, (ed.), *Behavioural Effects of Nicotine*. Basel: Karger.

Erwin, C.W. (1971). Cardiac rate responses to cigarette smoking: a study utilising radiotelemetry. *Psychophysiology*, **8**, 75–81.

Eysenck, H.J. (1967). *The Biological Basis of Personality*. Springfield, IL: Charles C. Thomas.

Eysenck, H.J. (ed.) (1971). *Readings in Extraversion–Introversion. 3: Bearings on Basic Psychological Processes*. London: Staples Press.

Eysenck, H.J. (1973). Personality and the maintenance of the smoking habit. In: W.L. Dunn (ed.), *Smoking Behaviour: Motives and Incentives*, New York: John Wiley & Sons, pp. 113–46.

Eysenck, H.J. (1980). *The Causes and Effects of Smoking*. London: Maurice Temple Smith.

Eysenck, H.J., Nias, D.K.B., and Cox, D.N. (1982). Sport and personality. *Advances in Behaviour Therapy and Research*, **4**, 1.

Freeman, G.L. (1948). *The Energetics of Human Behaviour*. New York: Cornell University Press.

Friedman, J., and Meares, R. (1980). Tobacco smoking and cortical evoked potentials: an opposite effect on auditory and visual systems. *Clinical and Experimental Pharmacology and Physiology*, **7**, 609–615.

Friedman, J., Goldberg, H., Horvath, T.B., and Meares, R.A. (1974). The effect of tobacco smoking on evoked potentials. *Clinical and Experimental Pharmacology and Physiology*, **1**, 249–258.

Friedman, S., and Fletcher, C.M. (1976). Changes in smoking habits and cough in men smoking cigarettes with 30% NSM tobacco substitute. *British Medical Journal*, **1**, 1427–1430.

Frith, C.D. (1967). The effects of nicotine on tapping, I and II. *Life Sciences*, **6**, 313–325.

Frith, C.D. (1971). Smoking behaviour and its relation to the smoker's immediate experience. *British Journal of Social and Clinical Psychology*, **10**, 73–78.

Froehlich, W. (1978). Stress, anxiety and the control of attention: a psychophysiological approach. In: C.D. Spielberger and I.G. Sarason (eds), *Stress and Anxiety*, pp. 99–130. Washington, DC: Hemisphere.

Fuller, R.G.C., and Forrest, D.W. (1973). Behavioural aspects of cigarette smoking in relation with arousal level. *Psychological Reports*, **33**, 115–121.

Gale, A. (1981). EEG studies of extraversion–introversion: what's the next step? In: R. Lynn (ed.), *Dimensions of Personality. Papers in honour of H.J. Eysenck*. Oxford: Pergamon Press.

Gilbert, D.G. (1979). Paradoxical tranquilizing and emotion reducing effects of nicotine. *Psychological Bulletin*, **86**, 643–661.

Goldfarb, T.L., and Jarvik, M.E. (1972). Accommodation to restricted tobacco smoke intake in cigarette smokers. *International Journal of the Addictions*, **7**, 559–565.

Hall, G.H., and Morrison, C.F. (1973). New evidence for a relationship between tobacco smoking, nicotine dependence and stress. *Nature*, **243**, 199–201.

Heimstra, N.W. (1973). The effects of smoking on mood change. In: W.L. Dunn (ed.), *Smoking Behaviour: Motives and Incentives*, pp. 197–208. New York: John Wiley & Sons.

Hughes, J.R., Crow, R.S., Jacobs, D.R., Mittlemark, M.B., and Leon A.S. (1984). Physical activity, smoking and exercise induced fatigue. *Journal of Behavioural Medicine*, **7**, 217–230.

Hultberger, M. (1974). Smoking habits as related to personality and situational variables. Unpublished thesis, University of Stockholm.

Hutchinson, R.R., and Emley, G.S. (1973). Effects of nicotine and avoidance condition suppression and aggression response measures in animals and man. In: W.L. Dunn (ed.), *Smoking Behaviour: Motives and Incentives*, New York: John Wiley & Sons, pp. 171–196.

Janssen, R.H.C., Mattie, H., Plooij Van Gorsen, P., and Werre, P.F. (1978). The effects of a depressant and a stimulant drug on the contingent negative variation. *Biological Psychology*, **6**, 209–218.

Jarvik, M.E. (1973). Further observations on nicotine as the reinforcing agent in the smoking habit. In: W.L. Dunn (ed.), *Smoking Behaviour, Motives and Incentives*, New York: John Wiley & Sons, pp. 33–50.

Jarvik, M.E. (1977). Biological factors underlying the smoking habit. In: M.E. Jarvik, J.W. Cullen, E.R. Gritz, T.M. Vogt, and J. West (eds), *Research on Smoking*

Behavior, NIDA Research Monograph 17, US Department of Health, Washington, pp. 122–148.

Jarvik, M.E., Glick, S.D., and Nakaruma, R.K. (1970). Inhibition of cigarette smoking by orally administered nicotine. *Clinical Psychology and Therapeutics*, **11**, 574–576.

Kahneman, D. (1973). *Attention and Effort*. Hillsdale, NJ: Prentice-Hall.

Knott, V.J. (1979). Psychophysiological correlates of smokers and non-smokers: studies of cortical, autonomic and behavioural responsivity. In: A. Remond and C. Izard (eds), *Electrophysiological Effects of Nicotine*, Amsterdam: North-Holland, pp. 99–116.

Kucek, P. (1975). Effect of smoking on performance under load. *Studia Psychologica*, **17**, 204–212.

Kumar, R. (1979). Tobacco smoking: tests of the nicotine hypothesis. In: A Remond and C. Izard (eds), *Electrophysiological Effects of Nicotine*, Amsterdam: North-Holland, pp. 245–54.

Kumar, R., Cooke, E.C., Lader, M.H., and Russell, M.A.H. (1978). Is tobacco smoking a form of nicotine dependence? In: R.E. Thornton (ed.), *Smoking Behaviour: Physiological and Psychological Influences*, Edinburgh: Churchill Livingstone, pp. 244–258.

Lang, P.J., Kozak, M.J., Miller, G.A., Levin, D.D., and McLean, A.J.R. (1980). Emotional imagery: conceptual structure and pattern of somato-visceral response. *Psychophysiology*, **17**, 179–192.

Mangan, G.L. (1982). The effects of cigarette smoking on vigilance performance. *Journal of General Psychiatry*, **106**, 77–84.

Mangan, G.L., and Golding, J. (1978). An enhancement model of smoking maintenance. In: R.E. Thornton (ed.), *Smoking Behaviour: Physiological and Psychological Influences*, Edinburgh: Churchill Livingstone, pp. 87–114.

Manser, R. (1972). Relation between some central effects of nicotine and its brain levels in the mouse. *Annals of Medical and Experimental Biology*, **50**, 205–212.

McCleary, R.A. (1966). Response-modulating functions of the limbic system-initiation and suppression. In: E. Stellar and J. Sprague (eds), *Progress in Physiological Psychology*. New York: Academic Press.

McKennell, A.C. (1970). Smoking motivation factors. *British Journal of Social and Clinical Psychology*, **9**, 8–22.

McMorrow, F.S., and Foxx, T.L. (1983). Nicotine's role in smoking: an analysis of nicotine regulation. *Psychological Bulletin*, **93**, 302–327.

Murray, M. (1958). Response of oligodendrocytes to serotonin. In: W. Windle (ed.), *Biology of Neuroglia*. Springfield, IL: Charles C. Thomas.

Myrsten, A.L., Anderssen, K., Frankenhaeuser, M., and Elgerot, A. (1975). Immediate effects of cigarette smoking as related to different smoking habits. *Perceptual Motor Skills*, **40**, 515–523.

Nelsen, J.M. (1978). Psychobiological consequences of chronic nicotinisation. A focus on arousal. In: K. Bättig (ed.), *Behavioural Effects of Nicotine*. Basel: Karger.

Nesbitt, P.D. (1973). Smoking, physiological arousal and emotional response. *Journal of Personality and Social Psychology*, **25**, 137–145.

Ney, T., and Gale, A. (1984). Smoking and performance. I: Studies of learning and memory. Unpublished manuscript, University of Southampton, Psychology Department.

Nicolis, J.S. (1978). Influences of intrapersonal conflict on interpersonal communication. In: C.D. Spielberger and I.G. Sarason (eds), *Stress and Anxiety*, Washington, DC: Hemisphere, pp. 337–44.

O'Connor, K.P. (1983). Individual differences in slow cortical potentials: implications for models of information processing. *Personality and Individual Differences*, **4**, 403–410.

O'Connor, K.P. (1984). Cognitive and psychophysiological aspects of smoker motivation. Unpublished doctoral thesis, University of London.

O'Connor, K.P. (1985). A model of situational preference amongst smokers. *Personality and Individual Differences*, **6**, 151–160.

O'Connor, K.P. (1986). Motor potentials and motor performance associated with introverted and extraverted smokers. *Neuropsychobiology*, **16**, 109–116.

O'Connor, K.P., and Stravynski, A. (1982). Evaluation of a smoking typology by use of a specific behavioural substitution method of self-control. *Behaviour Research and Therapy*, **20**, 279–288.

Paisey, T., and Mangan, G.L. (1982). NeoPavlovian temperament theory and the biological basis of personality. *Personality and Individual Differences*, **3**, 189–203.

Paton, W.D.M., and Perry, W.L.M. (1953). The relationship between depolarisation and block in the cat's superior cervical ganglion. *Journal of Physiology (London)*, **119**, 43–57.

Pivik, R.T., Stelmack, R.M., and Bylsma, F.W. (1988). Personality and individual differences in spinal motor neuronal excitability. *Psychophysiology*, **25**, 16–24.

Raw, M., Jarvis, M.J., and Russell, M.A.H. (1980). Comparison of nicotine chewing-gum and psychological treatment for dependent smokers. *British Medical Journal*, **281**, 481–482.

Remond, A., Martinerie, J., and Baillon, J.F. (1979). Nicotine intake compared with other psychophysiological situations through quantitative EEG analysis. In: A. Remond and C. Izard (eds), *Electrophysiological Effects of Nicotine*, Amsterdam: North-Holland, pp. 61–88.

Roos, S.S. (1977). Psychophysiological re-evaluation of Eysenck's theory concerning cigarette smoking. Part I. The central nervous system. *South African Medical Journal*, **52**, 237–240.

Rosencrans, J.S., Spencer, R.M., Krynock, G.M., and Chance, W.T. (1978). Discriminative stimulus properties of nicotine and nicotine-related compounds. In: K. Bättig (ed.), *Behavioral Effects of Nicotine*. Basel: Karger.

Russell, M.A.H. (1978). Self-regulation of nicotine intake by smokers. In: K. Bättig (ed.), *Behavioral Effects of Nicotine*. Basel: Karger.

Russell, M.A.H., Peto, J., and Patel, V.A. (1974). The classification of smoking by factorial structure of motives. *Journal of the Royal Statistical Society*, **137**, 313–346.

Russell, M.A.H., Raw, M., and Jarvis, M.J. (1980). Clinical use of nicotine chewing gum. *British Medical Journal*, **280**, 1599–1602.

Russell, M.A.H., Sutton, S.R., Feyerabend, C., and Cole, P.V. (1978). Addiction Research Unit: nicotine titration studies. In: R.E. Thornton (ed.), *Smoking Behaviour: Physiological and Psychological Influences*, Edinburgh: Churchill Livingstone, pp. 336–348.

Sabat, S.R. (1979). Selective attention, channel capacity and the average evoked response in human subjects. *Neuropsychologia*, **17**, 103–106.

Schachter, S. (1973). Nesbitt's paradox. In: W.L. Dunn (ed.), *Smoking Behaviour: Motives and Incentives*, Washington, DC: Winston, pp. 147–156.

Segal, M.J. (1979). The role of conditioning in drug tolerance and addiction. In: J.D. Keehn (ed.), *Psychopathology in Animals*. New York: Academic Press.

Smith, K.V. (1973). Physiological and sensory feedback of the motor system: neural–metabolic integration for energy regulation in behavior. In: J.D. Maser (ed.),

Efferent Organization and the Integration of Behavior, New York: Academic Press, pp. 18–65.

Smith, K.V., and Putz, V. (1970). Feedback analysis of learning and performance in steering and tracking behavior. *Journal of Applied Psychology*, **54**, 239–247.

Stanaway, R.G., and Watson, D.W. (1980). Smoking motivation: a factor analytical study. *Personality and Individual Differences*, **2**, 117–132.

Strelau, J. (1983). *Temperament–Personality–Activity*. London: Academic Press.

Suter, T.W. (1981). Psychophysiological effects of cigarette smoking and responding to conflict inducing stimuli in habitual smokers. Unpublished doctoral dissertation, Zurich University, Swiss Federal Institute of Technology.

Sutton, S., Russell, M.A.H., Feyerabend, C., and Saloojee, Y. (1978). Smokers' response to dilution of smoke by ventilated cigarette holders. In: R.E. Thornton (ed.), *Smoking Behaviour: Physiological and Psychological Influences*, Edinburgh: Churchill Livingstone, pp. 330–335.

Tecce, J.J. (1972). The contingent negative variation and psychological processes in man. *Psychological Bulletin*, **77**, 73–108.

Tecce, J.J. (1980). A rebound effect of the CNV. *Electroencephalography and Clinical Neurophysiology*, **51**, 631–642.

Tomkins, S.S. (1966). Psychological model for smoking behavior. *American Journal of Public Health*, **56** (Suppl.), 17–20.

Venables, P.H. (1955). Changes in motor response with increase and decrease in task difficulty in normal industrial and psychiatric patient subjects. *British Journal of Psychology*, **46**, 101–110.

Waller, D. (1975). Studies in smoking motivation. Unpublished doctoral thesis, University of Stockholm.

Warburton, D.M., and Wesnes, K. (1978). Individual differences in smoking and attention performance. In: R.E. Thornton (ed.), *Smoking Behaviour: Physiological and Psychological Influences*, Edinburgh: Churchill Livingstone, pp. 19–43.

Wesnes, K., and Warburton, D.M. (1978). The effects of cigarette smoking and nicotine tablets upon human attention. In: R.E. Thornton (ed.), *Smoking Behaviour: Physiological and Psychological Influences*, Edinburgh: Churchill Livingstone, pp. 131–147.

Wiemer, W.B. (1977). A motor theory of mind. In: R. Shaw and J. Bransford (eds), *Perceiving, Acting and Knowing: Towards an Ecological Psychology*, Hillsdale, NJ: Erlbaum, pp. 270–308.

Williams, G. (1980). Effects of cigarette smoking on immediate memory and performance in different kinds of smoker. *British Journal of Psychology*, **71**, 83–90.

Wine, J. (1971). Test anxiety and the direction of attention. *Psychological Bulletin*, **76**, 92–104.

Woodson, P.P., Buzzi, R., and Bättig, K. (1983). Effects of smoking on vegetative reactivity to noise. *Social and Preventative Medicine (Schweiz)*, **28**, 240–241.

8

Emotion, Anxiety and Smoking

David G. Gilbert
and
Richard Welser

ABSTRACT

Nicotine reduces anxiety and negative affect in chronic smokers. These effects may be accounted for by any of a large number of hypothesized biobehavioral mechanisms. Tobacco use is in part a function of nicotine's effects on mood, and smoking relapse is especially likely when the ex-smoker is experiencing negative affect.

Emotional factors have long been thought to be associated with smoking and have frequently been hypothesized to contribute to the subtle, yet highly persistent motivation to smoke. The present chapter evaluates evidence testing the hypothesis that smoking influences emotional states. It then describes and evaluates psychological and biological mechanisms proposed to explain nicotine/smoking's mood-altering effects. Finally, it hypothesizes additional mediating mechanisms and suggests how affect may relate to smoking motivation and relapse.

Smoking and Human Behavior, Edited by T. Ney and A. Gale
© 1989 John Wiley & Sons Ltd

SMOKING, NICOTINE AND AFFECT REGULATION

Nicotine, Smoking and Affect

Self-reported affect

A majority of smokers believe that smoking is pleasurable (Spielberger, 1986), helps them relax, and reduces negative affect (Kleinke, Staneski and Meeker, 1983; Spielberger, 1986). Many smokers also report smoking for the purpose of stimulation and to help them think and concentrate (Russell, Peto and Patel, 1974; Spielberger, 1986).

Experimental studies support the view that smoking and other means of nicotine administration reduce negative affect in certain conditions. However, because studies evaluating the effects of intravenous (i.v.) and similar means of nicotine administration on subjective experience have not manipulated environmental stressors, these studies offer relatively little to our understanding of the effects of nicotine on affect. In an early study (Johnston, 1942) nonsmokers given 1.3 mg nicotine reported an unpleasant lightheadedness or muzziness, whereas smokers described the same sensations as pleasant. No placebo injections or expectational controls were included. However, Lukas and Jasinski (1983) reported that initially nicotine produced 10 to 20 seconds of dysphoria, followed by episodes of 'euphoric' or 'high' feelings (30 to 90 seconds in duration) with i.v. nicotine, but not with i.v. saline. Rosenberg, Benowitz, Jacob and Wilson (1980) reported that sensations of arousal followed the first series of injections of nicotine in smokers, but complete tolerance to the subjective effects occurred by the third series of injections (an hour later). No effects on sense of well-being were noted.

It is likely that the above-noted divergence of effects of nicotine on affect resulted from failures to control environmental, expectational, tolerance and dose factors. The literature on drug–emotion interactions makes it clear that these factors are critical determinants of drug effects (Erdmann, 1983). For example, administration of tranquilizers in low-stress environments frequently leads to heightened, rather than reduced, tension and negative affect (Janke, Debus and Longo, 1979).

Smoking-deprived habitual smokers report more negative affect than do smokers allowed to smoke in situations producing mild-to-moderate negative affect. Individuals allowed to smoke, relative to those deprived for from one to twelve hours, have reported reduced feelings of anxiety while watching a stressful movie (Heimstra, 1973), while anticipating failure on an anagram task (Pomerleau, Turk and Fertig, 1984; Jarvik, Caskey, Rose, Herskovic and Sadeghpour, in press), while anticipating a cold pressor task (Jarvik et al., in press), when engaged in a mildly stressful social interaction (Gilbert and Spielberger, 1987), and during a competitive mental arithmetic task (Pomerleau and Pomerleau, 1987). Decreased anger and irritation have been reported by smokers allowed to smoke, compared to smoking-deprived smokers, while viewing stressful movies (Cetta, 1977; Heimstra, 1973) and while performing complex motor tasks (Neetz, 1979). Smoking deprivation is also associated with self-reports of less mental efficiency and increased boredom and irritation during a variety of cognitive tasks (Frankenhaeuser, Myrsten, Post and Johansson, 1971; Myrsten, Post, Frankenhaeuser and Johansson, 1972; Heimstra, 1973). Smoking may also reduce the subjective arousing effects of caffeine (Rose, 1986).

A recent study using specially designed cigarettes of similar construction, 'tar' delivery, and taste, but greatly different nicotine deliveries provides support for the view that nicotine is an important mechanism by which smoking modulates affect. Habitual smokers who smoked a medium-nicotine-delivery cigarette (0.8 mg FTC nicotine) reported experiencing significantly less anxiety during a stressful movie than did smokers of the identically appearing and tasting, but extremely-low nicotine delivery (0.1 mg FTC), cigarette (Gilbert, Robinson, Chamberlin and Spielberger, in press). Perlick (1977) found that high-nicotine-delivery cigarettes, relative to low-nicotine ones, reduced irritation associated with aircraft noise in heavy, but not light, smokers.

Mood-modulating effects of nicotine-containing gum have also been evaluated and found to support the view that nicotine has negative-affect-reducing properties in habitual smokers (Hughes, Hatsukami, Pickens, Krahn, Malin and Luknic, 1984; Jarvis, Raw, Russell and Feyerabend, 1982; West, Jarvis, Russell, Carruthers and Feyerabend, 1984). However, nicotine-containing gum has been reported to produce nausea, dizziness or anxiety to varying degrees in nonsmokers (Nyberg, Panfilov, Sivertsson and Wilhelmsen, 1982).

Some studies have not found negative-affect-reducing effects of smoking high- versus low-nicotine cigarettes (Bowen, 1969; Dubren, 1975; Fleming and Lombardo, 1987; Gilbert and Hagen, 1980, 1985; Hatch, Bierner and Fisher, 1983; Nesbitt, 1969; Shiffman and Jarvik, 1984). There are a number of potential reasons for these failures. Dubren's (1975) subjects, in both the smoking and abstaining conditions, smoked a mean of more than eleven cigarettes on the day of the experiment prior to the experimental session, thus minimizing differences between smoking and abstaining groups in blood levels of nicotine. Thus, high blood levels of nicotine combined with a minimal period of abstinence may have precluded differences in anxiety between the smoking and abstaining groups. Subjective distress induced by the smoking of two or more cigarettes in rapid succession may account for the failure of several of these studies to find tranquilizing effects. In addition to these possible explanations it appears that stressor parameters are of importance in determining whether or not nicotine has tranquilizing effects.

A comparison of studies finding tranquilizing effects with those that did not, suggests that the proximity and potency of the stressor in part determine whether or not nicotine has tranquilizing effects. Procedures that introduce mild or moderate distal (anticipatory) anxiety and/or ambiguous stressors (for example, a movie with anticipatory anxiety, expectations of failure, noise, and social interaction) tend to find tranquilizing effects for nicotine. On the other hand, the direct presentation of brief, proximal, and/or intense stressors is generally not associated with reductions of negative affect by anxiolytic medications (Janke et al., 1979) or by nicotine. For example, in one recent study (Jarvik et al., in press) smoking reduced anxiety prior to, but not during, stressful tasks. Similarly, the failure of Fleming and Lombardo (1987) to find anxiolytic effects may be attributable to the use of a very potent stressor—presentation of live rats to rat-phobic subjects. Studies finding reductions in anxiety have used milder stressors of a more ambiguous and distal nature. Consistent with our hypothesis of the importance of potency, proximity, and ambiguity, studies using highly threatening and proximal electrical shock have also failed to demonstrate smoking or nicotine-dependent reductions in self-reported anxiety (Nesbitt, 1969; Shiffman and Jarvik, 1984). The finding that antianxiety drugs such as the benzodiazepines reduce the expression of conditioned fear (distal threats) but generally not unconditioned responses (Gray, 1982) is also consistent with the view that proximity, potency and ambiguity are important stimulus parameters in determining whether or not nicotine will reduce negative affect. In non-stressful conditions the effects of nicotine on anxiety/tension are very slight relief (Agué, 1973) or nonexistent (Herning, Jones and Bachman, 1983; MacDougall, Musante, Howard, Hanes and Dembrowski, 1986).

There are several possible reasons why the negative affect caused by mild, moderate, distal and ambiguous stressors is reduced while that associated with more intense, proximal and definitive stressors is not. The common denominator across the intensity, distance and ambiguity dimensions is that of internal versus external drivenness of cognitive processes. One would expect environmentally driven cognitive–affective processes to be relatively independent of internal biases and interpretive processes, including those influenced by nicotine. On the other hand, in circumstances where the environment is relatively ambiguous and/or does not demand immediate coping, cognitive–affective processes would be expected to be relatively largely influenced by internal biases including those produced by nicotine. Thus, it seems reasonable to hypothesize that nicotine influences affective processes by priming neutral and/or positive affect-related processing and/ or by inhibiting processing contributing to negative affect. Experimental results suggest that nicotine may bias information processing away from negative and toward positive content by decreasing the activation of the right hemisphere relative to the left hemisphere (Gilbert, 1985; Gilbert et al., in press).

Behavioral indices of affect

Behavioral measures of anxiety and anger/irritation suggest that nicotine has tranquilizing effects. Nesbitt (1969) and Silverstein (1982) found that habitual smokers were willing to endure stronger intensities of electrical shock when smoking than when not smoking, and when smoking a high-nicotine than when smoking a low-nicotine cigarette. They interpreted low shock endurance as being indicative of anxiety, even though self-report findings were not consistent with this hypothesis. This interpretation has been questioned (Gilbert, 1979) since evidence suggests that in some situations nicotine increases detection thresholds for tactile stimuli, including electrical shock (Mendenhall, 1925; Wenusch and Scholler, 1936). It may be, therefore, that nicotine decreases the perception of shock and that this, rather than reduced anxiety, accounts for the increased willingness to endure shocks subsequent to smoking. Furthermore, the reliability of smoking's increasing shock endurance thresholds is questionable, since some studies have failed to find such an effect (Jarvik et al., in press; Milgrom-Friedman, Penman and Meares, 1983; Shiffman and Jarvik, 1984). The use of more sophisticated techniques than used till now, for example signal detection paradigms, may be of help in determining whether these effects are more due to changes in perceptual threshold or in terms of anxiety.

One of the best approaches to the assessment of nicotine's effects on affect is the one used by Hughes et al. (1984). Smokers were randomly assigned to chew either nicotine or placebo gums *ad libitum*, starting when they abruptly quit smoking. Daily ratings of subject's irritability and anxiety revealed increased tension and anxiety in individuals on the placebo gum. Subjects chewing placebo gum also reported increased anger and tension, whereas nicotine gum chewers noted significantly less tension and anger. Schechter and Rand (1974) and Cherek (1981) found that smoking and smoking a high- relative to a low-nicotine delivery cigarette was associated with reduced aggression as assessed with a Buss aggression machine task. However, Jones and Lieser (1976) found no effects of smoking on aggressive behavior.

THE MEASUREMENT AND NATURE OF AFFECT

Affect, like other psychological constructs, can be assessed by three different means: self-reported experience, behavioral observations and psychophysiological changes. These three means of assessing affect correlate with each other only moderately (Eysenck, 1975). There are several reasons for these low correlations, including individual differences in self-reporting, behaviorally expressing and physiologically responding to emotion (Buck, 1979); individual differences in coping and coping-associated physiology (Henry, 1986); and unreliability and invalidity of measurement devices. Some individuals (externalizers) are prone to be relatively more facially expressive of emotion, but relatively underreactive as assessed by heart rate and skin conductance activity. In contrast, internalizers tend to be relatively highly reactive as assessed by autonomic nervous system activation, but underreactive in their facial expression of emotion (Buck, 1979). Thus, the conclusions one makes concerning individual differences in emotional responsivity to the effects of nicotine may be a function of the dependent measure of emotion that one uses.

Given the complexity of the emotional construct and the relatively low correlations among differing indices of affective constructs it is important that multiple, standardized and validated measures be used. Investigators have, in some cases, inferred changes in affect on the basis of behavioral measures even though self-report measures did not support this interpretation. In other cases smoking has been compared with nonsmoking. Such studies do not allow one to determine what aspects of smoking contributed to the modulation of affect. Ideally, experimental investigations of nicotine's effects on affect should simultaneously assess self-reported affect, a behavioral measure such as facial expression, and several physiological measures. In order to avoid the many expectational and attributional effects known to influence emotional states and the effects of psychoactive drugs (Erdmann, 1983), studies assessing the effects of nicotine should minimize the ability of subjects to determine what nicotine condition they are in.

Considering the mediating role that cognition is hypothesized to play in emotional states (Ellis, 1962; Lazarus, 1981), studies assessing nicotine-induced changes in affect-related information processing might be informative. It would be helpful to know the effects of nicotine on self-reported thoughts, attributions and cognitive performance in a variety of situations varying in the degree and nature of stress.

Finally, nicotine-induced changes in basic biological drives such as eating and sex, and in preferences such as preferred intensity and quality of sensory input, need to be thoroughly assessed, since changes in such preferences and drives may lead to changes in affective response to a given environment.

EFFECTS OF NICOTINE AND SMOKING ON PHYSIOLOGICAL PROCESSES

Dose–response issues and problems

Rapid smoking, and smoking the first cigarette of the day, frequently lead to nausea and subjective distress even in habitual smokers (Silvette, Hoff,

Larson and Haag, 1962; Kozlowski, Director and Harford, 1981). Thus, the possibility of nicotine toxicosis should be formally assessed when addressing the ecological validity and generalizability of the effects of smoking. Nicotine overdose toxicosis may result when studies involve high-nicotine-delivery cigarettes, first cigarettes of the day and/or cigarettes smoked in rapid succession. Consistent with the caveat, the most intense subjective effects following the smoking of two 1.6 mg nicotine-delivery cigarettes in rapid succession are nausea and cold sweating, respectively (Redmond, Martinerie and Baillon, 1979).

Effects on hormones and neuromodulators

Problems of overdose are evident in studies evaluating the effects of smoking on hormones and neuromodulators. Until recently it appeared that smoking reliably produced increases in a number of stress-related hormones and other neuromodulators including cortisol (Cryer, Haymond, Santiago and Shaw, 1976; Hill and Wynder, 1974; Seyler, Fertig, Pomerleau, Hunt and Parker, 1984), growth hormone (Cryer et al., 1976), beta-endorphin (Pomerleau, Fertig, Seyler and Jaffe, 1983; Seyler, Pomerleau, Fertig, Hunt and Parker 1986), arginine vasopressin (Pomerleau et al., 1983), and catecholamines (Baer and Radichevich, 1985; Frankenhaeuser et al., 1971).

Relatively strong evidence suggests that many of the above-noted elevations in neuromodulators were a function of nicotine overdose toxicosis and associated nausea and feelings of stress (Gilbert and Jensen, 1987). For example, Benowitz, Kuyt and Jacob (1984) reported that their subjects did not have any higher plasma levels of cortisol on days on which they smoked *ad libitum* than on days on which they abstained. Furthermore, they noted that studies showing smoking to elevate cortisol evaluated

> smokers who, after several hours, smoked two or more cigarettes over a relatively short time. In contrast, our study and the findings of Tucci and Sode indicated that under more usual smoking conditions, plasma cortisol levels do not rise as a function of smoking. The cortisol level rises reported by others might have resulted from the stresses of the experimental situation or from rapid smoking procedures, which are known to induce effects that differ from those when smoking at normal rates (Benowitz et al., 1984, page 80).

Tucci and Sode (1972) also failed to find elevations in catecholamine levels in smokers during normal smoking conditions.

Neuromodulator release may occur in a stepwise fashion such that with normal smoking-sized doses no elevations in neuromodulator concentrations occur. Above a critical threshold dose linear increases in toxicosis/stress, and subsequent release of neuromodulators are likely (Gilbert and Jensen, 1987). It is yet to be determined whether normal smoking increases these neuromodulators, and if so, the dose–response functions and conditions in which increases occur. The question of whether normal smoking typically increases neuromodulator concentrations might be best assessed by a combination of naturalistic and more highly controlled studies. Naturalistic studies of smoking and abstaining days in a variety of settings, differing in their stress and activity demands, would allow for an adequate ecologically valid assessment of the effects of natural smoking on a variety of neuromodulators. Smoking may produce elevations in neuromodulators when individuals are in mildly to moderately stressful conditions that do not by themselves have such an effect, by overdosing with nicotine in nonstressful situations, and by a lack of an acute or chronic tolerance to nicotine. More generally, the question is that of what neuromodulators are released in what smokers, with what subjective and behavioral effects, in what situations, by what doses of nicotine administered over what period of time, after what period of tobacco deprivation. Greater articulation of the effects of the interactions of these numerous parameters will be obtained only by carefully designed systematic multivariate parametric studies.

Autonomic nervous system effects

Increased sympathetic nervous system end-organ activity is one of the most reliable effects of smoking-sized doses of nicotine. Mechanisms that produce these effects include: stimulation of the sympathetic ganglia, interaction with brain centers related to autonomic processes, release of hormones that then activate ANS end-organ receptors, and direct activation of end-organs (Meyers, Jawetz and Goldfien, 1974). Heart rate (HR) increases with cigarette nicotine delivery if the smoker is seated and has not smoked for an hour or more (Epstein and Jennings, 1986). Repeated doses produce an acute tolerance to nicotine's effects so that HR increases produced by cigarettes occurring at intervals of less than an hour are greatly attenuated (Rosenberg et al., 1980). There is some evidence that motor activity may attenuate HR increases associated with smoking (Gilbert and Spielberger, 1987; Suter, Buzzi, Woodson and Bättig, 1983). The relationship between HR and nicotine may be an inverted 'U'-shaped function. Nicotine initially has strong HR increasing effects, but at the very high doses associated with rapid smoking there may be a lessened increase and/or actual decrease in HR (Sachs, 1987). Since HR is determined by both parasympathetic and sympathetic mechanisms in a reciprocal fashion, and is also influenced by circulating hormones, it is difficult to pinpoint the ANS mechanisms associated with changes in HR in stressful situations. Increases in blood pressure associated with smoking have been found in quiescent (Epstein and Jennings, 1986) and active coping situations (MacDougall et al., 1986). Although the predominant effects of smoking-sized doses of nicotine are sympathetic, parasympathetic activation also occurs (Meyers et al., 1974).

Effects on the central nervous system (CNS)

The effects of smoking-sized doses of nicotine on the CNS are more complex than is frequently recognized. Nicotine interacts with a number of important neurotransmitter and neuromodulatory systems (Balfour, 1984) and it is reasonable to hypothesize that different neurotransmitter systems and neuromodulators are differentially influenced by different doses of nicotine within the smoking-size dose range. Furthermore, evidence suggests that the physiological, subjective and behavioral effects of a given dose of nicotine depend upon the physiological state of the CNS, which in turn is a function of environmental and trait factors. The fact that the CNS subsystems influence each other by direct and indirect inhibitory and stimulatory interactions with differing time courses (Guha and Pradhan, 1976) complicates the study of nicotine's effects. Interactions between personality and electrocortical responses to nicotine have been found in low-to-medium arousal conditions (Ashton, Millman, Telford and Thompson, 1974; Gilbert, 1987; O'Connor, 1982). In contrast, no personality by nicotine interactions have been noted for either EEG or self-reported affect during stressful situations (Gilbert et al., in press; Gilbert and Hagen, 1985).

Historically it has been assumed by many that nicotine's CNS effects result from stimulation of cholinergic pathways in the mesencephalic reticular formation that terminate in the sensory cortex and produce electrocortical activation (Warburton, 1981). In addition to these cholinergic processes, dopaminergic (Balfour, 1984), noradrenergic (Guha and Pradhan, 1976), serotonergic (Balfour, 1984), and neuromodulator-based (Gilbert, 1979; Pomerleau and Pomerleau, 1984) mechanisms may mediate nicotine's affect-modulating effects. Numerous additional studies will be necessary before nicotine's complex effects on the CNS are understood (Balfour, 1984).

Nicotine doses within the typical smoking range have been reported to either stimulate or depress cortical arousal, depending upon dose and rate of administration (Armitage, Hall and Sellers, 1969; Guha and Pradhan, 1976), time since smoking/nicotine dose (Guha and Pradhan, 1976), environmental stress (Gilbert et al., in press; Golding and Mangan, 1982), and individual differences in personality (Ashton et al., 1974). In a low-stress, relaxing environment, smoking produces EEG activation suggestive of increased mental alertness (Edwards and Warburton, 1983; Gilbert, 1987; Herning et al., 1983). In contrast to relaxing conditions, two studies have reported smoking and high- relative to low-nicotine cigarettes to increase the amount of slow (alpha) wave activity in stressful conditions (Gilbert et al., in press; Golding and Mangan, 1982). In situations eliciting an intermediate level of activation, the effects of smoking and nicotine on electrocortical activation are complex and cannot be described as activating or deactivating (Woodson, 1984).

Like background EEG activity, the effects of nicotine on event-related potentials (ERPs) vary as a function of stimulus intensity and dose. Consistent with the view that nicotine enhances vigilance and related forms of information processing, nicotine has been found to reduce the latency of the P_{300} component of the visual evoked potential (VEP) during a rapid information processing task (Edwards, Wesnes, Warburton and Gale, 1985). Reduced latency of the P_{300} suggests increased speed of information processing. Smoking enhances the amplitude of certain components of the VEP (Friedman and Meares, 1980; Knott, 1985), but may decrease the amplitude of some while increasing other components of auditory ERPs (Friedman and Meares, 1980). Such modality-specific effects suggest that the effects of nicotine on information processing may vary as a function of stimulus modality. Unfortunately, many studies of the electrocortical effects of nicotine have not simultaneously assessed behavioral and/or subjective effects. Possible psychological and behavioral correlates of electrocortical changes in such studies can only be inferred with great caution.

Effects on skeletal muscle activity

Smoking and other means of nicotine administration reduce muscular tension (EMG) in spastic patients (Webster, 1964) and substantially depress reflexive muscular activity (patellar and startle) in humans and primates (Clark and Rand, 1968; Domino, 1973; Hutchinson and Emley, 1973). Reduced EMG activity in both low- and high-stress situations was reported by Fuller and Forrest (1977), while the flexor reflex has been found to be enhanced by nicotine (Silvette et al., 1962). Tonic and phasic EMG responses to stress were relatively unaffected by cigarette nicotine delivery (Gilbert and Hagen, 1980), while the trapezius muscle EMG levels were enhanced when high-nicotine cigarettes were smoked very rapidly (Fagerstrom and Gotestam, 1977). However, the latter two studies are difficult to interpret since they required smoking of high-nicotine-delivery cigarettes at a rate that was likely to have produced nicotine overdose toxicosis in some individuals.

MECHANISMS TO EXPLAIN NICOTINE'S ABILITY TO REDUCE NEGATIVE AFFECT

Many mechanisms have been proposed to account for nicotine's mood-enhancing effects, and a number have been systematically investigated.

Mechanisms based on nicotine withdrawal models

The suggestion has been made that nicotine's effects on negative affect are simply a function of the elimination of nicotine withdrawal symptoms (Schachter, 1979). However, while there is little question that the process of quitting smoking is frequently associated with increases in irritability, anger and anxiety, such increases would be expected whether nicotine relieves withdrawal symptoms or has primary negative-affect-reducing properties analogous to those of minor tranquilizers. The nicotine withdrawal process is not well understood, and the psychological symptoms associated with withdrawal are highly variable from one individual to another (Murray and Lawrence, 1984) and possibly within given individuals over time and situations. Though a vast majority of smokers say they smoke to reduce negative affect, and to relax, some studies have found that a third or more who quit smoking report experiencing no postcessation symptoms other than that of craving for cigarettes (Murray and Lawrence, 1984).

Schachter (1979) has attempted to account for these varied effects by suggesting that some smokers are not addicted to nicotine, and that these smokers show no withdrawal symptoms or negative-affect-reducing effects from nicotine. In support of this view, Perlick (1977) found normal-nicotine-delivery cigarettes to alleviate annoyance in heavy but not light smokers. While some studies have failed to find differences in withdrawal symptomatology between heavy and light smokers (Shiffman and Jarvik, 1976), Wynder and associates found more symptoms in ex-smokers who had smoked 40 or more cigarettes per day than those smoking 20–39 per day, who in turn experienced more withdrawal symptoms than those who smoked fewer than 20 per day. The absence of withdrawal symptoms in 26 percent of heaviest smokers and 62 percent of light smokers in the Wynder et al. study suggests that mechanisms other than withdrawal may contribute to nicotine's negative-affect-reducing properties since most smokers report that smoking reduces negative affect (Wynder, Kaufman and Lesser, 1967).

Studies have not effectively addressed the possibility that nicotine has mood-enhancing effects independent of those that might be associated with withdrawal. However, it has been argued that the reduction of negative affect following smoking is not simply a consequence of withdrawal relief, since a number of studies used smokers who were minimally deprived and showed no difference in withdrawal when compared with *ad libitum* smoking sessions (Pomerleau, 1986). Studies of the effects of nicotine in animals also tend to support the view that nicotine has tranquilizing effects independent of withdrawal relief (Gilbert, 1979). Future studies of nicotine's effects on affect should compare level of withdrawal symptoms prior to smoking/nicotine administration with those in *ad libitum* conditions. Withdrawal-independent, mood-enhancing effects of nicotine could also be assessed by evaluating responses of ex-smokers and nonsmokers.

The mechanisms described below generally do not make any assumptions as to whether nicotine is alleviating negative affect associated with withdrawal, or whether nicotine has inherent anxiolytic or mood-enhancing effects. Many of the subjective and physiological effects of withdrawal are similar to those alleviated by nicotine. Thus, the mechanisms described in the following pages may mediate the negative affect associated with the withdrawal process and/or any inherent tranquilizing effects of nicotine.

Mechanisms based on altered perceptions of bodily activity

One or more of three mechanisms based on altered perceptions of bodily activity may contribute to nicotine's reduction of negative emotion in spite of its increasing ANS activity. The first suggests that nicotine reduces emotional experience by elevating perceptual thresholds for bodily arousal and tension (Gilbert, 1979). This hypothesis is based on evidence suggesting that under certain conditions nicotine increases the detection threshold for electrical shock (Mendenhall, 1925; Wenusch and Scholler, 1936) and on the observation that nicotine-induced increases in cardiovascular activity do not produce corresponding increases in perceived heart activity (Gilbert and Hagen, 1980).

Evidence for this hypothesis is mixed. One study found smoking to reduce sensitivity to muscle activity in females, but not in males (Epstein, Dickson, McKenzie and Russell, 1984). Others have reported a tendency to elevate detection and pain thresholds in males, but not females (Mueser, Waller, Levander and Schalling, 1984). Levine and Lombardo (1985) showed that smoking interferes with the perception of corrugator muscle EMG activity. This is of special relevance since the corrugator muscle is associated with negative affect (Fridlund and Izard, 1983). Smoking has been reported to increase (Nesbitt, 1969; Pomerleau et al., 1984; Silverstein, 1982), decrease (Milgrom-Friedman et al., 1983), and have no effect on pain endurance thresholds (Jarvik et al., in press; Shiffman and Jarvik, 1984; Waller, Schalling, Levander and Erdman, 1983; Sult and Moss, 1986). Lombardo and Epstein (1986) recently failed to demonstrate that nicotine interferes with the perception of heart beat; however, they did not partial out the effects of possible nicotine-induced increases in cardiac contractility.

The mechanisms mediating these variable effects of nicotine on somatic perception are far from clear. It has been suggested that smoking-induced beta-endorphin release causes a decreased experience of pain (Pomerleau et al., 1984); yet, as noted earlier in this chapter, it is not clear that smoking typically produces increases in beta-endorphin. It is possible that smoking and other forms of nicotine administration increase perceptual thresholds only in those conditions where beta-endorphin and/or other neuromodulators are released. Thus, rapid smoking of high-nicotine cigarettes and/or the combination of stress and smoking may increase neuromodulator concentrations and thereby increase perceptual thresholds. The elevation of perceptual thresholds might decrease the perception of bodily arousal.

The second of the proposed mechanisms based on altered perceptions of bodily activity assumes that nicotine's effects on emotions are a consequence of muscular-action-reducing properties of nicotine. While nicotine usually produces acute increases in ANS activation, it reduces some forms of muscular activity (see review earlier in this chapter). Hence, it may be that people who report that smoking tranquilizes them may be more influenced by the muscle-relaxing effects of nicotine than by the ANS-arousing effects (Gilbert, 1979).

The final of the three mechanisms is based on the law of initial values, the finding that response magnitude is related to prestimulation level in such a manner that high ANS activation preceding stimulation is associated with lower ANS and subjective response upon stimulation. Schachter (1973) has suggested that, since nicotine leads to arousal, the additional arousal induced by an emotional situation is less with nicotine than without it. Smoking a moderate- or high-nicotine-delivery cigarette produces elevations in tonic heart rate, but reduces phasic responses to stress (Gilbert et al., in press; Woodson, Buzzi, Nil and Bättig, 1986).

Sensory gratification and attributional models

Sensory experiences related to smoking and other forms of tobacco use may counteract negative affect. A significant number of smokers report enjoying smoking because they like handling cigarettes, watching smoke, and the sensory experience of something in the mouth, throat, and lungs (Russell, Peto and Patel, 1974). Experimental studies support the view that sensory factors are important in making the smoking habit a pleasant one (Rose, Tashkin, Ertle, Zinser and Lafer, 1985). The strong sensory impact of nicotine may also provide distraction from negative thoughts and stimulation that relieves boredom.

It has been suggested that the tranquilizing effects of smoking might be the result of smokers' misattributing emotion-induced sympathetic activation to smoking, since both emotion and smoking produce such activation (Schachter, 1973). However, this hypothesis appears unlikely given the inability of smokers to discriminate high- and low-nicotine-delivery cigarettes in some of the studies showing nicotine to produce tranquilization (Gilbert et al., in press) and given that individuals generally do not perceive increased arousal or ANS end-organ activity when they smoke (Gilbert and Hagen, 1980; Surawy and Cox, 1986).

CNS arousal modulation models

The CNS arousal modulation model of nicotine's effects on psychological processes (Eysenck, 1973) hypothesizes that nicotine's effects depend on the state of the cortex. When prenicotine arousal is high the effects are dearousing; when arousal is low the effects are arousing. Since cortical arousal is frequently elevated during emotional states (Lindsley, 1970) nicotine is predicted to reduce cortical and subjective arousal in such circumstances. Decreased cortical arousal is assumed to be related to reductions in emotionality. CNS sedation-induced alterations of perceptual and/or cognitive processes could produce a decreased response to and/or perception of external and/or proprioceptive input. Nicotine's effects on detection and tolerance thresholds may well be mediated by its effects on cortical arousal. A covariation between increased threshold and decreased EEG activation would be consistent with such a causal mechanism.

Increased positive mood should also result from smoking when one is tired or drowsy because smoking should stimulate one to a more hedonically pleasing level of cortical arousal. A modest number of studies (reviewed earlier in this chapter) support the hypothesis that nicotine has bidirectional effects on arousal that are consistent with this CNS-arousal modulation hypothesis. Smoking/nicotine may help the user achieve more ideal levels of cortical arousal which facilitate task performance by reducing decreases in vigilance over time (Wesnes and Warburton, 1983). Such enhanced performance may lead to lessened frustration and a greater sense of self-esteem (Ashton and Stepney, 1982; Wesnes and Warburton, 1983).

CNS pleasure center models

Brain pleasure center activation also has been hypothesized to account for the pleasurable and negative-affect-reducing properties of smoking. Three different hedonic systems have been hypothesized: the primary reward and aversion systems and the secondary reward system (Eysenck, 1973). Activation of the primary systems leads to increased peripheral and central arousal, while activation of the secondary reward system produces rewarding effects indirectly, by inhibiting the aversion system. Eysenck (1973) proposed that nicotine administered in emotionally arousing situations may improve mood by means of the secondary reward system. However, during low-arousal conditions nicotine may produce pleasure by directly stimulating the primary reward system. Unfortunately, pleasure-center-stimulation models are difficult to test because the concept of pleasure systems is so nonspecific.

Endogenous opioid/neuromodulator models

Neuromodulator models of the emotional and motivational effects of nicotine (Gilbert, 1979; Pomerleau and Pomerleau, 1984) hypothesize mechanisms to account for a variety of the effects of smoking and nicotine. Doses of nicotine exceeding those typical of normal smoking increase concentrations of plasma glucocorticoids and beta-endorphin. Nicotine-induced release of glucocorticoids and/or other neuromodulators could account for nicotine's mood-enhancing effects, its ability to facilitate habituation of EEG alpha-desynchronization orienting responses, and its ability to increase sensory, perceptual and pain thresholds (Gilbert, 1979). It has been argued that beta-endorphin is a likely mediator of these effects (Pomerleau and Pomerleau, 1984).

While normal smoking during nonstress conditions does not appear to cause an increase in plasma corticosteroids, beta-endorphin concentrations and related neuromodulators, and normal smoking in combination with mild-to-moderate stress, may result in increases in these neuromodulators. Studies systematically varying nicotine dose and level of stress could provide evidence critical to the neuromodulator hypothesis of smoking motivation and affect regulation.

Lateralized affective processors model

Cognitive and affective subprocessing systems to some extent rely on different neurotransmitter systems that are relatively localized and lateralized (Tucker and Williamson, 1984). Evidence reviewed earlier in this chapter is consistent with the view that nicotine interacts differentially with various neurotransmitter systems at different doses and organismic states. Thus, Gilbert (1987) hypothesized that nicotine has dose- and state-dependent psychological effects and relatively localized and lateralized CNS effects. Consistent with this hypothesis, relatively lateralized effects of nicotine on electrocortical measures have been reported (Elbert and Birbaumer, 1987; Gilbert, 1987; Gilbert et al., in press). These three electrocortical studies found the right hemisphere (RH) is more influenced by nicotine than the left hemisphere (LH). During stress, increased alpha power has been reported in the RH relative to the LH subsequent to smoking of a normal-nicotine-delivery cigarette, but not a very low-nicotine-delivery one (Gilbert et al., in press). In a nonstress situation subsequent to smoking a slightly greater activating effect (reduced alpha and theta band power) has been found in the RH than in the LH (Gilbert, 1987). Elbert and Birbaumer (1987) showed contingent negative variation (a slow electrocortical wave associated with the anticipation of an event) to be more activated in the RH than in the LH. Lateralized effects of nicotine on electrodermal activity during smoking have also been interpreted as indicating that smoking has a stronger effect on the RH than the LH (Boyd and Maltzman, 1984). Consistent with the results of electrophysiological studies, performance on cognitive and behavioral tasks suggests differential effects of nicotine on the two hemispheres.

During moderately stressful tasks, predominantly LH-based performances are enhanced by nicotine, while RH-based processes, including those hypothesized to be associated with negative affect, are relatively impaired. Schultze (1982) found smoking to improve anagram performance, a LH verbal task, but to decrease performance on digit symbol substitution and recall of Bender–gestalt forms (both tasks emphasize RH processing). Improved Stroop Word-Color Task and vigilance performance subsequent to smoking (Wesnes and Warburton, 1978, 1983) can be interpreted in the Tucker and Williamson (1984) model of hemispheric functioning as reflecting an increase in LH activation, as well as general cortical arousal. Nicotine-induced RH deactivation is also suggested by decreased performance on jigsaw puzzles (Schneider, 1978) and decreased accuracy in identifying facial emotional cues (Hertz, 1978) subsequent to smoking.

In contrast with the decrement in RH-based performance seen in moderately stressful situations, performance during low-stress tasks suggests that RH-based processes may be facilitated in such conditions. If the Tucker and Williamson (1984) model of hemispheric functioning is correct, nicotine's apparent ability to facilitate habituation (Golding and Mangan, 1982) and to reduce recall of irrelevant cues during nonstressful situations (Andersson and Hockey, 1977) reflects enhanced RH activation. Thus, whether RH or LH processes are activated or depressed by normal smoking may be a function of stress level and/or processing demands.

Lateralized effects may play a role in nicotine's modulation of affect (Gilbert, 1985, 1987; Gilbert et al., in press). Converging lines of evidence support the view that the LH is the biological seat of nonemotional, rational processes, while the RH is associated with negative affect and global, undifferentiated information processing (Davidson, 1984). Nicotine may facilitate activation of LH-based rational processes and/or inhibit RH-based emotional responses (Gilbert, 1985; Gilbert et al., in press). Effects of smoking on hemispheric asymmetry of EEG activation were found to depend upon level of stress and the nicotine delivery of the cigarette (Gilbert, 1985). Viewing a stressful movie subsequent to smoking a higher-nicotine-delivery cigarette was associated with reduced anxiety and enhanced left relative to right parietal activation. Gilbert's (1985) left-hemisphere-priming hypothesis suggests that nicotine directly stimulates LH-dominant cholinergic receptors, and that LH activation then tends to produce relative deactivation in RH emotional processes by inhibiting neural connections. Thus one might expect the observed increase in LH relative to RH activation ratio to be due to an increase in LH activation and a proportional decrease in RH activation. However, this was not the case. Most of the L-relative-to-R-enhancement was associated with decreased RH parietal activation, which suggests that nicotine's anxiolytic effects during the stressor may have been directly mediated by RH-dominant receptors. Nicotine-induced reduction in RH-based emotional activity could account for the lower level of anxiety experienced when smoking. Such decreased emotional information processing could allow the LH to process certain types of rational information without emotional interference.

Recent evidence suggesting that noradrenergic and serotonergic systems are relatively more dense in the right than the left hemisphere (Tucker and Williamson, 1984) implies that one of these largely inhibitory neurotransmitter systems could be the biological basis of nicotine's influence on the RH and emotion. As noted earlier, nicotine has been shown to influence both noradrenergic and serotonergic release (Balfour, 1984). Support for a serotonergically based mechanism is provided by the fact that the apparently serotonergically based symptoms of the clinical syndrome of depression are reminiscent of those seen during nicotine withdrawal (irritation, depressed mood, trouble concentrating, altered appetite). It appears likely that antidepressant medications alleviate depression by stimulating serotonergic systems (Gerner and Bunney, 1986). Support for the possible role of noradrenergic mechanisms is provided by findings that, like nicotine, noradrenergic processes facilitate habituation and reduce muscle tone (Tucker and Williamson, 1984). An alternative RH interpretation of the smoking-induced reductions of anxiety during stressful tasks is based on the observation that the right parietal cortex is important in the recognition of emotional expressions of the face (Ley and Strauss, 1986). Smoking-induced decrease in sensitivity to facial cues indicative of emotion (Hertz, 1978) is one mechanism by which RH-deactivation might decrease emotional responsivity. Nicotine-induced reduced processing of facial and other visual social cues could lead to anxiety reductions in certain settings, but would not account for nicotine's ability to reduce anxiety in situations free of anxiety-eliciting visual cues.

In summary, we suggest that some of nicotine's affect-modulating and performance-influencing effects are mediated by lateralized and localized CNS subprocessors. Findings suggest that the RH has a higher density of nicotinic receptors than the LH. During moderately to highly stressful conditions smoking-sized doses of nicotine appear to depress RH activation and RH-mediated performance. During low-stress conditions such doses of nicotine appear to produce primarily stimulant and performance-enhancing effects.

Hypothalamic model of nicotine, affect and consummatory drive

The hypothalamus is heavily involved in the regulation of many of the affective and other psychological processes related to smoking. Lesions of the ventromedial hypothalamus and/or stimulation of the dorsolateral hypothalamus in animals have been found to produce heightened emotionality and sensitivity to external stimuli, low activity level, hyposexuality, high taste responsivity, and weight gain (Nisbett, 1972). Nicotine withdrawal produces similar symptoms, while nicotine and smoking produce the opposite effects. Thus it seems reasonable to hypothesize that nicotine is acting to stimulate the ventromedial hypothalamus and/or deactivate the dorsolateral hypothalamus.

Consistent with this hypothalamic model, there are a number of relationships of nicotine with food consumption, affect and hunger. Food consumption, like nicotine, reduces anxiety (Schachter, 1971). Individuals also tend to smoke (Rose, Ananda and Jarvik, 1983) and eat (Morley, Levine and Rowland, 1983) more when anxious. Furthermore, smoking and nicotine produce weight loss in humans and animals (Grunberg and Baum, 1985) and it has been suggested that nicotine may be related to eating in a fashion that relieves the hunger drive (Grunberg and Baum, 1985).

Summary of models of smoking and affect

Individuals report that they smoke because it improves their affective state, reducing negative and/or increasing positive affect (Spielberger, 1986). Experimental studies reviewed above support the view that the nicotine provided by smoking and other forms of tobacco use reduces negative affect in habitual tobacco users. It is not yet clear whether negative reinforcement of tobacco use is provided only by the relief of withdrawal symptoms or whether nicotine has inherent negative-affect-reducing properties. However, it seems likely that nicotine has some inherent reinforcing properties since many cigarettes appear to be smoked independent of withdrawal effects. Furthermore, experimental studies suggest that nicotine has negative-affect-reducing properties after periods of very short smoking deprivation, but prior to the onset of any clear signs of withdrawal.

The question of whether nicotine has inherent positively reinforcing effects is not clear. Under highly specified conditions animals and humans will self-administer i.v. nicotine (Henningfield and Goldberg, 1985). However, the specific subjective and motivational processes cannot be clearly determined from these studies. The subjective effects of smoking-sized doses of nicotine are subtle, and are dependent upon a variety of expectational, environmental, physiological state and trait factors (Hughes, Pickens, Spring and Keenan, 1985). It is clear that individuals characterized by high degrees of psychopathology are more likely to take up the smoking habit (Seltzer and Oechsli, 1985). Thus some smokers may be self-medicating their psychopathology in an attempt to reduce negative affect and/or improve their cognitive performance. Smoking and relapse would be expected to be especially likely to occur when subjective well-being and self-control are threatened. For example, experiencing depressive and/or withdrawal symptoms may entail a special vulnerability to smoking and relapse.

Evidence reviewed earlier in this chapter suggests that different doses of nicotine may stimulate different biological systems. Small doses may produce stimulant effects in cholinergic and autonomic systems in low-arousal situations, intermediate doses are likely to stimulate systems with slightly higher thresholds, and still higher doses additional systems. Stressful situations are likely to alter thresholds for the nicotine-induced release of a variety of neurotransmitters and neuromodulators. Such stress- and dose-dependent activation of different physiological systems is likely to be carefully titrated by the experienced smoker so as to produce the desired subjective effects. The ability of the smoker to precisely control the blood dose of nicotine (and assumedly subjective state) on a minute-to-minute basis is likely to provide immediate gratification and well-being by allowing the individual to alter in a positive direction a variety of cognitive and affective states.

RECOMMENDATIONS FOR FUTURE WORK

One of the most basic questions that needs to be addressed by future work is whether nicotine has tranquilizing properties independent of those associated with relief of withdrawal symptoms. This question is important in that it relates to the onset and maintenance of tobacco use, as well as to cessation techniques. Future studies should assess the effects of nicotine on emotional states in individuals who do not habitually use tobacco products; for example, in nonsmokers and in ex-smokers. The possibility that nicotine has inherent negative-affect-reducing properties only in certain individuals who may tend to use nicotine as a form of self-medication, should be seriously addressed.

Our review suggests that systematic studies of the effects of various stimulus parameters, including stressor proximity, intensity and ambiguity, would be highly profitable. Evidence reviewed above suggests that we would expect the effects of nicotine to vary as a function of these stimulus parameters, and of individual differences in trait factors such as personality and degree of tolerance to nicotine. Parametric stressor stimulus studies could benefit from the simultaneous assessment of the effects of nicotine on cognitive and lateralized electrocortical processes, as well as behavioral task performance. Such complex studies should more effectively capture some of the complexity of interactions among cognitive, affective and behavioral processes.

Careful parametric studies of different doses of nicotine on subjective experience and other affect-related processes also need to be made. We noted above that studies of nicotine's effects on neuromodulators may be flawed in that they have typically used exceptionally high doses of nicotine; doses so high that we believe that they have typically caused nicotine-induced subjective and physiological stress. It is likely that the stress associated with these high-dose conditions, rather than ecologically valid nicotine-specific effects, is the cause of neuromodulator release in such studies. It is important that future studies assessing the effects of nicotine on hormones carefully assess the subjective correlates (including formal psychometric assessment of nausea and other signs of subjective distress) of their experimental procedures. However, this is not to say that the neuromodulator hypothesis should be rejected. Instead, studies should assess the possibility that nicotine reduces the threshold for the release of stress-induced neuromodulators.

We expect that quantified smoke delivery systems (Gilbert, Jensen and Meliska, in press) will be used extensively during the next decade to assess individual differences in affective and physiological response to known doses of nicotine. An understanding of such individual differences may be helpful in understanding individual differences in response to withdrawal symptoms and the motivation for tobacco use.

Appreciation of the large effects of slight changes in nicotine dose, stressor stimulus parameters and individual difference variables are needed if investigators are to significantly enhance our understanding of nicotine's effects on affective processes. It is hoped that this chapter will contribute to such an appreciation and to this understanding.

REFERENCES

Agué, C. (1973). Nicotine and smoking: effects upon subjective changes in mood. *Psychopharmacologia*, **30**, 323–328.

Andersson, K., and Hockey, G.R. (1977). Effects of cigarette smoking on incidental memory. *Psychopharmacology*, **52**, 223–226.

Armitage, A.K., Hall, G.H., and Sellers, C.M. (1969). Effects of nicotine on electrocortical activity and acetylcholine release from the rat cerebral cortex. *British Journal of Pharmacology*, **35**, 157–160.

Ashton, H., and Stepney, R. (1982). *Smoking: Psychology and Pharmacology*. London: Tavistock.

Ashton, H., Millman, J.E., Telford, R., and Thompson, J.W. (1974). The effect of caffeine, nitrazepam, and cigarette smoking on the contingent negative variation in man. *Electroencephalography and Clinical Neurophysiology*, **37**, 59–71.

Baer, L., and Radichevich, I. (1985). Cigarette smoking in hypertensive patients: blood pressure and endocrine responses. *American Journal of Medicine*, **78**, 564–568.

Balfour, D.J.K. (1984). The effects of nicotine on brain neurotransmitter systems. In: D.J.K. Balfour (ed.), *Nicotine and the Tobacco Smoking Habit*. Oxford: Pergamon Press.

Benowitz, N.L., Kuyt, F., and Jacob III, P. (1984). Influence of nicotine on cardio-vascular and hormonal effects of cigarette smoking. *Clinical Pharmacology and Therapeutics*, **36**, 74–81.

Bowen, M.E. (1969). Responses to smoking in the presence of anxiety-eliciting cues. *Dissertation Abstracts International*, **31/02-B**, 895.

Boyd, G.M., and Maltzman, I. (1984). Effects of cigarette smoking on bilateral skin conductance. *Psychophysiology*, **21**, 334–341.

Buck, R. (1979). Individual differences in nonverbal sending accuracy and electro-dermal responding: the externalizing–internalizing dimension. In: R. Rosenthal (ed.), *Skill in Nonverbal Communication*. Cambridge, MA: Oelgeschlager, Gunn & Hain.

Cetta, M.F. (1977). The effects of cigarette smoking upon variation in anxious, aggressive, and pleasant mood states. *Dissertation Abstracts International*, **38/01-B**, 349.

Cherek, D.R. (1981). Effects of smoking different doses of nicotine on human aggressive behavior. *Psychopharmacology*, **75**, 339–345.

Clark, M.S.G., and Rand, M.J. (1968). Effect of tobacco smoke on the knee-jerk reflex in man. *European Journal of Pharmacology*, **3**, 294–302.

Cryer, P.E., Haymond, M.W., Santiago, J.V., and Shaw, S.D. (1976). Norepi-nephrine and epinephrine release and adrenergic mediation of smoking-associated hemodynamic and metabolic events. *New England Journal of Medicine*, **295**, 573–577.

Davidson, R.J. (1984). Hemispheric asymmetry and emotion. In: K.R. Scherer and P. Ekman (eds), *Approaches to Emotion*. Hillsdale, NJ: Lawrence Erlbaum.

Domino, E.G. (1973). Neuropsychopharmacology of nicotine and tobacco smoking. In: W.L. Dunn, Jr (ed.), *Smoking Behavior: Motives and Incentives*. Washington, DC: Winston.

Dubren, R. (1975). The effects of smoking on anxiety. *Dissertation Abstracts International*, **36/11-B**, 5786.

Edwards, J.A., and Warburton, D.M. (1983). Smoking, nicotine, and electrocortical activity. *Pharmacology and Therapeutics*, **19**, 147–164.

Edwards, J.A., Wesnes, K., Warburton, D.M., and Gale, A. (1985). Evidence of more rapid stimulus evaluation following cigarette smoking. *Addictive Behaviors*, **10**, 113–126.

Elbert, T., and Birbaumer, N. (1987). Hemispheric differences in relation to smoking. In: A. Glass (ed.), *Individual Differences in Hemispheric Specialization*. New York: Plenum.

Ellis, A. (1962). *Reason and Emotion in Psychotherapy*. New York: Lyle Stuart.

Epstein, L.H., and Jennings, J.R. (1986). Smoking, stress, cardiovascular reactivity, and coronary heart disease. In: K.A. Matthews, S.M. Weiss, T. Detre, T.M. Dembroski, B. Falkner, S.B. Manuck and R.B. Williams, Jr (eds), *Handbook of Stress, Reactivity, and Cardiovascular Disease*. New York: John Wiley & Sons.

Epstein, L.H., Dickson, B.E., McKenzie, S., and Russell, P.O. (1984). The effect of smoking on perception of muscle tension. *Psychopharmacology*, **83**, 107–113.

Erdmann, G. (1983). Autonomic drugs as tools in differential psychopharmacology. In: W. Janke (ed.), *Response Variability to Psychotropic Drugs*. Oxford: Pergamon Press.

Eysenck, H.J. (1973). Personality and the maintenance of the smoking habit. In: W.L. Dunn, Jr (ed.), *Smoking Behavior: Motives and Incentives*. Washington, DC: Winston.

Eysenck, H.J. (1975). The measurement of emotion: psychological parameters and methods. In: L. Levi (ed.), *Emotions—Their Parameters and Measurement*. New York: Raven Press.

Fagerstrom, K., and Gotestam, K.G. (1977). Increase of muscle tonus after tobacco smoking. *Addictive Behaviors*, **2**, 203–206.

Fleming, S.E., and Lombardo, T.W. (1987). Effects of cigarette smoking on phobic anxiety. *Addictive Behaviors*, **12**, 195–198.

Frankenhaeuser, M., Myrsten, A., Post, B., and Johansson, G. (1971). Behavioural and physiological effects of cigarette smoking in a monotonous situation. *Psychopharmacologia*, **22**, 1–7.

Fridlund, A.J., and Izard, C.E. (1983). Electromyographic studies of facial expressions of emotions. In: J.T. Cacioppo and R.E. Petty (eds), *Social Psychophysiology*. New York: Guilford.

Friedman, J., and Meares, R. (1980). Tobacco smoking and cortical evoked potentials: an opposite effect on auditory and visual systems. *Clinical and Experimental Pharmacology and Physiology*, **7**, 609–615.

Fuller, R.G.C., and Forrest, D.W. (1977). Cigarette smoking under relaxation and stress. *Irish Journal of Psychology*, **3**, 165–180.

Gerner, R.H., and Bunney, W.E. (1986). Biological hypotheses of affective disorders. In: S. Arieti (ed.), *American Handbook of Psychiatry*, vol. 8. New York: Basic Books.

Gilbert, D.G. (1979). Paradoxical tranquilizing and emotion-reducing effects of nicotine. *Psychological Bulletin*, **86**, 643–661.

Gilbert, D.G. (1985). Nicotine's effects on lateralized EEG and emotion. Paper presented at the March 1985 Meeting of the Society of Behavioral Medicine.

Gilbert, D.G. (1987). Effects of smoking and nicotine on EEG lateralization as a function of personality. *Personality and Individual Differences*, **8**, 933–941.

Gilbert, D.G., and Hagen, R.L. (1980). The effects of nicotine and extraversion on self-report, skin conductance, electromyographic, and heart responses to emotional stimuli. *Addictive Behaviors*, **5**, 247–257.

Gilbert, D.G., and Hagen, R.L. (1985). Electrodermal responses to movie stressors: Nicotine × extraversion interactions. *Personality and Individual Differences*, **6**, 573–578.

Gilbert, D.G., and Jensen, R. Determinants of nicotine-induced release of neuromodulators: possible confounds of dose and stress. Manuscript in preparation.

Gilbert, D.G., Jensen, R.A., and Meliska, C.J. (in press). A system for administering quantified doses of tobacco smoke to human subjects: Plasma nicotine and filter pad validation. *Pharmacology, Biochemistry and Behavior*.

Gilbert, D.G., and Spielberger, C.D. (1987). Effects of smoking on heart rate, anxiety, and feelings of success during social interaction. *Journal of Behavioral Medicine*, **10**, 629–638.

Gilbert, D.G., Robinson, J.H., Chamberlin, C.L., and Spielberger, C.D. (in press). Effects of smoking/nicotine on anxiety, heart rate, and lateralization of EEG during a stressful movie. *Psychophysiology*.

Golding, J., and Mangan, G.L. (1982). Arousing and de-arousing effects of cigarette smoking under conditions of stress and mild sensory isolation. *Psychophysiology*, **19**, 449–456.

Gray, J.A. (1982). *The Neuropsychology of Anxiety*. New York: Oxford University Press.

Grunberg, N.E., and Baum, A. (1985). Biological commonalities of stress and substance abuse. In: S. Shiffman and T.A. Wills (eds), *Coping and Substance Use*. Orlando, FL: Academic Press.

Guha, D., and Pradhan, S.N. (1976). Effects of nicotine on EEG and evoked potentials and their interactions with autonomic drugs. *Neuropharmacology*, **15**, 225–232.

Hatch, J.P., Bierner, S.M., and Fisher, J.G. (1983). The effects of smoking and cigarette nicotine content on smokers' preparation and performance of a psychosocially stressful task. *Journal of Behavioral Medicine*, **6**, 207–216.

Heimstra, N.W. (1973). The effects of smoking on mood change. In: W.L. Dunn (ed.), *Smoking Behavior: Motives and Incentives*. Washington, DC: Winston.

Henningfield, J.E., and Goldberg, S.R. (1985). Stimulus properties of nicotine in animals and human volunteers: A review. In: *Behavioral Pharmacology: The Current Status*. Baltimore, MD: Alan R. Liss.

Henry, J.P. (1986). Neuroendocrine patterns of emotional response. In: R. Plutchik and H. Kellerman (eds), *Emotions: Theory, Research, and Experience*, vol. 3. Orlando, FL: Academic Press.

Herning, R.I., Jones, R.T., and Bachman, J. (1983). EEG changes during tobacco withdrawal. *Psychophysiology*, **20**, 507–512.

Hertz, B.F. (1978). The effects of cigarette smoking on perception of nonverbal communications. *Dissertation Abstracts International*, **39/2501B-2502B** (University Microfilms No. 78-21,400)

Hill, P., and Wynder, E.L. (1974). Smoking and cardiovascular disease. *American Heart Journal*, **87**, 491–496.

Hughes, J.R., Hatsukami, D.K., Pickens, R.W., Krahn, D., Malin, S., and Luknic, A. (1984). Effect of nicotine on the tobacco withdrawal syndrome. *Psychopharmacology*, **83**, 82–87.

Hughes, J.R., Pickens, R.W., Spring, W., and Keenan, R.M. (1985). Instructions control whether nicotine will serve as a reinforcer. *Journal of Pharmacology and Experimental Therapeutics*, **235**, 106–112.

Hutchinson, R.R., and Emley, G.B. (1973). Effects of nicotine on avoidance, conditioned suppression and aggression response measures in animals and man. In: W.L. Dunn, Jr (ed.), *Smoking Behavior: Motives and Incentives*. Washington, DC: Winston.

Janke, W., Debus, G., and Longo, N. (1979). Differential psychopharmacology of tranquilizing and sedating drugs. In: T.A. Ban, F.A. Freyhan, P. Pichot and W. Poldinger (eds), *Modern Problems of Pharmacopsychiatry*, vol. 14. Basel: Karger.

Jarvik, M.E., Caskey, N.H., Rose, J.E., Herskovic, J.E., and Sadeghpour, M. (in press). Anxiolytic effects of smoking associated with four stressors. *Addictive Behaviors*.

Jarvis, M.J., Raw, M., Russell, M.A.H., and Feyerabend, C. (1982). Randomized controlled trial of nicotine chewing-gum. *British Medical Journal*, **285**, 537–540.

Johnston, L.M. (1942). Tobacco smoking and nicotine. *Lancet*, **2**, 742.

Jones, B.W., and Leiser, R.L. (1976). Reported in Dunn, W.L. (1978). Smoking as a possible inhibitor of arousal. In: K. Bättig (ed.), *Behavioral Effects of Nicotine*. New York: Karger.

Kleinke, C.L., Staneski, R.A., and Meeker, F.B. (1983). Attributions for smoking behavior: comparing smokers with nonsmokers and predicting smokers' cigarette consumption. *Journal of Research in Personality*, **17**, 242–255.

Knott, V.J. (1985). Tobacco effects on cortical evoked potentials to distracting stimuli. *Neuropsychobiology*, **13**, 74–80.

Kozlowski, L.T., Director, J., and Harford, M.A. (1981). Tobacco dependence, restraint and time to the first cigarette of the day. *Addictive Behaviors*, **6**, 307–312.

Lazarus, R.S. (1981). A cognitivist's reply to Zajonc on emotion and cognition. *American Psychologist*, **36**, 222–223.

Levine, R.L., and Lombardo, T.W. (1985). *Smoking affects perception of EMG in facial muscles associated with mood.* Paper presented at the March 1985 meeting of the Society of Behavioral Medicine, New Orleans, LA.

Ley, R.G., and Strauss, E. (1986). Hemispheric asymmetries in the perception of facial expressions in normals. In: R. Bruyer (ed.), *The Neuropsychology of Face Perception and Facial Expression.* Hillsdale, NJ: Lawrence Erlbaum.

Lindsley, D.B. (1970). The role of nonspecific reticulo-thalamo-cortical systems in emotion. In: P. Black (ed.), *Physiological Correlates of Emotion.* New York: Academic Press.

Lombardo, T.W., and Epstein, L.H. (1986). The nicotine paradox: effect of smoking on autonomic discrimination. *Addictive Behaviors*, **11**, 341–344.

Lukas, S.E., and Jasinski, D.R. (1983). EEG power spectral effects of intravenous nicotine administration in humans. *Federation Proceedings*, **42**, 1018.

MacDougall, J.M., Musante, L., Howard, J.A., Hanes, R.L., and Dembrowski, T.M. (1986). Individual differences in cardiovascular reactions to stress and cigarette smoking. *Health Psychology*, **5**, 531–544.

Mendenhall, W.L. (1925). A study of tobacco smoking. *American Journal of Physiology*, **72**, 549–557.

Meyers, F.H., Jawetz, E., and Goldfien, A. (1974). *Review of Medical Pharmacology*, 4th edn. Los Altos, CA: Lange Medical Publications.

Milgrom-Friedman, J., Penman, R., and Meares, R. (1983). A preliminary study of pain perception and tobacco smoking. *Clinical and Experimental Pharmacology and Physiology*, **10**, 161–169.

Morley, J.E., Levine, A.S., and Rowland, N.E. (1983). Stress induced eating. *Life Sciences*, **32**, 2169–2182.

Mueser, K., Waller, D., Levander, S., and Schalling, D. (1984). Smoking and pain— a method of limits and sensory decision theory analysis. *Scandinavian Journal of Psychology*, **25**, 289–296.

Murray, A.L., and Lawrence, P.S. (1984). Sequelae to smoking cessation: a review. *Clinical Psychology Review*, **4**, 143–157.

Myrsten, A., Post, B., Frankenhaeuser, M., and Johansson, G. (1972). Changes in behavioral and physiological activation induced by cigarette smoking in habitual smokers. *Psychopharmacologia*, **27**, 305–312.

Neetz, R.A. (1979). The effect of smoking deprivation on psychomotor performance, mood, and task perception of female smokers. *Dissertation Abstracts International*, **40/06-B**, 2879.

Nesbitt, P.D. (1969). Smoking, physiological arousal, and emotional response. *Dissertation Abstracts International*, **31/04-A**, 4395.

Nisbett, R. (1972). Hunger, obesity, and the ventromedial hypothalamus. *American Psychologist*, **79**, 433–453.

Nyberg, G., Panfilov, V., Sivertsson, R., and Wilhelmsen, L. (1982). Cardiovascular effects of nicotine chewing gum in healthy non-smokers. *European Journal of Clinical Pharmacology*, **23**, 303–307.

O'Connor, K. (1982). Individual differences in the effect of smoking on frontal-central distribution of the CNV: some observations on the smoker's control of attentional behaviors. *Personality and Individual Differences*, **3**, 271–285.

Perlick, D.A. (1977). The withdrawal syndrome: nicotine addiction and the effects of stopping smoking in heavy and light smokers. *Dissertation Abstracts International*, **38/01-B**, 409.

Pomerleau, C.S., and Pomerleau, O.F. (1987). The effects of a psychological stressor on cigarette smoking and subsequent behavioral and physiological responses. *Psychophysiology*, **24**, 278–285.

Pomerleau, O.F. (1986). The 'Why' of tobacco dependence: underlying reinforcing mechanisms in nicotine self-administration. In: J.K. Ockene (ed.), *The Pharmacologic Treatment of Tobacco Dependence: Proceedings of the World Congress November 4–5, 1985*. Cambridge, MA: Harvard University Press.

Pomerleau, O.F., and Pomerleau, C.S. (1984). Neuroregulators and the reinforcement of smoking: towards a biobehavioral explanation. *Neuroscience and Biobehavioral Reviews*, **3**, 503–513.

Pomerleau, O.F., Fertig, J.B., Seyler, L.E., and Jaffe, J. (1983). Neuroendocrine reactivity to nicotine in smokers. *Psychopharmacology*, **81**, 61–67.

Pomerleau, O.F., Turk, D.C., and Fertig, J.B. (1984). The effects of cigarette smoking on pain and anxiety. *Addictive Behaviors*, **9**, 265–271.

Redmond, A., Martinerie, J., and Baillon, J. (1979). Nicotine intake compared with other psychophysiological situations through quantitative EEG analysis. In: A. Redmond and C. Izard (eds), *Electrophysiological Effects of Nicotine*. New York: Elsevier.

Rose, J.E. (1986). Cigarette smoking blocks caffeine-induced arousal. *Alcohol and Drug Research*, **7**, 49–55.

Rose, J.E., Ananda, S., and Jarvik, M.E. (1983). Cigarette smoking during anxiety-provoking and monotonous tasks. *Addictive Behaviors*, **8**, 353–359.

Rose, J.E., Tashkin, D.P., Ertle, A., Zinser, M.C., and Lafer, R. (1985). Sensory blockade of smoking satisfaction. *Pharmacology, Biochemistry and Behavior*, **23**, 289–293.

Rosenberg, J., Benowitz, N.L., Jacob, P., and Wilson, K.M. (1980). Disposition kinetics and effects of intravenous nicotine. *Clinical Pharmacological Therapy*, **28**, 517–522.

Russell, M.A.H., Peto, J., and Patel, U.A. (1974). The classification of smoking by factorial structure of motives. *Journal of the Royal Statistical Society*, **137**, 313–346.

Sachs, D.P.L. (1987). Pharmacologic, neuroendocrine, and biobehavioral basis for tobacco dependence. *Current Pulmonology*. Chicago: Year Book Medical Publishers.

Schachter, S. (1971). *Emotion, Obesity and Crime*. New York: Academic Press.

Schachter, S. (1973). Nesbitt's paradox. In: W.L. Dunn, Jr (ed.), *Smoking Behavior: Motives and Incentives*. Washington, DC: Winston.

Schachter, S. (1979). Regulation, withdrawal, and nicotine addiction. In: N.A. Krasnegor (ed.), *Cigarette Smoking as a Dependence Process*. Rockville, MD: National Institute of Drug Abuse.

Schechter, M.D., and Rand, M.J. (1974). Effect of acute deprivation of smoking on aggression and hostility. *Psychopharmacologia*, **35**, 19–28.

Schneider, N.G. (1978). The effects of nicotine on learning and short-term memory. *Dissertation Abstracts International*, **39/10B** (University Microfilms No. 79–06,196).

Schultze, M.J. (1982). Paradoxical aspects of cigarette smoking: physiological arousal, affect, and individual differences in body cue utilization. *Dissertation Abstracts International*, **42/11B** (University Microfilms No. 82-08,416.)

Seltzer, C.C., and Oechsli F.W. (1985). Psychosocial characteristics of adolescent smokers before they started smoking: evidence of self-selection. *Journal of Chronic Disease*, **38**, 17–26.

Seyler, L.E., Fertig, J., Pomerleau, O., Hunt, D., and Parker, K. (1984). The effects of smoking on ACTH and cortisol secretion. *Life Sciences*, **34**, 57–65.

Seyler, L.E., Pomerleau, O.F., Fertig, J., Hunt, D., and Parker, K. (1986). Pituitary hormone response to cigarette smoking. *Pharmacology, Biochemistry, and Behavior*, **24**, 159–162.

Shiffman, S., and Jarvik, M.E. (1976). Smoking withdrawal symptoms in two weeks of abstinence. *Psychopharmacology*, **50**, 35–39.

Shiffman, S., and Jarvik, M.E. (1984). Cigarette smoking, physiological arousal, and emotional response: Nesbitt's paradox re-examined. *Addictive Behaviors*, **9**, 95–98.

Silverstein, B. (1982). Cigarette smoking, nicotine addiction, and relaxation. *Journal of Personality and Social Psychology*, **42**, 946–950.

Silvette, H., Hoff, E.C., Larson, P.S., and Haag, H.B. (1962). The actions of nicotine on central nervous system functions. *Pharmacological Reviews*, **14**, 137–173.

Spielberger, C.D. (1986). Psychological determinants of smoking behavior. In: R.D. Tollison (ed.), *Smoking and Society: Toward a More Balanced Assessment*. Lexington, MA: D.C. Heath.

Sult, S.C., and Moss, R.A. (1986). The effects of cigarette smoking on the perception of electrical stimulation and cold pressor pain. *Addictive Behaviors*, **11**, 447–451.

Surawy, C., and Cox, T. (1986). Smoking behaviour under conditions of relaxation: a comparison between types of smokers. *Addictive Behaviors*, **11**, 187–191.

Suter, Th.W., Buzzi, R., Woodson, P.P., and Bättig, K. (1983). Psychophysiological correlates of conflict solving and cigarette smoking. *Activitas Nervosa Superior*, **25**, 261–272.

Tucci, J.R., and Sode, J. (1972). Chronic cigarette smoking: Effect on adrenocortical and sympathoadrenomedullary activity in man. *Journal of the American Medical Association*, **221**, 282–285.

Tucker, D.M., and Williamson, P.A. (1984). Asymmetric neural control systems in human self-regulation. *Psychological Review*, **91**, 185–215.

Waller, D., Schalling, D., Levander, S., and Erdman, R. (1983). Smoking pain tolerance, and physiological activation. *Psychopharmacology*, **79**, 193–198.

Warburton, D.M. (1981). Neurochemistry of behavior. *British Medical Bulletin*, **37**, 121–125.

Webster, D.D. (1964). The dynamic quantification of spasticity with automated integrals of passive motion resistance. *Clinical Pharmacology and Therapeutics*, **5**, 900–908.

Wenusch, A., and Scholler, R. (1936). Über den Einfluss des Rauchens auf die Reizschwelle des Drucksinnes. *Medizinische Klinik*, **32**, 356–358.

Wesnes, K., and Warburton, D.M. (1978). The effects of cigarette smoking and nicotine tablets upon human attention. In: R.E. Thornton (ed.), *Smoking Behaviour: Physiological and Psychological Influences*. Edinburgh: Churchill Livingstone.

Wesnes, K., and Warburton, D.M. (1983). Smoking, nicotine and human performance. *Pharmacology and Therapeutics*, **21**, 189–208.

West, R.J., Jarvis, M.J., Russell, M.A.H., Carruthers, M.E., and Feyerabend, C. (1984). Effect of nicotine replacement on the cigarette withdrawal syndrome. *British Journal of Addiction*, **79**, 215–219.

Woodson, P.P. (1984). The neuropharmacological double action of nicotine: mediation of cigarette smoking's energizing yet stabilizing effects on psychophysiological function. Unpublished dissertation, Swiss Federal Institute of Technology.

Woodson, P.P., Buzzi, R., Nil, R., and Bättig, K. (1986). Effects of smoking on vegetative reactivity to noise in women. *Psychophysiology*, **23**, 272–282.

Wynder, E.L., Kaufman, P.L., and Lesser, R.L. (1967). A short-term follow-up study on ex-cigarette smokers, with special emphasis on persistent cough and weight gain. *American Review of Respiratory Diseases*, **96**, 645–655.

Part Three

Smoking Behavior and Human Performance

9

Smoking Behavior: A Multivariate Process

RICO NIL
and
KARL BÄTTIG

ABSTRACT

Multivariate assessments of smoking behavior reveal low levels of inter-relationships between single measures. This suggests that multiple modes of control operate to determine smoking behavior. We suggest that inter-individual variance in smoking behavior reflects individual differences in the relative importance of the several determinants of smoking. Apart from nicotine, which seems to act in a differential way depending on the route of administration and dose, and individual sensitivity (tolerance effects), non-nicotinic smoking motives deserve more attention in future research.

INTRODUCTION

Dose of cigarette smoke is said to be an important factor in the development of smoking-related diseases. The precise measurement of dosage is particularly difficult because dosage is the result of a complex interaction between the smoker and his or her type of cigarette. Apart from the complexity of smoking behavior, the smoke itself contains thousands of constituents and the measurement of dosage must therefore be a multifactorial problem.

Smoking behavior is a process involving several steps or stages: selection

Smoking and Human Behavior, Edited by T. Ney and A. Gale
© 1989 John Wiley & Sons Ltd

of the type of cigarette, frequency of smoking, intensity of puffing, intensity of inhalation and absorption of smoke constituents into the blood. Operational measurement procedures have been developed for each of these behavioral components taken separately. But it is rare to find them combined in a comprehensive fashion in smoking research.

Measures of smoking behavior

In epidemiological studies the most widely used parameters are type of cigarette (for example, machine standard smoke yield for nicotine and tar; filter or nonfilter) and consumption. But laboratory studies reveal quite clearly that such global measures fail to describe adequately interindividual variability in smoking behavior and smoke absorption. We now describe the research methods which have been developed, and focus on their relevance.

Cigarette puffing behavior

Puffing behavior describes the interaction between smoker and cigarette. It not only controls the temporal patterning and quantity of smoke intake into the mouth, but also influences the quality of smoke. Schlotzhauer and Chortyk (1983) showed that a variety of smoke components were differentially affected when puffing frequency or volume were changed with a smoking machine. The shape of the puff pressure profile during a single puff affects the concentration of tar, nicotine, carbon monoxide and their interactions (Creighton and Lewis, 1978).

Cigarette holders are typically used to measure puffing parameters. To measure temporal characteristics, Henningfield and Griffiths (1979) inserted a thermistor in one study, and in another they used a pressure transducer connected to the holder by thin plastic tubes. Several techniques are available to measure puff volume and pressure (see Herning, Hunt and Jones, 1983a); and puff flow (volume integrated over time) can be assessed by pressure drop across a small resistance. Holders producing laminar flow of air/smoke (Rawbone, Murphy, Tate and Kane, 1978) or turbulent flow (Creighton, Noble and Whewell, 1978) have differential effects on the relation between pressure drop and flow. Confounding is also possible because the characteristics of the holder can change during smoking as a result of condensation, or because the gas smoke characteristics alter with increasing temperature toward the end of the cigarette (Adams, Lee, Rawbone and Guz, 1983; Woodman, Newman, Pavia and Clarke, 1984). It is possible to approximate puff flow by assessing puff pressure, but such a technique involves complex, nonlinear relations between pressure and flow, and is affected by the characteristics of particular cigarettes (Herning, Jones, Bachman and Mines, 1981).

Gritz, Rose and Jarvik (1983) estimated flow by measuring the temperature drop of a heated thermistor inserted in the holder.

In all such methods the holder itself can influence smoking behavior (Rawbone et al., 1978; Tobin and Sackner, 1982; Adams et al., 1983). Alternatives to holders include a pyrometer (Guillerm and Radziszewski, 1978) and an inductive plethysmographic cheek coil (Tobin and Sackner, 1982). These authors claim that holders increase the intensity of puffing behavior. Nevertheless, the holder, in spite of its problems, remains the most commonly used technique. We have obtained high test–retest reliability of puffing behavior using the pressure-drop method (Nil, Buzzi and Bättig, 1984). The technique is sensitive to variation in smoke delivery (Bättig, Buzzi and Nil, 1982; Nil, Buzzi and Bättig, 1986a), acute alcohol loading (Nil et al., 1984) and differential nicotine dependence in a selected group of smokers (Nil, Woodson and Bättig, 1986b).

Nicotine absorption

There are two ways of measuring nicotine absorption via the mouth: butt nicotine analysis (Schulz and Seehofer, 1978) and duplication. The former can allow comparison between laboratory and extra-laboratory smoking (Ashton, Stepney and Thompson, 1979); the latter allows exact measurement of the characteristics of the smoke reaching the mouth (Creighton et al., 1978; Stepney, 1981).

Measurement of respiratory inhalation

Although respiratory smoke inhalation is a crucial step in smoke absorption, few attempts have been made to measure its dynamics. Such measures could provide information about the dilution and distribution of the smoke bolus in the respiratory system. Respiratory traces on a polygraph, given prior calibration with a spirometer, can provide quantitative estimates of inhalation. Transducers in use include strain gauges (Rawbone et al., 1978; Herning, Jones, Benowitz and Mines, 1983b; Nil et al., 1984); transthoracic impedance (Guillerm and Radziszewski, 1978; Nil et al., 1986a); and inductive plethysmography (Tobin and Sackner, 1982; Herning et al., 1983a; McBride, Guyatt, Kirkham and Cumming, 1984). Our own experience is that such techniques are sensitive to body movement, and that sitting position can affect calibration (Nil et al., 1986a,b). We have therefore required subjects to maintain their sitting position during both calibration and smoking. Adams et al. (1983) have used the most direct and elaborate method, a head and arm-out whole-body volume displacement plethysmograph. While very precise and overcoming calibration problems, it is, of course, a most unnatural arrangement for smoking.

Apart from volume, inhalatory techniques have been used to estimate latency (time of mouth smoke exposure to the bolus; Medici, Unger and Rüegger, 1985); inhalation and exhalation time (Nil et al., 1986a), as well as a smoke exposure index (integrated inhalatory cycle over time; Rawbone et al., 1978).

Biochemical markers of smoke absorption

Four substances widely used are: nicotine; its main metabolite, cotinine; COHb; and thiocyanate (a metabolic product of hydrogen cyanide in cigarette smoke). Because the four substances vary in absorption and elimination their analysis, and the information they provide, differ greatly. Given that nicotine is so prominent in models of smoking motivation it is a good candidate (Bättig, 1980, 1981; Henningfield, 1984; Wesnes and Warburton, 1983). Nicotine is efficiently absorbed in the alveolar space, but it can also be absorbed through the mucus membranes in the mouth and the bronchial tree. Mucosal absorption increases with alkaline smoke (cigars) and decreases with acidic smoke (most cigarettes); see Armitage and Turner (1970). Plasma nicotine concentration peaks immediately after each cigarette, declining in a first phase rather rapidly (alpha phase, with a half-life of about 5 to 10 min) as a consequence of distribution into the tissues. The beta phase which follows (with a half-life of about 2 h) is due to metabolic clearance (Benowitz, Jacob, Jones and Rosenberg, 1982a; Feyerabend, Ings and Russell, 1985). Pre- and postnicotine plasma differences represent a useful measure of the nicotine absorption of a single cigarette; but potential problems for such a measure are the rapid decrease in plasma nicotine after smoking and the time patterning of the last few puffs. Measurement of nicotine exposure during the day should include both absorption and elimination (Benowitz and Jacob, 1985). Because invasive methods, such as blood sample collection, are perceived as stressful by subjects, plasma sampling has been restricted to postsmoking periods (Russell, Jarvis, Iyer and Feyerabend, 1980; Gori and Lynch, 1985). Such problems might be overcome with the use of venous catheters, inserted prior to smoking.

Cotinine can be extracted from plasma, saliva or urine, and is a marker of semichronic nicotine intake. Its half-life is about 15 to 20 h (Benowitz, Kuyt, Jacob, Jones and Osman, 1983). It should be remembered that cotinine is not the only metabolite of nicotine, and also that men seem to metabolize nicotine faster than women.

Nicotine and cotinine are markers of the smoke particle phase, while thiocyanate and COHb are markers of the gas phase. Because thiocyanate has a half-life of about fourteen days it can be used as a marker of chronic cigarette smoke exposure. Thiocyanate levels are higher in smokers, but it is not as specific a marker as nicotine and cotinine, since cyanide is present in several foods.

The most widely used marker of alveolar smoke uptake, and of the gas phase of smoke absorption, is COHb, whose half-life varies between 30 min and several hours, depending on the actual activity level of the proband. Carbon monoxide can be absorbed only in the alveolar space, and it thus represents alveolar smoke absorption only (Cumming, Guyatt and Holmes, 1978). Invasive measurement is by estimating COHb in the blood, and non-invasive measurement by expired air carbon monoxide concentration. The latter is highly correlated with blood COHb (Rawbone et al., 1978; Jarvis, Russell and Saloojee, 1980). Carbon monoxide has also been measured daily as an index of chronic smoke exposure (Wald, Idle, Boreham and Bailey, 1980) or as an index of single cigarette alveolar smoke absorption (Bättig et al., 1982). Given that carbon monoxide is both present in the environment and endogenously produced, it is not specific to cigarette smoke, but it does separate smokers from nonsmokers (Saloojee, Vesey, Cole and Russell, 1982).

Regional deposition of smoke particles in the respiratory system

Studies of deposition in the respiratory system are rare. Pearson, Chamberlain, Morgan and Vinitski (1985) used a radioaerosol technique. A special device was inserted into a holder to mix radioaerosol and cigarette smoke. The regional particle tar deposition did not necessarily parallel regional ventilation. A greater apical and central deposition was observed than that expected from normal breathing. Such findings are important, for they suggest that exposure of the pulmonary system to the particle and gas phase might be different, and that inhalation patterns might create differential effects. The increase of particle size during inhalation is important.

Physiological responses to smoking as a measure of smoke uptake

The magnitude of heart rate response to smoking is often used as an index of smoke/nicotine dosage. Blood pressure, peripheral vasoconstriction and skin temperature have also been used, but less frequently. Plasma nicotine and heart rate responses to smoking are correlated (Hopkins, Wood and Sinclair, 1984) as are heart rate and mouth nicotine intake (Suter, Buzzi and Bättig, 1983). While such findings hold in within-subject studies varying nicotine delivery, it is clear that tolerance affects the relationship of nicotine intake to heart rate (Rosenberg, Benowitz, Jacob and Wilson, 1980; Epstein, Ossip, Coleman, Hughes and Wiist, 1981; Pomerleau and Pomerleau, 1984). In contrast, skin temperature shows no effect of tolerance (Benowitz et al., 1982a). Such physiological responses to smoking are, however, small in magnitude. Moreover, even when subjects are inactive the effects are not specific to nicotine. This is particularly the case for peripheral vasoconstriction, which reacts sensitively to a variety of external psychological influences including the anticipation of smoking (Saumet and Dittmar, 1985).

INTERDEPENDENCE OF DIFFERENT SMOKING BEHAVIOR VARIABLES

It is clear that each of the variables considered so far explains only a part of smoking. The question arises as to whether the variables are interrelated, the extent of the relationships, and the degree to which one variable may be predicted by one or more other variables. Smoking occurs in two steps: puffing the smoke bolus of a variable size from the cigarette; and inhaling it, or part of it, with a variable amount of postpuff inspiratory air (Tobin and Sackner, 1982; McBride et al., 1984). We have conducted comprehensive studies of the interrelationships among smoking variables (Nil et al., 1986a); 117 regular smokers smoked their own cigarette in the laboratory. A wide range of variables was subjected to multiple regression analysis. A hierarchical analysis began with the determination of cigarette consumption by smoke delivery variables, followed by determination of presmoking CO air level, puff volume, estimated nicotine mouth intake, respiratory inhalation volume, and alveolar CO absorption. Each step in the analysis included all variables already used in the earlier stages.

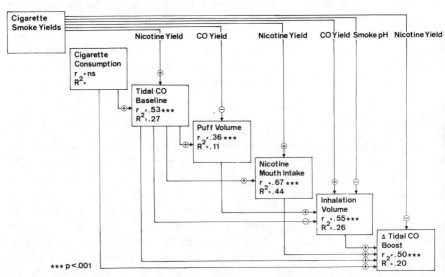

Fig. 1   Interrelationships between smoking behavior measures, evaluated by means of multiple regression analyses ($n=117$)

Figure 1 shows the results of these analyses. It is evident that cigarette consumption is not affected by the cigarette smoke delivery variables of nicotine, condensate, or CO, or by the smoke pH. Presmoking CO baseline, puff volume per cigarette, respiratory volume per cigarette, and even alveolar CO absorption (tidal CO boost) were only modestly predicted by other variables, as can be suggested from the amounts of explained variance (R^2). Nicotine mouth intake, estimated by extrapolating the machine smoking nicotine with the total puff volume per cigarette, was the only variable which was predicted by the nicotine yield of the cigarette and by presmoking CO air level. We therefore conclude, as have others, that the single components of smoking behavior are independent. This in turn suggests different modes of control for cigarette consumption, puffing, respiratory inhalation and alveolar smoke absorption. Moreover, there is even evidence for a differential control of different puffing variables as suggested by a principal-component analysis; puff volume, frequency and shape emerging as the key factors. Experimental manipulation of puffing conditions suggests that duration, and not interval, depend on the length of the tobacco rod and on draw resistance, in the absence of an effect for visual control, distance to the burning ember, smoke temperature or smoke delivery (Nemeth-Coslett and Griffiths, 1984a,b). The same authors (1985) showed that puff volume, and not duration, was sensitive to the pharmacological delivery of smoke, and suggested that volume and duration are insufficient to predict CO absorption.

DETERMINANTS OF SMOKING BEHAVIOR AND REGULATORY MECHANISMS OF SMOKE INTAKE

Over the past 20 years there has been a continuous decrease in cigarette smoke yields and a parallel tendency to claim a lower health risk from such cigarettes (Lubin, Blot, Berrino, Flamant, Gillis, Kunze, Schmahl and Visco, 1984). There is therefore an urgent need to measure the impact of smoke delivery on smoke behavior and absorption. The smoking of lighter cigarettes leads to a marginal increase in consumption (Stepney, 1980; Garfinkel, 1979). But single cigarette smoke absorption, as assessed biochemically, varies enormously between subjects. This makes it difficult to find parallel decreases in cross-sectional studies (Bättig et al., 1982; Russell et al., 1980; Benowitz, Jacob, Yu, Talcott, Hall and Jones, 1986; Ebert, McNabb, McCusker and Snow, 1983). However, closer inspection of such cross-sectional data suggests that low, and in particular, ultra-low yield cigarettes (less than 0.5 mg nicotine yield) might prevent high values of absorption (Russell, Jarvis, Feyerabend and Saloojee, 1986; Benowitz et al., 1986; Nil et al., 1986b). Figure 2 shows a similar trend for a single cigarette, tidal air CO boosts, for a pooled subject sample of 350 smokers, derived from several studies in our laboratory,

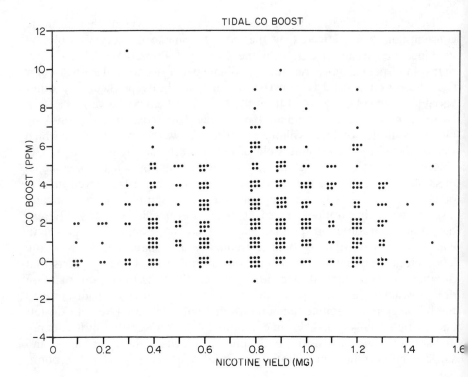

Fig. 2   Tidal CO boost in relation to machine nicotine yields, obtained from 350 regular smokers smoking their own cigarettes

smoking their own brand. It is clear that high values of smoke absorption are absent from smokers with low and ultra-low smoke yield cigarettes.

The variability, even among smokers of the same cigarette type, together with the absence of clear relationships between smoke yields and biochemical absorption markers, imply a wide range of regulatory mechanisms for smoke absorption. Both cross-sectional and switching studies demonstrate compensatory adaptations in smoking behavior in response to changes in smoke delivery. The nicotine titration hypothesis therefore suggests that the smoker hunts for his or her individual and homeostatic nicotine dose by varying the parameters of smoking.

The study by Nil et al. (1986a) already described, required subjects, in one session, to smoke their own cigarette and one with about 50 percent less smoke yield but with similar taste qualities, having had three days of prior familiarization. This allowed both a cross-sectional and a within-subject switching analysis. The results are shown in Figure 3. We concluded that estimated mouth intake of CO depends on cigarette strength, expressed in terms of nicotine yield. Similar relationships hold between CO mouth intake and CO yield, and nicotine mouth intake and yield. Compensatory puff volume increases occurred with decreasing yield, but were not sufficient for complete compensation, which at the level of alveolar CO absorption was virtually ideal. Respiratory inhalation volumes were on average unchanged from the switching comparison, with the exception of increased values when switching from low to ultra-low yields. A tendency toward a positive, rather than negative, relationship with increasing smoke delivery was observed in the cross-sectional analysis, a result which we found hard to explain. It does suggest, however, that inhalation volumes do not necessarily represent inhalation efficiency. We speculated that smokers might dilute concentrated smoke with increasing inhalation volumes. Yet it is difficult to explain how ultra-light smokers can have reached a CO boost of a magnitude similar to that of the other smokers. CO and plasma nicotine boost could be dissociated in light and ultra-light cigarettes. While our findings support other attempts to relate respiratory inhalation volume to smoke delivery or alveolar absorption (Adams et al., 1983; McBride et al., 1984), they do not address the issue of titration, since changes in nicotine delivery of the cigarettes used were often accompanied by corresponding changes in tar and CO delivery.

MULTIVARIATE ATTEMPTS TO SEPARATE EFFECTS OF CIGARETTE NICOTINE, TAR AND CARBON MONOXIDE DELIVERY

Using partial correlation Bättig et al. (1982) found a negative correlation in a male sample between tar yield and total puff volume, which suggests a slight compensatory adaptation for tar rather than nicotine. In a female sample nicotine yield correlated negatively with alveolar CO absorption (mixed expiratory air CO boost) and inhalation efficiency (CO boost per CO yield) but positively with puff interval. Nicotine yield therefore affected smoking only in females. Sutton, Russell, Iyer, Feyerabend and Saloojee (1982), using multiple regression, found that nicotine delivery of the cigarette correlated positively with puff volume, while tar delivery correlated negatively. Plasma nicotine boost was directly related to tar delivery and inversely related to nicotine delivery. Such results go against the nicotine titration hypothesis, supporting more the notion of tar compensation. But tar, nicotine and CO yields are highly intercorrelated, and their differentiation within multivariate analyses has to be interpreted with caution. The results of such analyses require validation by direct experimental manipulation.

Effects of variation in cigarette delivery relationships between nicotine, tar and CO

Nicotine effects can be separated from those of other smoke constituents in several ways, including independent manipulation of nicotine in experimental

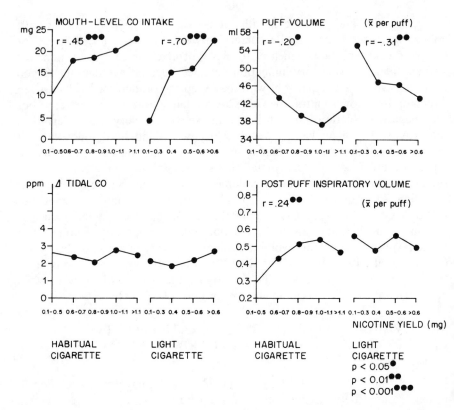

Fig. 3 Smoking behavior in relation to machine nicotine yield. The 117 regular smokers were classified into groups according to the nicotine yields of their own cigarettes (left) and a 40 percent lighter test cigarette (right) which was smoked for comparison during the same test session

cigarettes, preloading with nicotine prior to smoking, and the use of nicotine antagonists.

Nicotine:tar and nicotine:CO ratios

Table 1 reviews studies using cigarettes in which nicotine:tar or nicotine: CO ratios were varied, to see whether smoking behavior would vary. Most of the studies show nicotine to be important, while at the same time showing incomplete compensation for nicotine. But most of the studies suffer from the serious defects of failing to use biochemical markers and failing to take multivariate measures of smoke intake. The best-designed study (Stepney, 1981) provided evidence for mouth regulation of tar intake rather than for nicotine absorption.

Table 1 Effects of varying relations of nicotine to tar or CO deliveries of experimental cigarettes

Reference	n	Cigarettes and design	Changes with decreasing nicotine yields	
Goldfarb, Jarvik and Glick, 1970	15	Lettuce cig. with added nic.: 0.00 mg; 1.26 mg; 2.25 mg Each cig. for 1 week	Decrease in: Unchanged: Conclusion:	subjective strength cig. consumption 'fair degree of functional autonomy of smoking from nic.'
Jarvik, Popek, Schneider, Baer-Weiss and Gritz, 1978	28	2.0 mg nic.; 0.2 mg nic.; with equal tar delivery 2 × 2 (nic. yield × cig. length) repeated measures design	Increase in: Conclusion:	cig. consumption, N puffs smoking satisfaction not related to nic. Nic. controls smoking
Dunn and Freiesleben, 1978	4	1.01 mg nic.; 19.5 mg tar; 2.4 mg CO 1.32 mg nic.; 21.4 mg tar; 21.2 mg CO Each cig. during 5 days Analysis during working hours	Decrease in: Unchanged: Conclusion:	CO air butt length, N puffs, puff duration, cig. consumption, 'maximum puff effort' nic. regulation supported
Stepney, 1981	19	0.7 mg nic.; 11.0 mg tar; 13.0 mg CO 1.1 mg nic.; 10.0 mg tar; 6.0 mg CO 3-week switching periods Puff duplication	Decrease in: Unchanged: Conclusion:	mouth nic. intake, urine nic. cig. consumption, butt lengths, N puffs, puff volume, mouth level tar intake tar intake compensation?
Herming, Jones, Bachman and Mines, 1981	24	0.4 mg nic.; 1.2 mg nic.; 2.5 mg nic.; equal tar delivery 3 test days 1st cig./day tested	Decrease in: Increase in: Unchanged: Conclusion:	smoking time puff volume, CO boost, heart rate response N puffs, puff interval incomplete regulation

(*Continued*)

Table 1 (*Continued*)

Reference	n	Cigarettes and design	Changes with decreasing nicotine yields
Fagerström, 1982	12	0.53 mg nic.; 4.8 mg tar; 4.0 mg CO 1.10 mg nic.; 4.8 mg tar; 4.0 mg CO 4-week switching periods	Decrease in: CO level Unchanged: cig. consumption, plasma nic., plasma cotinine, heart rate Conclusion: nic. regulation depends on nic. dependence
Benowitz, Kuyt and Jacob, 1982b	7	0.4 mg nic.; 31.8 mg tar; 14.9 mg CO 2.5 mg nic.; 29.6 mg tar; 16.1 mg CO 3-day switching periods	Decrease in: plasma nic. Increase in: CO level Conclusion: down-regulation more effective than up-regulation
Griffiths, Henningfield and Bigelow, 1982	3	0.2 mg nic.; 25.4 mg tar; 13.7 mg CO 0.7 mg nic.; 27.1 mg tar; 14.1 mg CO 0.9 mg nic.; 27.1 mg tar; 17.0 mg CO 1.6 mg nic.; 28.1 mg tar; 15.0 mg CO 12-hour sessions	Decrease in: subjective strength Unchanged: interbeat interval, N puffs
Gust and Pickens, 1982	6	0.32 mg nic.; 24.7 mg tar; 14.9 mg CO 1.25 mg nic.; 24.5 mg tar; 14.9 mg CO 2.50 mg nic.; 29.6 mg tar; 16.1 mg CO	Increase in: puff volume, puff duration, N puffs, CO boost Conclusion: insufficient regulation
Sepkovic, Haley, Axelrad and Wynder, 1983	7	Subject's standard brand cig. Cig. with relative nic. increase of 0.34 mg	Increase in: With increased nic. yield: plasma nic., thiocyanate, COHb, heart rate response Unchanged: cigarette consumption Conclusion: incomplete down-regulation
McBride, Guyatt, Kirkham and Cumming, 1984	9	0.55 mg nic.; 8.1 mg tar; 10.3 mg CO 0.90 mg nic.; 7.8 mg tar; 9.8 mg CO 4 sessions 2 cig. per session	Decrease in: salivary nic., butt nic. Increase in: puff duration, puff volume, CO baseline Unchanged: CO boost, respiratory inhalation Conclusion: incomplete regulation

Reference	n	Cigarettes and design	Changes with decreasing nicotine yields
Robinson, Young and Rickert, 1984	22	0.92 mg nic.; 10.3 mg tar; 10.8 mg CO 1.03 mg nic.; 15.4 mg tar; 10.8 mg CO 5-week switching period Analyses after 15-hour deprivation	Decrease in: CO air, COHb, (slight) salivary thiocyanate Unchanged: cig. consumption, salivary cotinine, plasma cotinine Conclusion: incomplete regulation

Abbreviations. cig.: cigarette; nic.: nicotine; N puffs: number of puffs per cigarette

Table 2 Effects of nicotinic-pharmacologic manipulation on smoking behavior

Author	n	Treatment	Results	
Lucchesi, Schuster and Emley, 1967	4	i.v. nic. bitartrate 1 mg over 20 min every 60 min 6-hour sessions	Unchanged:	cig. consumption
	5	2 mg for the 1st hour 1 mg during each of the following hours	Decrease in: Increase in:	cig. consumption butt weight
	4	1 mg over 14 min every 46 min	Decrease in:	cig. consumption
Jarvik, Glick and Nakamura, 1970	7	Capsules with 10 mg nic. tartrate 5 capsules per day	Decrease in: Unchanged:	cig. consumption butt weight, 'strength,' 'quality'
Stolerman, Goldfarb, Fink and Jarvik, 1973	6	Mecamylamine hydrochloride: 7.5 to 22.5 mg in 5-mg increments Pentolinium: 100 mg; 150 mg 2-hour sessions	Decrease in: Increase in: Conclusion:	satisfaction (only by mecamylamine) cig. consumption nic. acts as the primary reinforcer
Kozlowski, Jarvik and Gritz, 1975	56	Nic.-containing chewing gum: 1 mg nic.; 4 mg nic. Nic.-containing cig.: 0.3 mg nic.; 14 mg tar 1.3 mg nic.; 19 mg tar	Decrease in: Increase in: Conclusion:	N puffs; effect greater after 4-mg nic. gum than after 1-mg nic. gum latency to smoking greater after high- than low-nic. cig. nic. regulation supported
Kumar, Cooke, Lader and Russell, 1977	12	12 puffs with 5-s inhalation: 2.6-mg nic. cig. (2×1.3 mg); 1.3-mg nic. cig. i.v. nic. in 10 5-s pulses: 0 mg nic.; 0.035 mg/kg; 0.07 mg/kg	Decrease in: Unchanged: Conclusion:	total puff volume, volume per puff, N puffs with inhalation preload no effects for i.v. preloads other rewarding tobacco constituents than nic.?

Author	n	Treatment	Results
Russell, Wilson, Feyerabend and Cole, 1976	41	Nic.-containing chewing gum	Decrease in: cig. consumption, COHb Increase in: plasma nic.
Henningfield, Miyasato and Jasinski, 1983	6	i.v. nic. hydrogen tartrate Self-administration according to a FR-10 schedule 0 mg; 0.75 mg; 1.5 mg; 3.0 mg per injection	Decrease in: cig. consumption, N puffs (analysed in three subjects) Conclusion: self-administration occurs; nic. acts as an integral part of cig. smoking behavior
Rose, Herskovic, Trilling and Jarvik, 1985a	10	Transdermal nic.: 0 mg; 4 mg; 8 mg	Decrease in: craving, nic. preference (after 8 mg nic.) Unchanged: total particulate matter intake
Nemeth-Coslett, Henningfield, O'Keeffe, and Griffiths, 1986	8	Mecamylamine: 2.5 mg; 5.0 mg; 10.0 mg; 20.0 mg 90-min sessions	With increasing dose of mecamylamine: Decrease in: puff interval Increase in: N puffs, number of puffs per session, session CO boost, cig. consumption
Nemeth-Coslett and Henningfield, 1986	5	Nic.-containing chewing gum: 0 mg; 2 mg; 4 mg Nine 12-hour sessions	Decrease in: cig. consumption, N puffs Unchanged: CO level

Abbreviations. cig.: cigarette; nic.: nicotine; N puffs: number of puffs per cigarette; i.v.: intravenous

Pharmacological manipulations

Table 2 reviews studies employing nicotine-specific pharmacological agents. The majority of the studies was successful in influencing smoking behavior by presmoking administration of nicotine, or by the centrally acting nicotine antagonist, mecamylamine. The route used for preloading is important, since intravenous injection gave less clearcut effects than loading by smoke inhalation. Unfortunately, in several cases there is no nicotine plasma measurement and several samples are small.

The role of nicotine: some preliminary conclusions

The studies in Tables 1 and 2 demonstrate that nicotine has an important role in the maintenance of smoking behavior. But the absence of evidence for the perfect behavioral compensation for nicotine suggests that smokers do not titrate to an exactly determined level of plasma nicotine or nicotine bolus. Rather, titration operates within a range which is acceptable to the smoker. In a study involving switching to ultra-low nicotine cigarettes West, Russell, Jarvis and Feyerabend (1984) found that a drop in plasma nicotine of about 60 percent was associated with a reduction in heart rate and an increase in hunger, in the absence of other common withdrawal symptoms such as irritability, depression or ability to concentrate. Such data confirm our view that subject reactions to nicotine variation operate within a range of tolerance. The results summarized in Tables 1 and 2 must lead us to consider factors other than nicotine which could be responsible for unexplained effects in smoking studies. These might include other pharmacologically active substances in the smoke, such as acetaldehyde, or motivational aspects of smoking such as taste of the smoke, draw resistance, or yet unknown satiation mechanisms including perhaps a crucial role for tar intake.

INDIVIDUAL VARIABILITY IN SMOKING BEHAVIOR

Several authors have claimed that patterns of puffing and respiratory inhalation are highly invariant characteristics of individual smokers (Creighton et al., 1978; Nil et al., 1984; McBride et al., 1984). As Figure 2 demonstrates such intraindividual invariance contrasts strongly with interindividual variability. Different motivations for smoking could underlie the between-smoker differences in smoking pattern. It follows that a taxonomy of subgroups of smokers would be worthwhile, since such groups might not only have different motives for smoking, but would respond differentially to experimental manipulations.

The most obvious characteristic for differentiation could be nicotine dependence. A few studies have compared smokers on the basis of objective biochemical measures of smoke intake; for example, Pomerleau, Fertig and Shanahan (1983) compared smokers with high and low levels of plasma cotinine and found that high and low cotinine smokers differed in several ways: cigarette consumption; craving on withdrawal; compensation during smoking after switching; and degree of nicotine heart rate tolerance. Our own study, comparing smokers on the basis of CO absorption, revealed that high absorbers showed a more intensive pattern of puffing (volume, peak flow and peak pressure), a higher daily cigarette consumption, and a shorter latency to smoking the first cigarette of the day (Nil et al., 1986b). Daily consumption and latency to first cigarette have been found to be useful variables for classifying subjects (Fagerström and Bates, 1981; Kozlowski, Director and Harford, 1981). Indeed, group differences extend to variables such as daily coffee consumption (higher for high CO absorbers) or a healthy eating habit index (lower for high CO absorbers) but, interestingly, not to personality measures or Type A (coronary-prone) behavior.

Our two groups of smokers showed differences in smoking behavior and heart rate response after fifteen-hour (overnight–morning) and four-hour (afternoon) deprivation. While both groups increased puff volume and duration and their score on a subjective need to smoke scale, high CO absorbers decreased CO boost following fifteen-hour deprivation, with a concomitant increase in heart rate response. The low CO group showed no such effects (Nil, Woodson and Bättig, 1987). Thus there was little evidence for compensatory adaptation on all measures, and our findings again demonstrate the low interdependence between puffing variables and alveolar smoke absorption. It is possible that the two groups, either because of nicotine consumption or dependence, develop a different relationship between nicotine intake and heart rate response.

A recent study by Michel, Nil, Buzzi, Woodson and Bättig (1987) compared high and low CO absorbers on information processing performance while monitoring ERPs, and found a lower baseline performance but a somewhat greater smoking-induced increase in performance in the high CO absorbers.

CONCLUSIONS AND FUTURE RESEARCH TRENDS

The studies reviewed so far lead to the conclusion that the effects of nicotine on smoking motivation must be seen in close interaction with other non-nicotinic factors which, in turn, can act as potent smoking behavior determinants. A recent experiment showed independent effects of cigarette smoke taste and cigarette smoke yields on puffing and inhalation (Nil and Bättig, unpublished results). Similar conclusions come from other lines of research showing that the manipulation of the sensory cues of smoking significantly affect craving and smoking behavior (Rose and Hickman, in press; Rose, Tashkin, Ertle, Zinser and Lafer, 1985b).

The great individual variance in smoking behavior thus seems to reflect individual equilibria in the importance of a possibly wide range of smoking motives. Furthermore, it appears that changes in smoking patterns in response to different smoking situations (stress) produce shifts in the importance of smoking motives on an individual basis. This multivariate model of smoking behavior may be related briefly to current problems in smoking cessation. Over recent years much effort has been spent in developing alternate routes of nicotine administration, including nicotine-containing chewing gums (Russell et al., 1976; Schneider, Jarvik, Forsythe, Read, Elliott and Schweiger, 1983), nasal nicotine (Russell, Jarvis, Devitt and Feyerabend, 1981), transdermal nicotine (Rose et al., 1985a) or nicotine-containing aerosols (Perkins, Epstein, Stiller, Jennings, Christiansen and McCarthy, 1986). It is beyond the scope of this chapter to review the outcome of such attempts; however, it has become clear that these methods have failed to drastically improve cessation rates (Schwartz, 1987). Further research should therefore lead to a better differentiation between routes of nicotine administration and dose, as well as between nicotinic and non-nicotinic smoking motives. This might lead to a better understanding of individual differences in smoking behavior which, in turn, might help to offer more specific and individually tailored smoking cessation strategies.

A series of other questions, however, requires further attention in future research. What is the impact of nicotine tolerance, as demonstrated for heart rate and blood pressure, on smoking behavior? Can similar tolerance effects be suggested for psychopharmacological smoking effects? What is the impact of learning and conditioned responses on smoking? Are such processes involved in the development of smoking withdrawal symptoms, as has been suggested to be the case for alcohol and opiate withdrawal?

Finally, almost nothing is known about possible relationships between patterns of puffing and respiratory inhalation and the development of smoking-related diseases. In a retrospective study Medici et al. (1985) described lower smoking-induced CO boosts in lung cancer patients than in controls, and shorter puff inhalatory intervals (time during which the puffed smoke bolus remains in the mouth before being inhaled) in patients suffering from chronic bronchitis. Prospective studies are needed to further clarify such relations.

REFERENCES

Adams, L., Lee, C., Rawbone, R., and Guz, A. (1983). Patterns of smoking: measurement and variability in asymptomatic smokers. *Clinical Science*, **65**, 383–392.

Armitage, A.K., and Turner, D.M. (1970). Absorption of nicotine in cigarette and cigar smoke through the oral mucosa. *Nature*, **226**, 1231–1232.

Ashton, H., Stepney, R., and Thompson, J.W. (1979). Self-titration by cigarette smokers. *British Medical Journal*, **2**, 357–360.

Bättig, K. (1980). The smoking habit and psychopharmacological effects of nicotine. *Activitas Nervosa Superior*, **22**, 274–288.

Bättig, K. (1981). Smoking and the behavioral effects of nicotine. *Trends in Pharmacological Sciences*, **2**, 145–147.

Bättig, K., Buzzi, R., and Nil, R. (1982). Smoke yield of cigarettes and puffing behavior in men and women. *Psychopharmacology*, **76**, 139–148.

Benowitz, N.L., and Jacob, P. (1985). Nicotine renal excretion rate influences nicotine intake during cigarette smoking. *Journal of Pharmacology and Experimental Therapeutics*, **234**, 153–155.

Benowitz, N.L., Jacob, P., Jones, R.T., and Rosenberg, J. (1982a). Interindividual variability in the metabolism and cardiovascular effects of nicotine in man. *Journal of Pharmacology and Experimental Therapeutics*, **221**, 368–372.

Benowitz, N.L., Kuyt, F., and Jacob, P. (1982b). Circadian blood nicotine concentrations during cigarette smoking. *Clinical Pharmacology and Therapeutics*, **32**, 758–764.

Benowitz, N.L., Kuyt, F., Jacob, P., Jones, R.T., and Osman, A.-L. (1983). Cotinine disposition and effects. *Clinical Pharmacology and Therapeutics*, **34**, 604–611.

Benowitz, N.L., Jacob, P., Yu, L., Talcott, R., Hall, S., and Jones, R.T. (1986). Reduced tar, nicotine, and carbon monoxide exposure while smoking ultralow- but not low-yield cigarettes. *Journal of the American Medical Association*, **256**, 241–246.

Creighton, D.E., and Lewis, P.H. (1978). The effect of smoking pattern on smoke deliveries. In: R.E. Thornton (ed.), *Smoking Behaviour: Physiological and Psychological Influences*, Edinburgh: Churchill Livingstone, pp. 301–314.

Creighton, D.E., Noble, M.J., and Whewell, R.T. (1978). Instruments to measure, record and duplicate human smoking patterns. In: R.E. Thornton (ed.), *Smoking Behaviour: Physiological and Psychological Influences*, pp. 277–288. Edinburgh: Churchill Livingstone.

Cumming, G., Guyatt, A.R., and Holmes, M.A. (1978). The absorption of carbon monoxide from the conducting airways of the human lung. In: R.E. Thornton (ed.), *Smoking Behaviour: Physiological and Psychological Influences*. Edinburgh: Churchill Livingstone, pp. 168–170.

Dunn, P.J., and Freiesleben, E.R. (1978). The effects of nicotine-enhanced cigarettes on human smoking parameters and alveolar carbon monoxide levels. In: R.E. Thornton (ed.), *Smoking Behaviour: Physiological and Psychological Influences*. Edinburgh: Churchill Livingstone, pp. 195–202.

Ebert, R.V., McNabb, M.E., McCusker, K.T., and Snow, S.L. (1983). Amount of nicotine and carbon monoxide inhaled by smokers of low-tar, low-nicotine cigarettes. *Journal of the American Medical Association*, **250**, 2840–2842.

Epstein, L.H., Ossip, D.J., Coleman, D., Hughes, J., and Wiist, W. (1981). Measurement of smoking topography during withdrawal or deprivation. *Behavior Therapy*, **12**, 507–519.

Fagerström, K.O. (1982). Effects of a nicotine-enriched cigarette on nicotine titration, daily cigarette consumption, and levels of carbon monoxide, cotinine, and nicotine. *Psychopharmacology*, **77**, 164–167.

Fagerström, K.O., and Bates, S. (1981). Compensation and effective smoking by different nicotine dependent smokers. *Addictive Behaviors*, **6**, 331–336.

Feyerabend, C., Ings, R.M.J., and Russell, M.A.H. (1985). Nicotine pharmacokinetics and its application to intake from smoking. *British Journal of Clinical Pharmacology*, **19**, 239–247.

Garfinkel, L. (1979). Changes in the cigarette consumption of smokers in relation to changes in tar/nicotine content of cigarette smoked. *American Journal of Public Health*, **69**, 1274–1276.

Goldfarb, T.L., Jarvik, M.E., and Glick, S.D. (1970). Cigarette nicotine content as a determinant of human smoking behavior. *Psychopharmacologia*, **17**, 89–93.

Gori, G.B., and Lynch, C.J. (1985). Analytical cigarette yields as predictors of smoke bioavailability. *Regulatory Toxicology and Pharmacology*, **5**, 314–326.

Griffiths, R.R., Henningfield, J.E., and Bigelow, G.E. (1982). Human cigarette smoking: manipulation of number of puffs per bout, interbout interval and nicotine dose. *Journal of Pharmacology and Experimental Therapeutics*, **220**, 256–265.

Gritz, E.R., Rose, J.E., and Jarvik, M.E. (1983). Regulation of tobacco smoke intake with paced cigarette presentation. *Pharmacology, Biochemistry and Behavior*, **18**, 457–462.

Guillerm, R., and Radziszewski, E. (1978). Analysis of smoking pattern including intake of carbon monoxide and influences of changes in cigarette design. In: R.E. Thornton (ed.), *Smoking Behaviour: Physiological and Psychological Influences*, Edinburgh: Churchill Livingstone, pp. 361–370.

Gust, S.W., and Pickens, R.W. (1982). Does cigarette nicotine yield affect puff volume? *Clinical Pharmacology and Therapeutics*, **32**, 418–422.

Henningfield, J.E. (1984). Behavioral pharmacology of cigarette smoking. *Advances in Behavioral Pharmacology*, **4**, 131–210.

Henningfield, J.E., and Griffiths, R.R. (1979). A preparation for the experimental analysis of human cigarette smoking behavior. *Behavior Research Methods and Instrumentation*, **11**, 538–544.

Henningfield, J.E., Miyasato, K., and Jasinski, D.R. (1983). Cigarette smokers self-administer intravenous nicotine. *Pharmacology, Biochemistry and Behavior*, **19**, 887–890.

Herning, R.I., Hunt, J.S., and Jones, R.T. (1983a). The importance of inhalation volume when measuring smoking behavior. *Behavior Research Methods and Instrumentation*, **15**, 561–568.

Herning, R.I., Jones, R.T., Bachman, J., and Mines, A.H. (1981). Puff volume increases when smoking low nicotine cigarettes. *British Medical Journal*, **283**, 181–189.

Herning, R.I., Jones, R.T., Benowitz, N.L., and Mines, A.H. (1983b). How a cigarette is smoked determines blood nicotine levels. *Clinical Pharmacology and Therapeutics*, **33**, 84–90.

Hopkins, R., Wood, L.E., and Sinclair, N.M. (1984). Evaluation of methods to estimate cigarette smoke uptake. *Clinical Pharmacology and Therapeutics*, **36**, 788–795.

Jarvik, M.E., Glick, S.D., and Nakamura, R.K. (1970). Inhibition of cigarette smoking by orally administered nicotine. *Clinical Pharmacology and Therapeutics*, **11**, 574–576.

Jarvik, M.E., Popek, P., Schneider, N.G., Baer-Weiss, V., and Gritz, E.R. (1978). Can cigarette size and nicotine content influence smoking and puffing rates? *Psychopharmacology*, **58**, 303–306.

Jarvis, M.J., Russell, M.A.H., and Saloojee, Y. (1980). Expired air carbon monoxide: a simple breath test of tobacco smoke intake. *British Medical Journal*, **1**, 484–485.

Kozlowski, L.T., Director, J., and Harford, M.A. (1981). Tobacco dependence, restraint and time to the first cigarette of the day. *Addictive Behaviors*, **6**, 307–312.

Kozlowski, L.T., Jarvik, M.E., and Gritz, E.R. (1975). Nicotine regulation and cigarette smoking. *Clinical Pharmacology and Therapeutics*, **17**, 93–97.

Kumar, R., Cooke, E.C., Lader, M.H., and Russell, M.A.H. (1977). Is nicotine important in tobacco smoking? *Clinical Pharmacology and Therapeutics*, **21**, 520–529.

Lubin, J.H., Blot, W.J., Berrino, F., Flamant, R., Gillis, Ch. R., Kunze, M., Schmahl, D., and Visco, G. (1984). Patterns of lung cancer risk according to type of cigarette smoked. *International Journal of Cancer*, **33**, 569–576.

Lucchesi, B.R., Schuster, C.R., and Emley, G.S. (1967). The role of nicotine as a determinant of cigarette smoking frequency in man with observations of certain cardiovascular effects associated with the tobacco alkaloid. *Clinical Pharmacology and Therapeutics*, **8**, 789–796.

McBride, M.J., Guyatt, A.R., Kirkham, J.T., and Cumming, G. (1984). Assessment of smoking behaviour and ventilation with cigarettes of differing nicotine yields. *Clinical Science*, **67**, 619–631.

Medici, T.C., Unger, S., and Rüegger, M. (1985). Smoking pattern of smokers with and without tobacco-smoke-related lung diseases. *American Review of Respiratory Disease*, **131**, 385–388.

Michel, Ch., Nil, R., Buzzi, R., Woodson, P.P., and Bättig, K. (1987). Rapid information processing and concomitant event-related brain potentials in smokers differing in CO absorption. *Neuropsychobiology*, **17**, 161–168.

Nemeth-Coslett, R., and Griffiths, R. (1984a). Determinants of puff duration in cigarette smokers: I. *Pharmacology, Biochemistry and Behavior*, **20**, 965–971.

Nemeth-Coslett, R., and Griffiths, R.R. (1984b). Determinants of puff duration in cigarette smokers: II. *Pharmacology, Biochemistry and Behavior*, **21**, 903–912.

Nemeth-Coslett, R., and Griffiths, R.R. (1985). Effects of cigarette rod length on puff volume and carbon monoxide delivery in cigarette smokers. *Drug and Alcohol Dependence*, **15**, 1–13.

Nemeth-Coslett, R., and Henningfield, J.E. (1986). Effects of nicotine chewing gum on cigarette smoking and subjective and physiologic effects. *Clinical Pharmacology and Therapeutics*, **39**, 625–630.

Nemeth-Coslett, R., Henningfield, J.E., O'Keeffe, M.K., and Griffiths, R.R. (1986). Effects of mecamylamine on human cigarette smoking and subjective ratings. *Psychopharmacology*, **88**, 420–425.

Nil, R., Buzzi, R., and Bättig, K. (1984). Effects of single doses of alcohol and caffeine on cigarette smoke puffing behavior. *Pharmacology, Biochemistry and Behavior*, **20**, 583–590.

Nil, R., Buzzi, R., and Bättig, K. (1986a). Effects of different cigarette smoke yields on puffing and inhalation: is the measurement of inhalation volumes relevant for smoke absorption? *Pharmacology, Biochemistry and Behavior*, **24**, 587–595.

Nil, R., Woodson, P.P., and Bättig, K. (1986b). Smoking behaviour and personality patterns of smokers with low and high CO absorption. *Clinical Science*, **71**, 595–603.

Nil, R., Woodson, P.P., and Bättig, K. (1987). Effects of smoking deprivation on smoking behavior and heart rate response in high and low CO absorbing smokers. *Psychopharmacology*, **92**, 465–469.

Pearson, M.G., Chamberlain, M.J., Morgan, W.K.C., and Vinitski, S. (1985). Regional deposition of particles in the lung during cigarette smoking in humans. *Journal of Applied Physiology*, **59**, 1828–1833.

Perkins, K.A., Epstein, L.H., Stiller, R., Jennings, J.R., Christiansen, C., and

McCarthy, T. (1986). An aerosol spray alternative to cigarette smoking in the study of the behavioral and physiological effects of nicotine. *Behavior Research Methods, Instruments and Computers*, **18**, 420–426.

Pomerleau, O.F., Fertig, J.B., and Shanahan, A.O. (1983). Nicotine dependence in cigarette smoking: an empirically-based, multivariate model. *Pharmacology, Biochemistry and Behavior*, **19**, 291–299.

Pomerleau, O.F., and Pomerleau, C.S. (1984). Neuroregulators and the reinforcement of smoking: towards a biobehavioral explanation. *Neuroscience and Biobehavioral Reviews*, **8**, 503–513.

Rawbone, R.G., Murphy, K., Tate, M.E., and Kane, S.J. (1978). The analysis of smoking parameters: inhalation and absorption of tobacco smoke in studies of human smoking behaviour. In: R.E. Thornton (ed.), *Smoking Behaviour: Physiological and Psychological Influences*, pp. 171–194. Edinburgh: Churchill Livingstone.

Robinson, J.C., Young, J.C., and Rickert, W.S. (1984). Maintain levels of nicotine but reduce other smoke constituents: a formula for 'less-hazardous' cigarettes? *Preventive Medicine*, **13**, 437–445.

Rose, J.E., and Hickman, C.S. Citric acid aerosol as a potential smoking cessation aid. *Chest* (In press).

Rose, J.E., Herskovic, J.E., Trilling, Y., and Jarvik, M.E. (1985a). Transdermal nicotine reduces cigarette craving and nicotine preference. *Clinical Pharmacology and Therapeutics*, **38**, 450–456.

Rose, J.E., Tashkin, D.P., Ertle, A., Zinser, M.C., and Lafer, R. (1985b). Sensory blockade of smoking satisfaction. *Pharmacology, Biochemistry and Behavior*, **23**, 289–293.

Rosenberg, J., Benowitz, N.L., Jacob, P., and Wilson, K.M. (1980). Disposition kinetics and effects of intravenous nicotine. *Clinical Pharmacology and Therapeutics*, **28**, 517–522.

Russell, M.A.H., Wilson, C., Feyerabend, C., and Cole, P.V. (1976). Effect of nicotine chewing-gum on smoking behavior and as an aid to cigarette withdrawal. *British Medical Journal*, **2**, 391–393.

Russell, M.A.H., Jarvis, M., Iyer, R., and Feyerabend, C. (1980). Relation of nicotine yield of cigarettes to blood nicotine concentrations in smokers. *British Medical Journal*, **280**, 972–976.

Russell, M.A.H., Jarvis, M.J., Devitt, G., and Feyerabend, C. (1981). Nicotine intake by snuff users. *British Medical Journal*, **283**, 814–817.

Russell, M.A.H., Jarvis, M.J., Feyerabend, C., and Saloojee, Y. (1986). Reduction of tar, nicotine and carbon monoxide intake in low tar smokers. *Journal of Epidemiology and Community Health*, **40**, 80–85.

Saloojee, Y., Vesey, C.J., Cole, P.V., and Russell, M.A.H. (1982). Carboxyhaemoglobin and plasma thiocyanate: complementary indicators of smoking behaviour. *Thorax*, **37**, 521–525.

Saumet, J.L., and Dittmar, A. (1985). Heat loss and anticipatory finger vasoconstriction induced by a smoking of a single cigarette. *Physiology and Behavior*, **35**, 229–232.

Schlotzhauer, W.S., and Chortyk, O.T. (1983). Effects of varied smoking machine parameters on deliveries of total particulate matter and selected smoke constituents from an ultra low-tar cigarette. *Journal of Analytical Toxicology*, **7**, 92–95.

Schneider, N.G., Jarvik, M.E., Forsythe, A.B., Read, L.L., Elliott, M.L., and Schweiger, A. (1983). Nicotine gum in smoking cessation: a placebo-controlled, double-blind trial. *Addictive Behaviors*, **8**, 253–261.

Schulz, W., and Seehofer, F. (1978). Smoking behaviour in Germany—the analysis of cigarette butts (KIPA). In: R.E. Thornton (ed.), *Smoking Behaviour: Physiological and Psychological Influences*, Edinburgh: Churchill Livingstone, pp. 259–276.

Schwartz, J.L. (1987). Review and evaluation of smoking cessation methods: The United States and Canada, 1978–1985. Department of Health and Human Services, USA: Division of Cancer Prevention and Control, NIH Publication No. 87–2940.

Sepkovic, D.W., Haley, N.J., Axelrad, C.M., and Wynder, E.L. (1983). Cigarette smoking as a risk for cardiovascular disease III: Biochemical effects with higher nicotine yield cigarettes. *Addictive Behaviors*, **8**, 59–66.

Stepney, R. (1980). Consumption of cigarettes of reduced tar and nicotine delivery. *British Journal of Addiction*, **75**, 81–88.

Stepney, R. (1981). Would a medium-nicotine, low-tar cigarette be less hazardous to health? *British Medical Journal*, **283**, 1–12.

Stolerman, I.P., Goldfarb, T., Fink, R., and Jarvik, M.E. (1973). Influencing cigarette smoking with nicotine antagonists. *Psychopharmacologia*, **28**, 247–259.

Suter, T.W., Buzzi, R., and Bättig, K. (1983). Cardiovascular effects of smoking cigarettes with different nicotine deliveries. *Psychopharmacology*, **80**, 106–112.

Sutton, S.R., Russell, M.A.H., Iyer, R., Feyerabend, C., and Saloojee, Y. (1982). Relationship between cigarette yields, puffing patterns, and smoke intake: evidence for tar compensation? *British Medical Journal*, **285**, 600–603.

Tobin, M.J., and Sackner, M.A. (1982). Monitoring smoking patterns of low and high tar cigarettes with inductive plethysmography. *American Review of Respiratory Disease*, **126**, 258–264.

Wald, N.J., Idle, M., Boreham, J., and Bailey, A. (1980). Inhaling habits among smokers of different types of cigarette. *Thorax*, **35**, 925–928.

Wesnes, K., and Warburton, D.M. (1983). Smoking, nicotine and human performance. *Pharmacology and Therapeutics*, **21**, 189–208.

West, R.J., Russell, M.A.H., Jarvis, M.J., and Feyerabend, C. (1984). Does switching to an ultra-low nicotine cigarette induce nicotine withdrawal effects? *Psychopharmacology*, **84**, 120–123.

Woodman, G., Newman, S.P., Pavia, D., and Clarke, S.W. (1984). Temperature and calibration corrections to puff volume measurements in cigarette smoking. *Physiology and Medical Biology*, **29**, 1437–1440.

10

Attentional Processing

DAVID M. WARBURTON
and
ANNE C. WALTERS

ABSTRACT

This chapter discusses the effects of smoking on human attentional processing both in the laboratory and at work. The underlying physiology which may give rise to these effects is examined with reference both to animal and human studies. Individual differences in the effects of smoking are also discussed, and it is argued that smokers use the attentional effects in order to manipulate the efficiency of their mental processing and thus improve performance.

INTRODUCTION

This chapter deals with the effects of smoking on human attentional processing. The first section discusses the main paradigms used to measure attentional processing. Succeeding sections consider the effects of smoking on performance in sustained attention, selective attention and perceptual intrusion situations.

While the effects of smoking clearly improve group performance in laboratory studies, it is important to assess whether smoking has benefits in more 'natural situations' and for all individuals. Thus we also consider the question of ecological validity and individual differences.

The final sections discuss how smoking acts on the neural mechanisms that

Smoking and Human Behavior, Edited by T. Ney and A. Gale
© 1989 John Wiley & Sons Ltd

are believed to be involved in attentional processing, and considers how smokers use nicotine as a resource to control their brain state to obtain more efficient attentional processing.

MEASUREMENT OF ATTENTION

In many discussions of the concept of attention it is implied that attention is a unitary process of selecting information, but it is not, and modern theorizing emphasizes that attention should not be 'thought of as a single entity' (Kinchla, 1980, page 214). In his cogent discussion Kinchla (1980) suggests that three kinds of investigation bear on the issue of selectivity in information processing. The first group are sustained attention tasks, which include selective monitoring. Second are studies of 'attention switching' or selective attention, which involve a shift from processing information from one source to processing that from another. The third are experiments studying 'perceptual intrusions' and principally involve the Stroop test.

SUSTAINED ATTENTION

Vigilance tasks are the fundamental paradigm for defining sustained attention as a behavioral category (Jerison, 1977). Vigilance tasks require attention to be directed to one or more sources of input for long periods of time, and the subject is required to detect and respond to small and infrequent changes in the input. Performance in vigilance situations is often assessed in terms of the hit rate, i.e. the proportion of signals correctly detected and the false-alarm rate, i.e. the number of occasions on which a signal is reported when one has not been presented. Measures of stimulus sensitivity and response criterion can be derived from the hit rate and the false alarm rate using signal detection theory to assess performance.

During a typical vigilance session the hit rate decreases (known as the vigilance decrement), but it is important to know if there is also a decrease in false alarms, which would mean a criterion shift. On the other hand, if the hit rate falls but the false-alarm rate does not, there is a reduction in stimulus sensitivity. In some of our studies of smoking and vigilance we have used the Mackworth clock test (Mackworth, 1950), which produces a reliable vigilance decrement. We found that smoking helped smokers to reduce the decrement and maintain their stimulus sensitivity to experimental targets in the 80-min visual vigilance task, whereas sensitivity dropped markedly for a group of nonsmokers and also for a group of smokers who were not allowed to smoke (Wesnes and Warburton, 1978).

In a second study, smokers maintained their initial level of stimulus sensitivity to auditory targets over an 80-min vigilance session when they smoked cigarettes, but when they performed the task smoking nicotine-free cigarettes, their sensitivity decreased over time (Wesnes and Warburton, 1978). A similar study with a higher target density, by Mangan and Golding (1978), found essentially the same result, that smoking maintained stimulus sensitivity.

If nicotine is the essential smoke ingredient, nicotine tablets should be effective in the visual vigilance task. Nicotine tablets helped reduce the vigilance decrement which occurred over time in a placebo control condition by maintaining stimulus sensitivity (Wesnes, Warburton and Matz, 1983). Further, the tablets produced the same effects in nonsmokers, light smokers and heavy smokers.

The effects of smoking on sustained reaction-time performance were studied by Frankenhaeuser, Myrsten, Post and Johansson (1971). The experimental sessions lasted 80 min, during which subjects continually performed a simple visual reaction time test. The task therefore had several properties of a vigilance task. In the nonsmoking condition the speed of reaction decreased over time, whereas in the smoking condition there was little change over the session, and the difference in reaction times between the two conditions was significant.

Another similar study of reaction times (Myrsten and Andersson, 1978) compared the effects of smoking in simple and complex reaction time tasks. In a simple reaction time task, smoking prevented the significant increase in reaction time which occurred over time in the nonsmoking condition. In a complex reaction time task, smoking significantly reduced reaction time, whereas reaction times increased nonsignificantly over the periods in the nonsmoking condition.

Williams (1980) tested the effects of smoking on crossing out each letter E found in sheets of randomly ordered letters arranged in lines of 30 letters. A highly significant effect of smoking was found for letter cancellation.

One of the most widely used cognitive vigilance tasks is the Bakan task (Bakan, 1959), in which a series of digits are presented at the rate of one per second, from which subjects are required to detect certain specified three-digit sequences. This task was originally derived from Wittenborn's (1943) factor analysis of attention tests, in which Wittenborn found that picking out various sequences of numbers or letters was most heavily loaded on what he called an 'attention' or 'mental concentration' factor.

We have used a version of the Bakan test, the rapid visual information processing test, to assess vigilance performance, both before and after smoking. We measured the speed and the accuracy of cognitive processing in terms of hit rate. In this test, measures of stimulus sensitivity and response criterion cannot be calculated because the number of false alarms is too low. Smoking improved speed and accuracy above baseline levels, whereas both not smoking, or smoking nicotine-free cigarettes, resulted in a decline in speed and accuracy below baseline levels (Wesnes and Warburton, 1983b).

Higher nicotine-delivery cigarettes improved performance more than low-delivery ones, suggesting once again that nicotine is the important smoke constituent for such effects (Wesnes and Warburton, 1984b).

Accordingly, we gave a range of nicotine tablets to nonsmokers, who then performed the rapid visual information processing task used to study cigarette smoking (Wesnes and Warburton, 1984a). We found that the highest dose of nicotine produced a performance improvement closely resembling that produced by smoking. Unpublished studies have shown that a lower plasma nicotine is obtained with the tablets, compared with pulmonary absorption from tobacco smoke (Russell, unpublished). Thus this study provides strong evidence that nicotine plays a major role in the improvements in sustained attention tasks that are produced by smoking.

SELECTIVE ATTENTION

Sustained and selective attention abilities seem largely independent. Moray (1969) correlated performance on the rapid visual information process with shadowing efficiency in a selective listening task. Although some correlation was found between performance on the tests, Moray concluded that the relation between the two kinds of attention was negligible.

Selective-attention tasks involve either focused or divided attention (Kahneman, 1973). Focused attention tasks require subjects to attend to one source of information to the exclusion of others. Divided attention tasks require subjects to divide their monitoring between two or more sources of information. Resource theories (Kahneman, 1973; Navon and Gopher, 1979; Norman and Bobrow, 1975) were designed to explain limitations on performance in dual tasks, where the subject is required to work at more than one thing at a time. They assume that the total amount of resources which can be deployed at any time is limited.

Evidence that smoking and, by inference, that nicotine, increases resources, comes from a study by Andersson and Hockey (1977). They presented words in different positions on a computer screen. In one condition, subjects had to remember the words in presentation order only. In the second condition, subjects were asked to remember the words, word order and location. In the first (words-only) condition, there were no differences between the nicotine and no-nicotine groups for the percentage of words recalled in the correct order, or for the percentage recalled correctly, regardless of word order. However, position on the screen was recalled significantly less well with nicotine. When the subjects were asked to attend to all three aspects of the material, the groups did not differ significantly in their recall, although there was a trend for location to be recalled better after nicotine than when deprived. This study suggests that nicotine can enable more selective processing of information, but only of information that is thought to be relevant by the subjects, i.e. nicotine is not acting via a passive processing system which merely responds to all information presented, but is making resources available for active and priority allocation by a 'top-down' system.

In one of our studies (Warburton, Wesnes and Ansboro, unpublished) we devised a divided attention task that was based on the Bakan visual information task. In one condition, subjects were presented with two series of digits at a rate of 50 per minute in the visual and auditory modality, using a different sequence for each modality. In a second condition, subjects were presented with numbers at the same rate in the visual modality only. It was emphasized in the first condition that subjects were to attend equally to both inputs. Detection of sequences in the divided attention task improved significantly after smoking a cigarette. The number detected was greater in the test period compared to the baseline period. Smoking a cigarette also prevented the increase in reaction times that occurred in the nonsmoking condition.

These two experiments provide evidence that smoking improves the selective attention aspects of human information processing. They also demonstrate that the beneficial effects of nicotine are not specific to sustained attention tasks.

PERCEPTUAL INTRUSIONS

The task which epitomizes perceptual intrusion effects is the Stroop test, and this is the one which has been used most frequently in smoking research. The Stroop test uses three sets of display, a list of color words printed in black, a set of color patches and a list of color words with the words printed in incongruent colors (for example the word GREEN printed in blue). Word reading is faster than color naming, while naming the incongruently printed color words takes much longer than naming the background color patches. The time difference between naming the colors in the two conditions is the Stroop effect. This score indicates the subject's ability to focus attention on a relevant stimulus dimension of print color and ignore an irrelevant semantic one.

The effects of two doses of nicotine, administered in tablet form, were studied on the Stroop performance of smokers and nonsmokers (Wesnes and Warburton, 1978). Both doses of nicotine reduced the size of the Stroop effect. No differences were found between the effects of the two doses of nicotine on the improvement of smokers and nonsmokers. The latter finding adds support to the argument that the smokers and nonsmokers do not differ in their response to nicotine, i.e. there was no evidence of tolerance to the effects of nicotine in nonsmokers.

The evidence from this section is in complete accord with the studies of sustained attention and selective attention. Thus it seems that nicotine enhances general attentional processing capacity, and its effects are not limited to one specific type.

ECOLOGICAL VALIDITY

Given such evidence of a generalized improvement in information processing by nicotine, it is of interest to consider whether this improvement can be produced in other tasks involving attention, including performance at work.

Tarriere and Hartemann (1964) used a task which combined central guiding with peripheral visual monitoring over a 150 min period. The measure of performance reported was the percentage of the peripheral visual signals missed. Monitoring performance was maintained by smoking, in contrast to the large increase in the percentage of omissions of the signals when not smoking.

In a study of smoking and simulated driving, Heimstra, Bancroft and DeKock (1967) measured four aspects of performance: steering efficiency, reaction time, brake light vigilance and meter vigilance. Two groups of 20 smokers and one group of 20 nonsmokers performed the task continuously for a 6 h period. One of the smoker groups was allowed to smoke cigarettes of unspecified delivery as often as they liked throughout the task, while the other group was not allowed to smoke.

Tracking error was greatest in the deprived smoker group throughout the experiment, but no significant differences were found between the other two groups over time. Reaction times increased significantly over time in the nonsmoker and deprived smoker groups, but not for the smoking group. Brake light vigilance was significantly lower for the deprived smokers than for the other two groups. In the meter vigilance task there were no between-group differences but the nonsmokers made significantly more errors as time progressed, whereas performance remained at a constant level for the smoker group.

Major surveys carried out in our laboratory and other laboratories have indicated that the vast majority of smokers respond positively to the statement 'smoking helps me to relax' and 'smoking helps me to think and concentrate' (Russell, Peto and Patel, 1974; Warburton and Wesnes, 1978). We have also surveyed a student population, and we specifically asked them whether smoking helped them concentrate, and if so whether this was a motive for smoking. Seventy-four percent of student smokers reported that this help is a motivation to smoke.

We have investigated whether smoking did have any benefits for academic performance that might be expected from the laboratory studies. While we have not found any effects on gross measures like percentage pass rates and final degree class, we have found significant differences in examination marks and a set of tutorial marks between smokers and nonsmokers (Warburton, Wesnes and Revell, 1984), which give some evidence for an association between smoking and academic success.

Very few studies of the effects of smoking on productivity at work have been carried out. In one recent study on the productivity of managers in a credit services company, the influence of smoking on performance of a variety of measures of health and lifestyle was assessed (Dahl, Gunderson and Kuehnast, 1984). It was hypothesized that those managers with the more healthy lifestyles would be more productive, and smoking was thought to be one indicator of poorer health. The researchers were therefore expecting that those managers who smoked would be less productive than those who did not. The effects they found overall were not very strong, with five major variables (including smoking) explaining only 11 percent of the variation in performance. However, four indices of health were positively correlated with improved productivity and, contrary to the investigators' expectations, smoking was one of the variables correlated with higher productivity.

It is clear that smokers report that smoking helps them to concentrate, and laboratory tests confirm this belief. Consequently, if this is a major motive for smoking, then it would be expected that smokers will smoke more during work than at other times, especially in the afternoon when attention tends to decrease. Evidence in support of this comes from two studies. A survey of smoking at work, by Meade and Wald (1977), showed that cigarette smoking was frequent during the working day. When there were no restrictions on smoking at work, male and female office workers smoked 56 percent of their cigarettes during working hours, no matter whether they were light or heavy smokers. The highest smoking rate per hour (about 30 percent greater than the average hourly rate for the whole day) occurred at work in the immediate post-lunch period, and so did the second-highest hourly rate. This occurrence of peak smoking rates during the working day is consistent with the idea that smoking is used by people to help cope with the demands of work, especially work which involves thinking and concentration, and may be used to counteract the effects of daily variations in attention (e.g. the 'post-lunch dip').

We have studied the smoking patterns of students during examination periods when high levels of concentration are needed for revision (Warburton et al., 1984). In comparison with a nonexamination period, the students smoked more cigarettes and, while they generated slightly less smoke from the cigarettes, the total nicotine intake was greater. They also claimed that they inhaled more of the smoke they generated, which can be interpreted as an attempt to maximize nicotine absorption for attentional processing.

Of course the results of these experiments do not allow us to infer that smoking produces higher achievement. However, we have already cited some studies from our laboratory that have demonstrated that cigarette smoking improves mental efficiency in tasks involving sustained concentration. It would seem to be a valid extrapolation that academic work performance, such as studying and essay writing, would be facilitated by smoking.

However, there is also some evidence that one of the personality characteristics of smokers is a need for achievement (Warburton et al., 1984) so an alternative hypothesis could be devised. Smoking may be one of the coping strategies adopted by people with a high need for achievement to help them achieve their goals. This hypothesis would also be consistent with other evidence that smokers adjust their smoking behavior to match their needs.

INDIVIDUAL DIFFERENCES IN THE EFFECTS OF SMOKING ON ATTENTION

The aspect of individual differences that has been explored most, with respect to attention, is the dimension of introversion–extraversion. Theoretical speculations (Eysenck, 1957) suggest that introverts are better at prolonged and monotonous tasks, and that extraverts show a greater decrement in performance over time in attentional performance. The majority of studies have reported such differences between introverts and extraverts on attentional performance (Warburton and Wesnes, 1978). When significant differences have been reported, introverts make more correct detections and fewer false alarms, and exhibit less decrement. In one experiment carried out in our laboratory (Warburton and Wesnes, 1978) we examined the relation between extraversion and neuroticism and vigilance performance in a situation where subjects were given varying doses of nicotine. The subjects in this experiment were nonsmokers, light smokers and heavy smokers, and they were tested on the Mackworth clock test (Mackworth, 1950). Smoking prevented the larger vigilance decrement in extravert smokers. Prior to smoking, subjects with a high degree of neuroticism performed less well than emotionally stable subjects. When performance during the 20 min after smoking was examined, improvement on the task was correlated significantly with the neuroticism scores, i.e. smoking was producing greater improvement in the more neurotic subjects. Results consistent with our findings were obtained by Kucek (1975), where subjects were tested under conditions of information overload. Kucek also found that smoking had a beneficial effect on the performance of neurotic subjects who were allowed to smoke. In a later study in our laboratory, consistent results were also found using nicotine tablets; the more neurotic subjects performed better in the drug than in a placebo control condition.

At first sight this may appear unrelated to the hypothesis that nicotine improves attention. However, Warburton and Wesnes (1978) suggested the neurotic subjects may be more preoccupied with the stressful aspects of the laboratory procedure and with their own fear of failure, and nicotine may be acting to reduce the effect of these preoccupations by allowing the subjects to more effectively focus their attention on the task.

SMOKING AND EEG

We now explore the neural bases for the effects that we have reported in the previous sections, and show that nicotine-improved attentional processing can be fitted into the known psychophysiology and psychopharmacology of attention.

It is commonly asserted that a shift from high-amplitude (8–13 Hz or alpha activity) to low-amplitude (13–20 Hz or beta) activity indicates an increase in alertness and attention (Edwards and Warburton, 1983). A number of studies have explored the effects of smoking on the EEG to see if it produces these sorts of shifts. The typical approach has been to examine the changes in either the level of alpha activity or the dominant alpha frequency after smoking in either deprived or nondeprived smokers.

Smoking has been shown to affect both the frequency and amplitude of alpha waves. Ulett and Itil (1969) showed a decrease in mean dominant EEG frequency from 10.5 to 9.5 Hz, and a significant increase in 3.5 to 7.0 Hz activity in deprived smokers, which was returned to baseline after smoking. The deprived smokers also expressed subjective sensations of drowsiness and fatigue, and showed a slower pulse and increased systolic blood pressure which was reversed after smoking.

Knott and Venables (1977) also studied deprived smokers, but compared them with a group of nondeprived smokers and nonsmokers. Half the smokers smoked a cigarette, while the other half and the nonsmokers inhaled through an unlit cigarette. Dominant alpha frequency was lower for the deprived group than for the nondeprived or nonsmokers, but smoking produced a significant increase for the former group. In a later experiment, Knott and Venables (1979) examined the effect of alcohol in conjunction with smoking, and found that alcohol produced a reduction of 0.2 Hz in dominant alpha frequency, but that smoking counteracted this effect.

Warburton and Wesnes (1979) demonstrated that the shift in dominant alpha frequency after smoking was related to performance on an information processing task, while Caille and Bassano also demonstrated that this effect was accompanied by an improvement in performance on a driving task (Caille and Bassano, 1976, 1977). Similarly, Warburton and Wesnes (1979) found that both cigarettes and nicotine tablets increased the dominant alpha frequency (11.5–13.5 Hz) and beta activity (13.5–20 Hz), and that these changes were correlated with more efficient performance in the rapid visual information processing task described earlier.

In a further study the P_{300} component of the event-related brain potential, produced by the target stimuli in a rapid information processing task, was recorded (Edwards, Wesnes, Warburton and Gale, 1985). The P_{300} reflects the activation of controlled processing for selection of an appropriate response (Picton, Donchin, Ford, Kahneman, and Norman, 1984). The P_{300} is related to attention, and is not elicited by an input which is irrelevant to the subject, i.e. an unattended stimulus (Donchin, 1984). The occurrence of the P_{300} wave depends on the completion of certain stimulus evaluation processes (Kutas, McCarthy and Donchin, 1977). McCarthy and Donchin (1981) have argued that the latency of the P_{300} component 'reflects the duration of stimulus evaluation processes and is relatively insensitive to response selection processes' (McCarthy and Donchin, 1981, page 77).

Stimulus evaluation involves the encoding, evaluating and categorization of the input—including memory search and identification of the stimulus. These studies suggest that nicotine is acting on the cortical mechanisms involved in information processing.

THE NEUROPSYCHOPHARMACOLOGY OF SMOKING

While smoking a cigarette, the principal method of taking nicotine into the body is by smoke inhalation. During inhalation the nicotine passes down the bronchi and into the alveoli, where it diffuses rapidly across the alveolar membrane. The velocity of the blood flow through the capillaries is slow, so that equilibrium is reached between alveolar nicotine and capillary nicotine. The nicotine-loaded blood then passes out of the lungs to the left atrium and left ventricle of the heart and the aorta, from which the carotid arteries branch off, the major branch going direct to the brain. The nicotine passes unmetabolized to the brain in about ten seconds from the time of the first puff. About 20 percent of the blood containing nicotine goes to the brain. It has been estimated that about 1.3 mg of nicotine is taken up from a medium-delivery cigarette (Armitage, Dollery, George, Houseman, Lewis and Turner, 1974) and approximately 20 percent of that (250 μg) enters the blood supply of the brain. Nicotine passes freely over the blood–brain barrier and well over 90 percent reaches the brain (Oldendorf, Hyman, Braun and Oldendorf, 1972). From a medium-delivery cigarette the amount of nicotine which will reach the brain is therefore over 200 μg. Neurons in many areas of the brain respond to the iontophoretic application of acetylcholine (Phillips, 1970). However, the majority of cholinergic neurons at the cortex are muscarinic rather than nicotinic. Nevertheless, smoking doses of nicotine (e.g. 200 μg/kg i.p. in the cat) do produce excitation of cortical cells and release of acetylcholine (Armitage, Hall and Sellars, 1969). Nicotine depletes whole-brain acetylcholine, and evidence from *in vivo* studies in the rat and mouse (Essman, 1971; Pepeu, 1965) suggests that this depletion results from increased release from storage and subsequent deactivation by acetylcholinesterase.

Cortical acetylcholine release and activation seems to result from an action at the mesencephalic reticular formation where receptors, sensitive to nicotine, are found. Certainly, destruction of the tegmental region of the midbrain prevents the activation of the cortex by nicotine at doses up to five times that which is sufficient in the intact animal (Domino, 1967; Kawamura and Domino, 1969). It would seem likely, therefore, that the action of nicotine on the cortex, in both the release of acetylcholine in this area and in the cortical desynchronization of the EEG found in cats and in humans, is via an indirect action of the ascending cholinergic pathways from the nucleus basalis of Meynert to the cortex.

Thus improvements in attentional processing during smoking can be seen as the outcome of changes in activity in the pathways which converge on the cortical sensory neurons (Robinson, 1985). This activity is seen as alterations in acetylcholine release and changes in electrocortical arousal. Warburton (1981) has proposed that the release of acetylcholine at the cortex increases the size of evoked potentials, and thus improves the probability of their being distinguished from the background cortical activity.

The cholinergic system has links with the vasoactive intestinal peptide (VIP) neurons at the cortex. These VIP neurons are concentrated particularly in the forebrain and cerebral cortex (Emson, Hunt, Rehfeld, Golterman and Fahrenkrug, 1980). The cortical VIP neurons have terminals ending close to pial and other cerebral blood vessels, and exogenously applied VIP relaxes the muscle cells of the cerebral arteries so that cerebral blood flow is increased (Lee, Saito and Berezin, 1984). Thus there is a coordination of two systems, whereby the cholinergic neurons are enhancing the activity of the sensory neurons and the linked VIP neurons are increasing cortical blood flow to make more energy sources available for the increased metabolic activity of the processing neurons.

This system can be seen as providing a state appropriate for information processing as state models of cognitive function describe (Hockey and Hamilton, 1983; Warburton, 1986). Here 'state' does not refer to discrete states of the organism but to a continuum of states, and argues that parts of the continuum may be more appropriate for some sorts of cognitive operations than other parts. The balance of activity of one particular type will depend on the requirements of the situation.

Normally the brain is not fixed in a 'state', but the states are varying from moment to moment. It has been suggested that there may be mechanisms that have evolved to enable switching from state to state to enable a balance of cognitive functions to occur (Warburton, 1986). Given this processing state system, how does nicotine improve attentional processing? The answer seems to be that it maintains the cortex in a desynchronized state by driving the ascending cholinergic pathway. The release of acetylcholine at the cortex enables the more efficient processing in sustained attention, selective attention and perceptual intrusion tests.

SUMMARY

Although a great many studies have been carried out to examine the effects of smoking on attention and performance, relatively few of these have looked at performance in the context of work which is relevant and meaningful for the smokers. The argument is always possible that the effects of smoking on attention are confined to the rigidly controlled laboratory situation. However, when studies are conducted in the context of the normal work situation then these are necessarily of a correlational nature, and do not permit direct conclusions of causality.

It is only when the full spectrum of the research, including experimental laboratory studies, correlational studies, EEG studies and physiological studies, is considered, that a more convincing picture emerges of the effects of smoking on human attentional processing. Examination of these studies has led us to conclude that smoking does improve attention, and that this phenomenon is recognized and manipulated by smokers.

In real life smokers use nicotine to improve the efficiency of their mental processing, particularly when undertaking tasks which require sustained attention, and help them achieve more at work. This description is consistent with the functional model of smoking behavior (Warburton, 1987). The functional model sees smoking as an important resource for the person. A resource refers not to what people do, but to what is available to them for managing their lives. In terms of attentional processing, smoking can be seen as being maintained by the personal control that smokers have over this specific aspect of their psychological state. Thus, smoking can be seen as purposeful activity for smokers; it provides them with nicotine as a resource for managing their lives.

REFERENCES

Andersson, K., and Hockey, G.R.J. (1977). Effects of cigarette smoking on learning and retention. *Psychopharmacologia*, **41**, 1–5.

Armitage, A.K., Dollery, C.T., George, C.F., Houseman, T.H., Lewis P.J., and Turner, D.M. (1974). Absorption and metabolism of nicotine by man during cigarette smoking. *British Journal of Clinical Pharmacology*, **1**, 180.

Armitage, A.K., Hall, G.H., and Sellars, C.M. (1969). Effects of nicotine on electrocortical activity and acetylcholine release from the cat cerebral cortex. *British Journal of Pharmaceutical Chemotherapy*, **35**, 152–160.

Bakan, P. (1959). Extraversion–introversion and improvement in an auditory vigilance task. *British Journal of Psychology*, **50**, 325–332.

Caille, E.J., and Bassano, J.L. (1976). Le geste du fumeur dans une tache de vigilance monotone. *Psychologie Medicale*, **8**, 631–638.

Caille, E.J., and Bassano, J.L. (1977). La nicotine dans le champ cerebral. *Psychologie Medicale*, **9**, 1005–1012.

Dahl, T., Gunderson, B., and Kuehnast, K. (1984). *The Influence of Health Improvement Programs on White Collar Productivity*. Minneapolis: University of Minnesota.

Domino, E.F. (1967). Electroencephalographic and behavioral arousal effects of small doses of nicotine. A neuropsychopharmacological study. *Annals of the New York Academy of Sciences*, **142**, 216–244.

Donchin, E. (1984). Dissociation between electrophysiology and behavior—a disaster or a challenge? In: E. Donchin (ed.), *Cognitive Psychophysiology*, vol. 1, Hillsdale, NJ: Lawrence Erlbaum, pp. 107–118.

Edwards, J., and Warburton, D.M. (1983). Smoking, nicotine and electrocortical activity. *Pharmacological Therapeutics*, **19**, 147–163.

Edwards, J.A., Wesnes, K., Warburton, D.M., and Gale, A. (1985). Evidence of more rapid stimulus evaluation following cigarette smoking. *Addictive Behaviors*, **10**, 113–126.

Emson, P.C., Hunt, S.P., Rehfeld, J.F., Golterman, N., and Fahrenkrug, J. (1980). Cholectystokinin and vasoactive intestinal polypeptide in the mammalian CNS: distribution and possible physiological roles. In: E. Costa and M. Trabucchi (eds), *Neural Peptides and Neural Communication*. New York: Raven Press.

Essman, W.B. (1971). Metabolic and behavioral consequences of nicotine. In: W.L. Smith (ed.), *Drugs and Cerebral Function*. Springfield, IL: Charles C. Thomas.

Eysenck, H.J. (1957). *The Dynamics of Anxiety and Hysteria*. New York: Praeger, Warburton.

Frankenhaeuser, M., Myrsten, A.-L., Post, B., and Johansson, G. (1971). Behavioral and physiological effects of cigarette smoking in a monotonous situation. *Psychopharmacologia (Berl.)*, **22**, 1–7.

Heimstra, N.W., Bancroft, N.R., and DeKock, A.R. (1967). Effects of smoking upon sustained performance in a simulated driving task. *Annals of the New York Academy of Sciences*, **142**, 295–307.

Hockey, G.R.J., and Hamilton, P. (1983). The cognitive patterning of stress states. In: G.R. Hockey (ed.), *Stress and Fatigue in Human Performance*. Chichester: John Wiley & Sons.

Jerison, H.J. (1977). Vigilance: biology, psychology, theory and practice. In: R.R. Mackie (ed.), *Vigilance: Theory, Operational Performance and Physiological Correlates*. New York: Plenum.

Kahneman, D. (1973). *Attention and Effort*. Englewood Cliffs, NJ: Prentice-Hall.

Kawamura, H., and Domino, E.F. (1969). Differential actions of m and n cholinergic agonists on the brainstem activating system. *International Journal of Neuropharmacology*, **8**, 105–115.

Kinchla, R.A. (1980). The measurement of attention. In: R.S. Nickerson (ed.), *Attention and Performance. VIII*. Hillsdale, NJ: Lawrence Erlbaum.

Knott, V.J., and Venables, P.H. (1977). EEG alpha correlates of non-smokers, smoking and smoking deprivation. *Psychophysiology*, **14**, 150–165.

Knott, V.J., and Venables, P.H. (1979). EEG alpha correlates of alcohol consumption in smokers and non-smokers. Effects of smoking and smoking deprivation. *Journal of Studies on Alcohol*, **40**, 247–257.

Kucek, P. (1975). Effect of smoking on performance under load. *Studia Psychologica*, **17**, 204–212.

Kutas, M., McCarthy, G., and Donchin, E. (1977). Augmenting mental chronometry: The P300 as a measure of stimulus evaluation time. *Science*, **197**, 792–795.

Lee, T.J.F., Saito, A., and Berezin, I. (1984). Vasoactive intestinal polypeptide-like substance: the potential transmitter for cerebral vasodilation. *Science*, **224**, 898–901.

Mackworth, N.H. (1950). Researches on the measurement of human performance. Medical Research Council Special Report No. 268. London: HMSO.

Mangan, G., and Golding, J. (1978). An 'enhancement' model of smoking maintenance? In: R.E. Thornton (ed.), *Smoking Behaviour: Physiological and Psychological Influences*. Edinburgh: Churchill Livingstone.

McCarthy, G., and Donchin, E. (1981). A metric for thought: a comparison of P300 latency and reaction time. *Science*, **211**, 77–80.

Meade, T.W., and Walde, N.J. (1977). Cigarette smoking patterns during the working day. *British Journal of Preventative and Social Medicine*, **31**, 25–29.

Moray, N. (1969). *Attention: Selective Processes in Vision and Hearing*. London: Hutchinson.

Myrsten, A.-L., and Andersson, K. (1978). Effects of smoking on human performance. In R.E. Thornton (ed.), *Smoking Behaviour: Physiological and Psychological Influences*, Edinburgh: Churchill Livingstone.

Navon, D., and Gopher, D. (1979). On the economy of the human processing system. *Psychological Review*, **86**, 214–255.

Norman, D.A., and Bobrow, D.G. (1975). On data-limited and resource-limited processes. *Cognitive Psychology*, **7**, 44–64.

Oldendorf, W.H., Hyman, S., Braun, L., and Oldendorf, S.Z. (1972). Blood–brain barrier: penetration of morphine, codeine, heroin and methadone after carotid injection. *Science*, **176**, 984–987.

Pepeu, G. (1965). Nicotina e acetilcolina cerebrale. *Archivio Italiano di Scienze Farmacolacologiche*, **15**, 93–94.

Phillips, W. (1970). *The Pharmacology of Synapses*. Oxford: Pergamon Press.

Picton, T., Donchin, E., Ford, J., Kahneman, D., and Norman, D. (1984). Report of Panel 11: The ERP and decision and memory processes. In: E. Donchin (ed.), *Cognitive Psychophysiology: Event Related Potentials and the Study of Cognition*. Hillsdale, NJ: Lawrence Erlbaum.

Robinson, S.E. (1985). Cholinergic pathways in the brain. In: M.M. Singh, D.M. Warburton and H. Lal (eds), *Central Cholinergic Mechanisms and Adaptive Dysfunctions*. New York: Plenum, pp. 37–61.

Russell, M.A.H., Peto, J., and Patel, U.A. (1974). The classification of smoking by a factorial structure of motives. *Journal of the Royal Statistical Society*, **137**, 313–333.

Tarriere, H.C., and Hartemann, F. (1964) Investigations into the effects of tobacco smoke on a visual vigilance task. *Proceedings of the Second International Congress of Ergonomics, Dortmund* (Supplement to *Ergonomics*), pp. 525–530.

Ulett, J.F., and Itil, T.M. (1969). Quantitative electro-encephalogram in smoking and smoking deprivation. *Science*, **164**, 969–970.

Warburton, D.M. (1981). Neurochemical bases of behaviour. *British Medical Bulletin*, **37**, 121–125.

Warburton, D.M. (1986). A state model for mental effort. In: G.R.J. Hockey, A.K.W. Gaillard and M.G.H. Coles (eds), *Energetics and Human Processing*. Dordrecht: Martinus Nijhoff.

Warburton, D.M. (1987). The functions of smoking. In: W.R. Martin, G.R. Van Loon, E.T. Iwamoto and D.L. Davis (eds), *Tobacco Smoke and Nicotine: A Neurobiological Approach*. New York: Plenum.

Warburton, D.M., and Wesnes, K. (1978). Individual differences in smoking and attentional performance. In: R.E. Thornton (ed.), *Smoking Behaviour: Physiological and Psychological Influences*. Edinburgh: Churchill Livingstone, pp. 19–43.

Warburton, D.M., and Wesnes, K. (1979). The role of electrocortical arousal in the smoking habit. In: A. Remond and C. Izard (eds), *Electrophysiological Effects of Nicotine*. Amsterdam: Elsevier.

Warburton, D.M., Wesnes, K., and Ansboro, M. The effects of smoking on divided attention. (Unpublished.)

Warburton, D.M., Wesnes, K., and Revell, A. (1984). Smoking and academic performance. *Current Psychological Research and Reviews*, **3**, 25–31.

Wesnes, K., and Warburton, D.M. (1978). The effects of cigarette smoking and nicotine tablets upon human attention. In: R.E. Thornton (ed.), *Smoking Behaviour: Physiological and Psychological Influences*. Edinburgh: Churchill Livingstone, pp. 131–147.

Wesnes, K., and Warburton, D.M. (1984a). Effects of scopolamine and nicotine on human rapid information processing performance. *Psychopharmacology*, **82**, 147–150.

Wesnes, K., and Warburton, D.M. (1984b). The effects of cigarettes of varying yield on rapid information processing performance. *Psychopharmacology*, **82**, 338–342.

Wesnes, K., Warburton, D.M., and Matz, B. (1983). Effects of nicotine on stimulus sensitivity and response bias in a visual vigilance task. *Neuropsychobiology*, **9**, 41–44.

Williams, G.D. (1980). Effect of cigarette smoking on immediate memory and performance in different kinds of smokers. *British Journal of Psychology*, **71**, 83–90.

Wittenborn, J.R. (1943). Factorial equations for tests of attention. *Psychometrika*, **8**, 19–35.

11

A Critical Evaluation of Laboratory Studies of the Effects of Smoking on Learning and Memory

TARA NEY
ANTHONY GALE
and
HAYDN MORRIS

ABSTRACT

Laboratory studies of the effects of smoking on human memory and learning are critically reviewed. While results are mixed, including a number of findings which are hard to explain, there is evidence that deprived smokers, allowed to smoke prior to a memory task, show enhanced recall after a delay. The results are in part consistent with Walker's neural consolidation theory, which suggests that high arousal at the time of learning protects the consolidation process. While none of the studies reviewed is perfect it is possible to make constructive proposals for future research.

INTRODUCTION

Learning and memory are central to human experience. We store information about the world and plan our actions on the basis of past learning. Any drug which facilitates learning and memory will therefore enhance human performance. This chapter reviews empirical studies of the effects of smoking

Smoking and Human Behavior, Edited by T. Ney and A. Gale
© 1989 John Wiley & Sons Ltd

on learning and memory in laboratory tasks. According to Edwards and Warburton (1983) it is nicotine which 'is the significant component of cigarette smoke that results in more efficient information processing' (page 189). If this is indeed the case, then enhancement of performance could be a good reason for sustaining the smoking habit. Two questions need to be asked: Does smoking affect efficiency of learning and memory, and if so, which component or components of smoking are responsible? We review existing studies and consider what conclusions can be drawn from their findings. We also identify a number of methodological problems with the research and make recommendations for future studies. Two general conclusions can be drawn: that orally administered nicotine has a facilitative effect on aspects of learning and memory, and that, in some studies, smoking prior to a memory task does lead to enhancement of long-term recall. However, it cannot be concluded that nicotine is the crucial agent in effects obtained with smoking; current evidence supports the view that smoking, via its capacity to increase subject arousal, may aid the consolidation process. This is an important area for future research, but new research strategies are essential.

EMPIRICAL RESEARCH FINDINGS

Rote learning

There have been several studies of rote learning, involving the repetition of lists of single or paired words up to some specified criterion of performance. Two early studies of rote learning of nonsense syllables (Andersson and Post, 1974; Andersson, 1975) showed no benefit for smoking. Subjects viewed repeated lists of nonsense syllables and the measure of performance was their ability to anticipate each item on the list. Recall was actually worse immediately following smoking. Other authors (Mangan, 1983; Mangan and Golding, 1984; Peeke and Peeke, 1984) have claimed that the Andersson (1975) study showed a delayed improvement following smoking, but our reading of her paper does not confirm that view since the improvement, 45 min after initial learning, was not statistically significant. Andersson and Hockey (1977) asked subjects to recall a list of words projected on different quadrants of a screen; smoking had no effect on performance. However, subjects were then asked in which quadrant individual words had appeared; this incidental aspect of the task was adversely affected by smoking. An experiment by Peeke and Peeke (1984) also showed no benefit to incidental learning. In a set of tasks including learning, Stevens (1976) showed that smokers were worse than nonsmokers and that heavier smokers were worse than lighter smokers. Houston, Schneider and Jarvik (1978) also showed poor performance following smoking. Their subjects heard lists of nouns which they were then required to recall immediately and after a delay; on both occasions deprived smokers performed better than smokers. In a complex experimental design, involving a set of tasks, Williams (1980) obtained no effect for smoking where subjects had to recall a series of nine digits. Carter (1974) also found no effects for smoking in a serial learning task.

Mangan and Golding (1978) and Mangan (1983) reported a paired-associate (PAL) and a serial learning (SL) task; they varied task difficulty (two levels) and the nicotine content of cigarettes (two levels). Acquisition learning (performance over a sequence of trials) was impeded in the easier PAL task by a medium (1.3 mg) cigarette, but was enhanced in the harder PAL task; the lower-value cigarette (0.7 mg) had no effects. However, by later test trials, smoking had improved performance. In Mangan's SL task recall of the first four words in a 20-word list benefited from smoking. Such a primacy effect could be due either to increased opportunity for rehearsal or reduced possibility of retroactive interference from later items. Mangan, in reviewing his findings, accepts that they are not straightforward, and are difficult to explain in terms of direct effects of nicotine. We note at this point that complex ANOVA designs, with several factors and levels within factors, and employing repeated measures over trials or sessions, may well lead to very complex data sets, which in their turn are not easy to explain in simple terms. Critics of the use of repeated-measures designs suggest that they provide artificial enhancement of effects (Johnson and Lubin, 1972) and some journals insist on correction formulae (Jennings, Cohen, Ruchkin and Fridlund, 1987).

The most complex series of studies available is by Peeke and Peeke (1984). Their general finding was that pre-trial smoking reliably enhanced recall of a word list, not immediately, but after 10 and 45 min and after 24 h. Post-trial smoking was not beneficial. In one study use of a higher-nicotine cigarette (1.38 mg), again in pre-trial smoking, improved both immediate and delayed recall. Recognition tasks (as opposed to recall tasks) gained no benefit from smoking. We cannot do justice here to the four experiments and detailed analyses; the reader is referred to the original paper, which contains the most detailed and careful discussion of their findings and of the smoking and learning literature. Peeke and Peeke (1984) used no-smoking controls and suggest that, rather than enhance performance, smoking might return the deprived smoker to a stable condition. They also suggest that the benefit from smoking is not a direct effect on memory *per se* but upon attentional capacity (see below). Thus the most comprehensive sequence of studies published ends with very cautious conclusions.

Mangan and Golding (1983) report a complex study in which smokers and nonsmokers were tested at intervals ranging from ½ h to 1 month. Subjects performed a paired-associate task. In this study, smoking occurred *after* the initial learning trial, including four treatments for smokers (abstention, low-, medium-, and high-nicotine cigarette). After a careful analysis of different measures of performance the authors selected 'trials to criterion' and 'initial errors,' the latter reflecting errors when initially presented with the material at retest. At 30 min after learning, nonsmokers performed better than all smoking groups. At 1 day and at 1 week, nonsmokers still performed better than smokers, but not all comparisons were statistically significant. There was considerable attrition among the smoking subjects for the 1-month test, almost half the sample withdrawing from the study. When the remaining smokers were entered into the analysis, low- and medium-nicotine subjects performed better than either nonsmokers or high-nicotine smokers on the initial errors measure (meeting the material again for the first time at retest); nevertheless, for the more typical measure of trials to criterion, smokers still performed at a worse level. From these results Mangan and Golding (1983) claim that smoking (in the low- and medium-nicotine groups) has aided an aspect of the consolidation process. Unfortunately, as they concede, the direction of the effect depends on the measure taken, and is based upon a self-selecting sample which chose to be available for retest (although the performance of this nonattrition group was no different on earlier trials than the quitters). Given the large number of statistical tests performed, and the repeated measurements on the subjects, this study would need replication before the crossover effect for memory can be accepted with confidence. Moreover, since subjects were tested on four occasions it is hard to attribute consolidation merely to events which occurred (smoking) at the initial session. Finally, we should note that previous work, including their own, demonstrated superior effects for nicotine/smoking at the shorter test periods. Thus their study contradicts earlier findings. The most persistent finding among their data is that smoking and smokers do worse than the nonsmoker group.

Summarizing so far, it is clear that taking the studies as a whole, smoking can improve rote memory, can make memory worse, or can have null effects. The positive effects seem to occur after a delay. Recognition and incidental learning do not benefit. Dose of nicotine can have null, positive or negative effects. Smoking after deprivation, but before and not during the task, seems to convey a long-term benefit. In the Peeke and Peeke study (1984) it matters whether the smoker is light, moderate or heavy. Different memory tasks give different results, and different measures of performance taken from the same data set can give different results.

Questionnaire studies reveal a belief by smokers that their attentional capacity is enhanced by smoking. At this point we can consider what evidence smokers themselves might have for their belief that smoking aids attention, or that, when deprived of smoking, attention is reduced. The studies reviewed so far indicate that some smokers may actually be worse off for smoking so far as memory is concerned. Those who are benefiting are doing so at some *delay* after learning, and given that the improvements are modest (see Mangan, 1983 and Peeke and Peeke, 1984) they must be particularly sensitive observers of their own performance. In other words, smokers must be able to detect a slight increment in their performance, which is not immediate but appears after initial learning occurred.

State-dependent learning

In the above studies subjects were allowed to smoke at some point prior to or during the task, and then tested for recall. The question arises whether the *state* of the subject (smoking or nonsmoking) is important. Does smoking during recall enhance performance if it recaptures the state of the subject during learning trials? State-dependent learning experiments employ manipulations of subject state during both initial learning and subsequent recall. Peters and McGee (1982) varied the nicotine content of cigarettes smoked on two consecutive testing sessions. They found that one condition (high nicotine followed by low nicotine) was worse than the other three combinations. Their finding is an embarrassment for state-dependent learning theory since both conditions involving different states (namely high–low and low–high) should have been inferior to learning and recall in identical states. A similar manipulation was used by Warburton, Wesnes and Shergold (1982), who in two studies used smoking/nonsmoking and nicotine tablet/placebo respectively to control state at initial learning or recall. The smoking study showed some state-dependent learning effects since smoking or nonsmoking at *both* sessions was superior to changing state for the second session. However, not all the appropriate comparisons were statistically significant. The nicotine tablet study failed to show state-dependent learning effects, but did demonstrate that nicotine raised performance at the initial session. These three studies, therefore, do not provide conclusive evidence of state-dependent learning, although it is clear that nicotine tablets do enhance initial learning.

A briefly reported recent study by Kunzendorf and Wigner (1985), using a more realistic task than the rote learning studies, provides good support for state-dependent learning approaches. Subjects read a short article and then had to answer six factual questions about it. There were four conditions, with smoking or nonsmoking either during study of the article or during the test. For identical conditions performance was higher (smoking–smoking 4.1 words, nonsmoking–nonsmoking 3.6) with scores of 2.9 and 2.6 words for the mixed conditions. Relief from deprivation cannot be a source of the results, since recall for nonsmoking on the two occasions was inseparable from smoking on the two occasions. Yet at the same time it is hard to claim that smoking helped performance. Their simple design could be replicated using manipulations of nicotine and/or degree of smoking habit. We note that their study contained a broad range of smokers (mean of 15.2 cigarettes per day but with a standard deviation of 8.8) and it is encouraging that they obtain their effect given the differential findings in previous studies for smoking habit and/or nicotine level.

State-dependent learning studies call for clearcut results. Ideally, smoking followed by smoking should be best and then nonsmoking followed by nonsmoking, with mixed conditions yielding the worst effects. No study has given such results so far. However, there are two possible reasons for data not falling in line with prediction. The first is asymmetrical transfer effects; particular combinations, say, smoking on initial encounter with a new task, *may* yield better outcomes than nonsmoking at the first session. A possible control would be to have testing points at both sessions, thus enabling comparison of performance prior to the second session. The second reason for questioning existing studies is their failure to monitor smoking; subjects might use titration methods to ensure a constant intake of nicotine, in spite of the experimenter's attempts. This latter criticism clearly only applies to studies in which subjects are required to smoke different nicotine concentrations at different sessions.

Enhancement via attention?

If smoking has any effect on learning and memory it might be via an indirect route, by either facilitating or disrupting the subject's capacity to attend to the task (Peeke and Peeke, 1984). The Andersson and Hockey (1977) study indicates that attention to incidental features of the task was disrupted by smoking. It is possible to suggest, therefore, that smoking might reduce distraction caused by irrelevant task features even though, in the Andersson and Hockey study, performance on the main task was not thereby enhanced. The Stroop test involves perceptual conflict in which a color word is printed in an ink of another color. Good performance involves concentrated attention on the subject's part as the task is very distracting. Wesnes and Warburton (1978) showed that nicotine enhanced the performance of both smokers and nonsmokers. However, another Stroop study yielded no benefit for smoking, as opposed to nicotine (Myrsten, Elgerot and Edgren, 1977). Using a tracking task, again requiring attention, Schori and Jones (1975) showed no effect for smoking on the subjects' capacity to track under either low- or high-demand conditions.

Finally, in an unpublished study, Ney and Gale asked subjects to solve Raven's matrices problems while smoking *ad libitum* or not smoking. This task involves considerable attention to the stimuli, and induces bodily stilling with cardiac deceleration which varies in duration as a function of task difficulty. While concentrating on the items smoking activity ceased (Ney, Gale and Weaver, 1988). In both an independent subjects and repeated measures design smoking had no beneficial effect on either speed or accuracy of problem solution. We mention this study because it involves considerable attention on subjects' part. While concentrating (i.e. while working on the tasks) subjects chose *not* to smoke, thus showing that they did not consider smoking to be helpful. At the same time, cessation from smoking when under mental pressure reveals a capacity for self-regulation.

Conclusion on the research studies

We return to our initial two questions: Does smoking enhance learning and memory and if so why? Given the lack of clearcut findings showing that smoking has beneficial effects it would be perverse to argue that it is the nicotine in cigarettes which enhances performance! In the independent studies manipulating nicotine (rather than smoking) improvement may be the result of introducing a drug into the nervous system, and may not be specific to nicotine; to test for specificity a variety of stimulants needs to be used. In the Ney and Gale study referred to above, task difficulty caused heart rate to decelerate given the need for information intake (see Lacey, 1967). Given that smoking raises heart rate it creates psychophysiological conditions incompatible with the intake of information. Moreover, in many tasks, acts associated with smoking (inhalation, tapping, gaze aversion during exhalation) may act as distractors, reducing the smoker's capacity to observe and attend to task materials.

Nevertheless, the several studies indicating a longer-term positive effect of smoking on later recall must cause us to speculate on the consolidation processes involved in these tasks. Studies which have been theoretically related to Walker's neural consolidation theory (1958) have shown that high or low arousal at the time of learning (manipulated via task materials, presence of noise, etc.) can have differential effects on immediate or longer-term recall. Higher arousal at the time of learning is seen to protect the memory trace so that immediate access is impeded until the trace is established. Lower arousal at the time of learning allows the material to be accessed, thus disrupting it in the longer term (Eysenck, 1984; Gregg, 1986). To be consistent with such findings it would have to be shown that smoking has arousing effects, a view which is commonly shared. One possible avenue for future studies is a combination of learning trials with later recall, but with physiological monitoring of subject state (see Peeke and Peeke, 1984). Few, if any, of the authors referred to seem to be aware of Walker's theory, but it has clear implications both for rote learning and for state-dependency studies. In the latter case there should be relationships not only with state variation over learning and testing, but state variation at initial learning, as well as with the delay inserted prior to recall. Walker's theory predicts crossover effects, with high arousal being beneficial in the long term and low arousal being beneficial for immediate recall.

CONCEPTUAL AND METHODOLOGICAL PROBLEMS

We now consider whether indeed further work on the relationship between smoking and memory or learning tasks is justified. Our brief account of relevant research studies has obscured several methodological problems, and it is to these which we now turn. Perhaps the tasks and manipulations which have been employed are not wholly appropriate?

What is memory?

Serial rote learning tasks are very convenient for laboratory studies for several reasons: material-to-be-learned is broken into discrete units; subjects' attention can be specifically related to the device delivering the material; the laboratory can be stripped of all distraction; performance improves in increments over trials; associative meaning of the items (e.g. by use of nonsense syllables) can be eliminated; and trial onset and duration can be controlled, so that smoking can be inserted or withheld as required. Unfortunately, such tasks lack ecological validity. We do not deny that actors have to learn their lines, or that medical students have to rote learn their anatomy, but in everyday living learning typically occurs in different ways. People remember many things without having to make a voluntary effort and without an instruction to recall them subsequently. Material-to-be-learned is not organized in discrete parcels, association is an aid not a disadvantage, subjects do not come new to the material but apply existing cognitive frameworks, voluntary direction of attention is not necessary, learning can occur in major one-trial leaps not several tiny incremental steps, and learning is not organized in terms of discrete chunks but in terms of episodes. Much of our learning is more like the incidental learning component of the Andersson and Hockey task (where did the word appear?) than the consciously directed component (remember the words we show you!). Moreover, the serial linear information process model implied by the majority of the experiments we have used is certainly not fashionable in contemporary psychology, even if it was once considered worthwhile to construct elaborate theories around it (Rabbitt, 1979).

At the same time it is clear there are several types of memory (for example, working memory, episodic memory, autobiographical memory and so on) which are much more part of everyday human subjective experience of memory than are the tasks used in the smoking and memory literature.

In each context, the term 'memory' is a gross oversimplification of existing models. For example, contemporary models of working memory include notions such as a central executive, the articulatory loop, the inner ear, the visuospatial scratchpad, voluntary and automatic attention, and so on. It is in our view unlikely that smoking will have equivalent effects on all aspects of working memory, and indeed it is possible that it might have differential effects, improving, decrementing or leaving untouched, particular components. In such contexts the notion that smoking enhances information processing (Edwards and Warburton, 1983) seems far too generous and all-encompassing. In our view such an approach implies a commitment to a biological view of smoking in which the nicotine is the key constituent; driven by such a reductionist approach, notions of context, relevance and salience, and other aspects of smoking, such as the motoric aspects, the social relevance, or the smoker's attributions to smoking, become neglected. While the nicotine model does lead to titration studies and the notion of self-regulation, it implies that the smoker is a relatively passive receptacle of chemical substances.

As we have shown, existing research is equivocal. But even if the results were wholly consistent they would have little bearing on learning and memory in everyday experience, and could not help us to understand why smokers believe that smoking helps them.

How to set up hypotheses

It is clear, therefore, that studies of the effects of nicotine on performance are for us somewhat different in conception from studies of the effects of *smoking*. Within the research traditions which have developed, the former seems to be the driving force, but a focus on smoking as opposed to nicotine can lead to different task manipulations, different dependent variables and, as has already been shown, to different results. In many of the studies we have reviewed there is no set of specific predictions concerning outcome, so that much of the interpretation of the effects or noneffects of manipulation (dosage, task difficulty, time of smoking, degree of smoking habit, etc.) comes *post hoc* rather than *ante hoc*. Such failure to make predictions reveals the poverty of theory in the field. In the case of a specific aspect of memory, predictions need to be couched in terms of particular hypothetical processes or mechanisms. We have found it very difficult indeed, partially because of the lack of hypotheses and the tendency to *post hoc* theorizing, to impose any overall framework on existing findings.

Sources of variation in learning and memory studies

Yet even where the same task has been used in two different studies, is the picture more clear? Let us consider when the subject is allowed to smoke. The Peeke and Peeke (1984) study is one of the few to insert smoking as a systematically manipulated variable. The typical procedure is to allow a cigarette to be smoked, then to introduce the learning task, and then to test the subject for what has been learned (Andersson and Hockey, 1977; Houston et al., 1978; Mangan, 1983; Peters and McGee, 1982). But in some studies the subject does not obtain nicotine until after learning (Warburton et al., 1982) or in others smoking occurs in between learning sessions (Andersson, 1975; Kucek, 1975) or during learning (Kunzendorf and Wigner, 1985). In other studies two cigarettes are smoked during different points of learning (Schori and Jones, 1975) and in yet others smoking occurs before or during both learning and retrieval (Kunzendorf and Wigner, 1985; Stevens, 1976). Clearly, there are countless permutations of when to ask subjects to smoke, how much to smoke, and whether *ad libitum* or under precise instruction. A good-quality theory, which allowed precise testable hypotheses, would surely not allow for such anarchy in manipulation of the central variable in the research?

Even within rote learning, variations are endless, allowing: different numbers of trials, different trial lengths, different types of task, varied intervals between learning and retrieval, number of occasions when recall is required, how long is allowed for recall, and whether retrieval is in the form of recall or recognition. Within such varying schedules different demands are made on subjects: to smoke one or more times, to smoke cigarettes with varying nicotine delivery, and/or to smoke freely or on a prescribed schedule.

If we take the various groups employed, and the comparisons made, the inferences which can be drawn are different. Thus various combinations of the following groups appear in the literature: nonsmokers, nonsmokers smoking, deprived smokers not smoking, deprived smokers smoking, nondeprived smokers smoking, deprived smokers sham smoking, deprived smokers smoking nicotine-free cigarettes, nonsmokers absorbing nicotine orally, smokers absorbing nicotine orally, nonsmokers absorbing placebo, smokers absorbing placebo, and so on. Where smokers are used variable-quality descriptions are given by authors in terms of: length of smoking history; whether light, heavy and medium smokers; the descriptions often overlapping (in terms of cigarettes per day, or nicotine delivery) from study to study.

What is a good design?

There is no such thing as a perfect design, each approach having its own advantages and disadvantages. It is therefore important for the weaknesses of the design employed to be recognized. For example, between-subject designs can be affected by constitutional or personality differences, while differences between deprived and nondeprived subjects may be due to the withdrawal effects of abstention (see Ashton and Stepney, 1982; Mangan and Golding, 1978; Wesnes and Warburton, 1978). A within-subjects design in which each subject acts as his or her own control by participating in all conditions, is probably the best compromise, but it needs also a group of nonsmokers, a sham smoking condition (to control for motoric effects) and systematic counterbalancing. Variation in nicotine levels should also strengthen the inferential framework. But even within-subject designs can introduce asymmetrical transfer effects, as we have already mentioned; for example, a subject encountering the task for the first time when smoking may have a different reaction from encountering the task when deprived. There is reason to believe that such asymmetrical effects are particularly powerful in learning tasks.

What subjects are used?

In some of the earlier studies, sample sizes were very small. In most studies samples tend to be of young students, who are largely male. Of thirteen studies in which sex is specified, eight used exclusively male subjects, while in another three studies males far outnumbered the females. On those rare occasions where both males and females are used (Carter, 1974; Elgerot, 1976; Houston et al., 1978; Myrsten et al., 1977; Peeke and Peeke, 1984; Schori and Jones, 1975) tests are not always made for sex differences. Yet there is evidence that gender affects inhalation patterns and contexts in which smoking occurs (Batten, 1985; Frith, 1971). University students are not likely to have a long history of smoking, they tend to be middle-class in origin, and may well smoke in a different fashion and in different contexts, say, from a production-line worker. A housewife and office worker may also differ in the preferred situations and style of smoking. Such subtleties may be overlooked if one has a reductionist view of smoking, attributing its psychological effects to the impact of chemicals on the brain, since presumably one brain functions very much like another.

Not all studies actually mention the habitual smoking pattern of subjects. Some studies do not document this (e.g. Carter, 1974; Mangan, 1983; Peters and McGee, 1982; Warburton et al., 1982); others include samples varying from less than five per day (Andersson and Post, 1974), through fifteen (Kunzendorf and Wigner, 1985), to as many as 40 (Houston et al., 1978). It is likely that personality differences dictate level of smoking, and that number taken per day could be confounded with extraversion–introversion, which in its turn may influence task performance.

Abstention instructions

Many studies instruct subjects to abstain from smoking prior to attending the experimental session. Thus all smokers should have similar nicotine levels in the body prior to the beginning of an experiment. This procedure eliminates a possible source of error. It is reasonable to assume that there would be an interaction between different existing levels of nicotine in the body and the effects of the cigarette(s) smoked in the experiment. An abstention period ensures that all subjects come to the laboratory with similar amounts of nicotine in the body. The use of an abstention period is a sensible component of experimental design in smoking studies.

Most studies reviewed employed an abstention period. This period ranged from 1 hour (Mangan, 1983), through 3 hours (Houston et al., 1978) to 1 week (Myrsten et al., 1977). However Elgerot (1976) and Stevens (1975) did not include any abstention period. There are strong arguments against long abstention periods. Most smokers do not typically go for hours without smoking a cigarette. Thus smokers who come to the laboratory up to 1 week deprived will be in a very atypical physiological and psychological state. The effects of smoking on subjects in such a state of deprivation cannot be generalized to the normal smoking population, nor is it likely that allowing them then to smoke and requiring them to engage in a learning task will tap into their normal learning or attentional styles.

It is routine to request subjects not to take other substances containing drugs which affect physiology, such as tea, coffee and alcoholic beverages, prior to an experimental session. Again there is great variability between studies in the time period during which subjects are asked to abstain from these substances. It is typical for there to be the same deprivation period for tobacco and other drugs in a study. The rationale for drug deprivation is simple. There could be interactions between the effects of drugs taken prior to the experiment and the effects of the cigarette(s) smoked in the study. Thus drug deprivation removes another possible source of noise from the experiment. However, again it is likely that the deprivation from everyday drugs such as caffeine further reduces the ecological validity of the experiment. In the smoker's normal environment smoking interacts with the other drugs routinely taken in our culture.

There is a further problem with the use of an abstention period. Subjects may not comply with the instructions. This could be due to them deliberately ignoring the instructions. It is also possible that smoking is such an habitual action that it has become an invisible behavior to the smoker. The subject may have smoked a cigarette during the abstention period and not be aware of having done so. A reliable index of how recently a cigarette has been smoked can be gained by measuring exhaled carbon monoxide. It is unfortunate that devices for measuring exhaled carbon monoxide are expensive, and are not part of the equipment of most psychophysiological laboratories. To test for the presence of the other proscribed substances would typically be regarded as unacceptable. It would involve blood or urine testing, and would be an unreasonable expectation of most experimental subjects.

The arguments for a nonsmoking period prior to an experiment are sensible. It is desirable that effects during the experiment should not be contaminated by smoking prior to the session. However, a long abstention period would reduce ecological validity as the smoker would be in an abnormal state. A reasonable compromise is to ask smokers to deprive themselves for an hour. In an hour the immediate effects of nicotine have dissipated, so the experiment will not be badly contaminated by previously smoked cigarettes. Furthermore, it must be routine for the majority of smokers not to smoke for an hour, particularly the student subjects used in so many studies. A similar argument would apply for other drugs.

Control for smoking behavior

In all the studies reviewed it is assumed that nicotine is the psychologically significant element in smoking. The sensory and motoric aspects of smoking are neglected. However, if the effects of smoking are to be attributed only to nicotine the possible effects of the sensory and motoric aspects must be eliminated. This is done with the use of a control group.

A control group is a normal requirement in psychological and pharmacological research. When a new drug or treatment is tested it is important that any change induced can be attributed directly to the specific action of the drug or treatment. The actual administration of the tablet must be ruled out as the cause of the change. This is done by use of a control group which undergoes exactly the same procedure as the experimental group except for the substitution of an inert substance for the active drug. If there is a difference observed between the groups it is then fair to attribute this to the action of the drug and not the effect of administration. In smoking research, when there is no control for the motoric aspects of smoking (i.e. lighting up, the action of drawing), it is not possible to attribute any observed changes in smokers' behavior or physiology to nicotine. It could be that the motoric aspects are responsible for any or part of the changes observed in both physiology and behavior. If the effects of smoking are to be attributed to nicotine the other constituents of cigarette smoke must also be eliminated as possible causes of change following smoking.

Houston et al. (1978) used nicotine-free cigarettes as a control for both the motoric aspects of smoking and the sensory effects of smoking. Thus they hoped to attribute any differences in physiology and behavior between the nicotine-free cigarettes and tobacco cigarettes to the presence of nicotine in the tobacco cigarettes. But nicotine-free cigarettes are not an adequate control for either the motoric aspects of the cigarette or the sensory aspects of the cigarette. Because the draw characteristics of nicotine-free cigarettes are completely different from normal cigarettes their use is not an adequate control for the motoric aspects. The sensory aspects of the nicotine-free cigarette also differ from tobacco cigarettes, so that they represent no sort of control for the sensory component of tobacco smoke. The smoker will also react to the novelty of smoking a different type of cigarette with such different properties to his/her normal brand.

It has been found in psychological and pharmacological research that a control group is necessary. However, in some psychological and pharmacological research it is also necessary to prevent knowledge that the substance given is inert or active. We know that it is the expectation of the subject which leads to the placebo effect, even though we do not understand the mediating process. To counter the effects of expectation single- and double-blind procedures have been developed. In a single-blind design the subject does not know whether he/she is taking the active or inert substance. A double-blind procedure requires that both the subject and the experimenter are unaware of the nature of the substance used. This technique is used because the experimenter, as well as the subject, can bias experimental results by their expectations. In smoking research where comparisons are being made between cigarettes it is not possible to use a single- or double-blind technique. Smokers can tell the type of cigarette they are smoking. Smokers are aware if they are smoking their own brand or something weaker or stronger (Comer and Creighton, 1978). It is not possible to prevent smokers having knowledge of what they are smoking. An unusual single-blind procedure can be adopted in which the experimenter is blind while the smoker is not. In smoking research to date every attempt to use a control for either the motoric aspects of smoking, or the sensory aspects of smoking, has not prevented the subject from knowing that the control cigarette is different from his/her normal brand. If the smoker knows the control cigarette is different this knowledge could lead to some form of placebo or self-fulfilling prophecy effect. The nature and extent of the effect would depend on the expectations of the particular smoker, and is therefore unpredictable.

Given the current state of tobacco processing technology there is no effective control for either the motoric aspects of smoking or the sensory aspects of smoking. The only adequate control would be a cigarette which was in all respects similar to a normal tobacco cigarette apart from the absence of nicotine. Such a cigarette cannot be manufactured at present.

Manipulation of nicotine levels

While there are studies which intentionally set out to manipulate the dosage of nicotine (for example, Peters and McGee, 1982; Mangan, 1983; Peeke and Peeke, 1984; Warburton et al., 1982) there are others which arbitrarily select a nicotine dosage. For example, Andersson and Hockey (1977) used a nicotine dosage of 2.3 mg, which is very high, while Houston et al. (1978) used cigarettes with only 1.5 mg nicotine, apparently without justification. In the light of those studies which demonstrate that dosage may affect physiology and performance (i.e. Peters and McGee, 1982; Williams, 1980) some theoretical rationale should be given for the nicotine dosage used. Furthermore, the effect of administering a high nicotine dosage cigarette (for example, 2.3 mg) to a light smoker (less than five cigarettes per day) as in the Andersson and Post (1974) study, will be different from that of administering a lower nicotine dosage cigarette (e.g. 1.5 mg) to a heavy smoker (two packs/day) as in the Houston et al. (1978) study. Although information about machine smoking estimates may be of limited value (Edwards, 1983, page 11), the argument here is that such information is essential not only so that comparisons across studies may be made, but so that individual differences may be examined.

Instructions to smoke

It is often difficult to tell whether instructions given to subjects regarding how to smoke have been omitted from the written paper or the actual experiment! This information is important, otherwise it is not possible to tell whether subjects were pressured, felt obliged, or truly were free to smoke. One finds that instructions vary from none (Peters and McGee, 1982; Suter and Bättig, 1982) to free smoking (for example, 'S's were free to smoke or not at all times,' Stevens, 1976) to more contrived smoking ('S's took a puff every 25 seconds and held the smoke in for 5 seconds. This was done for 12 puffs,' Houston et al., 1978), and so the generalizability of their results is limited. It is quite plausible that the inconsistent results from the same research group, for example, between Elgerot (1976) and Myrsten et al. (1977), may be due to when subjects were and were not able to smoke. Furthermore, instructions about when to smoke will determine the time between smoking and task performance. During concomitant activity, one set of behaviors may be seen to be primary while others are secondary. This, after all, is the rationale for the use of secondary tasks in the study of mental load. Yet during the task in Kucek's (1975) experiment, no consideration was made of the extra mental load effect of cigarette smoking during a loaded task. Wesnes and Warburton (1983) maintain that, at this stage in research, control over smoking is necessary, and in their own research they maintain a compromise is made: they allow smokers to smoke test cigarettes in their own way at specified times during the experiment. However, such compromising constraint *is* a constraint, and creates a situation which does not represent the subject's habitual smoking patterns or the habitual integration of smoking acts with task performance.

Habitual cigarette consumption

Another problem is the lack of information regarding nicotine content of the cigarettes the subject *normally* smokes (e.g. Carter, 1974). This is a different problem from neglecting categorization of subjects based upon cigarette consumption per day (e.g. light, moderate, heavy) as discussed above. For example, a subject who smokes ten nonfiltered cigarettes with 2.5 mg nicotine delivery will almost certainly be receiving a different amount of nicotine per cigarette or per day than an individual smoking ten filtered cigarettes with 1.0 mg nicotine delivery. To assume that two such smokers are a part of the same smoking population may be incorrect. Regardless of the deprivation time, a dosage of nicotine given to two such subjects may react more as a function of the nicotine level the individual is accustomed to receiving rather than the nicotine dosage *per se*. Some studies have even neglected information on nicotine delivery of cigarettes given during the experiment (e.g. Myrsten et al., 1977; Schori and Jones, 1975).

CONCLUSIONS AND RECOMMENDATIONS

From the criticisms we have made about research into the effects of smoking upon learning and memory, a number of guidelines can be identified for future research. While existing data do not provide convincing evidence that smoking has beneficial effects on memorial performance, there are sufficient grounds to carry out further research both in terms of *some* of the research findings and the claims smokers themselves make.

We have already suggested: appropriate designs for abstention from smoking prior to experimentation; greater sensitivity in the choice of subjects and in the partitioning of data for smoking habits, gender and other sources of individual variation; the need for experimental manipulations based on specific hypotheses, derived from theory; and the use of experimental paradigms which offer superior generalization from laboratory to real-life contexts.

Titration presents a special problem. Both the psychological tool model and the addiction model would predict that subjects will manipulate their smoking rate as a function of the delivery of the cigarette and of the situational demands. Subjects who are asked to learn material in the laboratory face a considerable challenge. Cigarettes which deliver nicotine at a rate different from those to which the smoker is accustomed will lead to inhalation patterns which either reduce or increase intake as is appropriate. It is essential, therefore, to monitor the intensity of the subject's smoking under all conditions to ensure that nicotine delivery is at the level intended by the experimenter. Unfortunately, there are clear indications that subjects *will* titrate and that experimenter control will never be achieved (see Nil and Bättig, Chapter 9 in this volume). However, studies which do not report on the smoker's smoking behavior cannot assume that obtained effects are due to nicotine manipulation by the experimenter.

So far as experimental tasks go, it is important to select procedures relating to memory, around which theoretical frameworks have been built within experimental psychology. For example, in the case of serial recall, explanatory models have been constructed to explain the overall shape of the recall/error curve and to partition components of the curve. Such models have been tested by systematic manipulation. Mangan (1983), for example, obtains primacy effects yet does not go on to speculate about why this may be so. Yet early parts of the serial recall curve are likely to reflect opportunities for active rehearsal; recency effects can be manipulated by the use of suffixes and other devices which disturb the integrity of temporary memory buffers, and so on. Existing knowledge from experimental psychology can therefore be used to dictate key factors such as type of materials, inter-item interval, type of distractor and so on. The aim would be to determine which aspect of tasks is particularly affected by smoking.

For example, using serial digit strings Gale, Jones and Smallbone (1974) demonstrated very specific EEG changes correlated both with individual differences in recall performance and in discriminating between high-recall and low-recall trials. Allowing subjects to smoke between trials, for example, would enable measurement of EEG consequences of smoking, recall performance as affected by smoking or nonsmoking, and the relationship between smoking, the EEG and improvements in performance as the experiment proceeds.

Only a small proportion of the studies we have reviewed included the use of physiological measures (Andersson, 1975; Andersson and Hockey, 1977; Elgerot, 1976; Kucek, 1975; Myrsten et al., 1977; Peeke and Peeke, 1984). Typically, heart rate is measured as an indication of overall arousal; no study reviewed has successfully related physiological change to memorial performance in spite of a considerable literature in the field (for example, Levonian, 1972). If electrocortical measures are taken, then it is important to bear in mind the time course of the action of nicotine on the brain and the duration of its likely effects. Again, the use of physiological measures needs to be planned in advance, so that specific hypotheses can be constructed. In the case of heart rate, for example, a distinction needs to be drawn between task aspects which involve stimulus intake and those which involve stimulus rejection, since such psychological demands move heart rate in opposite directions (Lacey, 1967).

Apart from measurement of performance and the use of physiological monitoring, few studies of the effects of smoking on memory have sought to tap into the subjects' phenomenal view of the laboratory task and their interaction with it. Yet it is subjective report which leads us to think that smokers use smoking as a means of increasing cognitive efficiency (Wesnes and Warburton, 1983), or for reducing stress (Gilbert, 1979), or differentially in different situations (O'Connor, 1980). We have already suggested that subjects' reactions to different cigarettes (for example, no-nicotine, or varying in nicotine concentration) may affect their appraisal of the situation. Measures of taste satisfaction would at least provide a test of the subject's awareness or otherwise of experimental manipulations (Moss and Prue, 1982). Finally, subjective measures may provide us with estimates of the degree of effort involved in particular tasks. In the Ney and Gale study referred to above it is reasonable to infer that subjects found the cognitive task so demanding and absorbing that smoking actually stopped; if subjects have limited capacity for information processing then smoking might impose additional burdens as a secondary and low-priority task.

We accept that subjects may not have direct access to sensory or other information; that they might construct answers to please the experimenter; or that they might accept common stereotypes of smoking as facilitating attention and therefore confirm that it does so in their case; or that, indeed, subjects might repress their reactions or even lie, as part of the justification for their smoking habit. Nevertheless, we believe that the use of subjective report provides access to nonredundant data (Mackay and Cox, 1987).

Peeke and Peeke (1984) observe that not all their subjects demonstrate the group effects. Workers like O'Connor (for example, 1980) have developed a style of smoking research which focuses upon individual differences. There is evidence that extraverts tend to be heavier smokers than introverts (Eysenck and Eaves, 1980), or take shorter, more frequent drags (Ashton, Millman, Telford and Thompson, 1974). O'Connor (1980) shows that extraverts and introverts differ both in the pattern of smoking and in the pattern of the CNV. Several studies show that there is considerable variation in smoking styles and patterns (Frith, 1971; McKennel, 1970; Russell, 1974; Tomkins, 1966). Such findings reinforce the notion that smoking can be used as a tool to manipulate the individual's state. The learning experiment is surely an occasion for seeking to enhance one's performance and therefore to deploy established personal strategies for coping with task demands? None of the studies we have reviewed measures how smokers smoked during the smoking period, and whether that pattern was predictive of efficiency in learning.

Smoking should be treated as a set of behaviors in its own right. The psychological tool model (Ashton and Stepney, 1982) encourages us to think of smoking as an elaborated behavior, dovetailed into task demands or environmental circumstances with a view to stabilizing the smoker's hedonic state or bodily reactions. Individual smokers appear to have quite stable smoking patterns (Ashton, Stepney and Thompson, 1979). It may be necessary, however, to stabilize subjects' reactions to the laboratory itself to ensure that normal smoking patterns are observed. The laboratory itself may constitute a special threat to subjects so that they refrain from smoking (Myrsten, Andersson, Frankenhaeuser and Elgerot, 1975) or smoke more vigorously than in natural settings (Ossip-Klein, Martin, Lomax, Prue and

Davis, 1983). A useful strategy for future research may be to take individual differences in the patterning of smoking as one of the key independent variables. For example, rapid smoking may create distractions which disturb the subject's attentional control, while more deliberate and slow smoking might reflect the subject's capacity to integrate task and smoking demands.

In conclusion, there is some evidence that for some subjects, in some learning tasks and with some nicotine concentrations, smoking just prior to learning (and following a period of deprivation) has modest and delayed positive effects on verbal rote learning. None of the authors whose work we have reviewed has come up with a convincing explanation of why this particular benefit is gained or, more important perhaps, why other manipulations or other memory tasks yield either negative or null effects. Researchers into smoking and memory would do well to study contemporary views of the consolidation process and to integrate their data with psychophysiological studies of memory.

REFERENCES

Andersson, K. (1975). Effects of cigarette smoking on learning and retention. *Psychopharmacologia*, **41**, 1–5.

Andersson, K., and Hockey, R. (1977). Effects of cigarette smoking on incidental memory. *Psychopharmacology*, **52**, 223–226.

Andersson, K., and Post, B. (1974). Effects of cigarette smoking on verbal rote learning and physiological arousal. *Scandinavian Journal of Psychology*, **15**, 263–267.

Ashton, H., and Stepney, R. (1982). *Smoking: Psychology and Pharmacology*. London: Tavistock.

Ashton, H., Millman, J.E., Telford, R., and Thompson, J.W. (1974). The effects of caffeine, nitrazepam and cigarette smoking on the contingent negative variation in man. *Electroencephalography and Clinical Neurophysiology*, **37**, 263–267.

Ashton, H., Stepney, R., and Thompson, J.W. (1979). Self-titration by cigarette smokers. *British Medical Journal*, **2**, 357–360.

Batten, L. (1985). Addiction and perceived dependence as smoking motivations: an empirical analysis. Unpublished manuscript. University of Southampton.

Carter, G.L. (1974). Effects of cigarette smoking on learning. *Perceptual and Motor Skills*, **39**, 1344–1346.

Comer, A.K., and Creighton, D.E. (1978). The effect of experimental conditions on smoking behaviour. In: R.E. Thornton (ed.), *Smoking Behavior: Physiological and Psychological Influences*. Edinburgh: Churchill Livingstone.

Edwards, J.A., and Warburton, D.M. (1983). Smoking, nicotine and electrocortical activity. *Pharmacology and Therapeutics*, **21**, 189–208.

Elgerot, A. (1976). Note on selective effects of short-term tobacco-abstinence on complex versus simple mental tasks. *Perceptual and Motor Skills*, **42**, 413–414.

Elliot, R., and Thysell, R. (1968). A note on smoking and heart rate. *Psychophysiology*, **5**, 280–283.

Eysenck, H.J., and Eaves, L.S. (1980). *The Cause and Effects of Smoking*. London: Maurice Temple Smith.

Eysenck, M.W. (1984). *A Handbook of Cognitive Psychology*. London: Erlbaum.

Frith, C.D. (1971). Smoking behaviour and its relation to the smoker's immediate experience. *British Journal of Social and Clinical Psychology*, **10**, 73–78.

Gale, A., Jones, D.M., and Smallbone, A. (1974). Short term memory and the EEG. *Nature*, **248**, 433–440.

Gilbert, D.G. (1979). Paradoxical tranquilising and emotion-reducing effects of nicotine. *Psychological Bulletin*, **36**, 643–661.

Gregg, V.H. (1986). *Introduction to Human Memory*. London: Routledge & Kegan Paul.

Houston, J.P., Schneider, N.G., and Jarvik, M.E. (1978). Effects of smoking on free recall and organization. *American Journal of Psychiatry*, **135**, 220–222.

Jennings, J.R., Cohen, M.J., Ruchkin, D.S., and Fridlund, A.J. (1987). Editorial policy on analyses of variance with repeated measures. *Psychophysiology*, **24**, 474–478.

Johnson, L.C., and Lubin, A. (1972). On planning psychophysiological experiments: design, measurement, and analysis. In: N.S. Greenfield and R.S. Sternbach (eds), *Handbook of Psychophysiology*. New York: Holt, Rinehart & Winston.

Kucek, P. (1975). Effects of smoking on performance under load. *Studia Psychologica*, **17**, 204–211.

Kunzendorf, R., and Wigner, L. (1985). Smoking and memory: state-specific effects. *Perceptual and Motor Skills*, **61**, 558.

Lacey, J.I. (1967). Somatic response patterning and stress: Some revisions of activation theory. In: M.G. Appley and R. Trumbell (eds), *Psychological Stress: Issues in Research*. New York: Appleton-Century Crofts.

Levonian, B. (1972). Retention over time in relation to arousal during learning: an explanation of discrepant results. *Acta Psychologica*, **36**, 290–321.

Mackay, C., and Cox, T. (1987). Self-report techniques. In: A. Gale and B. Christie (eds), *Psychophysiology and the Electronic Workplace*. Chichester: John Wiley & Sons.

Mangan, G.L. (1983). The effects of cigarette smoking on human verbal learning and retention. *Journal of General Psychology*, **108**, 203–210.

Mangan, G.L., and Golding, J. (1978). An 'enhancement' model of smoking maintenance? In: R.E. Thornton (ed.), *Smoking Behavior: Physiological and Psychological Influences*. Edinburgh: Churchill Livingstone.

Mangan, G.L., and Golding, J.F. (1983). The effects of smoking on memory consolidation. *Journal of Psychology*, **115**, 65–77.

Mangan, G.L., and Golding, J.F. (1984). *The Psychopharmacology of Smoking*. Cambridge: Cambridge University Press.

McKennel, A.C. (1970). Smoking motivation factors. *British Journal of Social and Clinical Psychology*, **9**, 8–22.

Moss, R.A., and Prue, D.M. (1982). Research on nicotine regulation. *Behaviour Therapy*, **13**, 31–46.

Myrsten, A.-L., Andersson, K., Frankenhaeuser, M., and Elgerot, A. (1975). Immediate effects of cigarette smoking as related to different smoking habits. *Perceptual and Motor Skills*, **40**, 515–523.

Myrsten, A.-L., Elgerot, A., and Edgren, B. (1977). Effects of abstinence from tobacco smoking on physiological and psychological arousal levels in habitual smokers. *Psychosomatic Medicine*, **39**, 25–38.

Ney, T., Gale, A., and Weaver, M. (1988). Smoking patterns during cognitive performance. *Addictive Behaviors*, **13**, 291–296.

O'Connor, K. (1980). Individual differences in situational preference amongst smokers. *Personality and Individual Differences*, **1**, 249–257.

Ossip-Klein, D.J., Martin, J.E., Lomax, B.D., Prue, D.H., and Davis, C.J. (1983). Assessment of smoking topography generalization across laboratory, clinical and naturalistic settings. *Addictive Behaviors*, **8**, 11–17.

Peeke, S.C., and Peeke, H.V.S. (1984). Attention, memory and cigarette smoking. *Psychopharmacology*, **76**, 232–235.

Peters, R., and McGee, R. (1982). Cigarette smoking and state-dependent memory. *Psychopharmacology*, **76**, 232–235.

Rabbitt, P.M.A. (1979). Current paradigms and models in human information processing. In: V. Hamilton and D.M. Warburton (eds), *Human Stress and Cognition: An Information Processing Approach*. Chichester: John Wiley & Sons.

Russell, M.A.H. (1974). Realistic goals for smoking and health. *Lancet*, **1**, 254–258.

Schori, T.R., and Jones, B.W. (1975). Smoking and work load. *Journal of Motor Behaviour*, **7**, 113–120.

Stevens, H.A. (1976). Evidence that suggests a negative association between cigarette smoking and learning performance. *Journal of Clinical Psychology*, **32**, 896–898.

Suter, Th.W., and Bättig, K. (1982). Vegetative effects of Stroop-test solving and cigarette smoking. *Activitas Nervosa Superior*, **2**, 264–267.

Tomkins, S.S. (1966). Psychological model for smoking behaviour. *American Journal of Public Health*, **56**, 17–20.

Walker, E.L. (1958). Action decrement and its relation to learning. *Psychological Review*, **65**, 129–142.

Warburton, D.M., Wesnes, K., and Shergold, K. (1982). Facilitation of learning and state dependency with nicotine. Presented at the Colloquium International Neuropharmacologium Congress, Jerusalem, Israel.

Wesnes, K., and Warburton, D.M. (1978). The effects of cigarette smoking and nicotine tablets upon human attention. In: R.E. Thornton (ed.), *Smoking Behaviour: Physiological and Psychological Influences*. New York: Churchill.

Williams, D.G. (1980). Effects of cigarette smoking on immediate memory and performance in different kinds of smoker. *British Journal of Psychology*, **71**, 83–90.

Part Four

Attitudes, Interventions and Social Policy

12

Passive Smoking: Attitudes, Health and Performance

ROY J. SHEPHARD

ABSTRACT

Acute effects of passive smoke exposure include not only annoyance, but also various disturbances of vision, an increased liability to respiratory infections, and provocation of asthmatic attacks in sensitive individuals. Chronic effects include an increased risk of various cancers, emphysema and obstructive lung disease. Maternal smoking also increases perinatal mortality and impairs child development. Such serious health effects far outweigh the impact of passive smoking upon performance. It is as yet unclear whether there is any 'safe' threshold exposure level that could be achieved by costly ventilation systems. The optimum solution thus seems regulations prohibiting smoking in public places, with an attempt to offer similar protection to the fetus. The Fishbein behavioral model merits application in the analysis of responses to the regulation of smoking.

INTRODUCTION

Passive smoking (Shephard, 1982) is generally defined as unwanted exposure of individuals to smoke coming from cigarettes, cigars and pipes of smokers. On a very still day, tobacco smoke can cause mild annoyance even in the open air, but complaints become more frequent in closed spaces, particularly if a substantial number of smokers are present and ventilation has been

Smoking and Human Behavior, Edited by T. Ney and A. Gale
© 1989 John Wiley & Sons Ltd

limited to reduce costs of heating or air-conditioning. Technical distinctions are drawn between *mainstream* smoke (which is somewhat filtered by the smoker's inhalation and subsequent exhalation) and the more irritant *sidestream* smoke which escapes from a smoldering cigarette held in the hand or placed in an ashtray (Shephard, 1982). However, such distinctions are unimportant in our present context. Some authors have also considered bloodstream exposure of the fetus to combustion products inhaled by a smoking mother as a form of passive smoking. Damage to the unborn child certainly has important psychological connotations, and thus merits consideration.

Interest in passive smoking is a relatively recent phenomenon. Twenty years ago, nonsmokers regarded a substantial daily dose of passive smoke on the underground, at the restaurant, and in the cinema, as an unfortunate but inevitable consequence of life in a large city. However, as the lethal impact of cigarettes upon smokers became widely appreciated, nonsmokers began to realize that passive smoking, also, was more than annoying—it had adverse effects on personal health. Demands for legislation of smoke-free air have accelerated as adult nonsmokers have become a sizeable majority of most populations, as an increased risk of lung cancer has been demonstrated in spouses exposed to smoke from their partners' cigarettes (Hirayama, 1981), and as public health authorities have recognized that the progressive creation of smoke-free zones is a powerful weapon in the campaign to make smoking a socially unacceptable form of behavior.

This chapter will consider certain key issues, including current models of attitude formation and attitude change, the influence of the smoker upon the passive smoker, passive smoking effects on the smoker and ex-smoker, passive smoking and health, and passive smoking and performance.

KEY ISSUES

Attitude formation and change

During the past decade our understanding of health behavior has been influenced substantially by the theory of rational behavior (Fishbein and Ajzen, 1974; Jaccard, 1975) and the health belief model of Becker and Maiman (1975).

Fishbein and his associates have argued that the intention to adopt a given pattern of behavior is shaped by an appropriately weighted combination of 'attitudes' and 'subjective norms.' 'Attitudes' in turn are determined by a series of specific beliefs and their personal evaluation. In the context of passive smoking, for example, one such belief might be 'that regular exposure to cigarette smoke for at least three hours a day increases the risk of lung cancer'; respondents could be asked to rate the strength of their belief on a seven-level likely/unlikely scale. One corresponding evaluation might be 'the increased risk of developing lung cancer by regular exposure to cigarette smoke for at least three hours per day would cause me very great/very little concern' (also rated on a seven-level multiple-choice scale). The product of this belief and its evaluation measures the individual's attitude toward the risk of causing or developing lung cancer from passive smoking. Other statements might examine the individual's attitudes toward such issues as eye irritation, nasal irritation and an increased risk of chronic chest disease. Summation of the products of the specific beliefs and their evaluation gives a measure of the overall attitude of the individual toward passive smoke accumulation.

'Subjective norms' reflect the perceived beliefs of significant others and the individual's motivation to comply with these beliefs. For example, one specific normative statement for a smoker might be 'my doctor thinks I should not smoke when I am in the same room as a small child.' The subject would be invited to rate this proposition on a seven-point likely/unlikely scale. The motivation to comply with this item might be explored using a statement of the type 'I will not smoke when I am in the same room as a small child because my doctor has suggested that I should not.' Again, a seven-point likely/unlikely scale could be used. A similar pair of questions might substitute 'husband' or 'wife' for 'doctor.' The summed product of norms and motivation to comply with the norms establishes a score for the individual's overall subjective norm with regard to passive smoking. Notice that while many of the attitude items are essentially similar for the smoker and the nonsmoker, the subjective norms are generally diametrically opposed (the smoker evaluating whether it is socially permissible to cause smoke exposure, and the nonsmoker deciding whether it is socially desirable to accept smoke exposure).

The relative contribution of attitudes and subjective norms to the shaping of behavioral intent depends in part on the behavior which is under consideration. Although there have been no formal studies of passive smoking, it is a matter of daily experience that the antagonism between the smoker and the nonsmoker is much more marked than that which exists, for instance, between the exerciser and the nonexerciser. One might thus anticipate a larger relative influence of subjective norms for passive smoke exposure than for some other forms of behavior. Prior use of the Fishbein model suggests that inter-individual differences arise from sociodemographic factors (age, sex, occupation, socioeconomic status, cultural background, level of education) and personality variables (introversion/extraversion, neuroticism, dominance, self-efficacy, locus of control, authoritarianism). In general, the Fishbein model provides a less satisfactory description of behavior in those subjects who are sensitive to the opinions of others (an *external locus of control*—Saltzer, 1981, and a weak *self-efficacy*—Dishman, 1982) than in those who have an internal locus of control. The model is particularly likely to break down in a situation where a person feels alienated and unwilling to consider the needs of others, for example, inner-city youths who apparently find pleasure in smoking in a railway coach where smoking is prohibited.

Both attitudes and subjective norms are usually assessed by the observation of overt behavior rather than by the measurement of behavioral intentions. This approach assumes the individual under observation is free to translate behavioral intentions into immediate behavior (Newman, 1974; Stutzman and Green, 1982). In fact, intentions and behavior are not always congruent (Jaccard, 1975). In the specific case of a heavy cigarette smoker, the force of previous habits, plus a strong physiological or psychological dependence upon tobacco, may severely limit the possibility of rational behavior.

Modifications of the Fishbein model have stressed the situational nature of many forms of behavior (Beardon and Woodside, 1978; Rokeach, 1968; Triandis, 1977). Triandis (1977) explored role beliefs for those playing particular roles in society. For example, a member of the clergy might be less likely to smoke in a nonsmoking area while wearing clerical garb. Likewise, a parishioner might be more willing to observe regulations in the company of the pastor. On the other hand, a youth in the company of other young people who seemed willing to defy regulations would be more likely to ignore a prohibition of smoking. The number of individuals who are present also influences smoking behavior—defiance of the regulations concerning smoking in a train, for example, is much more likely late at night (when the train is relatively empty).

The health belief model (Becker and Maiman, 1975) bears a certain resemblance to the attitudinal component of the Fishbein model. Becker and Maiman (1975) argue that behavior is influenced by perceived susceptibility to an illness, by the severity of the consequences of the illness and by the likelihood that the behavior in question will reduce either the susceptibility to illness or the severity of an attack. In the context of passive smoking, a person is thus more likely to react against passive smoke exposure if there has been a family history of lung cancer. Likewise, action is more likely to be provoked by fears about lung cancer than by the annoyance and general irritation associated with passive smoking. The reports of Hirayama (1981) and Trichopoulos, Kalandidi, Sparros and MacMahon (1981), establishing a substantial risk of lung cancer with secondary smoke, thus mark an important watershed in the campaign against passive smoke exposure. Susceptibility to cancer reflects frequent rather than occasional exposure; thus rational protest becomes most likely where there is heavy smoke exposure in the workplace and the home.

Attitude change is commonly a slow process, to the point that programs of health education have sometimes been thought ineffective. However, campaigns that were initiated some 20 years ago to reduce the consumption of animal fat, and to reduce the number of smokers, are now having a substantial impact upon population behavior. In the past five years there has also been a substantial shift in attitudes with respect to passive smoking (Shephard, 1982).

Factors contributing to the change in public attitudes can be deduced from the behavioral models discussed above. There has firstly been a substantial increase of scientific knowledge concerning the risks of passive exposure to cigarette smoke (US Surgeon General, 1986). In the United States for example, the Environmental Protection Association has estimated that passive smoking causes 5000 cancer deaths per year. This has led to campaigns of health education by groups such as National Cancer societies, with a view to updating the beliefs of the general public. As in the earlier issue of cancer in the smoker, those who are interested in the continued sale of cigarettes have invested much money in countercampaigns, attempting to discredit the new information. Although the key studies of Hirayama (1981), Trichopoulos et al. (1981) and Trichopoulos, Kalandidi and Sparros (1983) were all statistically significant and have been supported by many subsequent authors (Table 1), cigarette manufacturers have suggested that the population studied were of 'inadequate' size (Glantz, 1985). Attempts have been made to direct attention away from cigarette smoke to other materials which accumulate in poorly ventilated buildings (Wilson and Farant, 1985), and all employees of some cigarette manufacturing companies have been given a book (Canadian Tobacco Manufacturers' Council, 1985) providing detailed arguments to confound recent evidence on the health effects of passive smoke exposure.

A further basis for change in public attitudes has been a shift in subjective norms. It is no longer considered socially acceptable behavior to expose the nonsmoker to cigarette smoke. Factors inducing this shift in social norms include: (1) a decrease in the proportion of adult smokers (from a majority to a shrinking minority of the population), (2) a recognition that smoking is more than a minor annoyance for the nonsmoker, (3) the progressive extension of legislation prohibiting smoking in public air space and (4) a desire on the part of many smokers to see regulations that will control what they recognize as an otherwise ungovernable and irrational urge to smoke.

In general, new regulations guaranteeing smoke-free air have been exceedingly well received both by smokers and nonsmokers. Particularly when combined with the offer of a smoking withdrawal program, the prohibition of smoking at work has provided many smokers with a valuable incentive to escape from their addiction. Cigarette manufacturing companies have naturally viewed the widespread acceptance of smoke-free shops, offices, cinemas and restaurants with growing alarm, and have invested much money in advertisements aimed specifically at impeding the introduction and implementation of such regulations.

Table 1 Relative risk of lung cancer through passive smoking (all subjects non-smokers *except* in study of Sandler et al., 1985; who used a mixed population)

Reference	Exposure	Risk ratio
Hirayama (1983)	Spouse (ex-smoker or 1–19 cigarettes/day)	1.61
	Spouse (>20 cigarettes/day)	2.08
Trichopoulos et al. (1983)	Spouse (ex-smoker)	1.90
	(1–20 cigarettes/day)	1.95
	(>21 cigarettes/day)	2.50
Correa et al. (1983)	Spouse (1–40 pack-years)	1.48
	(>40 pack-years)	3.11
Koo and Ho (1985)	Spouse smoker	1.48
Garfinkel (1981)	Spouse smoker	'No significant increase'
Chan and Fung (1982)	Spouse smoker	0.75
Kabat and Wynder (1984)	Work exposure	3.27 (male)
		0.68 (female)
	Home exposure	1.26 (male)
		0.92 (female)
Sandler et al. (1985)	Spouse smoker	1.90*

* Mixture of smokers and nonsmokers

Smoker effects on the passive smoker

The effects of passive smoking upon the nonsmoker are numerous (Shephard, 1982). The characteristic odor of burning tobacco can be detected at extremely low concentrations (for instance, when the ambient carbon monoxide concentration is as low as 1.5–2.0 ppm or less). A slight increase over this threshold is sufficient to cause various annoying symptoms, including irritation of the eyes and nose, watering of the eyes, and running of the nose (Weber, 1984). A further increase of the smoke concentration induces coughing, wheezing, tightness in the chest and nausea. Some individuals are particularly sensitive to the respiratory effects of tobacco smoke; while such sensitivity may be linked to a history of asthma (Dahms, Bolin and Slavin, 1981; Shephard, Collins and Silverman, 1979a), attempts to demonstrate a specific respiratory allergy to tobacco (Savel, 1970; Zussman, 1970) have not been very convincing, partly because supposed antigens (prepared from unpurified extracts of tobacco leaves or cigarette smoke condensate) have been contaminated by other noxious materials (Becker, Levi and Zavecz, 1979).

Objective responses to acute smoke exposure include an increase of resting heart rate in some subjects (Pimm, Shephard and Silverman, 1978), a deterioration in cognitive processes (Oborne, 1983), a speeding in the break-up of the conjunctival tear film of the eyes (Basu, Pimm, Shephard and Silverman, 1978), minor increases of nasal and pulmonary resistance (Cockcroft, MacCormack, Tarlo, Hargreave and Pengelly, 1979; Urch, Silverman and Shephard, accepted for publication, 1988) and a moderate increase of blood carboxyhaemoglobin levels (to a maximum of 2.0–2.5 percent, even under the worst-likely conditions—Aronow, 1978; Shephard, 1982). A carboxyhaemoglobin level of 2.5 percent is itself at the borderline for effects on psychomotor performance, physical work capacity, and the risk of a cardiac crisis (Shephard, 1982), although Oborne (1983) suggests that annoyance at discourteous smoking rather than smoking *per se* is responsible for the deterioration in mental performance.

Among chronic responses, several massive community studies have shown an increased risk of respiratory infections. This danger persists after control for socioeconomic status (Harlap and Davies, 1974) and respiratory infections in siblings (Leeder, Corkhill, Irwig, Holland and Colley, 1976); the results show a dose dependence (Fergusson, Horwood, Shannon and Taylor, 1981), with particularly marked effects in young children who cannot escape from smoking mothers (Fergusson et al., 1981; Holt and Turner, 1984; Samet and Speizer, 1985). In older children, some smaller studies (Colley, Holland and Corkhill, 1974; Dodge, 1982; Lebowitz and Burrows, 1976; Lebowitz, Armet and Knudson, 1982) have had negative findings, although others have noted a slowing of lung growth (Ferris, Dockery, Ware, Berkey and Speizer, 1984), smaller forced expiratory volumes (Hasselbad, Humble, Graham and Anderson, 1981; Schilling, Letai, Hui, Beck, Schoenberg and Bouhuys, 1977; Tager, Weiss, Rosner and Speizer, 1979) and an increased incidence of asthma (O'Connell and Logan, 1974; Weiss, Tager, Speizer and Rosner, 1980) if the mother in a household smokes. Among adults, Hirayama (1981) observed a 49 percent increase in the age and occupation standardized risk of death from emphysema and asthma if the spouse smoked more than 20 cigarettes/day. Those working alongside smokers have a dose-dependent 10–20 percent impairment of lung function relative to those without such exposure (White and Froeb, 1980); however, a statistically significant effect of spousal smoking on lung function has only been shown in two of five studies (Kauffmann, Tessier and Oriel, 1983; Stock, 1980). In asthmatic subjects, chamber exposure to cigarette smoke provokes more symptoms (Shephard, Collins and Silverman, 1979b) and a larger decrease of lung volumes (Dahms et al., 1981) than in nonasthmatic individuals.

Because cigarette smoke is so readily detected, it is impossible to carry out true double-blind experiments. The question thus arises as to whether the symptoms and physiological changes observed are influenced by suggestion and/or anticipation of a response. The tachycardia observed in women but not in men (Pimm et al., 1978) is one pointer in this direction, as is the existence of individuals who are particularly sensitive to cigarette smoke. Cameron (1972) noted that symptoms were reported twice as frequently by children who disliked smoke exposure as by those who were indifferent or enjoyed the experience. A number of authors have also demonstrated that suggestion can provoke asthmatic attacks, both in children (Weiss, Martin and Riley, 1970) and adults (Horton, Suda, Kinsman, Souhrada and Spector, 1978; Luparello, Lyons, Bleeker and McFadden, 1968; Savel, 1970). The main effect is thought to be on the large airways (Spector, Luparello, Kopetzky, Souhrada and Kinsman, 1976). Phillips, Wilde and Day (1972) also used suggestion to induce a 10.2 percent decrease of the one-second forced expiratory volume ($FEV_{1.0}$) in subjects without a history of allergic disease, while Horton et al. (1978) commented on correlations between the response to suggestion of bronchospasm and other measures of emotional response such as blood pressure, finger pulse amplitude and forehead electromyographic activity. However, our studies of normal subjects have not shown any relationship between physiological and psychological measures of suggestibility on the one hand, and symptoms or physiological responses to cigarette smoke exposure on the other hand (Urch, Silverman and Shephard, in preparation). A further argument against suggestibility as the main explanation of responses to cigarette smoke is that both symptoms and physiological responses generally show a dose–response relationship (Muramatsu, Weber, Muramatsu and Akermann, 1983; Shephard, Collins and Silverman, 1979a; Winneke, Plischke, Roscovanu and Schlipkoeter, 1984), even though the *difference* in concentration of the smoke between experiments would not really have been observed by the subjects in most instances.

Organic disease can hardly be dismissed as a response to suggestion. Much interest and controversy was thus aroused by reports of an increased risk of lung cancer with, or subsequent to, passive cigarette smoke exposure. Hirayama (1981) described a 61 percent increase of risk where the spouse was a former smoker, or consumed one to nineteen cigarettes per day, and a 108 percent increase of risk where the spousal consumption exceeded 20 cigarettes per day. He stressed that close contact between spouses augmented the risk in traditional Japanese homes. Nevertheless, some increase of risk appears almost inevitable, given that cigarettes emit a variety of carcinogens into the atmosphere (Repace, 1985). Grimmer, Boehnke and Harke (1977) estimated that passive smoking increased the body burden of cancer-causing polycyclic aromatic hydrocarbons such as benz(α)pyrene. The very dangerous nitrosamine carcinogens of the type $R(R)=N.NO$ are found mainly in sidestream smoke and, depending on the proximity of a smoking colleague, the nonsmoker can thus inhale the equivalent of 0.5 to 30 cigarettes per day (Brunnemann, Yu and Hoffmann, 1977). Other epidemiological studies have generally confirmed the order of risk of lung cancer suggested by Hirayama (Tables 1 and 2), with the important exception of the report of Garfinkel (1981). Moreover, passive smoking confers an increased risk for other types of cancer (including the breast, cervix and endocrine glands), both in smokers and in nonsmokers (Miller, 1984; Sandler, Everson and Wilcox, 1985).

Table 2 Relative risk of other forms of cancer through passive smoking

Reference	Exposure	Risk ratio †
Miller (1984)	Spouse smoker	1.40
Sandler et al. (1985)*	Spouse or other household occupants	
	1 smoker	1.4
	2 smokers	2.3
	3 or more smokers	2.6

* Risk assessed for both smokers and nonsmokers (combined population).
† Risk relative to household where no smokers.

Effects upon the fetus of smoking during pregnancy include a reduced birthweight, an increased risk of prematurity and perinatal complications, and possibly some retardation in the physical growth and mental development of the child over the first ten years of life (Yarnell and St Leger, 1979; US Surgeon General, 1980). However, the fetus has little opportunity to complain about these problems, and to date society has done relatively little to protect the unborn child from the insults which may be inflicted upon it by its mother.

The attitudes of the nonsmoker toward cigarette smoke have undoubtedly been influenced by the growing knowledge of acute and chronic ill-effects of passive smoke exposure. In 1976, Shephard and LaBarre (1978) found that relatively few nonsmokers perceived tobacco smoke as a major source of air pollution (3.5 percent of subjects in heavily polluted urban areas, and 6.3 percent in residential areas, respectively). However, the proportion with this perception increased with age, rising to 9.9 and 11.7 percent for heavily polluted and residential areas, respectively in those aged 60–80 years. Several possible hypotheses may be advanced regarding this age gradient: (1) the elderly may move mainly in residential areas of the city, and thus have less experience of other sources of pollution; (2) many of the 60–80-year age group no longer live in their own homes—they thus encounter unaccustomed passive smoke exposure from which there is little escape on a daily basis; and (3) failing vision may be particularly vulnerable to the effects of eye irritants. In support of this hypothesis, elderly smokers were more frequently bothered by cigarettes than by smoke from other types of fire, while in younger individuals the reverse was true (Shephard et al., 1979a). Despite the limited importance attached to smoking as a source of air pollution in 1976, 90.7 percent of nonsmokers were prepared to support municipal politicians who were prepared to introduce 'tougher' legislation to control smoking (Shephard and LaBarre, 1978). An analogy may perhaps be drawn with noise pollution, where 'unnecessary' noise is perceived as much more annoying than that which it is difficult to avoid (Shephard, 1974). As might be predicted from the 'evaluation' scale of Fishbein's model and the perceived susceptibility of the health belief model, support for legislation against passive smoking rose from 58.5 percent in those subjects with little concern about air pollution in general to 89.3 percent in those individuals who were greatly concerned about air pollution. Support was also related to the beliefs of the individual concerning the health effects of smoking (Table 3). Support for control legislation was particularly strong in those subjects who were aware of the less commonly appreciated dangers of smoking.

Table 3 Influence of health beliefs on attitudes towards a politician willing to enact 'tougher' legislation to control smoking in public places (after Shephard, 1982) (percentages)

Attitude towards politician	Scientists have proven that smoking causes:							
	Lung cancer		Chronic chest disease		Coronary disease		Problems to unborn babies	
	Yes	No	Yes	No	Yes	No	Yes	No
Strongly support	46.2	35.9	50.9	30.4	55.6	32.5	52.4	34.7
Opposed	7.3	11.2	7.4	9.7	6.7	9.7	7.2	9.3

The situational component of attitudes postulated by Rokeach (1968) is well illustrated by differences in reactions to the smoking habits of a spouse and a workmate. Some 55 percent of nonsmokers believed that their health was adversely affected by passive exposure to smoke from a spouse's cigarettes, but 66 percent thought that their health was adversely affected by a smoking workmate (Shephard and LaBarre, 1978). Other locations where annoyance was anticipated depended partly on smoke concentrations (the areas most frequently mentioned were restaurants, 72.7 percent, cinemas, 65.9 percent and bars 64.8 percent) and partly on personal experience (for example, businessmen complained about smoke on aircraft, housewives about smoke in shops, and students about smoke on buses). A surprisingly high percentage of nonsmokers (41.8 percent) were annoyed by smoke in medical facilities. This again is probably situational, reflecting in part a perceived dissonance between the purpose of the facility and the reality of its impact upon health, and in part the initial ill-health of those visiting a doctor's office.

As early as 1976, 73 percent of all nonsmokers and 90 percent of those aged over 40 years had already seen material on the health hazards of passive smoke exposure (Shephard and LaBarre, 1978). The proportion of nonsmokers who said they were unaffected by passive exposure to cigarette smoking (11.6 percent) matches these figures, but a rather low proportion (41.6 percent) accepted that it had a major effect upon health. This emphasizes the relatively slow formation of health beliefs through campaigns of health education. In the United States the percentage regarding the smoke as hazardous rose from 46 percent in 1974 to 72 percent in 1980 (Glantz, 1985). At the period of our 1976 survey, about a half of the nonsmoking public considered that the main responsibility for the control of smoke accumulation lay with the general public. However, an average of 44 percent already saw it as a problem for government or public health workers, with a substantial difference of percentages between those who considered it a nuisance (47 percent) or a hazard to health (47 percent) and those who were unaffected by the smoke (24 percent). Interestingly, only 1.6 percent saw the problem primarily as an exercise in room ventilation; when the possibility of control by segregation of smokers or the improvement of ventilation was raised, the majority of nonsmokers thought that any resultant costs should be borne by the smoker. However 6.8 percent were themselves prepared to accept a 5 percent increase in costs for fares, entertainment and the like, a further 3.9 percent a 10 percent increase in costs, and another 1.8 percent an even larger increase in costs as the price of clean air. The desire to direct costs toward the smoker was greater if the smoke was thought to affect health (53 percent) than if there was no perceived health effect (44 percent).

Passive smoke effects on the smoker and the ex-smoker

The ex-smoker appreciates all the effects of passive smoke exposure already noted for the nonsmoker. In theory, one might anticipate that reactions would be exaggerated, for several reasons: (1) tobacco addiction and a risk of recidivism persist for up to ten years after a successful cigarette withdrawal campaign—there might thus be a perceived or a subconscious fear that the smell of burning tobacco would renew the craving for a cigarette; (2) smoking might have been stopped because symptoms were developing in the chest or elsewhere; and (3) the learning process which led to successful cigarette withdrawal might have increased knowledge of susceptibility to tobacco smoke, thus strengthening the desire to escape its adverse effects.

However, in most locations ex-smokers actually express annoyance somewhat less frequently than habitual nonsmokers (Shephard and LaBarre, 1978). There seems to be some habituation, either psychological or physiological, to a smoky atmosphere which is lost progressively after cigarette withdrawal. In subjects who have not smoked for at least five years, effects are perceived as frequently as in a nonsmoker. As a category, 37.6 percent of ex-smokers said they were unaffected by cigarette smoke (compared with 11.6 percent of nonsmokers), while a major effect upon health was perceived by 23.6 percent (vs 41.6 percent of nonsmokers). Ex-smokers were also less well informed on the dangers of passive smoking, only 62 percent having read such material (vs 73 percent of nonsmokers).

Since the habitual smoker spends much of his or her day at no more than arm's length from a smoldering cigarette, unless there is also some habituation, smokers should be the group who are most vulnerable to passive smoke exposure. In fact, only 38 percent of smokers notice watering of the eyes in a smoky room, compared with 56 percent of nonsmokers. Moreover, the smokers are slower to report this symptom than the nonsmokers. However, as might be predicted from the relative composition of sidestream and mainstream smoke, the proportion is higher than that for active smoking (21 percent). The recent analysis of Sandler et al. (1985) suggests that the presence of other smokers in a household increases the risk of various types of cancer for the smokers as well as for the nonsmoker.

In our 1976 survey a surprisingly large number of smokers (79 percent of light cigarette smokers—less than five cigarettes per day—and 68 percent of heavier smokers—more than five cigarettes per day) supported legislation to control smoking in public places (Shephard, 1982). Even among the heavier smokers, less than 15 percent were opposed to such legislation. A gratifying 67 percent of smokers were aware of the risks of passive smoking, and were concerned about effects they were having on the nonsmoker. A further 9 percent of smokers had read such reports, but stated that they did not believe them. The percentage of concerned smokers increased with age, from 62 percent in those under 20 years to 84 percent in those over 60 years of age. Very few smokers felt that nonsmokers should bear the added costs of ventilation caused by their habit, but on the other hand, less than a quarter of smokers were themselves prepared to pay more in order to provide clean air for the nonsmoker. The willingness to pay increased from 21 percent in the lightest smokers (less than five cigarettes/day) to 38 percent in the heaviest smokers (more than 40 cigarettes/day). However, there was also an increase in the proportion of individuals suggesting that nonsmokers should bear the costs, from 5 percent in the lightest smokers to 13–15 percent in those smoking more than 20 cigarettes per day. Some 94 percent of continuing smokers suggested they would accept a polite request to stop smoking if they were in a nonsmoking area, and 88 percent said they would also accept such a request for other enclosed areas. The majority of smokers either favored (37 percent) or were indifferent (48 percent) to the establishment of more nonsmoking areas. Those who regarded such action as an intrusion upon their personal liberty were more numerous among those who did not wish to give up smoking (23 percent) than among those who had some wish to halt their addiction (9 percent).

The attitudes of women toward smoking during pregnancy provide an interesting commentary on the possibility of voluntary restraint in the interests of a nonsmoker. The attention of the mother is focused upon the developing fetus, and there are unique opportunities for advice from health professionals at antenatal clinics. Nevertheless, only a minority of women stop smoking, or even reduce their cigarette consumption during pregnancy (Landesman-Dwyer and Emmanuel, 1979; Langford, Thompson and Tripp, 1980; US Surgeon General, 1980). Possibly because much of their advertising revenue is derived from cigarette manufacturers, women's magazines have provided extremely limited coverage of risks to the fetus (Shephard and Lorimer, 1982). The great majority of young female smokers (including those who intend to continue to smoke during pregnancy) are aware that their habit has a harmful effect upon both the fetus and the newborn child (Langford et al., 1980; Yankelovich, Skelly and White, Inc., 1979). Nevertheless, the success of quitting is influenced by the firmness of the belief that the fetus will be harmed (Dohrenwend and Dohrenwend, 1974). An important obstacle to the strengthening of this belief has been a lack of knowledge on the part of physicians. Danaher (1978) found 24 percent of doctors denying any influence of maternal smoking upon neonatal death. Moreover, many physicians who have the necessary knowledge fail to take the necessary time to communicate this information to their patients; only 24 percent of American women who were pregnant between 1970 and 1975 remembered receiving advice on smoking from their doctors (Harris, 1979). Arguments against such instruction in prenatal classes have included not only lack of time and educational material, but fear of upsetting the patient and a lack of knowledge on the part of the teacher (McRae and Choi-Lao, 1978). Factors influencing the success of educational programs are in part predictable from the behavioral models discussed above, including peer expectations (Baric and MacArthur, 1977) and a history of previous birth complications (Danaher, Shisslak, Thompson and Ford, 1978). Other positive influences are person-to-person contact (Gastrin and Ramstrom, 1979) and a high socioeconomic status (Baris, MacArthur and Sherwood, 1976). As in nonpregnant women, a fear of excessive weight gain is an argument sometimes advanced against stopping smoking (Donovan, Burgess, Hossack and Yudkin, 1975).

Health effects

As with any public health issue where risks are long-term and relatively small in magnitude, it is difficult to establish the nature and extent of the dangers to health associated with various doses of smoke exposure.

An earlier break-up of the tear film may predispose individuals to more frequent conjunctival infections, but there is no evidence on this as yet. In exposure to other types of airborn contaminant, it has been argued (Bates, 1974) that any level of exposure which causes changes of pulmonary function is too high, and may lead to pathological changes in sensitive individuals (for example, patients with a history of asthma and 'twitchy' airways). The study of Hirayama (1981) suggested an increased mortality from emphysema and asthma if the spouse was a smoker, and the spirals of sticky mucus usually associated with chronic bronchitis have been demonstrated in nonsmokers who work in smoky office buildings (Stock, 1980). The rather limited evidence of chronic respiratory disease in humans is supported by findings of chronic bronchitis and emphysema in animals that have been passively exposed to cigarette smoke (Shephard, 1982).

Inhibition of the movement of the hairlike cilia lining the airways, and an inhibition of the action of particle-ingesting phagocytic cells, leads to an increased pulmonary retention of both bacteria and fine particles. This could explain the increased incidence of respiratory disorders in smoke-exposed children over the first year of life (Colley et al., 1974; Holt and Turner, 1984; Leeder et al., 1976). This effect of passive smoking cannot be attributed to parental chest disease, social class, or birthweight of the infant; it shows a convincing dose-dependence, varying with the daily cigarette consumption of the household and being most marked when both parents smoke.

In the worst cases, blood carboxyhemoglobin rises to 2.5 percent. There may then be some increase in liability to angina and ischemic heart disease (Shephard, 1983). The potential influence of carbon monoxide upon the heart is particularly great in mountain areas (where people are already subjected to some hypoxia); a carbon monoxide-related oxygen lack can also contribute to the harmful effects of smoking upon the developing fetus.

Direct evidence concerning cancer and smoking has already been discussed. An editorial in the *British Medical Journal* (1978) suggested that 75 percent of the benzpyrene emitted from cigarettes appeared in the sidestream smoke, and that under conditions of poor ventilation a nonsmoker could inhale smoke equivalent to the consumption of four cigarettes over a single hour. On this basis it was estimated that regular, heavy passive exposure to cigarette smoke could cause two cases of lung cancer per 100,000 nonsmokers per year. Animal experiments (Shephard, 1982) have generally supported the view that prolonged passive smoke exposure causes lung cancer, although the tumors tend to be adenocarcinomas, in contrast with the squamous cell carcinomas found in active smokers.

The infants born to smoking mothers are on average about 200 g lighter than those born to nonsmokers, and there is a two-fold increase in the likelihood of bearing an infant weighing less than 2.5 kg (US Surgeon General, 1980). Infants in this last category have a 30-fold increase in the risk of neonatal mortality. The subsequent growth and intellectual development of the child may be retarded to at least eleven years of age (Butler and Goldstein, 1973; Davies, Gray, Ellwood and Abernethy, 1976; Naeye, Herkness and Utts, 1977).

Effects on performance

The main effect of passive smoking on performance is probably a deterioration of cognitive function in the nonsmoker (Oborne, 1983). Arousal is increased by annoyance—particularly if the smoker is perceived as discourteous—and in keeping with the inverted-U relationship between the level of arousal and function, the optimum for performance is exceeded in many individuals. Disturbances are particularly likely in small, enclosed spaces (such as an aircraft cockpit), where the work is in itself very demanding (and thus arousing). Problems are also exacerbated if the subject has an introverted personality (and is thus already strongly aroused). Particularly in older individuals, conjunctival irritation and lachrymation may also impair vision (Shephard, Ponsford, Basu and LaBarre, 1979a,b).

Some reports have suggested that the psychomotor function of a nonsmoker is impaired with a 2.0–2.5 percent carboxyhemoglobin level (Shephard, 1983)—in particular some deterioration of vigilance, such as failure to detect differences in signal length, tone loudness and light brightness has been described. However, not all authors have been able to demonstrate such responses, and the threshold for hypoxic deterioration of psychomotor function remains a matter for vigorous debate.

Even a small increase of carboxyhemoglobin decreases the oxygen-carrying capacity of the blood. One would thus anticipate a proportional reduction of maximal performance in large muscle tasks dependent on oxygen delivery, with an earlier onset of fatigue in submaximal effort. Horvath, Raven, Dahms and Gray (1975) suggested that there was no effect until a blood level of 4 percent carboxyhemoglobin was attained. However, the threshold that they propose seems largely an error inherent in fitting a regression line. In fact, Horvath et al. did not present convincing evidence against a direct proportionality between maximum oxygen intake and carboxyhemoglobin levels. The potential for cigarette smoke to curtail physical performance in patients suffering from exercise-induced angina was clearly demonstrated by Aronow and Isbell (1973).

METHODOLOGICAL PROBLEMS

Attitude formation and change

For a long period, quantitative studies of attitude formation and attitude change remained in disrepute, because social scientists were able to explain only a very small proportion of the variance in their observations (5–10 percent). The situation has greatly improved with the development of clear, theoretical models and the use of precise, reliable and valid questionnaires. Nevertheless, the greatest success to date has been in describing fairly simple commercial operations such as the marketing of a particular brand of toothpaste. The value of 'rational behavior' models in exploring the complex issues of passive smoking behavior has yet to be established. As in other lifestyle applications, it is unlikely that more than 50 percent of the total variance will be explained by the model, leaving the challenge of discovering other instruments to explore the remainder of the behavioral equation.

Effects on the nonsmoker

The main difficulty in examining the effects of passive smoking on the nonsmoker is the impossibility of carrying out double-blind experiments. When observations are made in the community it is also extremely difficult to determine the extent of exposure. The spouse or working colleague is known simply as a 'smoker', but may consume anywhere from one to 50 cigarettes per day, with ten-fold variations in the nicotine and tar content of the smoke from one type of cigarette to another. The extent of contact with the smoker is equally varied, as is the degree of ventilation of the room. Measures of blood or urinary cotinine provide a more sensitive exposure index, but such studies are hardly feasible in the context of large epidemiological studies of passive smoking and cancer. Moreover, even blood measurements may not indicate the critical variable—the relative proportions of mainstream and sidestream smoke present in the inspired atmosphere.

Increasingly, the habit of smoking is concentrated among the poor and ill-educated sections of society who have a poor general lifestyle. This further complicates analyses where selection is based on the smoking habits of the marriage partner (or in the case of the fetus, the mother).

In terms of physiological response, changes of respiratory function may have a considerable health significance, but effects on the individual are small and at the borderline for detection by procedures which often have a test to test variation of 10 or even 20 percent.

Finally, there is a need for good instruments to rate the suggestibility of subjects.

Effects on the ex-smoker and smoker

The main experimental difficulty when dealing with the ex-smoker and the smoker is in separating the strong effects of direct exposure from what are probably the weaker effects of passive exposure to cigarette smoke.

In terms of attitudes there may also be a gap between the expressed behavioral intentions (which reflect the strong social pressure toward clean air) and the actual behavior in the presence of a nonsmoker. More work is needed on methods of examining the influence of addictions in: (1) modifying the truth of stated attitudes and subjective norms, and (2) interfering with the translation of a behavioral intention into overt behavior.

Health effects

Analysis of acute effects on respiratory health is complicated by an association between smoking households, poor socioeconomic conditions (including industrial exposure to air contaminants and contaminated residential areas), chronic coughs (which could pass a respiratory infection to a spouse or child) and poor general attitudes to health. The significance of minor changes in respiratory function is also far from clearly established, and where mother/child interactions are examined there may be a common genetic susceptibility to respiratory disease.

Likewise, when examining chronic changes of lung function, a complex multivariate equation is needed to adjust for such influences as age, sex, race, socioeconomic status and parental function. Given the errors of estimation at each step in this process it is hardly surprising that the effects of passive smoking sometimes seem small and of limited statistical significance, even if a large-scale survey has been completed.

The most dramatic chronic effect of smoke exposure is an increased risk of lung and other types of cancer. However, an enormous number of subjects must be scanned in order to find a single death from a histologically proven lung cancer where the victim is clearly established as a nonsmoker, the smoking habits of the spouse are clearly established and due adjustments can be made for such variables as occupation and socioeconomic status. Further, there seems to be some difference in the *type* of lung cancer between active and passive smokers, possibly because the air contaminants are carried further into the lung when passively inhaled by normal ventilation rather than a small puff on a cigarette.

Effects on performance

As with physiological tests, the main difficulty in describing psychological and psychomotor changes is that the disturbance of function is small relative to the error inherent in the test. However, there is the added complication of a probable inverted-U-shaped relationship between exposure and performance, with considerable difficulty in deciding whether a given individual carrying out a specific task is on the ascending or the descending portion of the curve (Shephard, 1974).

Secular trends

All research on smoking and health is complicated by secular trends. The nature of the average cigarette, its combustion properties, and its yields of tar and nicotine, have changed dramatically over the past ten years. As a reaction to such changes, and to deliberate modifications of packaging format, the average smoker has consumed a progressively larger number of cigarettes per day; the proportions of main and sidestream smoke have also altered, since low-nicotine cigarettes have encouraged the smoker to take longer, deeper and more frequent inhalations. Random exposure to cigarettes in restaurants, public service vehicles, offices and places of entertainment has been reduced by increased control legislation, but domestic exposure (where the spouse smokes) has probably been increased by the construction of more airtight houses. At the same time, the attitudes and beliefs of both the nonsmoker and the smoker about the dangers of passive smoking have undergone a very rapid change. All of these factors make it very difficult to compare results from one country to another, or even from one year to another within a given country.

FUTURE RESEARCH

Attitude formation and change

There is plainly scope for early application of a Fishbein-type research model to problems of attitude formation in passive smoking. It will be particularly interesting to assess the relative importance of attitudes versus subjective norms, and thus to decide the relative importance of individual education versus a modification of the social environment in dealing with problems of passive smoking. It will be particularly interesting to assess the influence of the various types of cigarette addiction (physiological, psychological and habit) upon the operation of a rational behavior model, and to evaluate the truthfulness of responses to an attitudinal questionnaire.

Effects on the nonsmoker

Given the complaints of acute visual impairment, it would seem useful to make measurements of visual thresholds and visual discriminating capacity at various ages before, during and after passive exposure to cigarette smoke. Discriminant analysis may prove a useful technique in combining various individually marginal changes of pulmonary or psychomotor function into an unequivocal index of physiological and psychological response. If the peripheral distribution of 'passive smoke' within the lungs is confirmed, it may be helpful to evaluate disturbances of pulmonary function using tests of small rather than large airway function. However, even if more sensitive laboratory tests can be devised, it seems likely that symptomatic responses will remain the best indicator of exposure. There is thus scope to develop a psychometric scale of exposure, analogous to Borg's scale for the rating of perceived exertion. Moreover, there seems a need to examine the potential contribution of preconceived beliefs to subjective, physiological and psychomotor responses to cigarette smoke.

There have already been some estimates of the minimum ventilation needed to keep a room clear of cigarette smoke (Cain, Leaderer, Isseroff, Berglund, Huey, Lipsitt and Perlman, 1983), together with at least one calculation of the extra energy needed for heating and refrigeration (Shephard, 1982). There seems a need for others to check these figures, even if the conclusion is drawn that this offers an unreasonably expensive solution to the problem.

Effects on the smoker

In terms of subjective responses the smoker seems capable of distinguishing between passive and active smoking. It will thus be of value to continue careful comparisons between the smoker and the nonsmoker, examining how far a lesser response in the smoker reflects an habituation to smoke, and how far it reflects an overreaction on the part of the nonsmoker. The excess mortality of smokers passively exposed to cigarette smoke during growth, or through the smoking habits of a spouse, should be further evaluated, since this may provide a valuable indication of the relative toxicity of mainstream and sidestream smoke. Control of cigarette smoke in the workplace is a current issue, and given that the majority of smokers express a wish to stop smoking, it would be interesting to make a careful analysis of companies where such schemes are being introduced, to examine (1) how far such action helps the process of smoking withdrawal, and (2) how far the smokers appreciate the advantages of a cleaner, safer and smoke-free working environment.

Effects on health

One key question, as with most toxic agents, is whether there is a threshold dose for adverse effects, or whether the deterioration in health is a continuous function of smoke exposure. If there is indeed a threshold, a related issue is an acceptable margin of safety. For most environmental problems a 100-fold margin is required. If society accepts such a margin for passive smoking, all passive exposure to cigarette smoke would be precluded. However, there remains a need to establish more clearly the relationship between measurable indices of passive exposure (such as carboxyhemoglobin, cotinine and thiocyanate) and the chemical agents which contribute to chronic bronchitic and carcinogenic change.

The long-term impact of maternal smoking during pregnancy demands further exploration. If problems are arising from a carbon monoxide-induced fetal hypoxia in the early weeks of pregnancy, the current trend to low-nicotine/low-tar cigarettes will likely worsen the situation of the fetus by increasing the maternal demand for the smoke.

Effects on performance

The interactions of personality, task difficulty, intelligence and the annoyance caused by passive exposure to cigarette smoke merit further analysis in the framework of the inverted-U-shaped relationship between performance and arousal. It seems obvious that work requiring fine vision must be impaired by conjunctival inflammation and watering of the eyes, but a dose–response relationship of this effect has yet to be clearly established in offices and factories where smoking is still allowed. The interpersonal conflicts between smokers and nonsmokers must also have a negative impact on productivity, and the extent of this loss deserves measurement. A full economic analysis should be undertaken in organizations where pollution control measures are being introduced, including an assessment of gains in productivity by smokers as the time-wasting ritual of the cigarette is avoided. Attitudes toward work among both smokers and nonsmokers should also be explored, before and after the introduction of smoke control regulations.

CONCLUSIONS

There is now sufficient evidence to show that passive exposure to cigarette smoke is not only annoying to the nonsmoker, but also has adverse effects upon health and performance. There are acute effects on vision, and liability to respiratory infections, while asthmatic attacks may be provoked in sensitive individuals. Long-term influences include an increased risk of various forms of cancer, with a probable increase in the chances of developing emphysema and chronic obstructive lung disease. Maternal smoking further imposes upon the developing fetus the hazards of increased perinatal mortality, with delays in subsequent physical and mental development. The costs of increased ventilation to limit smoke accumulation are very high, and the majority of both smokers and nonsmokers seem unwilling to bear such costs. Voluntary restriction of smoking also seems relatively ineffective. Given the general acceptance of regulation by both smokers and nonsmokers, the process of developing laws and bylaws to guarantee smoke-free air in public enclosed spaces should continue and, where possible, it should be accelerated.

RECOMMENDATIONS

(1) More precise methods of estimating personal exposure to the most toxic components of cigarette smoke should be developed.
(2) Dose–response curves should be obtained for both acute and chronic reactions to passive smoke, to see if there is a threshold dose.
(3) Attitudinal models of the Fishbein type should be applied in the context of passive smoking behavior.
(4) Concepts of the arousal curve should be applied to the impact of passive smoke exposure upon performance.
(5) Regulations to ensure smoke-free air in public places should be introduced as rapidly as feasible. Attitudinal studies should examine prospectively the impact of such measures upon the smoker and the nonsmoker.
(6) Comparable measures are needed to protect the unborn fetus against the immediate and long-term health effects of maternal smoking.

REFERENCES

Aronow, W.S. (1978). Effects of passive smoking on angina pectoris. *New England Journal of Medicine*, **299**, 21–24.

Aronow, W.S., and Isbell, M.W. (1973). Carbon monoxide: effect on exercise-induced angina pectoris. *Annals of Internal Medicine*, **79**, 392–395.

Baric, L., and MacArthur, C. (1977). Health norms in pregnancy. *British Journal of Preventive and Social Medicine*, **31**, 30–38.

Baric, L., MacArthur, C., and Sherwood, M. (1976). A study of health education aspects of smoking in pregnancy. *International Journal of Health Education (Suppl.)*, **19**, 1–16.

Basu, P.K., Pimm, P.E., Shephard, R.J., and Silverman, F. (1978). The effect of cigarette smoke on the human tear film. *Canadian Journal of Ophthalmology*, **13**, 22–26.

Bates, D.V. (1974). The Canadian air pollution problem in retrospect. In: R.J. Shephard, D. Pengelly and F. Silverman (eds), *Proceedings of First Canadian Conference on Research in Atmospheric Pollution*. Toronto: University of Toronto, 1974, pp. 84–91.

Beardon, W.O., and Woodside, A.G. (1978). Situational and extended attitude models as predictors of marijuana intentions and reported behavior. *Journal of Social Psychology*, **106**, 57–67.

Becker, C.G., Levi, R., and Zavecz, J. (1979). Induction of IgE antibodies to antigen isolated from tobacco leaves and from cigarette smoke condensate. *American Journal of Pathology*, **96**, 249–256.

Becker, M.H., and Maiman, L. (1975). Socio-behavioral determinants of compliance with health and medical care recommendations. *Medical Care*, **13**, 10–24.

British Medical Journal (1978). Breathing other people's smoke (Editorial). *British Medical Journal*, **ii**, 453–454.

Brunnemann, K.D., Yu, L., and Hoffmann, D. (1977). Assessment of carcinogenic volatile N-nitrosamines in tobacco and in mainstream and sidestream smoke from cigarettes. *Cancer Research*, **37**, 3218–3222.

Butler, N.R., and Goldstein, H. (1973). Smoking in pregnancy and subsequent child development. *British Medical Journal*, **iv**, 573.

Cain, W.S., Leaderer, B.P., Isseroff, R., Berglund, L.G., Huey, R.J., Lipsitt, E.D., and Perlman, D. (1983). Ventilation requirements in buildings. 1. Control of occupancy odor and tobacco smoke odor. *Atmospheric Environment*, **17**, 1183–1197.

Cameron, P. (1972). Second-hand tobacco smoke: children's reactions. *Journal of School Health*, **42**, 280–284.

Canadian Tobacco Manufacturers' Council (1985). *Tobacco Smoke and the Non-smoker*. Montreal: Canadian Tobacco Manufacturers' Council.

Chan, W.C., and Fung, S.C. (1982). Lung cancer in non-smokers in Hong Kong. In: E. Grundmann, J. Clemmesen and C.S. Moir (eds), *Geographical Pathology in Cancer Epidemiology. Cancer Campaign*, vol. 6. New York: Gustav Fischer Verlag, pp. 199–202.

Cockcroft, D.W., MacCormack, D.W., Tarlo, S.M., Hargreave, F.E., and Pengelly, L.D. (1979). Nasal airway inspiratory resistance. *American Review of Respiratory Disease*, **119**, 921–926.

Colley, J.R.T., Holland, W.W., and Corkhill, T.T. (1974). Influence of passive smoking and parental phlegm on pneumonia and bronchitis in early childhood. *Lancet*, **ii**, 1031–1034.

Correa, P., Pickle, L.W., Fontham, L.E., Lin, Y., and Haenszel, W. (1983). Passive smoking and lung cancer. *Lancet*, **ii**, 595–597.

Dahms, T.E., Bolin, J.F., and Slavin, R.G. (1981). Passive smoking: effects on bronchial asthma. *Chest*, **80**, 530–534.

Danaher, B.G. (1978). Ob. Gyn. intervention in helping smokers quit. In: J.L. Schwarz (ed.), *Progress in Smoking Cessation*. New York: American Cancer Society, pp. 316–328.

Danaher, B.G., Shisslak, C.M., Thompson, C.B., and Ford, J.D. (1978). A smoking cessation program for pregnant women: an explanatory study. *American Journal of Public Health*, **68**, 896–898.

Davies, D.P., Gray, O.P., Ellwood, P.C., and Abernethy, M. (1976). Cigarette smoking in pregnancy: associations with maternal weight gain and fetal growth. *Lancet*, **i**, 385–387.

Dishman, R. (1982). Compliance/adherence in health related exercise. *Health Psychology*, **1**, 237–267.

Dodge, R. (1982). The effects of indoor pollution on Arizona children. *Archives of Environmental Health*, **37**, 151–155.

Dohrenwend, B.S., and Dohrenwend, D.P. (1974). *Stressful Life Events: Their Nature and Effects*. New York: John Wiley & Sons.

Donovan, J.R., Burgess, P.L., Hossack, C.M., and Yudkin, G.D. (1975). Routine advice against smoking in pregnancy. *Journal of the Royal College of General Practitioners*, **15**, 264–268.

Fergusson, D.M., Horwood, L.J., Shannon, F.T., and Taylor, B. (1981). Parental smoking and lower respiratory illness in the first three years of life. *Journal of Epidemiology and Community Health*, **35**, 180–184.

Ferris, B.G., Dockery, D.W., Ware, J.H., Berkey, C.S., and Speizer, F.E. (1984). Effects of passive smoking on children in the six-cities study. In: G. Borglund, T. Lindvall and J. Sundell (eds), *Indoor Air, Radon, Passive Smoking, Particulates and Housing Epidemiology 2*. Stockholm: Swedish Council for Building Research.

Fishbein, M., and Ajzen, I. (1974). Attitudes towards objects as predictors of single and multiple behavioral criteria. *Psychological Review*, **81**, 59–74.

Garfinkel, L. (1981). Time trends in lung cancer mortality among non-smokers and a note on passive smoking. *Journal of the National Cancer Institute*, **66**, 1061–1066.

Gastrin, G., and Ramstrom, L.M. (1979). How to reach and convince pregnant women to give up smoking. In: J.L. Schwartz (ed.), *Progress in Smoking Cessation*. New York: American Cancer Society, pp. 154–159.

Glantz, S.A. (1985). The tobacco industry's response to scientific evidence on involuntary smoking. In: W.F. Forbes, R.C. Frecker and D. Nostbakken (eds), *Proceedings of the Fifth World Conference on Smoking and Health*. Ottawa: Canadian Council on Smoking and Health, pp. 278–292.

Grimmer, G., Boehnke, H., and Harke, H.P. (1977). Zum problem des Passivrauchens: Aufnahme von polycyclischen aromatischen Kohlenwasserstoffen durch Einatmen von zigarettentrauch-haltiger Luft. *International Archives of Occupational and Environmental Health*, **40**, 93–99.

Harlap, S., and Davies, A.M. (1974). Infant admissions to hospital and maternal smoking. *Lancet*, **i**, 529–532.

Harris, J.E. (1979). Smoking during pregnancy. Preliminary results from the National Clearing House on Smoking and Health, 1975 prevalence data. (Cited by US Surgeon General, 1979, *Smoking and Health*, Washington, DC: DHEW Publication, PHS79-50066.)

Hasselbad, V., Humble, C.G., Graham, M.G., and Anderson, H.S. (1981). Indoor environmental determinants of lung function in children. *American Review of Respiratory Disease*, **123**, 479–485.

Hirayama, T. (1981). Non-smoking wives of heavy smokers have a higher risk of lung cancer: a study from Japan. *British Medical Journal*, **282**, 183–185.

Hirayama, T. (1983). Passive smoking and lung cancer: consistency of association. *Lancet*, **ii**, 1425–1426.

Holt, P.G., and Turner, K.J. (1984). Respiratory symptoms in children of smokers: an overview. In: R. Rylander, Y. Peterson and M-C. Snella (eds), E.T.S.—environmental tobacco smoke. *European Journal of Respiratory Diseases* (Suppl.), **133**(65), 109–120.

Horton, D.J., Suda, W.L., Kinsman, R.A., Souhrada, J., and Spector, S. (1978). Bronchoconstrictive suggestion in asthma: a role for airways hyper-reactivity and emotions. *American Review of Respiratory Disease*, **117**, 1029–1038.

Horvath, S.M., Raven, P.B., Dahms, T.E., and Gray, D.J. (1975). Maximal aerobic capacity at different levels of carboxyhaemoglobin. *Journal of Applied Physiology*, **38**, 300–303.

Jaccard, J.J. (1975). A theoretical analysis of selected factors important to health education strategies. *Health Education Monographs*, **3**, 152–167.

Kabat, G.C., and Wynder, E.L. (1984). Lung cancer in non-smokers. *Cancer*, **53**, 1214–1221.

Kauffman, F., Tessier, J.F., and Oriol, P. (1983). Adult passive smoking in the home environment: a risk factor for chronic airflow limitation. *American Journal of Epidemiology*, **117**, 269–280.

Koo, L.C., and Ho, J.H.C. (1985). Cultural, environmental and familial backgrounds of female lung cancer patients in Hong Kong: a retrospective case control study. *Directory of On-Going Research in Smoking and Health*. Washington, DC: US Public Health Service, p. 81.

Landesman-Dwyer, S., and Emmanuel, I. (1979). Smoking during pregnancy. *Teratology*, **19**, 119–125.

Langford, E.R., Thompson, E., and Tripp, S.C. (1980). Smoking and health education during pregnancy: evaluation of a program for women in pre-natal classes. Unpublished report, Department of Health Administration, University of Toronto.

Lebowitz, M.D., and Burrows, B. (1976). Respiratory symptoms related to smoking habits of family adults. *Chest*, **69**, 48–50.

Lebowitz, M.D., Armet, B.D., and Knudson, R. (1982). The effect of passive smoking on pulmonary function in children. *Environment International*, **8**, 371–373.

Leeder, S.R., Corkhill, R., Irwig, L.M., Holland, W.W., and Colley, J.R.T. (1976). Influence of family factors on the incidence of lower respiratory illness during the first year of life. *British Journal of Preventive and Social Medicine*, **30**, 203–212.

Luparello, J., Lyons, H.A., Bleeker, E.R., and McFadden, E.R. (1968). Influence of suggestion on airway reactivity in asthmatic subjects. *Psychosomatic Medicine*, **30**, 819–825.

McRae, B.C., and Choi-Lao, A.T.H. (1978). National survey on smoking and health education in pre-natal classes in Canada. *Canadian Journal of Public Health*, **69**, 427–430.

Miller, G.H. (1984). Cancer, passive smoking and non-employed and employed wives. *Western Medical Journal*, **140**, 632–635.

Muramatsu, T., Weber, A., Muramatsu, S., and Akermann, F. (1983). An experimental study on irritation and annoyance due to passive smoking. *International Archives of Occupational and Environmental Health*, **51**, 305–317.

Naeye, R.L., Herkness, W.L., and Utts, J. (1977). Abruptio placentae and perinatal 'death': a prospective study. *American Journal of Diseases of Children*, **130**, 1207–1210.

Newman, J.E. (1974). Predicting absenteeism and turnover: a field comparison of Fishbein's model and traditional job attitude measures. *Journal of Applied Physiology*, **59**, 610–615.

Oborne, D. (1983). Cognitive effects of passive smoking. *Ergonomics*, **26**, 1163–1172.

O'Connell, E., and Logan, G.B. (1974). Parental smoking in childhood asthma. *Annals of Allergy*, **32**, 142–145.

Phillips, R.L., Wilde, G.J.S., and Day, J.H. (1972). Suggestion and relaxation in asthmatics. *Journal of Psychosomatic Research*, **16**, 192–204.

Pimm, P.E., Shephard, R.J., and Silverman, F. (1978). Psychological effects of acute passive exposure to cigarette smoke. *Archives of Environmental Health*, **33**, 201–213.

Repace, J.L. (1985). The dosimetry of passive smoking. In: W.F. Forbes, R.C. Frecker and D. Nostbakken (eds), *Proceedings of the Fifth World Conference on Smoking and Health*. Ottawa: Canadian Council on Smoking and Health, pp. 191–198.

Rokeach, M. (1968). *Beliefs, Attitudes and Values*. San Francisco, CA: Jossey Bass.

Saltzer, E.B. (1981). Cognitive moderators of the relationship between behavioral intentions and behavior. *Journal of Personality and Social Psychology*, **41**, 260–271.

Samet, J.M., and Speizer, F.E. (1985). Passive smoking and the lungs. A review of effects other than malignancy. *Proceedings of the Fifth World Conference on Smoking and Health*. Ottawa: Canadian Cancer Society, pp. 1–24.

Sandler, D.P., Everson, R.B., and Wilcox, A.J. (1985). Passive smoking in adulthood and cancer risk. *American Journal of Epidemiology*, **121**, 37–48.

Savel, H. (1970). Clinical hypersensitivity to cigarette smoke. *Archives of Environmental Health*, **21**, 146–148.

Schilling, R.S.F., Letai, A.D., Hui, S.L., Beck, G.J., Schoenberg, J.B., and Bouhuys, A. (1977). Lung function, respiratory disease and smoking in families. *American Journal of Epidemiology*, **106**, 274–283.

Shephard, R.J. (1974). *Men at Work*. Springfield, IL: Charles C. Thomas.

Shephard, R.J. (1982). *The Risks of Passive Smoking*. London: Croom Helm.

Shephard, R.J. (1983). *Carbon Monoxide—the Silent Killer*. Springfield, IL: Charles C. Thomas.

Shephard, R.J., and LaBarre, R. (1978). Attitudes of the public towards cigarette smoke in public places. *Canadian Journal of Public Health*, **69**, 302–310.

Shephard, R.J., and Lorimer, J. (1982). Attitudes towards the hazards of smoking: the influence of pregnancy. In: R. Viswanathan (ed.), *Smoking and Health*. Special issue of *Indian Journal of Chest Diseases and Allied Sciences*.

Shephard, R.J., Collins, R., and Silverman, F. (1979a). Responses of exercising subjects to acute 'passive' cigarette smoke exposure. *Environmental Research*, **19**, 279–291.

Shephard, R.J., Collins, R., and Silverman, F. (1979b). Passive exposure of asthmatic subjects to cigarette smoke. *Environmental Research*, **20**, 279–291.

Shephard, R.J., Ponsford, E., Basu, P.K., and LaBarre, R. (1979a). Effects of cigarette smoke on the eyes and airway. *International Archives of Occupational and Environmental Health*, **43**, 135–144.

Shephard, R.J., Ponsford, E., Basu, P.K., and LaBarre, R. (1979b). Effects of cigarette smoking on intraocular pressure and vision. *British Journal of Ophthalmology*, **62**, 682–687.

Spector, S., Luparello, T.J., Kopetzky, M.T., Souhrada, J., and Kinsman, R.A. (1976). Response of asthmatics to methacholine and suggestion. *American Review of Respiratory Disease*, **113**, 43–50.

Stock, S. (1980). The perils of second hand smoking. *New Scientist*, **2** (October), 10–13.

Stutzman, T.M., and Green, S.B. (1982). Factors affecting energy consumption: two field tests of the Fishbein–Ajzen model. *Journal of Social Psychology*, **117**, 183–201.

Tager, I.B., Weiss, S.T., Rosner, B., and Speizer, F.E. (1979). Effect of parental cigarette smoking on the pulmonary function of children. *American Journal of Epidemiology*, **110**, 14–26.

Triandis, H.C. (1977). *Interpersonal Behavior*. Monterey, CA: Brookes-Cole.

Trichopoulos, D., Kalandidi, A., and Sparros, L. (1983). Lung cancer and passive smoking. Conclusion of Greek study. *Lancet*, **ii**, 677–678 (letter).

Trichopoulos, D., Kalandidi, A., Sparros, L., and MacMahon, B. (1981). Lung cancer and passive smoking. *International Journal of Cancer*, **27**, 1–4.

United States Surgeon General (1980). *The Health Consequences of Smoking for Women*. Washington, DC: US Government Printing Office.

United States Surgeon General (1986). *The Health Consequences of Involuntary Smoking.* Washington, DC: US Government Printing Office.

Weber, A. (1984). Environmental tobacco smoke 3.4. Acute effects of environmental tobacco smoke. *European Journal of Respiratory Diseases*, **65** (Suppl. 133), 98–108.

Weiss, J.H., Martin, C., and Riley, J. (1970). Effects of suggestion on respiration of asthmatic children. *Psychosomatic Medicine*, **32**, 409–415.

Weiss, S.T., Tager, I.B., Speizer, F.E., and Rosner, B. (1980). Persistent wheeze. *American Review of Respiratory Disease*, **122**, 679–707.

White, J.R., and Froeb, H.F. (1980). Small airways dysfunction in non-smokers chronically exposed to tobacco smoke. *New England Journal of Medicine*, **302**, 720–723.

Wilson, A.G., and Farant, J.P. (1985). *Workshop on Indoor Air Quality: Canadian Issues and Opportunities.* Ottawa: Environment Canada.

Winneke, G., Plischke, K., Roscovanu, A., and Schlipkoeter, H-W. (1984). Patterns and determinants of reaction to tobacco smoke in an experimental exposure setting. In: G. Berglund, T. Lindvall and J. Sundell (eds), *Indoor Air, Radon, Passive Smoking, Particulates and Housing Epidemiology*, vol. 2. Stockholm: Swedish Council for Building Research.

Yankelovich, Skelly and White, Inc. (1977). *A Study of Cigarette Smoking Among Teen-age Girls and Young Women: Summary of the findings.* Washington, DC: National Cancer Institute, DHEW (NIH) Publication 77-1203.

Yarnell, J.W.G., and St Leger, A. (1979). Respiratory illness, maternal smoking habits and lung function in children. *British Journal of Diseases of the Chest*, **73**, 230–236.

Zussman, B.M. (1970). Tobacco sensitivity in the allergic patient. *Annals of Allergy*, **28**, 371–377.

13

Smoking Attitudes and Behavior: Applications of Fishbein and Ajzen's Theory of Reasoned Action to Predicting and Understanding Smoking Decisions

STEPHEN SUTTON

ABSTRACT

This chapter reviews applications of the Fishbein and Ajzen theory of reasoned action to predicting and understanding smoking decisions. The model is described and examples are given of how the components are operationalized. Applications to smoking are then reviewed and criticisms of the model are discussed. To date, all the studies in this area have been correlational and in most cases they have used a cross-sectional design with no behavioral follow-up. Although they have shown consistent support for the model, the correlations are lower than might have been expected and the model may need to be elaborated by incorporating additional explanatory variables and causal linkages. There is a pressing need for prospective experimental studies incorporating behavioral measures.

INTRODUCTION

The notion that attitudes are important in understanding and predicting smoking behavior has been pervasive in research on smoking. It also under-lies attempts to change smoking behavior by means of public information

Smoking and Human Behavior, Edited by T. Ney and A. Gale

campaigns. The literature on smoking attitudes is vast, amounting to thousands of published studies. However, the great majority of studies have been atheoretical in orientation and this has hampered progress toward developing a sound and cumulative body of knowledge on the subject of smoking attitudes. This chapter will not attempt to review all the literature. Instead, it will focus on a theory of attitude–behavior relations which has been influential in recent years, and has been applied with some success to topics as diverse as seat belt use (Wittenbraker, Gibbs and Kahle, 1983), family planning (Davidson and Jaccard, 1975), drug use (Bentler and Speckart, 1979), voting behavior (Fishbein, Ajzen and Hinkle, 1980), coupon usage (Shimp and Kavas, 1984), and infant-feeding behavior (Manstead, Proffitt and Smart, 1983). The theory is known as the Fishbein–Ajzen behavioral intention model or, more recently, as the theory of reasoned action (Ajzen and Fishbein, 1980; Fishbein and Ajzen, 1975). This chapter describes the model, reviews applications of the model to smoking decisions, and discusses the problems and potential of the model as applied to smoking.

THE THEORY OF REASONED ACTION

Fishbein and Ajzen make the assumption that most behaviors of social relevance are under volitional control, and that a person's intention to perform (or not to perform) a behavior is both the immediate determinant and the best single predictor of that behavior. Intention in turn is held to be a function of two basic determinants, one personal and the other reflecting social influence. The personal factor is the individual's positive or negative evaluation of performing the behavior. This is referred to as attitude toward the behavior (AB). The second determinant represents the perceived expectations of important others with regard to his/her performing the behavior in question, and is called the subjective norm (SN). Generally speaking, people will have strong intentions to perform a given action if they evaluate it positively, and if they believe that important others think they should perform it. These two components, attitude toward the behavior and subjective norm, are assumed to combine additively to determine behavioral intention (BI):

$$BI = w_1(AB) + w_2(SN),$$

where w_1 and w_2 are weights representing the relative importance of the personal–attitudinal and the social–normative components. The relative importance of the two factors will vary depending on the intention, the population and the individual in question. In some cases the attitudinal factor will be more important; in other cases normative considerations will predominate.

The theory also specifies the determinants of AB and SN. Attitude toward the behavior is held to reflect the person's salient beliefs concerning the possible consequences of the action. Generally speaking, a person who believes that performing a given behavior will lead to mostly positive outcomes will hold a favorable attitude toward the behavior, and, conversely, a person who believes that the action will result in mostly negative outcomes will hold an unfavorable attitude. Specifically, AB is held to be a function of the sum of the person's salient behavioral beliefs (b_i) concerning the outcomes of the action, each weighted by their evaluation (e_i) of that outcome:

$$AB = \sum_{i=1}^{n} b_i e_i,$$

where n is the number of salient outcomes. Subjective norm is also a function of beliefs, namely the person's beliefs that specific individuals or groups think he or she should or should not perform the behavior. Generally speaking, a person who believes that most significant referents think he or she should perform the behavior will perceive social pressure to do so. Specifically, SN is held to be a function of the sum of the person's salient normative beliefs (nb_j) concerning each referent, each weighted by their motivation to comply (mc_j) with that referent:

$$SN = \sum_{j=1}^{m} nb_j mc_j,$$

where m is the number of salient referents. In other words, a person's behavioral intentions, and hence behavior, depend ultimately on that person's beliefs concerning (a) the possible consequences of the behavior and (b) the expectations of important others. It follows that in order to change behavior it is necessary to change these underlying beliefs.

Figure 1 summarizes the theory of reasoned action in the form of a causal model or path diagram. Fishbein and Ajzen argue that variables other than BI, AB, SN and their component beliefs, that is variables 'external' to the model, can influence intentions, and hence behavior, only by influencing AB, SN or the relative importance of these two components. For example, the intention to perform a given action may be related to demographic variables such as age or social class, or to personality characteristics such as introversion–extraversion. However, according to Fishbein and Ajzen, the effects of these variables on intentions would be entirely mediated by their effects on AB and SN. Thus, the theory of reasoned action specifies the proximal determinants of intentions and behavior.

According to Fishbein and Ajzen a measure of intention will not always be an accurate predictor of behavior. There are at least two factors that

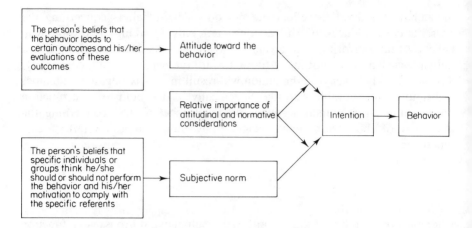

Fig. 1   Schematic representation of Fishbein and Ajzen's theory of reasoned action. (From Ajzen and Fishbein (1980), p. 8; reprinted by permission of Prentice-Hall, Englewood Cliffs, NJ.)

influence the strength of the observed relationship between intention and behavior. The first concerns the degree of 'correspondence' between the measures of intention and behavior. In order to accurately predict behavior, it is essential that the two concepts are measured at the same level of specificity or generality. For example, to predict whether or not a person will smoke cigarettes at the forthcoming Christmas party, the measure of intention should be phrased specifically in terms of 'smoking cigarettes at the forthcoming Christmas party'. The same principle of correspondence also applies to the operationalization of the other variables in the model. The second factor that influences the strength of the intention–behavior relationship is the stability of intentions. Clearly, if a person's intention changes in the interval between the measurement of intentions and behavior then this will reduce the accuracy of prediction. The longer the time interval, the greater the probability that events will occur that produce changes in intentions, and therefore the lower the observed relationship between intention and behavior.

Operationalization of the model's components

The components of the theory of reasoned action are typically operationalized using questionnaire ratings in semantic differential format. Table 1 shows what form the questionnaire items might take in a (hypothetical) study of the decision to stop smoking in the next two months, based on the recommendations made by Ajzen and Fishbein (1980, Appendix A, pp. 261–263). Note that both intentions and beliefs are conceived of as subjective probabilities, and measures of these concepts typically employ likelihood scales. Attitude toward the behavior is usually assessed using several evaluative ratings, whereas the measures of behavioral intentions and subjective norm are typically each based on a single item. The measures of behavioral beliefs, outcome evaluations, normative beliefs and motivations to comply, use multiple items—one for each salient outcome or referent. These are then combined according to the formulae given in the previous section. Except for the motivation to comply scales, which as unipolar scales would be scored from 1 (not at all) to 7 (very much), all the scales shown in Table 1 would be scored from −3 (unlikely, harmful, bad, punishing) to +3 (likely, beneficial, good, rewarding).

Table 1 Recommended operationalizations of the components of the theory of reasoned action for the decision to 'stop smoking in the next two months'

Behavioral intention (BI)
I intend to stop smoking in the next two months.
      likely ____ : ____ : ____ : ____ : ____ : ____ : ____ unlikely

Attitude toward the behavior (AB)
My stopping smoking in the next two months is
      harmful ____ : ____ : ____ : ____ : ____ : ____ : ____ beneficial
      good ____ : ____ : ____ : ____ : ____ : ____ : ____ bad
      rewarding ____ : ____ : ____ : ____ : ____ : ____ : ____ punishing

Subjective norm (SN)
Most people who are important to me think
      I should ____ : ____ : ____ : ____ : ____ : ____ : ____ I should not
      stop smoking in the next two months

Behavioral beliefs (b_i)
My stopping smoking in the next two months will lead me to put on weight.
      likely ____ : ____ : ____ : ____ : ____ : ____ : ____ unlikely

Outcome evaluations (e_i)
For me, putting on weight is
      good ____ : ____ : ____ : ____ : ____ : ____ : ____ bad

Normative beliefs (nb_j)
My parents think
      I should ____ : ____ : ____ : ____ : ____ : ____ : ____ I should not
      stop smoking in the next two months

Motivations to comply (mc_j)
Generally speaking, how much do you want to do what your parents think you should do?
      not at all ____ : ____ : ____ : ____ : ____ : ____ : ____ very much

---

APPLICATIONS OF THE MODEL TO SMOKING DECISIONS

This section reviews applications of the Fishbein–Ajzen model to predicting and understanding smoking decisions. These are discussed under three headings: studies of smokers' and nonsmokers' beliefs about smoking; studies predicting intention; and studies predicting behavior from intentions.

Table 2   Studies of smokers' and nonsmokers' beliefs about smoking

Study	Sample	Brief description of study
Jaccard (1975)	78 university students (USA)	Comparison of intenders and nonintenders with regard to twelve behavioral beliefs and outcome evaluations.
Roberts (1980)	142 college women (USA)	Comparison of smokers and nonsmokers with regard to fourteen behavioral beliefs and outcome evaluations.
Fishbein (1982)	193 young college women (USA)	Comparison of intenders and nonintenders with regard to sixteen behavioral beliefs and outcome evaluations and six normative beliefs and motivations to comply.
Loken (1982)	178 college women (USA)	Comparison of current smokers, occasional smokers, and never-smokers with regard to sixteen behavioral beliefs and outcome evaluations and eleven normative beliefs and motivations to comply.
Newman, Martin and Irwin (1982)	190 high-school students (USA and Australia)	Comparison of intenders and non-intenders with regard to seventeen behavioral beliefs and outcome evaluations and six normative beliefs and motivations to comply.
Newman, Martin and Ang (1982)	417 high-school students (USA and New Zealand)	Comparison of intenders and nonintenders with regard to ten behavioral beliefs and outcome evaluations and seven normative beliefs and motivations to comply.
Grube, McGree and Morgan (1984)	752 primary school children (Eire)	Comparison of regular smokers, occasional smokers, and nonsmokers with regard to fourteen behavioral beliefs and outcome evaluations and four normative beliefs.

Study	Sample	Brief description of study
Grube, McGree and Morgan (1986)	195 first-year student teachers (Eire)	Comparison of regular smokers, occasional smokers, and nonsmokers with regard to seventeen behavioral beliefs and outcome evaluations and four normative beliefs.
Budd (1986)	170 undergraduate psychology students (UK)	Comparison of never, experimental, occasional, and regular smokers with regard to eighteen behavioral belief–outcome evaluation products and nine normative beliefs.
de Vries and Kok (1986)	219 primary and secondary school children (Holland)	Comparison of smokers and nonsmokers with regard to 28 behavioral beliefs and outcome evaluations and sixteen normative beliefs and motivations to comply.

Note: Two other studies should be mentioned for the sake of completeness. Brubaker and Loftin (1987) applied the theory of reasoned action to smokeless tobacco use. Page and Gold (1983) examined sex differences in beliefs, evaluations and motivations to comply with respect to cigarette smoking in a sample of college students, but unfortunately did not include intention to smoke or smoking status in their analyses.

Studies of smokers' and nonsmokers' beliefs

Table 2 lists studies that have compared smokers and nonsmokers or intenders and nonintenders with regard to their behavioral beliefs and evaluations concerning the possible outcomes of smoking, and also in some cases their normative beliefs and motivations to comply with significant referents. I will illustrate this approach by describing one of these studies in detail (Fishbein, 1982). Table 3 summarizes the results of the Fishbein study, in which two groups of college women were compared, those whose intentions to smoke were stronger than their intentions not to smoke ('intenders') and those whose intentions not to smoke were stronger ('nonintenders'). The table gives the behavioral beliefs and outcome evaluations with respect to sixteen possible outcomes (eight positive, eight negative) of smoking. These are modal salient beliefs, identified by means of the standard elicitation procedure in which an independent sample of women were asked to list the advantages and disadvantages of their own smoking and not smoking using an open-ended format. The beliefs used for the final questionnaire were those elicited most frequently by this procedure. In Table 3, intenders and nonintenders are compared with regard to (a) their mean outcome evaluations, based on their ratings of each outcome on a seven-point bipolar scale ranging from -3 to $+3$, and (b) their mean differential beliefs; that is, the extent to which the women believed that a particular outcome was more likely to be a result of their smoking (positive score) or of their not smoking (negative score). In effect, differential beliefs were assessed on a thirteen-point scale ranging from −6 to +6.

Table 3 Mean outcome evaluations and behavioral beliefs for college women with intentions to smoke ('intenders') and not to smoke ('nonintenders'). (Adapted from Fishbein (1982), Table 8.4, p. 192)

	Outcome evaluations		Behavioral beliefs	
Outcomes	Intenders (*n* = 36)	Nonintenders (*n* = 150)	Intenders	Nonintenders
Negative				
Harmful to health	−2.17	−2.71*	4.53	5.37*
Increase cancer	−1.94	−2.75*	4.33	5.34*
Breathing problems	−2.33	−2.75*	3.89	4.90*
Offensive to others	−2.14	−2.65*	2.81	4.65*
Bad breath	−2.50	−2.51	3.44	5.09*
Bad odor on clothes	−1.83	−2.52*	3.67	5.26*
Increase dependency	−2.08	−2.88*	4.78	4.93
Expensive	−0.86	−0.79	4.17	5.05*
Positive				
Relieves tension	2.31	2.47	2.75	−0.48*
Relaxing	2.56	2.51	2.94	−1.40*
Helps concentrate	2.31	2.21	0.44	−2.29*
Helps interact	2.08	2.12	1.28	−1.65*
Acceptance by peers	1.67	1.57	−0.39	−2.03*
Something to do with hands	0.58	0.65	3.75	1.35*
Keeps weight down	2.72	2.50	1.00	−3.37*
Pleasant taste experience	2.13	2.03	0.14	−4.76*

*Difference between intenders and nonintenders significant at 0.01 level.

Considering first the evaluation scores, it is clear that both intenders and nonintenders rated the negative outcomes negatively and the positive outcomes positively, on average. Thus, the two groups agreed that 'being harmful to health' and 'increasing one's risk of cancer' were 'bad' and that 'relieving tension' and 'relaxing' were 'good'. Furthermore, there were no significant differences between intenders and nonintenders with regard to their ratings of the positive outcomes. The positive outcomes most valued by both groups were 'keep weight down,' 'relaxing,' 'relieves tension,' and 'helps concentrate'; the positive outcome that was valued least by both groups was 'having something to do with your hands.' In contrast to the findings for the positive outcomes there were significant differences between the two groups with regard to six out of the eight negative outcomes. Thus with the exception of 'bad breath' and 'expensive,' intenders rated the negative outcomes significantly less negatively than nonintenders.

The two groups also differed with regard to their behavioral beliefs. For both groups the scores for the negative outcomes were without exception positive, indicating that both intenders and nonintenders believed that each negative outcome was more likely to occur if they smoked than if they didn't smoke, though these beliefs were held significantly less strongly by intenders (with one exception: 'increase dependency'). An interesting pattern is evident for positive outcomes. With one exception, intenders believed that positive outcomes were more likely if they smoked, whereas nonintenders believed that they were more likely to achieve these outcomes (which they valued to the same extent as intenders) by not smoking. The single exception to this was 'acceptance by peers,' which both intenders and nonintenders believed would be more likely to be attained through not smoking.

This microanalysis of college women's beliefs about smoking indicates that the differences between intenders and nonintenders are not limited to any one belief or subset of beliefs, but occur across the whole range. The two groups differed significantly either in their beliefs or their evaluations of every outcome that was assessed. The implication for attempts to encourage people to stop smoking, or not to start, is that it may be helpful to provide information concerning a wide range of possible outcomes of smoking rather than focusing on one or two outcomes such as those related to health or money.

The other studies listed in Table 2 obtained results that were broadly similar to those reported by Fishbein (1982), despite variations in the operationalization of the variables and in the lists of consequences employed. In every case the criterion groups were found to differ with regard to their beliefs concerning the consequences of smoking, though differences in their evaluation of these consequences were less frequent.

It should be noted that, from the standpoint of the Fishbein–Ajzen model, comparing intenders and nonintenders with regard to their beliefs about smoking makes the implicit assumption that any differences observed are due to differences in attitude (AB) or subjective norm (SN); that is, that beliefs (behavioral beliefs together with outcome evaluations, and normative beliefs together with motivations to comply) determine attitude and subjective norm and these in turn determine intention. The second link in this presumed causal chain is considered in the following section. With respect to the first link, few studies in the domain of cigarette smoking have examined the relationship between beliefs and attitudes. Fishbein (1982) reports a correlation of 0.58 ($p < 0.01$) between a direct (semantic differential) measure of attitude toward 'my smoking cigarettes' and the sum of the products of behavioral beliefs and outcome evaluations ($\Sigma b_i e_i$) in a sample of 63 young college women. The corresponding correlation between SN and Σnb_jmc_j was 0.53 (p <0.01). Fishbein also states that significant correlations (ranging from 0.45 to 0.68) have also been obtained for several other smoking-related attitudes and subjective norms (for example, the attitude toward 'my starting to smoke cigarettes'), but he does not provide details of these studies. Budd (1986) found correlations of a similar order (0.56 and 0.72 for AB and SN, respectively; both p <0.001). Finally, de Vries and Kok (1986) reported correlations of 0.61 and 0.34 (p <0.001). Thus, in general less than 50 percent of the variance in AB and SN was accounted for.

Budd's study deserves further comment. As a measure of belief salience he asked his subjects to indicate which of eighteen behavioral beliefs were the five most important reasons for why they either did, or did not, smoke cigarettes. He found that the correlation between the direct measure of AB and the sum of the belief-evaluation products was significantly higher when the latter was based on salient rather than nonsalient beliefs (r = 0.615 vs. r = 0.073, p <0.001). He also showed that smokers and nonsmokers differed in regard to which beliefs they regarded as salient, with the health hazards of smoking tending to be more salient for the nonsmokers, and the pleasures of smoking tending to be more salient for the smokers. His conclusion that belief salience should be incorporated into the theory of reasoned action is unwarranted, however. According to the Fishbein–Ajzen model, attitudes are determined by salient beliefs, and one would therefore expect salient beliefs to be more closely related to attitudes than nonsalient beliefs. Furthermore, belief salience, as measured by Budd, may simply reflect belief strength and evaluation. If one compares the belief-evaluation products in Budd's Table 3 with the salience frequencies in his Table 5, they appear to be highly correlated for both smokers and nonsmokers. In other words, when smokers, for example, are asked which beliefs are the five most important reasons why they smoke, they tend to choose those positive outcomes that have the largest belief-evaluation products—that is, outcomes that they both strongly associate with smoking and value highly. Finally, it should be noted that Budd's finding that beliefs are differentially salient for smokers and nonsmokers is entirely consistent with the Fishbein–Ajzen model.

All the studies referred to in this section have been cross-sectional. Finding that beliefs about smoking are correlated with attitudes, intentions and behavior is consistent with the theory of reasoned action, but is not uniquely predicted by it. An observed correlation between beliefs and behavior, for example, is also consistent with the notion that beliefs are determined by behavior as well as vice-versa, as postulated by reasoned action theory. What is needed are experimental studies in which beliefs about the target behavior are manipulated and the effects on attitudes, intentions and behavior assessed. Fishbein, Ajzen and McArdle (1980) employed this approach in a study in which alcoholics were encouraged to sign up for an alcoholic treatment unit by means of persuasive communications. However, to my know-ledge no experimental tests of the Fishbein–Ajzen model have been conducted in the domain of cigarette smoking.

Studies predicting intention

A major postulate of the theory of reasoned action is that behavioral inten-tions (BI) are determined by attitude toward the behavior (AB) and the subjective norm (SN). A number of studies have examined this in relation to smoking. They are summarized in Table 4 in terms of the multiple corre-lation (R) for predicting intention and the beta-weights (standardized partial regression coefficients) for the two components. The studies are arranged so that those emanating from the same research group or using similar samples can be easily compared. The significance levels shown in Table 4 are as reported in the original publications except where otherwise indicated. Two studies by Grube and his colleagues (Grube, McGree and Morgan, 1984; Grube, Morgan and McGree, 1986) have been excluded because the analyses they used make it difficult to compare their findings with those of the other studies.

Most of the studies were conducted in the United States and all used either adolescents or college students as subjects. There were differences between the studies in the way that the model variables were operationalized, including a number of departures from the recommended format. For example, in the two studies by Chassin and her colleagues (Chassin, Presson, Bensenberg, Corty, Olshavsky and Sherman, 1981; Presson, Chassin, Sherman, Olshavsky, Bensenberg and Corty, 1984), behavioral intentions to smoke (or not to smoke) were assessed by means of four items (for example, 'I plan to smoke cigarettes a month from now') using a Likert response scale ranging from 'strongly agree' to 'strongly disagree.' The authors note that in their pilot studies the younger subjects had great difficulty with the more usual likelihood ratings. For their analysis they combine the four items into a single scale, but they do not report the correlations between them.

All the multiple correlations in Table 4 were statistically significant at the 0.05 level or better, and ranged from 0.43 to 0.83 (18–69 percent of the variance explained) with an overall mean correlation of 0.63 (40 percent of the variance). The predictability of intentions seems rather lower than one might expect, given that in all cases the measures of AB, SN, and BI were obtained at the same time on the same questionnaire, conditions that should maximize the correlations between measures. The observed relationships may be attenuated owing to imperfect reliability of the measures. Multiple indicator approaches that enable the effects of random measurement error to be taken into account offer the promise of increased predictive power. In the context of the Fishbein–Ajzen theory, such approaches have been applied

Table 4 Studies predicting smoking intentions from attitudes (AB) and subjective norms (SN)

Study	Intention	Sample	Beta weights		R
			AB	SN	
Chassin et al. (1981)[a]	To smoke/not smoke cigarettes a month/a year from now	2460 adolescents (6th–12th grade)			
		611 middle-school never-smokers[b]	0.50***	0.22***	0.60***
		488 high-school never-smokers	0.47***	0.22***	0.58***
		341 middle-school experimental smokers	0.46***	0.42***	0.72***
		638 high-school experimental smokers	0.44***	0.34***	0.66***
		134 middle-school regular smokers	0.39***	0.10 n.s.	0.43***
		248 high-school regular smokers	0.39***	0.28***	0.54***
Presson et al. (1984)[c]	As above	2904 adolescent never and experimental smokers (6th–12th grade)			
		520 middle-school midwest boys	0.37***	0.43***	0.67***
		599 middle-school midwest girls	0.53***	0.17***	0.63***
		143 middle-school southwest boys	0.70***	0.12*	0.76***
		159 middle-school southwest girls	0.64***	0.28***	0.77***
		554 high-school midwest boys	0.46***	0.34***	0.67***
		542 high-school midwest girls	0.43***	0.33***	0.63***
		198 high-school southwest boys	0.43***	0.43***	0.70***
		189 high-school southwest girls	0.56***	0.20***	0.66***
Jaccard (1975)[d]	To smoke cigarettes	78 university students	0.67 n.g.	0.02 n.g.	0.68***
Fishbein (1982)[d]	To smoke	63 young college women	—	—	0.83***
Fishbein (1982)[e,f]	To smoke and not to smoke cigarettes	193 young college women	0.50**	0.20*	0.62*
Newman, Martin and Irwin (1982)	To smoke cigarettes in the future	95 high-school students, 14–16 years (USA)	0.50**	0.25 n.s.	0.46**
		95 high-school students, 14–16 years (Australia)	0.52**	0.02 n.s.	0.52**

Study	Intention	Sample	Beta weights		R
			AB	SN	
Newman, Martin and Ang (1982)	As above	279 high-school students, 14–16 years (New Zealand)	0.26**	0.41**	0.43**
		138 high-school students, 14–16 years (USA)	0.37**	0.26 n.s.	0.52**
Budd (1986)[d]	To smoke cigarettes	170 undergraduate psychology students	—	—	0.73***
de Vries and Kok (1986)	To smoke cigarettes regularly[g]	221 primary and secondary school children, 10–15 years	0.48	0.23[h]	0.63***

Significance levels: $*p < 0.05$; $**p < 0.01$; $***p < 0.001$; n.s. = non-significant; n.g. = not given.

[a] See also Sherman et al. (1982) for analyses based on a different subsample drawn from the same initial sample of 4638 adolescents.

[b] Never-smokers were those who had 'never smoked a cigarette, not even a few puffs'; 'experimental smokers' were those who had 'smoked a cigarette or a few cigarettes "just to try"', but not in the past month'; 'regular smokers' were those who regularly smoked at least one cigarette a month.

[c] The sample used in this study overlapped with that used in the Chassin et al. (1981) study.

[d] Significance levels for R were not reported in these studies but the F values can be computed given R, the sample size, and the number of predictors (in this case, two).

[e] Fishbein (1982) also mentions a number of other studies of smoking intentions; see his Table 8.3, p. 189. See also Fishbein (1980).

[f] In this study differential intentions (intention to smoke minus intention not to smoke) were predicted from differential attitudes and subjective norms.

[g] A number of different measures of intention were obtained in this study. It is not clear which one was used in testing the model.

[h] The beta weights were calculated from the correlations given in Figure 2 in this study.

to alcohol, marijuana and hard drug use (Bentler and Speckart, 1979), but not as yet to smoking.

The arrangement of Table 4 reveals some similarities in results between studies conducted by the same research group, and using similar samples and similar operationalization of measures. For example, the results for the 'midwest' subsample in the Presson et al. (1984) study were similar to those for the comparable groups (never- and experimental smokers) in the earlier paper from the same research team (Chassin et al., 1981). Furthermore, the two studies by Newman and his colleagues (Newman, Martin and Ang, 1982; Newman, Martin and Irwin, 1982) produced consistent results.

Beta weights representing the independent contribution of attitudes and subjective norms to the prediction of intentions were reported in all but three studies. All the coefficients were positive. Where significance levels were reported, the coefficients were statistically significant in every case for AB, and in all but four cases for SN. With the exception of three instances the coefficient for AB was greater than that for SN (although a test of the significance of this difference was not reported in any of the studies). Thus, in general, the attitudinal component was a more important predictor of intention than the normative component. In interpreting these results the relationship between these two components should be taken into account. Although the correlation between AB and SN was reported in only one of the studies (de Vries and Kok, 1986), it is possible in nearly every case to calculate it from the information given. With few exceptions the correlations were positive and statistically significant.

The results from the Chassin et al. (1981) and Presson et al. (1984) studies provide some information on the variability of the findings across different subgroups. Apart from a difference between smoking groups (prediction of intentions was best amongst experimental smokers and worst amongst regular smokers), the pattern of prediction was very similar across subgroups with no indication of differences as a function of sex, region (midwest vs. southwest) or age (middle school vs. high school).

In their two studies, Chassin and her colleagues also examined the sufficiency of the Fishbein–Ajzen formulation—that is, the extent to which the model variables (AB and SN) on their own provide a sufficient explanation of behavioral intentions without the need to incorporate additional explanatory variables. The external variables they examined were drawn from Jessor and Jessor's (1977) problem behavior theory, which attempts to explain adolescent problem behaviors, such as smoking, drinking and drug use, in terms of a large number of psychosocial risk factors. Chassin and her associates found that adding seventeen variables from problem behavior theory to AB and SN increased the variance explained in intentions by less than 5 percent except among the regular smokers, where the increase was

12–15 percent. None of the other studies in Table 4 specifically examined the sufficiency question.

The Chassin et al. (1981) study is particularly interesting for another reason. Because they analyzed the results separately for each smoking group, they effectively controlled for the influence of previous or current behavior in examining the relationship between attitudes, norms and intentions. Thus, particularly for the never-smokers group, the rival hypothesis that the observed relationship between AB, for example, and intention contained a spurious component due to the effect of recent behavior on both can be ruled out.

Finally, a study by Sherman, Presson, Chassin, Bensenberg, Corty, and Olshavsky (1982) should be mentioned. They report analyses based on a different subsample drawn from the same initial sample of 4638 adolescents referred to by Chassin et al. (1981). They examined the hypothesis that the level of direct experience with smoking would moderate the attitude–intention relationship. Although they interpret their findings as supporting this hypothesis, their results in fact showed not only that direct experience had no effect on intentions over and above that due to attitude and subjective norms but, more importantly, that the interaction term (attitudes × direct experience) produced only a minute increase ($\leqslant 0.5$ percent) in the variance explained in intentions. Furthermore, their measure of direct experience had low internal consistency and lacked face validity. It is not clear why they did not base their measure of direct experience on the subjects' self-reported behavior (i.e. whether or not they had tried a cigarette) which would seem to be the obvious choice.

Studies predicting behavior from intentions

Several applications of the Fishbein–Ajzen model to smoking have included a behavioral follow-up and enabled an assessment to be made of the extent to which current intentions predict future behavior. In all cases the behavioral criteria were dichotomous and were based on self-reports assessed at varying intervals (one month to one year) after the measurement of intention. Fishbein (1982) briefly reported two studies based on small samples of college women. In the first, 41 women were asked to rate their intention to smoke cigarettes during the next month. One month later they were asked whether or not they had smoked during the past month. The correlation between intentions and behavior was 0.84. However, this apparently high level of support for the model may simply be a function of stable behavior patterns. Assuming that nonsmokers tend to have nonsmoking intentions, and smokers tend to have intentions to smoke, and given that few people change their smoking status over the course of a month, then one would expect to observe a strong relationship between intentions at time 1 and behavior at time 2.

This simple example indicates the importance of taking into account current or prior behavior, as well as behavioral intention, when attempting to explain future behavior.

In the second study, Fishbein asked a sample of 25 young women smokers to indicate their intention to quit smoking in the next two months, and then contacted them again two months later. He found no relationship between their initial intentions and whether or not they had stopped smoking at follow-up. However, he argued that in predicting whether or not a smoker will quit, it is necessary to take account of their intentions concerning other behavioral alternatives, namely to continue smoking at the same rate or to reduce their consumption. When the data were reanalyzed in terms of the relative strengths of these intentions, the results were more supportive of the model.

The only other application of the Fishbein–Ajzen model in this area that examined the relationship between intention and subsequent behavior was the study of Chassin, Presson, Sherman, Corty and Olshavsky (1984), who tested a large sample of adolescents (1207 never-smokers and 740 triers) on two occasions approximately one year apart. They employed the same four-item index of intentions that they used in their other studies. Despite imperfect correspondence in their measures and the relatively long follow-up period, they reported a correlation of 0.20 between the initial intentions of never-smokers and whether or not they had become a smoker (experimental or regular) by one year follow-up and a correlation of 0.28 between the initial intentions of experimental smokers and whether or not they had graduated to the status of regular smoker one year later. Chassin et al. also reported multiple correlations for predicting the transition to increased smoking status from AB, SN and intentions. These did not differ from the simple correlations reported above, indicating that AB and SN did not account for additional variance in behavior change over and above that due to intentions alone; that is, that in the context of the variables in the Fishbein–Ajzen model, intentions were a sufficient predictor of behavior. On the other hand, adding 17 variables from Jessor and Jessor's (1977) problem-behavior theory and eight 'smoking environment' variables significantly increased the multiple correlation, suggesting that it is possible to find variables whose effects on behavior are not mediated through attitudes, subjective norms or intentions.

Finally, a number of studies should be mentioned that were not designed as tests of the Fishbein–Ajzen model, but that nevertheless included a measure of intention (more accurately, behavioral expectation; see the following section) and a behavioral follow-up (Allegrante, O'Rourke and Tuncalp, 1977; Ary, Biglan, Gallison, Weissman and Severson, 1986; Eisinger, 1971, 1972; McCaul, Glasgow, O'Neill, Freeborn and Rump, 1982; National Institute of Education (NIE), 1979; Ockene, Benfari, Nuttall,

Hurwitz and Ockene, 1982; Pederson and Baskerville, 1983; Pederson, Baskerville and Lefcoe, 1981; Pederson, Baskerville and Wanklin, 1982; Pederson and Lefcoe, 1986, 1987; Salber and Abelin, 1967). All these studies reported a significant positive relationship between behavioral expectation and subsequent behavior. Several of these studies used very long follow-ups. In the NIE study, for example, adolescents' self-prediction of their future smoking status was found to be the best predictor of actual smoking status five years later ($r = 0.36$).

CRITICISMS OF THE FISHBEIN–AJZEN MODEL

The theory of reasoned action has stimulated a large amount of critical comment. Considerable attention has been paid to the issue of the definition and operationalization of the model variables. Warshaw and Davis (1985) have criticized research using the Fishbein–Ajzen model for failing to distinguish between behavioral intentions, which refer to a person's plans about his/her own future behavior, and what they call behavioral expectations or predictions, which refer to the person's perceived likelihood of performing a given behavior. They regard the latter as a more inclusive concept in the sense that plans imply expectations but expectations do not imply plans. Thus, one may think it likely that one will smoke in five years' time without necessarily having formed an intention to do so.

Fishbein and Ajzen's model departs from traditional expectancy-value approaches such as the subjective expected utility (SEU) model in that it incorporates not only personal behavioral beliefs concerning the possible consequences of adopting a particular course of action, but also normative beliefs concerning the perceived expectations of important others. So, for example, the smoker's belief that 'my husband thinks I should stop smoking' (normative belief) would be distinguished from 'my stopping smoking would please my husband' (behavioral belief). Assuming both beliefs were salient to the individual concerned, they would be regarded by Fishbein and Ajzen as making separate and independent contributions to that person's decision to stop smoking. Miniard and Cohen (1981) argue, on the other hand, that the attitudinal and normative components are not clearly separated in the model, leading to 'double-counting.' However, even if the two components can be considered to be conceptually distinct, empirically they are typically correlated, and the theory needs to be elaborated to account for this correlation. This can be done without incorporating additional variables into the model by positing additional causal linkages between behavioral beliefs, normative beliefs, attitude toward the behavior and subjective norm. Such additional causal paths would, of course, need to be supported by a suitable rationale.

A further problem with the model concerns the interpretation of the weights w_1 and w_2 of the two components. According to Fishbein and Ajzen, these may vary from individual to individual. If so, however, they must have a psychological interpretation which should be incorporated into the model. The recommended operationalizations of the normative component are also problematic. While the normative belief items are phrased specifically in terms of the behavior in question (e.g. 'my parents think I should/should not stop smoking in the next two months'), the motivation to comply items are not ('generally speaking, how much do you want to do what your parents think you should do?'), which seems to be inconsistent with the emphasis that Fishbein and Ajzen place on the correspondence of measures. In fact, multiplying normative beliefs by motivations to comply has sometimes been found to reduce the predictive power of the normative component (for example, Schlegel, Crawford and Sanborn, 1977). For this reason, motivations to comply are often not measured at all, the normative component being computed simply as the unweighted sum of the normative beliefs. Furthermore, the single item used to assess subjective norm seems to necessitate the assumption that everyone is motivated to comply with 'most people who are important to me.'

Such problems stem from the attempt to create a separate normative component which is homologous to the attitudinal component in the sense that it involves the multiplicative combination of two kinds of element (normative beliefs, motivations to comply) into a single overall judgement (subjective norm). In my view it would be better to revert to the traditional expectancy-value approach in which the normative aspects of behavior are regarded simply in terms of the perceived rewards and costs, and are not given any special status in the theory.

The Fishbein–Ajzen model postulates a simple chain structure (i.e. A influences B which in turn influences C). A number of commentators (for example, Liska, 1984) have made the point that tests of the model should consider and examine the possibility of additional linkages. For example, there is evidence that attitudes influence behavior not only through behavioral intentions but also directly (for example, Bentler and Speckart, 1979; Manstead, Proffitt and Smart, 1983). The possibility of reciprocal effects should also be considered (for example, behavior may influence attitudes as well as vice-versa) and also interactive effects (for example, the effect of attitudes on intentions may vary depending on the level of subjective norm).

The theory of reasoned action is parsimonious in that it postulates a limited number of proximal determinants of intentions and behavior. All other variables are assumed to influence intentions (and hence behavior, assuming a strong intention–behavior relationship) only by way of their effects on attitudes and subjective norms or the relative weights of these two components. A common criticism of the model is that other variables have direct effects on intentions and behavior, and should therefore be included in the model. Examples of these other variables are moral norms (Pomazal and Brown, 1977), behavioral norms (Grube, Morgan and McGree, 1986), ideal behavioral intentions (Budd and Spencer, 1984, 1985), and social structure (Liska, 1984).

In applying the model to smoking, a variable that may be of crucial importance in understanding current intentions and future behavior is the person's current or past behavior. In their study of drug use intentions and behavior, Bentler and Speckart (1979) found that recent past behavior (frequency of alcohol, marijuana or hard drug use in the past two weeks) had a substantial independent effect on current intentions and on behavior assessed two weeks later. The behavior–behavior effect was at least as large as the intention–behavior effect, suggesting that such behaviors are only partly under the control of intentions and reflect a substantial effect of inertia or habit. In the same vein, Huba, Wingard and Bentler (1981) found that adolescents' intentions to use drugs significantly predicted substance use one year later, but that the increase in prediction over and above that due to previous drug use was minimal. These findings raise the question of the applicability of the Fishbein–Ajzen model and related approaches to behaviors that may be regarded as having a large habitual component. Fishbein and Ajzen limit their theory to behaviors that are under volitional control, thus effectively excluding many behaviors that require skills, abilities, opportunities or the cooperation of other people. To the extent that aspects of smoking behavior are involitional, they may fall outside the explanatory range of the model. Liska (1984) argues that Fishbein and Ajzen have created a false dichotomy between volitional and involitional behavior, and suggests that variation in resources (i.e. skills, abilities, opportunities, social cooperation) be built into the model so as to accommodate both volitional and involitional behaviors.

In our own work on smokers' decisions to stop smoking using the subjective expected utility model, we have tried to deal with this problem by conceptualizing the smoker's decision as, initially, one of whether or not to try to stop smoking (Sutton, 1979, 1987; Sutton and Eiser, 1984; Sutton, Marsh and Matheson, 1987). This decision, I would argue, is under volitional control. Confidence, defined as the subjective probability of succeeding given that an attempt is made, is incorporated into the model in order to take account of the fact that many smokers anticipate difficulty in stopping smoking. In a similar attempt to solve the same problem, Schifter and Ajzen (1985) have developed an extension of the theory of reasoned action that incorporates the concept of perceived control. They apply this theory of planned behavior, as they refer to it, to the problem of predicting and understanding weight loss.

CONCLUSIONS

The theory of reasoned action implies that different behaviors within the same domain (for example, starting to smoke, stopping smoking) and behaviors in different domains (for example, stopping smoking, stopping drinking) do not require different theories, but are in principle explicable in terms of a single theoretical approach. According to this approach any behavior that can be regarded as a decision can be explained in terms of the same limited set of social-psychological concepts. The Fishbein and Ajzen approach also attempts to clearly define and distinguish different kinds of attitudes, and to organize them into a systematic framework. In effect, it categorizes variables into one of two groups: (a) a small set of proximal determinants of the decision, and (b) a larger, potentially infinite, set of distal factors that may influence the decision but only through their effects on the proximal factors.

This emphasis on clearly specified, testable theory is long overdue in the field of smoking attitudes. Furthermore, the theory of reasoned action brings with it two practical suggestions which, if adopted, would in themselves improve the quality of work in this area. The first concerns the use of personal rather than general measures of beliefs and attitudes. For instance, consider the following two statements: 'cigarette smoking is dangerous to health' (general belief); 'my cigarette smoking is dangerous to my health' (personal belief). Quite clearly, a smoker might endorse the first statement but not the second. (See Fishbein (1977) for further discussion of this point.) The second practical recommendation concerns the need for correspondence between measures. For example, if the aim is to predict whether or not someone will reduce smoking over a six-month period, then the most appropriate predictor, according to Fishbein and Ajzen, would be the person's intention to reduce smoking over the next six months.

To date there have been only a small number of applications of the model to smoking. These studies were correlational, and in most cases they used a cross-sectional design with no behavioral follow-up. In the main they provided support for the model by demonstrating correlations between the model's components. However, the observed relationships were lower than one might have expected. For instance, in the studies reported in Table 4, on average less than 50 percent of the variance in intention was accounted for. Furthermore, research using the model in other domains suggests that its parsimonious causal structure is too simple, and should be elaborated by incorporating additional explanatory variables (for example, past behavior) and additional causal linkages. Clearly there is immense scope for further research in this area, and a pressing need for prospective experimental studies incorporating behavioral measures. Such research should not only advance our understanding of smoking attitudes and behavior, and how to change them, but also contribute to social-psychological theories of decision-making and attitude–behavior relations.

ACKNOWLEDGEMENTS

I would like to thank my colleagues in the Smoking Section of the Addiction Research Unit for their helpful comments on an earlier draft of this chapter. The Medical Research Council and the Imperial Cancer Research Fund provided financial support.

REFERENCES

Ajzen, I., and Fishbein, M. (eds) (1980). *Understanding Attitudes and Predicting Social Behavior*. Englewood Cliffs, NJ: Prentice-Hall.

Allegrante, J.P., O'Rourke, T.W., and Tuncalp, S. (1977). A multivariate analysis of selected psychosocial variables on the development of subsequent youth smoking behavior. *Journal of Drug Education*, **7**, 237–247.

Ary, D.V., Biglan, A., Gallison, C.L., Weissman, W., and Severson, H.H. (1986). Longitudinal prediction of the onset and change of adolescent smoking. In: W.F. Forbes, R.C. Frecker and D. Nostbakken (eds), *Proceedings of the Fifth World Conference on Smoking and Health*, vol. 1. Ottawa: Canadian Council on Smoking and Health, pp. 641–648.

Bentler, P.M., and Speckart, G. (1979). Models of attitude–behavior relations. *Psychological Review*, **86**, 452–464.

Brubaker, R.G., and Loftin, T.L. (1987). Smokeless tobacco use by middle school males: a preliminary test of the reasoned action theory. *Journal of School Health*, **57**, 64–67.

Budd, R.J. (1986). Predicting cigarette use: the need to incorporate measures of salience in the theory of reasoned action. *Journal of Applied Social Psychology*, **16**, 663–685.

Budd, R.J., and Spencer, C.P. (1984). Predicting undergraduates' intentions to drink. *Journal of Studies on Alcohol*, **45**, 179–183.

Budd, R.J., and Spencer, C.P. (1985). Exploring the role of personal normative beliefs in the theory of reasoned action: the problem of discriminating between alternative path models. *European Journal of Social Psychology*, **15**, 299–313.

Chassin, L., Presson, C.C., Bensenberg, M., Corty, E., Olshavsky, R.W., and Sherman, S.J. (1981). Predicting adolescents' intentions to smoke cigarettes. *Journal of Health and Social Behavior*, **22**, 445–455.

Chassin, L., Presson, C.C., Sherman, S.J., Corty, E., and Olshavsky, R.W. (1984). Predicting the onset of cigarette smoking in adolescents: a longitudinal study. *Journal of Applied Social Psychology*, **14**, 224–243.

Davidson, A.R., and Jaccard, J.J. (1975). Population psychology: a new look at an old problem. *Journal of Personality and Social Psychology*, **31**, 1073–1082.

de Vries, H., and Kok, G.J. (1986). From determinants of smoking behaviour to the implications for a prevention programme. *Health Education Research*, **1**, 85–94.

Eisinger, R.A. (1971). Psychosocial predictors of smoking recidivism. *Journal of Health and Social Behavior*, **12**, 355–362.

Eisinger, R.A. (1972). Psychosocial predictors of smoking behavior change. *Social Science and Medicine*, **6**, 137–144.

Fishbein, M. (1977). Consumer beliefs and behavior with respect to cigarette smoking:

a critical analysis of the public literature. Report prepared for the staff of the Federal Trade Commission.

Fishbein, M. (1980). A theory of reasoned action: some applications and implications. In: M.M. Page (ed.), *Nebraska Symposium on Motivation, 1979*. Lincoln: University of Nebraska Press, pp. 65–116.

Fishbein, M. (1982). Social psychological analysis of smoking behavior. In: J.R. Eiser (ed.), *Social Psychology and Behavioral Medicine*. Chichester: John Wiley & Sons, pp. 179–197.

Fishbein, M., and Ajzen, I. (1975). *Belief, Attitude, Intention, and Behavior: An Introduction to Theory and Research*. Reading, MA: Addison-Wesley.

Fishbein, M., Ajzen, I., and Hinkle, R. (1980). Predicting and understanding voting in American elections: effects of external variables. In: I. Ajzen and M. Fishbein (eds), *Understanding Attitudes and Predicting Social Behavior*. Englewood Cliffs, NJ: Prentice-Hall, pp. 173–195.

Fishbein, M., Ajzen, I., and McArdle, J. (1980). Changing the behavior of alcoholics: Effects of persuasive communication. In: I. Ajzen and M. Fishbein (eds), *Understanding Attitudes and Predicting Social Behavior*. Englewood Cliffs, NJ: Prentice-Hall, pp. 217–242.

Grube, J.W., McGree, S., and Morgan, M. (1984). Smoking behaviours, intentions and beliefs among Dublin primary school children. *Economic and Social Review*, **15**, 265–288.

Grube, J.W., McGree, S., and Morgan, M. (1986). Beliefs related to cigarette smoking among Irish college students. *International Journal of the Addictions*, **21**, 701–706.

Grube, J.W., Morgan, M., and McGree, S.T. (1986). Attitudes and normative beliefs as predictors of smoking intentions and behaviours: a test of three models. *British Journal of Social Psychology*, **25**, 81–93.

Huba, G.J., Wingard, J.A., and Bentler, P.M. (1981). Intentions to use drugs among adolescents: a longitudinal analysis. *International Journal of the Addictions*, **16**, 331–339.

Jaccard, J. (1975). A theoretical analysis of selected factors important to health education strategies. *Health Education Monographs*, **3**, 152–167.

Jessor, R., and Jessor, S.L. (1977). *Problem Behavior and Psychosocial Development: A Longitudinal Study of Youth*. New York: Academic Press.

Liska, A.E. (1984). A critical examination of the causal structure of the Fishbein/Ajzen attitude–behavior model. *Social Psychology Quarterly*, **47**, 61–74.

Loken, B. (1982). Heavy smokers', light smokers', and nonsmokers' beliefs about cigarette smoking. *Journal of Applied Psychology*, **67**, 616–622.

McCaul, K.D., Glasgow, R., O'Neill, H.K., Freeborn, V., and Rump, B.S. (1982). Predicting adolescent smoking. *Journal of School Health*, **52**, 342–346.

Manstead, A.S.R., Proffitt, C., and Smart, J.L. (1983). Predicting and understanding mothers' infant-feeding intentions and behavior: testing the theory of reasoned action. *Journal of Personality and Social Psychology*, **44**, 657–671.

Miniard, P., and Cohen, J.B. (1981). An examination of the Fishbein–Ajzen behavioral intentions model's concepts and measures. *Journal of Experimental Social Psychology*, **17**, 309–339.

National Institute of Education (NIE) (1979). *Teenage Smoking: Immediate and Longterm Patterns*. Washington, DC: US Government Printing Office.

Newman, I.M., Martin, G.L., and Ang, J. (1982). The role of attitudes and social norms in adolescent cigarette smoking. *New Zealand Medical Journal*, **95**, 618–621.

Newman, I.M., Martin, G.L., and Irwin, R.P. (1982). Attitudinal and normative factors associated with adolescent cigarette smoking in Australia and the United States of America: a methodology to assist health education planning. *Community Health Studies*, **6**, 47–56.

Ockene, J.K., Benfari, R.C., Nuttall, R.L., Hurwitz, I., and Ockene, I.S. (1982). Relationship of psychosocial factors to smoking behavior change in an intervention program. *Preventive Medicine*, **11**, 13–28.

Page, R.M., and Gold, R.S. (1983). Assessing gender differences in college cigarette smoking intenders and nonintenders. *Journal of School Health*, **53**, 531–535.

Pederson, L.L., and Baskerville, J.C. (1983). Multivariate prediction of smoking cessation following physician advice to quit smoking: a validation study. *Preventive Medicine*, **12**, 430–436.

Pederson, L.L., and Lefcoe, N.M. (1986). Change in smoking status among a cohort of late adolescents: prediction and explanation of initiation, maintenance and cessation. *International Journal of Epidemiology*, **15**, 519–526.

Pederson, L.L., and Lefcoe, N.M. (1987). Short- and long-term prediction of self-reported cigarette smoking in a cohort of late adolescents: report of an 8-year follow-up of public school students. *Preventive Medicine*, **16**, 432–447.

Pederson, L.L., Baskerville, J.C., and Lefcoe, N.M. (1981). Change in smoking status among school-aged youth: impact of a smoking-awareness curriculum, attitudes, knowledge and environmental factors. *American Journal of Public Health*, **71**, 1401–1404.

Pederson, L.L., Baskerville, J.C., and Wanklin, J.M. (1982). Multivariate statistical models for predicting change in smoking behavior following physician advice to quit smoking. *Preventive Medicine*, **11**, 536–549.

Pomazal, R.J., and Brown, J.D. (1977). Understanding drug use motivation: a new look at a current problem. *Journal of Health and Social Behavior*, **18**, 212–222.

Presson, C.C., Chassin, L., Sherman, S.J., Olshavsky, R., Bensenberg, M., and Corty, E. (1984). Predictors of adolescents' intentions to smoke: age, sex, race, and regional differences. *International Journal of Addictions*, **19**, 503–519.

Roberts, S. (1980). Belief assessment as a component of curriculum planning: cigarette smoking as an example. *Journal of School Health*, **30**, 555–558.

Salber, E.J., and Abelin, T. (1967). Smoking behavior of Newton school children—5-year follow-up. *Pediatrics*, **40**, 363–372.

Schifter, D.E., and Ajzen, I. (1985). Intention, perceived control, and weight loss: an application of the theory of planned behavior. *Journal of Personality and Social Psychology*, **49**, 843–851.

Schlegel, R.P., Crawford, C.A., and Sanborn, M.D. (1977). Correspondence and mediational properties of the Fishbein model: an application to adolescent alcohol use. *Journal of Experimental Social Psychology*, **13**, 421–430.

Sherman, S.J., Presson, C.C., Chassin, L., Bensenberg, M., Corty, E., and Olshavsky, R.W. (1982). Smoking intentions in adolescents: direct experience and predictability. *Personality and Social Psychology Bulletin*, **8**, 376–383.

Shimp, T.A., and Kavas, A. (1984). The theory of reasoned action applied to coupon usage. *Journal of Consumer Research*, **11**, 795–809.

Sutton, S.R. (1979). Can subjective expected utility (SEU) theory explain smokers' decisions to try to stop smoking? In: D.J. Oborne, M.M. Gruneberg and J.R. Eiser (eds), *Research in Psychology and Medicine*, vol. 2. London: Academic Press, pp. 94–101.

Sutton, S.R. (1987). Social-psychological approaches to understanding addictive behaviours: attitude–behaviour and decision-making models. *British Journal of Addiction*, **82**, 355–370.

Sutton, S.R., and Eiser, J.R. (1984). Thè effect of fear-arousing communications on cigarette smoking: an expectancy-value approach. *Journal of Behavioral Medicine*, **7**, 13–33.

Sutton, S.R., Marsh, A., and Matheson, J. (1987). Explaining smokers' decisions to stop: test of an expectancy-value approach. *Social Behaviour*, **2**, 35–49.

Warshaw, P.R., and Davis, F.D. (1985). Disentangling behavioral intention and behavioral expectation. *Journal of Experimental Social Psychology*, **21**, 213–228.

Wittenbraker, J., Gibbs, B.L., and Kahle, L.R. (1983). Seat belt attitudes, habits, and behaviors: an adaptive amendment to the Fishbein model. *Journal of Applied Social Psychology*, **13**, 406–421.

14

Intervening and Preventing Cigarette Smoking

HOWARD LEVENTHAL
TIMOTHY BAKER
THOMAS BRANDON
and
RAY FLEMING

ABSTRACT

We review the stages, techniques and processes involved in secondary (cessation and maintenance) and primary prevention of smoking (preparation, initial tries and experimentation, occasional use and dependence). In discussing secondary prevention we review data on aversive conditioning, a key procedure for smoking cessation, and counselling, a key procedure for maintenance. It is suggested that both procedures affect multiple, underlying processes and influence both cessation and maintenance, as well as the stage for which they are specifically targeted (e.g. rapid smoking for cessation). The large-scale research efforts on primary prevention, which are based upon a revised medical perspective on prevention that recognizes the need for systematic clinical trials on large populations, have focused upon skills training and ignored motivation to use skills to reduce social pressures to smoke. Ways of introducing motivational factors to expand the skills approach are discussed. While the revised medical model assumes that knowledge of the intervention process is adequate to initiate large-scale trials, we argue that knowledge of process for both secondary and primary prevention is in its infancy, and that basic research is needed in both.

Smoking and Human Behavior, Edited by T. Ney and A. Gale
© 1989 John Wiley & Sons Ltd

313

INTRODUCTION

The National Cancer Institute (NCI) estimates that cigarette smoking contributes significantly to the onset of one-third of the cancers suffered by Americans. Thus, secondary (cessation) and primary prevention of smoking has become their number one priority (Greenwald and Cullen, 1985). The effort has resulted in health warnings on cigarette packs, the outlawing of cigarette advertising on TV, the establishment of smoking and nonsmoking sections in commercial aircraft and restaurants, and the prohibition of smoking in public buildings. While the promoters of public health can take comfort from their many successes, our review of the current state of affairs for both secondary and primary prevention of smoking suggests the odds are at best modest for the elimination of this health hazard and its $60,000,000,000 annual cost.

The current prevention strategy

The NCI has proposed a systematic, five-phase program for *cancer control*, i.e. 'the reduction of cancer incidence, morbidity, and mortality through an orderly sequence from research on interventions and their impact in defined populations to the broad, systematic application of the research results' (Greenwald and Cullen, 1985). The phases are as follows: (1) developing hypotheses respecting the behaviors that must be changed to prevent cancer (this is done on the basis of epidemiological studies that identify likely causative agents and physiological studies that describe how these agents initiate and promote cancer); (2) pilot trials of existent behavioral methods for conducting and assessing interventions; (3) controlled intervention trials— large-scale trials; (4) defined population studies—conducted in 'large, distinct, and well-characterized populations or in a sizeable sample of the population chosen in such a way that the study subjects and results are representative of the ultimate target population' (Greenwald and Cullen, 1985); and (5) demonstration and implementation.

The Greenwald and Cullen stepwise approach represents a major advance over earlier, medically oriented thinking that viewed prevention as a two-step process: (1) the scientific analysis of disease causation at the epidemiological and biological level; and (2) the intensive and enthusiastic use of mass media, community groups, and behavioral and social learning technologies, to alter behavior. But by arguing for the use of 'existent methods' (step 2), they assume that current knowledge of social, psychological and biological processes, and their interaction, is sufficient to initiate interventions, a view we regard as very optimistic. Our thesis is that *inadequate attention has been given to the basics of the social, psychological and biological aspects of the intervention process*, both for long-term smoking cessation and smoking prevention.

Three aspects of prevention programs

There are at least three broad sets of factors that are important for the evaluation of intervention programs (Leventhal, Safer, Cleary and Gutmann, 1980): (1) the level of intervention, i.e. whether the intervention aims at cultural or community change (e.g. anti-smoking ordinances), institutional change, group change or individual change; (2) the target populations (e.g. ethnicity, age, smoking status, pregnancy status, etc.); and (3) the underlying process targeted for intervention (e.g. developing motivation to quit, skills to maintain quitting, etc.). The processes underlying smoking in a specific target group will designate specific goals for intervention and will also determine the most appropriate level of intervention. For example, the decision to promote cessation among heavy smokers who have not considered quitting (Prochaska and DiClemente, 1983; DiClemente and Prochaska, 1982), suggests specific goals and further suggests various levels of communication to meet these goals.

As we shall see in our review of both secondary and primary prevention, few studies have addressed variables in more than one of these sets of factors, and very few indeed have considered the interaction between variables from more than one set.

SECONDARY PREVENTION

Virtually every procedure imaginable, from talk therapies (Leventhal, 1968) to behavioral therapies (Bernstein, 1969; Lichtenstein, 1971; Lichtenstein and Danaher, 1975), and drug treatments have been used to beat the smoking 'habit.' Leventhal and Cleary (1980) suggested that, regardless of strategy, all interventions must address at least two separate underlying mechanisms: (1) motivation to avoid smoking; and (2) coping skills to maintain avoidance. They also suggest that successful interventions must build upon thorough knowledge of the underlying behavioral and biological mechanisms involved in the development (initiation, experimentation, occasional smoking) and maintenance ('addiction' or dependence) of smoking if trial and error was to be replaced with a rational approach to the design and assessment of interventions. The review and analysis which follow suggest that interventions making conscious use of such knowledge are increasingly effective.

Processes mediating therapeutic success in smoking cessation

Though it is typical to posit a single model of action for each of the many treatments used to help individuals quit smoking, it has become increasingly clear to us that any particular treatment strategy can affect treatment outcomes in many different ways. Awareness of such possibilities has led to attempts to focus on a more limited number of processes by examining specific stages in quitting smoking (Brownell, Glynn, Glasgow, Lando, Rand, Gottlieb and Pinney, 1986; DiClemente and Prochaska, 1982). For the sake of simplicity we focus upon two broad phases: (1) initial cessation/short-term maintenance, and (2) long-term maintenance. The first phase encompasses a three-day to two-week period of time beginning with the complete cessation of smoking to the end of the nicotine withdrawal period and the disappearance of withdrawal signs (Hatsukami, Hughes and Pickens, 1985; Shiffman and Jarvik, 1979). Long-term maintenance refers to the period following nicotine withdrawal during which the threats to abstinence are typically less salient, and thus more insidious. A two-stage model is based on the premise that any treatment evaluation strategy that does not separate the effects of treatment on cessation and maintenance processes will yield an incomplete or inaccurate picture of treatment effects. For instance, long-term abstinence rates are a function of both cessation and maintenance processes, yet, typically, no attempt is made to examine cessation and maintenance effects separately.

We will examine the effects of two intervention techniques on these two phases; rapid smoking (aversion treatment), and coping response training. We contrast these interventions because they are targets of extensive research and the available data permit us to discuss the routes of their therapeutic actions (Erickson, Tiffany, Martin and Baker, 1983; Hall, Rugg, Tunstall and Jones, 1984; Tiffany, Martin and Baker, 1986). In rapid smoking therapy clients inhale on cigarettes at six-second intervals until they become too ill to continue (Schmahl, Lichtenstein and Harris, 1972). The coping response training (CRT) teaches clients to anticipate, prepare for and react to cigarette cravings through the use of cognitive and behavioral responses that alleviate craving or stress reactions without the use of nicotine (Marlatt, 1982; Shiffman, 1984a).

Rapid smoking: an emphasis on quitting

Because rapid smoking involves inhaling, it may aid smokers in their attempts to quit by the temporary alleviation of nicotine withdrawal symptoms (Erickson et al., 1983; Burns, 1969; Cummings, Gordon and Marlatt, 1980). Evidence suggests that withdrawal symptoms are formidable obstacles to quitting. Secondly, rapid smoking produces uncomfortable consequences such as dizziness, nausea, burning mouth and throat, numbness, tachycardia and negative affect, that are supposed to generate a conditioned aversion to cigarettes (Tiffany et al., 1986). Evidence for the decreased incentive value of cigarettes following aversion therapy is seen in the increased cardiac acceleration (a defensive response) in post-treatment test sessions when treated persons taste a cigarette. The magnitude of this response is predictive of positive long-term outcome (Baker, Cannon, Tiffany and Gino, 1984; Erickson et al., 1983; Tiffany et al., 1986). Several other factors may enhance the effectiveness of rapid smoking. For example, the physical sensations and peripheral irritation produced by rapid smoking may reduce the desire to smoke for a limited period of time, and it may increase clients' awareness of the health consequences of smoking, accentuating their own vulnerability, and further reducing the incentive value of smoking. Second, the procedure may extinguish the power of smoking cues to arouse the urge to smoke, an outcome suggested by the beneficial effect achieved with rapid puffing, in which the client does not inhale (Tiffany et al., 1986). Third, rapid smoking divorces smoking from its usual cognitive and affective precursors (e.g. negative affect) and thus may further reduce the incentive value of cigarettes in those situations. Finally, rapid smoking may benefit from nonspecific treatment effects, such as the value of a credible, highly complex treatment ritual. In summary, while rapid smoking achieves high rates of initial abstinence— rates often approaching 100 percent cessation, the experimental findings implicate more than one underlying process (Erickson et al., 1983; Hall et al., 1984; Hall, Sachs and Hall, 1979; Tiffany et al., 1986).

Once rapid smoking, or any treatment intervention, produces short-term cessation, long-term abstinence may then be affected in at least four ways: (1) by generating a sense of self-effectance; (2) by the extinction of urges; (3) by generating visible health benefits; and (4) by dissonance reduction. These generic effects should be distinguished from effects specific to the type of treatment.

For example, most nicotine withdrawal symptoms peak and diminish during the first seven to ten days, and the likelihood of relapse diminishes as these symptoms decline. It is likely that weathering this period of withdrawal affects success in quitting for the longer term by enhancing expectations of success at maintenance and creating an impression of high self-control (Brandon, Zelman and Baker, in press; Cummings, Giovino, Jaen and Emrich, 1985; Shiffman and Jarvik, 1979). Indeed, measures of self-efficacy (Bandura, 1977) or self-confidence are consistent predictors of long-term smoking treatment outcome (Condiotte and Lichtenstein, 1981; DiClemente, 1981; Tiffany et al., 1986), and increases in reported confidence over the first two weeks of abstinence have been found to predict the duration of abstinence during the year following treatment (Brandon, Zelman and Baker, 1987).

Unfortunately, the mechanism responsible for self-efficacy effects is unclear. Marlatt and Gordon (1980) suggested that self-efficacy aids maintenance by increasing the likelihood the ex-smoker would execute a coping response when confronted with temptation, but Shiffman (1984a) found no relationship between retrospectively reported efficacy levels and use of coping responses during a relapse crisis. Another possibility is that temptation may stimulate a stress response which enhances the urge to smoke, and the strength of this response may be inversely proportional to the ex-smoker's confidence in his or her ability to resist (e.g. Breier, Albus, Pickers, Zahn, Wolkowitz and Paul, 1987). On the other hand, Baer, Holt and Lichtenstein (1986) found self-efficacy ratings made little improvement in the prediction of long-term smoking outcome above and beyond clients' smoking behavior at the time the ratings were made. They argue from these findings that prediction of long-term success by self-efficacy is an artifact of the individual's current smoking behavior, and that it is a self statement that reflects the individual's current smoking level.

Second, if the cessation procedure leads the smoker to resist smoking in the presence of past smoking cues, these cues are less likely to trigger future urges to smoke (cf. Siegel, 1983). This may occur because cue exposure extinguishes conditioned drug responses that produce signs and symptoms of withdrawal (e.g. Sherman, Morse and Baker, 1987). Also, experience with nonsmoking may lead ex-smokers to cease attributing their emotional reactions to smoking or abstinence from smoking, thereby moving smoking down the hierarchy of stress-reducing responses.

Third, the immediate benefits of quitting smoking, e.g. increased endurance, enhanced gustatory sensitivity and clothes free of tobacco smoke, should further reinforce abstinence. Health benefits should be particularly rewarding, since the development of smoking-related symptomatology (e.g. a 'smoker's cough') is the most common precipitant of quitting attempts (cf. Pechacek and Danaher, 1979). Moreover, the longer an individual abstains from smoking, the greater is his or her perceived investment in quitting, and the greater would be the perceived loss should relapse occur.

Finally, dissonance reduction and lifestyle changes may augment the ex-smoker's motivation to stay off cigarettes. Thus, the behavior of quitting, and each success at quitting, may lead the individual to minimize incentives for continuing smoking. And if the ex-smoker adapts behaviors such as an exercise program, to sustain his or her nonsmoking, these behaviors will not only be evidence of his desire to be a nonsmoker, but will introduce him or her to new nonsmoking friends, and generate new motives to help sustain abstinence (McIntyre-Kingsolver, Lichtenstein and Mermelstein, 1986; Mermelstein, Lichtenstein and McIntyre, 1983; Mermelstein, Cohen, Lichtenstein, Baer and Kamarck, 1986) and new skills may be developed for obtaining substitute reinforcements through nonpharmacological means (Panksepp, Siviy and Normansell, 1985).

Our discussion of rapid smoking has emphasized its direct effects upon initial cessation and short-term maintenance, and has emphasized its indirect effects on long-term maintenance. We should not ignore the possibility, however, that rapid smoking may continue to affect long-term maintenance if its initial effects are of substantial magnitude. Thus, if rapid smoking produces taste aversion, it should have long-term benefits because taste aversions are persistent. Similarly, rapid smoking's impact upon the perceived, personal health risks of smoking may affect the ex-smoker long after treatment termination.

Coping response training: an emphasis on maintenance of cessation

Coping response training (CRT) is designed to have a direct influence upon initial cessation and long-term maintenance of nonsmoking by teaching skills needed to cope with both urges to smoke and life stressors. The training consists of two basic components: (1) instruction in recognition of situations that put one at risk for smoking, e.g. situations involving stress or negative affect, or situations highly associated with past smoking; and (2) preparation of behavioral and cognitive responses for managing situationally induced urges to smoke. Typical behavioral coping responses include avoiding or leaving a situation, distracting activities (e.g. chewing gum or exercising), relaxation, and direct attempts to change problem situations that precipitate urges. Cognitive coping responses include distracting thoughts, minimizing or restructuring the precipitating problem, reminding oneself of the benefits of quitting or the negative consequences of smoking a single cigarette, and identifying oneself as a nonsmoker. In addition, smokers can be taught 'lifestyle' coping responses to alter persistent behavior patterns and enhance their ability to reduce the magnitude of future stress responses that induce the urge to smoke (Marlatt, 1985).

The utility of coping response training is supported by evidence that subjects who report using coping responses are less likely to relapse in the face of temptation (Shiffman, 1984b). While CRT can be focused on skills specific to short- and long-term cessation, the major goal of CRT is to influence long-term maintenance by teaching skills that remain available long after treatment ends. In fact, if clients become more skillful with practice we might expect CRT subjects to acquire better and better coping skills relative to controls in the post-treatment period (e.g. Marlatt, 1983; Sobell and Sobell, 1976).

While the basic rationale of CRT is straightforward and reasonable, there is little experimental evidence that its therapeutic effects are dependent upon a smoker's acquisition of the skills that investigators identify, *a priori*, as important. For example, in studies where CRT has produced superior clinical outcomes, there is little evidence that such outcomes are dependent upon the acquisition of putative skills (Tiffany et al., 1986: in many studies there is no advantage of intensive CRT relative to less intensive treatments). Moreover, the enhanced use of coping skills and higher abstinence rates achieved by CRT, declines to the level of untreated clients once treatment ends (Brandon et al., 1987; Davis and Glaros, 1986). Thus, rather than showing improvement, clients appear to 'forget' their coping skills as time elapses.

Though CRT emphasizes coping skills, it may also influence motivation for smoking cessation. For instance, the information on the health risks of smoking provided in CRT programs is likely to increase the incentive value of quitting, and the emphasis on the addictive nature of smoking may highlight the importance of total abstinence from cigarettes. By encouraging clients to behave like nonsmokers, e.g. to discuss the negative aspects of smoking and to proclaim their commitment to quitting, CRT may lead clients to perceive themselves as motivated to behave in a way that is congruent with these self-perceptions (Bem, 1972).

CRT's most important contribution to motivation to quit and maintain cessation may arise because it is usually conducted with groups of smokers. A peer group of quitters may provide both social pressure and social support to resist challenges to quitting, and to maintain abstinence. A number of correlational studies have suggested that social support can facilitate smoking cessation and maintenance (Coppotelli and Orleans, 1985; Horwitz, Hindi-Alexander and Wagner, 1985); though Mermelstein and his colleagues (1983, 1986) concluded that both general social support and support for quitting smoking enhanced initial cessation and short-term maintenance, but did not affect long-term maintenance. Although the studies cited measured perceived support from the smokers' spouses or partners, it seems reasonable that a quit-smoking group could provide similar support, especially for clients who lack supportive partners. Etringer, Gregory and Lando (1984) investigated support from nonsmoking groups by manipulating group cohesion via verbal commitments and exercises designed to facilitate positive group interaction. They found that subjects who were assigned to an enriched cohesion group tended to be more successful over a short term (two months post-treatment), but not beyond—supporting the notion that social support exerts its effects early.

At least three different views have been advanced to explain the operation of support. The traditional view is that it buffers the effects of stress (Cobb, 1976; Dean and Lin, 1977). Since stress is a common precursor to relapse (Brandon, Tiffany and Baker, 1986; Marlatt and Gordon, 1980; Shiffman, 1982), such a buffer should be beneficial to the maintenance of abstinence (social supporting may also directly quell withdrawal stress; Panksepp et al., 1985). A second view is that social support functions simply through assisting cognitive and behavioral coping responses (Thoits, 1986).

Finally, support groups may generate social *pressure* to remain abstinent. Clients often tell us they refrained from smoking so they would not 'let the group down.' Hamilton and Bornstein (1979) maximized social pressure and social support by pairing subjects as 'buddies,' listing their names in the newspaper, having them wear 'I quit' buttons, and giving them a congratulatory letter signed by prominent members of the community. The combination of the above interventions with a behavioral treatment package led to greater reductions in smoking at three months post-treatment than the behavioral treatment alone. Once again, though, social support/pressure failed to exert any long-term outcome differences.

CRT also can affect long-term outcomes through many of the indirect processes enumerated previously with respect to rapid smoking (e.g. end of nicotine withdrawal, increased self-efficacy). In addition, CRT may produce indirect effects that do reflect its specific attributes (i.e. as opposed to indirect effects that reflect the specific attributes of rapid smoking). For example, since CRT emphasizes the temptation to smoke elicited by specific high-risk situations, clients would be expected to make external, specific and unstable attributions for their smoking urges (cf. Abramson, Seligman and Teasdale, 1978) attributions that imply that urges are not fixed or unalterable. At the same time, since CRT stresses the individual's ability to cope with urges, clients may make internal attributions for their success or failure to do so. In contrast, treatments that involve external manipulations (e.g. rapid smoking) should yield more external attributions for success or failure. The nature of the attributions is expected to influence clients' affect, attitudes and future behavior.

Conclusions

Both rapid smoking and CRT illustrate how treatments initially developed from a particular theoretical base, to meet a limited set of objectives, are likely to produce effects via multiple pathways. However, while both process measures and dismantling strategies have been used to validate the primary theoretical effects of both rapid smoking (Tiffany et al., 1986) and CRT (Davis and Glaros, 1986; Hall et al., 1984), they are rarely used to investigate the impact of treatment upon other variables that may influence outcome (e.g. social support, nicotine replacement, self-efficacy, self-perception, motivation to quit). These treatments need to be dismantled into their component parts to identify their prepotent elements. Moreover, process analyses need to be done at two stages of the quitting process: cessation and maintenance. This, of course, introduces a host of analytic problems. For example, if one studies maintenance among groups of abstinent smokers who had received different cessation treatments, differences in maintenance may be due to the fact that the cessation interventions yielded two very different populations of smokers (Harackiewicz, Samsone, Blau, Epstein and Mandorlink, 1987). Finally, our analysis suggests a reason for the difficulty in identifying specific, direct effects of a cessation treatment: indirect effects of treatment and the effects due to quitting *per se*, may overwhelm or mask important (but short-lived) initial effects.

The ultimate goal of such research is to develop more powerful interventions. We know, for example, that CRT combined with aversive or focused smoking produces some of the highest short-term and long-term abstinence rates. But we do not know if the high abstinence rates are due to the two treatments acting upon different stages of quitting, if the combined treatment package has a greater impact upon each individual smoker, or if it works by meeting different needs of different smokers. The absence of answers to these questions indicates that smoking cessation research remains in its infancy.

PRIMARY PREVENTION

School-based anti-smoking programs have been the focus of primary prevention in the United States, Canada and the United Kingdom. This reflects the access schools offer to the target audience (Leventhal, 1968), and the tradition of using public education to attack social problems (Leventhal, 1973; Wharton, 1982). Finally, the official recognition of the exceptional hazards of smoking (US Public Health Service, 1964), and the difficulty of achieving successful smoking cessation (Leventhal, 1973, Leventhal and Cleary, 1980) led to a major infusion of federal funds for research on primary prevention.

By the late 1970s, Thompson (1978) was able to locate and review nearly 200 published reports of anti-smoking studies and programs. He concluded that virtually none of these investigations presented convincing evidence of success in reducing the rate of recruitment to smoking among schoolchildren. Because many of these programs were conducted in health education courses, it was concluded that programs emphasizing long-term health risks were ineffective in persuading children not to smoke. Actually, Mittelmark, Murray, Luepker, Pechacek, Pirie and Pallonen (1987) point out that there is little clear evidence that health-related programs are ineffective, as the failures reviewed by Thompson could have occurred for many reasons. For example, most of the studies evaluated the effects of a program administered to a single group. Because they were done during a time of increasing rates of smoking among adolescents, an absence of change in post-treatment smoking initiation might actually represent a positive outcome. Moreover, there are many different types of health information, and many different ways of presenting the same information, and few published reports provided enough detail to allow Thompson to document whether some types of information were more effective than others.

The new generation of studies

School-based anti-smoking programs conducted in the past ten to fifteen years have produced more favorable outcomes. To see why this is so we need to examine their conceptual and methodological make-up.

Conceptual structure

Beginning in the early 1970s Richard Evans (Evans, 1976; Evans, Rozelle, Mittelmark, Hansen, Bane and Havis, 1978) began a series of studies of school interventions that avoided the health and/or threat-oriented approaches that had characterized many earlier school and laboratory studies of anti-smoking communications (Leventhal, 1968, 1970) and emphasized, instead, two theoretical approaches: (1) inoculation against inducements to smoke (McGuire, 1964) and (2) the development of specific action plans (Leventhal, 1970) and social skills (Bandura, 1969) to resist pressures to try cigarettes and/or to experiment with smoking. The approach of the Evans group was *response-focused*; i.e. it dealt with motives (attitudes) and responses specific to smoking (Ajzen and Fishbein, 1977). The films used to generate motivation focused on factors such as the socially undesirable aspects of smoking (cigarettes smell bad; kids who smoke are less competent), cigarette advertisements as a form of 'media rip-off,' and both immediate and remote health risks. The response component concentrated on rehearsal to improve skills for rejecting offers of cigarettes without alienating peers. Indeed, a substantial portion of the program focused on practice in how to 'Say NO.'

A second, *life skills* training approach, viewed adolescent dissatisfactions with self and environment as the root cause of a broad spectrum of problem behaviors including aggression against peers, defiance of authority, early sexual activity, and substance abuse including cigarette smoking (Jessor and Jessor, 1977). The program objective is to improve skills for defining and coping with life problems so as to alleviate the underlying dissatisfactions and distress which provides the motivation for problem behaviors including substance use (Botvin and Eng, 1982; Botvin, Eng and Williams, 1980; Botvin and Wills, 1985). Information specific to substance use, e.g. sessions encouraging the exploration of alternatives to drug use, is also included.

The strength of both the *response-focused* and *life skills* programs lies in their development of *procedural or 'how-to' knowledge*, and their weakness lies in a failure to elaborate the significant attributes of *representational or 'what-for' knowledge*. Thus, neither format suggests a clear approach for developing *personally* meaningful representations of the risks of smoking for youngsters of different ages, and maintaining this motivation through the developmental chaos of adolescence. Even studies of *life skills* programs provide few clues as to how one can link daily problem-solving to prevention. Thus, we do not know if the benefits in primary prevention of smoking that adolescents derive from the life skills program are a sign of (1) increased awareness of specific failures to cope successfully with other life problems; (2) redefinition and increased skill in coping with life problems; or (3) awareness that the skills they have acquired are meant to substitute for smoking.

Methodological structure

Flay (1985) divided the past decade and a half of *response-focused* and *life skills* interventions into four generations, each generation superior in methodological sophistication to that preceding it. For example, in the latest generation, as contrasted with the earliest, multiple schools are randomly assigned to treatment and control conditions to provide adequate statistical power when schools are treated as the sampling unit. This avoids the confound between school environment and program that arises when only a single school is used in both the experimental and control conditions. The most recent studies were also longitudinal, i.e. pre- and post-test were conducted on the same children and behavioral effects were computed on an individual basis. Independent, anonymous pre- and post-samples were commonly compared in the earlier studies.

By using multiple schools in each condition the new studies report results for very large samples, e.g. 1000 to 7000 or more youngsters in each of the experimental and control conditions (Best, 1987). Thus, the new studies will have much larger numbers of smokers (15 percent of 1000 to 7000 = 150 to 1050) in their control groups than did the earlier studies (often as few as 50) and comparisons between conditions will be more reliable. The larger sample allows the examination of effects on separate subsamples of smokers, and provides room for the inevitable loss in participants at each follow-up, e.g. 20 and 40 percent or more at each point under some studies (Murray, Richards, Luepker and Johnson, 1987). The loss rate is higher among smokers than nonsmokers (Murray, O'Connell, Schmid and Perry, 1987; Hirshman and Leventhal, in press). Many recent studies have also used special techniques such as the bogus pipeline which creates a false impression that physiological measures of smoking have been taken (Jones and Sigall, 1971; Murray et al., 1987) and physiological measures to enhance the validity of self-reports of smoking, though these procedures may be needed only in some conditions.

Finally, the most recent *response-focused* and *life skills* programs have attempted to increase the strength of their interventions by increasing the number of exposures to the program, e.g. as many as 18 to 20-hour long sessions during early grades and multiple booster sessions per year for the two to three years following. The time-intensive nature of the new programs raises serious questions about their adaptability to the typical school setting, where they must compete for time in an already overcrowded curriculum taught in understaffed classrooms by underpaid teachers.

Outcomes of recent studies

While not all of the results are in, sufficient data exist so that we can determine whether recent methodological improvements in research have generated improved prevention outcomes. A careful examination of both published and unpublished reports suggests reductions of 10 to 25 percent in the rates of recruitment to initiation and experimental smoking by nonsmokers (Flay, Ryan, Best, Brown, Kersall, D'Avernas and Zanna, 1985; Best, Perry, Flay, Brown, Towson, Kersell, Ryan and D'Avernas, 1984), and occasionally, moderate effects in the reduced movement from experimental to relatively heavy, daily smoking (Murray et al., 1987). The sample sizes, however, are still small, making for unstable comparisons (Flay, 1985).

But there are distinct failures. For example, no advantage was reported for the experimental groups in the very large and well-controlled studies by Best and his colleagues (1987), and no effect was reported for nonsmokers in the large study recently reported by Biglan and his colleagues (Biglan, Glasgow, Ary, Thompson, Severson, Lichtenstein, Weissman, Faller and Gallison, 1987). Thus, the methodological improvements fail to yield a 25 percent reduction in smoking on a consistent basis. The failures seem to be due to two factors: (1) lighter, experimental smokers in the experimental program conditions eventually (two or three years later) progress to heavier smoking; and (2) few youngsters who are regular smokers are able to quit (Ershler, Leventhal, Fleming and Glynn, in press).

Evaluation of current programs

While current programs have shown that skills training is of some benefit, they also suggest that school-based programs will not meet public health targets for the elimination of smoking by primary intervention. Moreover, it is not clear that where successes are reported for these programs, the program itself is the sufficient condition for the positive outcome. The social climate is far different now than it was at the time the older programs were conducted, and the necessary ingredients for primary prevention may be the combination of program and context. By assigning schools to conditions, current programs confound individual skills training with social context effects. This confounding creates at least three possible routes for program success. First, students may resist smoking because as individuals they have learned about the risks of smoking and have acquired skills to cope with life problems and/or social pressures to smoke. Second, students may resist smoking because they know that other students are exposed to the same information, and because their expectations or perceptions of group norms for smoking have changed. And third, the knowledge, skills and norms acquired by exposure to the program may be effective only when other students reinforce behaviors consistent with the program. With the important exception of the study by Biglan et al. (1987), none of the current studies has begun to examine these differential paths for influence.

Several parallels exist between the interventions for primary prevention and those for secondary prevention. For example, both the life skills interventions and CRT aim to reduce smoking by enhancing skills to reduce life stresses, and both the response-specific programs and CRT teach skills to manage specific urges. As is true for secondary intervention, each primary intervention is based upon a specific theoretical model, but each can impact upon prevention through multiple routes; some generic, i.e., true of all methods, and some specific to a particular method. Unfortunately, it is also true that virtually none of the existent primary intervention studies has been designed to vary or to assess these 'indirect' routes of influence. But unlike the studies of rapid smoking, where motivation to quit is a clear target of intervention, the school-based studies give little attention to varying and/or assessing young people's desire to remain nonsmokers. Even where primary interventions have used health information and special devices to enhance the immediacy and vividness of the danger of smoking, there are virtually no studies that attempt to identify the contribution of these particular program components to outcomes.

The development of smoking

Though we agree that current studies have established the importance of skills as *one* of the key components in primary prevention, we also believe that further methodological tuning will not result in an increase in the effectiveness of skills procedures. Thus, the NCI dictum that phase 2 studies should apply existent approaches to prevention is flawed, as it fails to recognize the need for basic research to elaborate the conceptual framework for motivation to avoid smoking. Steps in this direction can be seen in recent efforts to create a developmental framework that examines the functions of smoking at different stages in its developmental history.

The developmental theme

Retrospective reports by adult smokers and reports from children (Baugh, Hunter, Mac, Webber and Berenson, 1982; McKennel and Thomas, 1967, Wohlford and Giammona, 1969) suggest a median of two years for the development of smoking, with very considerable variance about that figure.

These observations imply that the development of smoking is shaped by a complex interaction between individual psychological and biological factors and the individual's social context. Thus it may be possible to identify temporal stages in the development of smoking, and to identify different subgroups of individuals who are moved toward regular smoking and dependence by somewhat different processes.

Building on prior suggestions (Dunn, 1973), investigators have defined and sought empirical evidence for the following four stages: (1) a *preparatory* stage; (2) a stage of *initiation and experimentation*; (3) a stage of *occasional to regular use*; and (4) a stage of *dependence and regular use* (Bigland and Lichtenstein, 1984; Flay, D'Avernas, Best, Kersall and Ryan, 1983; Leventhal and Cleary, 1980; Glynn, Leventhal and Hirschman, 1986). Smoking appears to have somewhat different functions at each of these stages, and it appears that different component processes may be involved at each. For example, during the preparatory stage youngsters learn about the presumed functions of smoking by observing parental and peer smoking. These models may establish expectations that affect attention and shape the child's initial smoking experience (Glynn et al., 1986). Exposure to secondary smoke may also result in physiological and psychological changes that inoculate the youngster against the noxious effects of the first smoking experience. Because the first cigarette is highly aversive it becomes the last for most adolescents (Biglan and Lichtenstein, 1984; Hirschman, Leventhal and Glynn, 1984); only one-third of those who try at first appear to overlook the coughing and burning throat and go on to a second cigarette (Biglan and Lichtenstein, 1984; Hirschman, Leventhal and Glynn, 1984; Silverstein, Kelly, Swan and Kozlowski, 1982). Compared to adolescents who experiment minimally, those who persist in experimenting report more highs and pleasant emotional experiences, though they do not report fewer negative experiences from smoking (Friedman, Lichtenstein and Biglan, 1985).

When we look at the later stages of regular use, we find that adolescents at this stage have the same problems quitting as do adults: i.e. adolescents who quit report unpleasant withdrawal sensations (McNeill, West and Jarvis, 1987) that lead to the resumption of smoking (Ershler *et al.*, in press). Data also suggest that the factors that encourage adolescents to attempt quitting may be different from those involved in success at quitting (Ershler et al., in press; Hansen, Collins, Anderson, Johnson and Graham, 1985; Presson, Chassin, Sherman, Olshavsky, Bensenberg and Corty, 1984).

Individual differences in the developmental process

The wide range of individual variation in rates of movement from initial tries to dependence suggests individual differences in the functional utility of smoking, though there is far less evidence to support this hypothesis for children than for adults (Jessor and Jessor, 1977; Kandel and Faust, 1975; Leventhal and Avis, 1976; McKennel, 1968; Mosbach and Leventhal, in press).

In a recent study, Mosbach and Leventhal (in press) asked 7th- and 8th-grade schoolchildren to identify the peer groups they most enjoyed doing things with. Two of the four groups identified had high rates of smoking. They were the 'dirts' (children from rural areas) and 'druggies' (young males who used substances and exhibited problem behaviors) who were most likely to experiment (94 percent) and to smoke regularly (62 percent), and the 'hot-shots' (mainly females who were good students and sociable who were somewhat less likely to try (67 percent) and to smoke regularly (28 percent)). The level of smoking was well under 10 percent for youngsters interested in athletics and in those who were called 'regulars.' The data suggest multiple and quite different functions for smoking in the first two groups. For the 'dirts,' smoking likely functioned to control frustration at inability to regulate rewards, and was maintained as an expression of solidarity and belongingness to a deviant group. For the 'hot-shots' smoking functioned as a way of defining themselves as mature and coping with achievement anxiety. Thus, the functions of smoking and its developmental history may be dependent upon group membership.

Implications for prevention

The analysis of stages and the recognition of subgroups has the potential for generating a number of new approaches to primary prevention. At the very least it is clear that any program should attempt to identify specific target subgroups and consider whether these groups demand different communication levels, styles and/or content. Secondly, it also seems reasonable for prevention programs to use intervention procedures appropriate to different stages. There is little reason to expect the same intervention to succeed both for adolescents at the preparatory stage and for adolescents who are already nicotine-dependent. An example of an intervention designed to make use of development notions, is the Hirschman and Leventhal attempt (in press) to influence adolescents' perceptions of their initial smoking experiences. For example, among their various misconceptions of smoking (Leventhal, Glynn, Fleming and Ershler, 1987), adolescents believe that adaptation to noxious effects is a sign of invulnerability. By reinterpreting adaptation as a sign that smoke has killed the body's warning system, making the smoker more vulnerable to harm, the adolescent's initial experience with cigarettes may become a deterrent to further use. An intervention based upon this procedure showed a reduction by half in movement from first to later tries, an effect that is especially encouraging because of the brevity of the program (three classroom sessions), and its minimal emphasis upon skills training. Thus, a combination of the developmental and skills approaches might produce still more powerful effects. Clearly, further efforts in this area are needed.

Finally, it seems likely that the way in which adolescents interpret their first failed quitting attempt might play a role in their subsequent motivation to quit, in their belief in the difficulty of quitting, and in their perception of their ability to do so (Eiser, van der Pligt, Raw and Sutton, 1985; Marlatt and Gordon, 1980).

CONCLUSION

As we increase our understanding of the processes involved in both cessation and the development of smoking, we should be able to formulate a wider range of effective intervention strategies for both secondary and primary prevention. These strategies will be targeted at multiple levels, e.g. the culture (its laws and media), social institutions (workplace and insurance rules), face-to-face groups, and the individual. The strategies used at each level will be better integrated to achieve positive health promotive effects for particular target audiences. This requires a major modification of the NCI phases; specifically, phase 1 studies are needed on the intervention process before we can move to phases 2 through 5. In short, our ultimate success will depend upon the richness of our basic knowledge regarding the behavioral mechanisms underlying the development of smoking and ways of modifying these mechanisms.

It appears that the critical factor in the underlying process may be the link between the organism's emotional system and the urge to smoke (Baker, Morse and Sherman, 1987; Leventhal and Cleary, 1980; Tomkins, 1968). As the adolescent smoker moves from his first to later cigarettes, a variety of subjective and overt reactions are experienced that continually reshape the individual's conditioned reactions and rational beliefs regarding smoking. These experiences play a key role in the movement toward becoming a smoker, and they play a key role when one attempts to reverse the process and move the smoker to a nonsmoking status. It is clear that cigarette smoke is a multicomponent activator whose effects depend, in part, upon the content of the smoke, what is its temperature, nicotine level, and the constitution and amount of the several thousand other products present in smoke (Pomerleau and Pomerleau, 1984). The impact of cigarette smoke would then vary as a function of differences between individual smokers with respect to their biology, psychology and social psychology.

For example, at the moment they smoke their first cigarette, adolescents may differ in their level of sympathetic, parasympathetic and pituitary adrenocorticotrophic activation, and in the reactivity of each of these systems. Such differences could reflect constitutional factors (both developmental and nondevelopmental) and psychological factors. The constitutional factors could be both genetic and acquired, and the psychological factors could be both dispositional (trait-like) and momentary or situationally induced states. Thus, socially induced excitement could vary the level of catecholamines, direct attention, and generate expectations, all of which might influence the impact of cigarette smoke on the individual's consciousness and motivation to smoke. In short, the impact of cigarette smoke on the individual will reflect biological and social psychological components that act by influencing the level and reactivity of the component systems. As our knowledge of this system improves, so too will our interventions.

ACKNOWLEDGMENT

Preparation of this manuscript was supported by the following grants: NIDA 2R01DA03530-04 and NIDA DA02336. Requests for reprints should be addressed to: Howard Leventhal, Ph.D., Rutgers–State University of New Jersey, Department of Psychology, Tillett Hall, Kilmer Campus, New Brunswick, New Jersey 08903, USA.

REFERENCES

Abramson, L.Y., Seligman, M.E.P., and Teasdale, J. (1978). Learned helplessness in humans: critique and reformulation. *Journal of Abnormal Psychology*, **87**, 49–74.

Ajzen, I., and Fishbein, M. (1977). Attitude–behavior relations: a theoretical analysis and review of empirical research. *Psychological Bulletin*, **84**, 888–918.

Baer, J.S., Holt, C.S., and Lichtenstein, E. (1986). Self-efficacy and smoking reexamined: construct validity and clinical utility. *Journal of Consulting and Clinical Psychology*, **54**, 846–852.

Baker, T.B., Cannon, D.S., Tiffany, S.T., and Gino, A. (1984). Cardiac response as an index of the effect of aversion therapy. *Behaviour Research and Therapy*, **22**, 403–411.

Baker, T.B., Morse, E., and Sherman, J.E. (1987). The motivation to use drugs: a psychobiological analysis of urges. In: P.C. Rivers (ed.), *Alcohol and Addictive Behavior*, Nebraska Symposium on Motivation, 1986. Lincoln, Nebraska: University of Nebraska Press.

Bandura, A. (1969). *Principles of Behavior Modification*. New York: Holt, Rinehart & Winston.

Bandura, A. (1977). Self-efficacy: toward a unifying theory of behavior change. *Psychological Review*, **84**, 191–215.

Baugh, J.G., Hunter, S., Mac, D., Webber, L.S., and Berenson, G.S. (1982). Developmental trends of first cigarette smoking experience of children: the Bogalusa Heart Study. *American Journal of Public Health*, **72**, 1161–1164.

Bem, D.J. (1972). Self-perception theory. In: L. Berkowitz (ed.), *Advances in Experimental and Social Psychology*, vol. 6. New York: Academic Press, pp. 1–62.

Bernstein, D.A. (1969). The modification of smoking behavior: an evaluative review. *Psychology Bulletin*, **71**, 418–440.

Best, J.A. (1987). From determinants to diffusion: program for developmental research for smoking prevention and cessation. Paper presented at the Hutchinson Smoking Prevention and Cessation Conference, Seattle, Washington, 9–10 March.

Best, J.A., Perry, C.L., Flay, B.R., Brown, K.S., Towson, S.M.J., Kersell, M.W., Ryan, K.B., and D'Avernas, J.R. (1984). Smoking prevention and the concept of risk. *Journal of Applied Social Psychology*, **14**, 257–273.
Biglan, A., and Lichtenstein, E. (1984). A behavior-analytic approach to smoking acquisition: some recent findings. *Journal of Applied Social Psychology*, **14**, 207–223.
Biglan, A., Glasgow, R., Ary, D., Thompson, R., Severson, H., Lichtenstein, E., Weissman, W., Faller, C., and Gallison, C. (1987). How generalizable are the effects of smoking and parent messages in a teacher-administered program. *Journal of Behavioral Medicine*, **10**, 613–628.
Botvin, G.J., and Eng, A. (1982). The efficacy of a multicomponent approach to the prevention of cigarette smoking. *Preventive Medicine*, **11**, 199–211.
Botvin, G.J., and Wills, T. (1985). Personal and social skills training: cognitive–behavioral approaches to substance abuse prevention. In: C.S. Bell and R. Battjes (eds), *Prevention Research: Deterring Drug Abuse Among Young Children and Adolescents*. NIDA Research Monograph No. 63. Washington, DC: US Government Printing Office pp. 8–49.
Botvin, G.J., Eng, A., and Williams, C.L. (1980). Preventing the onset of cigarette smoking through life skills training. *Preventive Medicine*, **9**, 135–143.
Brandon, T.H., Tiffany, S.T., and Baker, T.B. (1986). The process of smoking relapse. In: F.M. Tims and C.G. Leukefeld (eds), *Relapse and Recovery in Drug Abuse*. NIDA Research Monograph No. 72. Washington, DC: US Government Printing Office, pp. 104–117.
Brandon, T.H., Zelman, D.C., and Baker, T.B. (1987). Effects of maintenance sessions on smoking relapse: delaying the inevitable? *Journal of Consulting and Clinical Psychology*, **55**, 780–782.
Brandon, T.H., Zelman, D.C., and Baker, T.B. (in press). Delaying smoking relapse with extended treatment. In: T.B. Baker and D.S. Cannon (eds), *Addictive Disorders: Recent Research on Assessment and Treatment*. New York: Praeger.
Breier, A., Albus, M., Pickers, D., Zahn, T.P., Wolkowitz, O.M., and Paul, S.M. (1987). Controllable and uncontrollable stress in humans: alterations in mood and neuroendocrine and psychophysiological function. *American Journal of Psychiatry*, **144**, 1419–1425.
Brownell, K.D., Glynn, T.J., Glasgow, R., Lando, H., Rand, C., Gottlieb, A., and Pinney, J.M. (1986). Task force 5: Interventions to prevent relapse. *Health Psychology*, **5** (Suppl.), 53–68.
Burns, B.H. (1969). Chronic chest disease, personality, and success in stopping cigarette smoking. *British Journal of Preventive and Social Medicine*, **23**, 23–37.
Cobb, S. (1976). Social support as a moderator of life stress. *Psychosomatic Medicine*, **38**, 300–314.
Condiotte, M.M., and Lichtenstein, E. (1981). Self-efficacy and relapse in smoking cessation programs. *Journal of Consulting and Clinical Psychology*, **49**, 648–658.
Coppotelli, H.C., and Orleans, C.T. (1985). Partner support and other determinants of smoking cessation maintenance among women. *Journal of Consulting and Clinical Psychology*, **53**, 455–460.
Cummings, C., Gordon, J.R., and Marlatt, G.A. (1980). Relapse: strategies of prevention and prediction. In: W.T. Miller (ed.), *The Addictive Behaviors*. Oxford: Pergamon Press, pp. 291–321.
Cummings, K.M., Giovino, G., Jaen, C.R., and Emrich, L.J. (1985). Reports of smoking withdrawal symptoms over a 21-day period of abstinence. *Addictive Behaviours*, **10**, 373–381.

Davis, J.R., and Glaros, A.G. (1986). Relapse prevention and smoking cessation. *Addictive Behaviors*, **11**, 105–114.

Dean, A., and Lin, N. (1977). The stress-buffering role of social support. *Journal of Nervous and Mental Disease*, **165**, 403–417.

DiClemente, C.C. (1981). Self-efficacy and smoking cessation maintenance: a preliminary report. *Cognitive Therapy and Research*, **5**, 175–187.

DiClemente, C.C., and Prochaska, J.O. (1982). Self-change and therapy change of smoking behavior: A comparison of processes of change in cessation and maintenance. *Addictive Behaviors*, **7**, 133–142.

Dunn, W.L. (1973). Experimental methods and conceptual models as applied to the study of motivation in cigarette smoking. In: W.L. Dunn, Jr (ed.), *Smoking Behavior: Motives and Incentives*. Washington, DC: Winston, pp. 93–111.

Eiser, J.R., van der Pligt, J., Raw, M., and Sutton, S.R. (1985). Trying to stop smoking: effects of perceived addiction attributions for failure and expectancy of success. *Journal of Behavioral Medicine*, **4**, 321–341.

Erickson, L.M., Tiffany, S.T., Martin, E.M., and Baker, T.B. (1983). Aversive smoking therapies: a conditioning analysis of therapeutic effectiveness. *Behaviour Research and Therapy*, **21**, 595–611.

Ershler, J., Leventhal, H., Fleming, R., and Glynn, K. (in press). The quitting experience for smokers in 6th through 12th grade. *Addictive Behaviors*.

Etringer, B.D., Gregory, V.R., and Lando, H.A. (1984). Influence of group cohesion on the behavioral treatment of smoking. *Journal of Consulting and Clinical Psychology*, **52**, 1080–1086.

Evans, R.I. (1976). Smoking in children: developing a social psychological strategy to deterrence. *Journal of Preventive Medicine*, **8**, 122–127.

Evans, R., Rozelle, R., Mittelmark, M., Hansen, W., Banc, A., and Harvis, J. (1978). Deterring the onset of smoking in children: knowledge of immediate physiological effects and coping with peer pressure, media pressure and parent modeling. *Journal of Applied Social Psychology*, **8**, 126–135.

Flay, B.R. (1985). Psychosocial approaches to smoking prevention: a review of findings. *Health Psychology*, **4**, 449–488.

Flay, B.R., D'Avernas, J.R., Best, J.A., Kersall, M.W., and Ryan, K. (1983). Why young people smoke and ways to prevent them: the Waterloo study. In: P. Firestone and P. McGrath (eds), *Pediatric Behavioral Medicine*. New York: Springer-Verlag, 1983, pp. 132–183.

Flay, B.R., Ryan, K., Best, J.A., Brown, K.S., Kersell, M.W., d'Avernas, J.R., and Zanna, M.P. (1985). Are social psychological smoking prevention programs effective? The Waterloo study. *Journal of Behavioral Medicine*, **8**, 37–60.

Friedman, L.S., Lichtenstein, E., and Biglan, A. (1985). Smoking onset among teens: an empirical analysis of initial situations. *Addictive Behaviors*, pp. 1–13.

Glynn, K., Leventhal, H., and Hirschman, R. (1986). A cognitive developmental approach to smoking prevention. In: C.S. Bell and R. Battjes (eds), *Prevention Research: Deterring Drug Abuse Among Children and Adolescents*. NIDA Research Monograph No. 63. Washington, DC: US Government Printing Office, pp. 130–152.

Greenwald, P., and Cullen, J.W. (1985). The new emphasis in cancer control—an editorial. *Journal of the National Cancer Institute*, **74**(3), 543–551.

Greenwald, P., and Sondik, E.J. (1986). *Cancer Control Objectives for the Nation: 1985–2000*. NCI Research Monograph No. 2. A Publication of the National Cancer Institute, pp. 1–105.

Hall, R.G., Sachs, D.P.L., and Hall, S.M. (1979). Medical risk and therapeutic effectiveness of rapid smoking. *Behaviour Therapy*, **10**, 249–259.

Hall, S.M., Rugg, D., Tunstall, C., and Jones, R.T. (1984). Preventing relapse to cigarette smoking by behavioral skill training. *Journal of Consulting and Clinical Psychology*, **52**, 372–382.

Hamilton, S.B., and Bornstein, P.H. (1979). Broad-spectrum behavioral approach to smoking cessation: effects of social support and paraprofessional training on the maintenance of treatment effects. *Journal of Consulting and Clinical Psychology*, **47**, 598–600.

Hansen, W.B., Collins, L.M., Anderson Johnson, C., and Graham, J.W. (1985). Self-initiated smoking cessation among high school students. *Addictive Behaviors*, **10**, 265–271.

Harackiewicz, J.M., Samsone, C., Blair, L.W., Epstein, J.A., and Mandorlink, G. (1987). Attributional processes in behavior change and maintenance: smoking cessation and continued abstinence. *Journal of Consulting and Clinical Psychology*, **55**, 372–378.

Hatsukami, D., Hughes, J.R., and Pickens, R. (1985). Characterization of tobacco withdrawal: physiological and subjective effects. In: J. Grabowski and S.M. Hall (eds), *Pharmacological Adjuncts in Smoking Cessation*. NIDA Research Monograph No. 53. Washington, DC: US Government Printing Office, pp. 56–67.

Hirschman, R., and Leventhal, H. (in press). Preventing smoking behaviors in school children: a pilot test of a cognitive developmental program. *Journal of Applied Social Psychology*.

Hirschman, R.S., Leventhal, H., and Glynn, K. (1984). The development of smoking behaviors: conceptualization and supportive cross-sectional survey data. *Journal of Applied Social Psychology*, **14**, 184–206.

Horwitz, M.B., Hindi-Alexander, M., and Wagner, T.J. (1985). Psychosocial mediators of abstinence, relapse, and continued smoking: a one-year follow-up of a minimal intervention. *Addictive Behaviours*, **10**, 29–39.

Jessor, R., and Jessor, S.L. (1977). *Problem Behavior and Psychosocial Development: A Longitudinal Study of Youth*. New York: Academic Press.

Jones, E.E., and Sigall, H. (1971). The bogus pipeline: a new paradigm for measuring affect and attitude. *Psychological Bulletin*, **76**, 349–364.

Kandel, D., and Faust, R. (1975). Sequence and stages in patterns of adolescent drug use. *Archives of General Psychiatry*, **32**, 923–932.

Leventhal, H. (1968). Experimental studies of anti-smoking communications. In: E. Borgatta and R. Evans (eds), *Smoking, Health, and Behavior*. Chicago: Aldine, pp. 95–121.

Leventhal, H. (1970). Findings and theory in the study of fear communications. *Advances in Experimental Social Psychology*, **5**, 120–186.

Leventhal, H. (1973). Changing attitudes and habits to reduce chronic risk factors. *American Journal of Cardiology*, **31**, 571–580.

Leventhal, H., and Avis, N. (1976). Pleasure, addiction, and habit: factors in verbal report or factors in smoking behavior? *Journal of Abnormal Psychology*, **85**, 478–488.

Leventhal, H., and Cleary, P.D. (1980). The smoking problem: a review of the research and theory in behavioral risk modification. *Psychological Bulletin*, **88**, 370–405.

Leventhal, H., Glynn, K., Fleming, R., and Ershler, J. (1987). Is the smoking decision an 'informed choice?': effects of smoking risk factors on smoking beliefs. *Journal of American Medical Association*, **257**, 3373–3376.

Leventhal, H., Safer, M., Cleary, P., and Gutmann, M. (1980). Cardiovascular risk modification by community-based programs for life-style change: comments on the Stanford study. *Journal of Consulting and Clinical Psychology*, **48**, 150–158.

Lichtenstein, E. (1971). Modification of smoking behavior: good designs–ineffective treatment. *Journal of Consulting and Clinical Psychology*, **36**, 163–166.

Lichtenstein, E., and Danaher, B.G. (1976). Modification of smoking behavior: a critical analysis of theory, research and practice. In: M. Hersen, R.M. Eiseler and P.M. Miller (eds), *Progress in Behavior Modification*, vol. 3. New York: Academic Press, pp. 79–132.

Marlatt, G.A. (1982). Relapse prevention: a self-control program for the treatment of addictive behaviors. In: R.B. Stuart (ed.), *Adherence, Compliance and Generalization in Behavioral Medicine*. New York: Brunner/Mazel, pp. 329–378.

Marlatt, G.A. (1983). The controlled drinking controversy. *American Psychologist*, **38**, 1097–1110.

Marlatt, G.A. (1985). Lifestyle modification. In: G.A. Marlatt and J.R. Gordon (eds), *Relapse Prevention*. New York: Guilford Press, pp. 71–127.

Marlatt, G.A., and Gordon, J.R. (1980). Determinants of relapse: implications for the maintenance of behavior change. In: P.O. Davidson and S.M. Davidson (eds), *Behavioral Medicine: Changing Health Lifestyles*. New York: Brunner/Mazel, pp. 410–452.

McGuire, W.J. (1964). Inducing resistance to persuasion: some contemporary approaches. In: L. Berkowitz (ed.), *Advances in Experimental Social Psychology*. New York: Academic Press, pp. 191–229.

McIntyre-Kingsolver, K., Lichtenstein, E., and Mermelstein, R.J. (1986). Spouse training in a multicomponent smoking-cessation program. *Behaviour Therapy*, **17**, 67–74.

McKennel, A.C. (1968). British research into smoking behavior. In: E.F. Borgatta and R.R. Evans (eds), *Smoking, Health and Behavior*. Chicago, Aldine, pp. 140–164.

McKennel, A.C., and Thomas, R.K. (1967). *Adults' and Adolescents' Smoking Habits and Attitudes*. Government Social Survey. London: HMSO.

McNeil, A.D., West, R.J., and Jarvis, M. (1987). Subjective effects of cigarette smoking in adolescents. *Psychopharmacology*, **92**, 115–117.

Mermelstein, R., Lichtenstein, E., and McIntyre, K. (1983). Partner support and relapse in smoking-cessation programs. *Journal of Consulting and Clinical Psychology*, **51**, 465–466.

Mermelstein, R., Cohen, S., Lichtenstein, E., Baer, J.S., and Kamarck, T. (1986). Social support and smoking cessation and maintenance. *Journal of Consulting and Clinical Psychology*, **54**, 447–453.

Mittelmark, M.B., Murray, D.M., Luepker, R.V., Pechacek, T.F., Pirie, P.L., and Pallonen, U.E. (1987). Predicting experimentation with cigarettes: the childhood antecedents of smoking study (CASS). *American Journal of Public Health*, **77**, 206–208.

Mosbach, P., and Leventhal, H. (in press). Peer group identification: implications for intervention. *Journal of Abnormal Psychology*.

Murray, D.M., Luepker, R.V., Johnson, D.A., and Mittelmark, M.B. (1984). The prevention of cigarette smoking in children: a comparison of four strategies. *Journal of Applied Social Psychology*, **14**, 274–288.

Murray, D., O'Connell, C., Schmid, L., and Perry, C. (1987). The validity of smoking self-reports by adolescents: A reexamination of the bogus pipeline procedure. *Addictive Behaviors*, **12**, 7–15.

Murray, D.M., Richards, P.S., Luepker, R.V., and Johnson, C.A. (1987). The prevention of cigarette smoking in children: two and three year follow up comparison of four prevention strategies. *Journal of Behavioral Medicine*, **10**(6), 595–611.

Panksepp, J., Siviy, S.M., and Normansell, L.A. (1985). Brain opioids and social emotions. In M. Reite and T. Field (eds), *The Psychobiology of Attachment and Separation*. New York: Academic Press, pp. 3–49.

Pechacek, T.F., and Danaher, B.G. (1979). How and why people quit smoking: A cognitive–behavioral analysis. In: P.C. Kendall and S.D. Hollon (eds), *Cognitive–Behavioral Interventions: Theory, Research, and Procedures*, New York: Academic Press, pp. 389–422.

Pomerleau, C.S., and Pomerleau, O.F. (1984). Neuroregulators and the reinforcement of smoking: towards a biobehavioral explanation. *Neuroscience and Biobehavior Reviews*, **8**, 503–513.

Presson, C.C., Chassin, L., Sherman, S.J., Olshavsky, R., Bensenberg, M., and Corty, E. (1984). Predictors of adolescents' intentions to smoke: age, sex, race and regional differences. *International Journal of the Addictions*, **19**, 503–519.

Prochaska, J.O., and Di Clemente, C.C. (1983). Stages and processes of self-change of smoking: toward an integrative model of change. *Journal of Consulting and Clinical Psychology*, **51**, 390–395.

Schmahl, D.P., Lichtenstein, E., and Harris, D.E. (1972). Successful treatment of habitual smokers with warm, smoky air and rapid smoking. *Journal of Consulting and Clinical Psychology*, **38**, 105–111.

Sherman, J.E., Morse, E., and Baker, T.B. (1987). Urges/craving to smoke: preliminary results from withdrawing and continuing smokers. *Advances in Behaviour Research and Therapy*, **8**, 253–269.

Shiffman, S. (1982). Relapse following smoking cessation: a situational analysis. *Journal of Consulting and Clinical Psychology*, **50**, 71–86.

Shiffman, S. (1984a). Coping with temptations to smoke. *Journal of Consulting and Clinical Psychology*, **52**, 261–267.

Shiffman, S. (1984b). Cognitive antecedents and sequelae of smoking relapse crises. *Journal of Applied Social Psychology*, **14**, 296–309.

Shiffman, S.M., and Jarvik, M.E. (1979). Smoking withdrawal symptoms in two weeks of abstinence. *Psychopharmacology*, **50**, 35–39.

Siegel, S. (1983). Classical conditioning, drug tolerance, and drug dependence. In: R.G. Smart, F.B. Glaser, Y. Israel and H. Kalant (eds), *Research Advances in Alcohol and Drug Problems*. New York: Plenum Press, pp. 207–246.

Silverstein, B., Kelly, E., Swan, J., and Kozlowski, L.T. (1982). Physiological predisposition toward becoming a cigarette smoker: experimental evidence for a sex difference. *Addictive Behaviors*, **7**, 83–86.

Sobell, M.B., and Sobell, L.C. (1976). Second-year treatment outcome of alcoholics treated by individualistic behavior therapy: results. *Behavioral Research and Therapy*, **14**, 195–215.

Thoits, P.A. (1986). Social support as coping assistance. *Journal of Consulting and Clinical Psychology*, **54**, 416–423.

Thompson, E. (1978). Smoking education programs 1960–76. *American Journal of Public Health*, **68**, 250–257.

Tiffany, S.T., Martin, E.M., and Baker, T.B. (1986). Treatments for cigarette smoking: an evaluation of the contributions of aversion and counseling procedures. *Behaviour Research and Therapy*, **24**, 437–452.

Tomkins, S. (1968). A modified model of smoking behavior. In: E.F. Borgotta and R.R. Evans (eds), *Smoking, Health, and Behavior*. Chicago: Aldine, pp. 165–186.

US Public Health Service (1964). *Smoking and Health Report of the Advisory Committee to the Surgeon General of the Public Health Service.* US Department of Health Education and Welfare, Public Health Service, Center for Disease Control, PHS. Publication No. 1103, p. 387.

Wharton, J.C. (1982). *Crusaders for Fitness: A History of American Health Reformers.* Mount Vernon, New York: Consumers Union, Princeton University Press.

Wohlford, P., and Giammona, S.T. (1969). Personality and social variables related to the initiation of smoking cigarettes. *Journal of School Health*, **39**, 544–552.

15

The Future of Tobacco Use and Smoking Research

ROBERT B. COAMBS,
LYNN T. KOZLOWSKI
and
ROBERTA G. FERRENCE

ABSTRACT

The profiles of smokers will change with the decline of smoking. Smoking will be treated as drug use, and a greater proportion of smokers will abuse other substances. Theories of smoking as a psychopathology will become more prevalent, as the remaining smokers acquire a die-hard image. Smokers' health will grow worse.

INTRODUCTION

Smoking is declining in Canada, the United States and the United Kingdom. Anti-smoking advocates in these countries and elsewhere anticipate a nonsmoking generation by the year 2000 (e.g. Forbes, Frecker and Mastbakken, 1983). However, complete eradication of such a popular psychoactive drug would be unprecedented, and the rate of decline in smoking will probably level off well before it reaches zero. We can already see that some groups, such as problem drinkers, are resistant to anti-smoking pressures, and continue to smoke as much as they did 20 years ago (Kozlowski, Jelinek and Pope, 1986).

Smoking and Human Behavior, Edited by T. Ney and A. Gale
© 1989 John Wiley & Sons Ltd

Both popular and scientific conceptions of tobacco use have been changing. Smoking used to be viewed as a recreational habit and a private pleasure; it is increasingly viewed as drug addiction, deviant behavior and a public health hazard. While we do not foresee the elimination of smoking, its place in society will be transformed. In this chapter we look at some of these changes, and discuss their potential influence on tobacco research and health policy.

THE DECLINE IN SMOKING

The prevalence of smoking in adult men has declined from a high of about 70 percent in Canada in the 1950s to about 30 percent today (Jossa, 1985). Smoking among women peaked later, and at a lower rate, and is now only a few percentage points less than men's. Similar figures apply to the United States and Britain (UK Government Statistical Service, 1981; US Department of Health and Human Services, 1986).

The decline in smoking is likely to continue because more smokers quit and more individuals never start. In both Canada and the United States this decrease can be seen in a decline in smoking prevalence in the age range of 13 to 25, when most smoking begins (Jossa, 1985; US Department of Health and Human Services, 1987). Although the proportion of smokers has declined, the number of cigarettes smoked by individual smokers has not decreased (US Department of Health and Human Services, 1981).

The rate of decline in smoking differs among different subgroups of smokers. For example, in Britain the percentage of lighter smokers (less than 20 cigarettes per day) is declining faster than the percentage of heavier smokers (more than 20 cigarettes per day) (UK Government Statistical Service, 1981). Therefore a single statistic describing a unitary declining trend in smoking prevalence can be misleading; it is more accurate to consider a family of trends declining at very different rates.

THE DEMOGRAPHICS OF FUTURE SMOKERS

The social diffusion model

Psychoactive drug use involves the interaction of psychosocial and biological factors (Herman and Kozlowski, 1979; Kozlowski and Herman, 1984). Sometimes psychosocial and situational forces are much more important than biological forces. The circumstances in which nicotine is typically used are characterized by a rich and powerfully influential social environment. Some individuals will not voluntarily take a drug they believe is hazardous; others will knowingly take dangerous drugs, and the pressure from friends doing the same thing can strongly influence such decisions. Biological and psychological factors do not adequately account for the large variations in the prevalence of smoking by age, sex, region, social class and time period. For example,

88 percent of older, better-educated Canadian males living in Ontario and British Columbia have never smoked, whereas only 28 percent of older women with less education residing in the Prairies, Quebec and the Maritime provinces have smoked (Ferrence, 1988). Shifts in population genetics, or changes in personality traits in these populations, could not account for these patterns. Rather than biological or psychological traits, these differences appear to be determined by cultural fashion.

Of course, cultural fashions change, and the changes observed in smoking patterns share common properties with other changes in society. Rogers and Shoemaker (1983) have studied the 'diffusion of innovation' within societies, and found that new behaviors, techniques and ideas are adopted at a cumulative rate which conforms to an S-shaped curve. A particular behavior is adopted slowly at first, then increases rapidly, and finally slows and levels off or declines. Those who adopt a behavior early tend to be more exposed to external sources of communication, to be more cosmopolitan, to have higher social status and to be more innovative. When one applies this social diffusion model to patterns of smoking, one would expect males with higher education, living in more advantaged, urbanized areas to adopt smoking first, and women with less education, living in less advantaged, rural areas to be among the last to take up smoking. Now that the new fashion is to give up smoking, one would expect that the same groups who were the first to start would also be the first to quit.

Profiles of future smokers

As smoking declines, the remaining smokers will likely be the heavier, more addicted smokers who are less able to quit (Kozlowski, 1979). This is partly because those who found it easy to give up smoking would have already done so. The remainder would consist of those die-hard smokers who find quitting most difficult.

One would expect that this die-hard remainder would display characteristics which were the opposite of those who have quit successfully. Extensive research has been done regarding the characteristics associated with quitting smoking. Cherry and Kiernen (1976) report that high daily cigarette consumption and low extraversion scores were independently related to difficulty in giving up smoking. Neuroticism was related to difficulty in quitting in men, but not in women. In reviewing the research literature, Ashton and Stepney (1982, p. 172) note several characteristics associated with quitting. Former smokers had more education and greater emotional stability. When they did smoke, they were less likely to inhale, smoked fewer cigarettes, spent fewer years as a smoker, and drank less alcohol and coffee.

From these data one would expect future smokers to be those who smoke more heavily for a longer time, have less education, are less stable, and consume more alcohol and coffee. Kozlowski (1979) notes that heavy smokers are less likely to quit in smoking cessation programs. In a study of 2000 British smokers, McKennel (1973) found that those who had the most difficulty in stopping smoking consisted of individuals who tended to smoke heavily, had a manual occupation and had friends who smoked. Several studies confirm the relationship between smoking and other drug use. Smokers are more likely to be problem drinkers (Prendergast and Preble, 1973), heavy coffee consumers (Matarazzo and Saslow, 1960), and users of illegal drugs (Mello and Mendelson, 1986). Furthermore, the users of these drugs are less likely to quit smoking (Guildford, 1966; McArthur, Waldron and Dickinson, 1958; Mello and Mendelson, 1986; Thomas, 1973). Thomas (1973) found that heavier smokers drank more alcohol and coffee, and were more anxious, than lighter smokers.

Since health concerns also promote quitting (e.g. Green, 1977), future smokers may be less concerned about their health. Carmody, Brischetto, Pierce, Matarazzo and Conner (1986) found that a general concern with health was the most common reason given for quitting. Eisinger (1972) reported that having an acquaintance whose health had been affected by smoking increased the likelihood of quitting from 10 to 27 percent.

Future smokers as deviants

Smoking today is considered unhealthy, offensive to nonsmokers, and in some circles quite deviant. This was not always the case. Brill, a psychoanalyst and biographer of Freud, argued that, 'one is more justified in looking with suspicion at the [tobacco] abstainer . . . most of the fanatic opponents of tobacco I have known were all bad neurotics' (Brill, 1922). His view that nonsmokers were abnormal is understandable, given that smoking was gaining in popularity at the time, and the public was largely unaware of the health hazards of smoking. Smoking was considered a relaxing pastime, a 'habit' much like gum-chewing or nail-biting, with little or no stigma attached to it, at least for men. In fact a man was considered somewhat inadequate if he did not smoke.

Since Brill's time the tables have turned. Even now, new information about the hazards of tobacco use continues to influence individual attitudes and behavior. For example, evidence that nicotine is a psychoactive drug comparable to heroin and cocaine (Henningfield, Miyasato and Jasinski, 1983) may deter would-be smokers who are concerned about the association of smoking with drug use.

As the number of smokers dwindles it will be easier for the rest of society to isolate and stigmatize them (Nuehring and Markle, 1974). Changes in the demographics of those who continue to smoke mean that future smokers actually will be more abnormal or deviant. When the large majority of middle-aged men smoked, social pressure encouraged others to take up smoking. (All smokers were certainly not hopelessly addicted to nicotine.) When social pressure to smoke subsided in the mid-1960s (Warner, 1977), those who found it easiest to quit did so. An individual could be 'able' to quit smoking because of an assortment of factors (for example, high motivation or little withdrawal difficulty). The pool of remaining smokers, by definition, came to contain a higher and higher percentage of smokers who were 'unable' to quit smoking. These remaining smokers were those best able to resist the social disapproval and censure that accompanies tobacco use, and perhaps other types of deviant behavior.

Increasingly, the behavioral characteristics of those who continue to smoke are likely to be perceived as abnormal by nonsmokers. Smokers are reported to have greater antisocial tendencies, including belligerence, psychopathic deviance, misconduct, rebelliousness, defiance and disagreeableness (Lebovits and Ostfeld, 1971; Nesbitt, 1972; Reynolds and Nichols, 1976; Smith, 1970). Since smokers are more likely to be heavy users of alcohol, caffeine and illicit drugs, increasing proportions of smokers will display emotional instability and drug and alcohol abuse; and society may come to view smokers as they now view alcoholics and drug abusers.

The tendency of smokers to associate with other smokers will further isolate them from nonsmokers. For example, a major survey of the American Cancer Society shows that 68 percent of young female smokers have boyfriends or husbands who smoke, compared to 41 percent of nonsmokers (Clark, 1976). Other studies have shown that smokers with friends or a spouse who smokes are less likely to quit (e.g. Eisinger, 1971; Schwartz and Dubnitzky, 1968). As their numbers decline, future smokers will probably associate with other smokers even more exclusively than they do now. As society increasingly censures smokers, they may be more prone to form subcultures, to see themselves as deviant, and to appear defensive and secretive about their behavior, much as alcoholics and drug abusers are now.

The tendency to consider the drug use of a small minority to be deviant is exemplified in a comparison of types of alcohol use in certain counties in the Southern United States which are 'dry' (alcohol abstinent) with other counties that are 'wet' (nonabstinent). In the 'dry' regions there are fewer drinkers, but a high proportion of them have serious drinking problems. In contrast, there are more drinkers in the 'wet' regions, but few have serious drinking problems (Cahalan and Room, 1974). Thus, an observer in a 'dry' region would notice that most people who drink show patterns of alcohol abuse, and might conclude that most drinkers are abnormal individuals, and that prohibition is justified. An observer in a 'wet' region, however, would notice that few people who drink show patterns of alcohol abuse, and might conclude that most drinkers are normal individuals, and that prohibition would deny access to alcohol for many normal drinkers.

The health of future smokers

Less smoking will lead to lower rates of smoking-related diseases, but the health effects of smoking will likely worsen among those who continue to smoke. Smoking will be most common among the poor, who already have higher rates of many health problems than more advantaged groups (Health and Welfare Canada, 1981). Health problems are more prevalent among alcoholics and drug abusers than among the general population (Ashley, Olin, Harding le Riche, Kornaczewski, Schmidt and Rankin, 1981; Goldstein, Hunt, Des Jarlais and Deren, 1987; Schmidt and Popham, 1975), and these groups will form a larger proportion of those who smoke. The number of cigarettes consumed per smoker is likely to increase slightly, because it is the heaviest smokers who will continue to smoke. These smokers are not likely to switch to weaker brands of cigarettes (Kozlowski, 1987). Since risk to health is related to amount smoked, future smokers are likely to suffer more serious health problems than current smokers.

RESEARCH ISSUES

The declining number of smokers will change smoking research in important ways. Since smokers are more likely to be problem drinkers, heavy coffee consumers and users of illegal drugs, research subjects who use only tobacco will become harder to find.

The increasing overlap between the population of smokers and other drug users is likely to promote the view that smoking is another form of drug use. This presents opportunities for complementary enrichment of both areas of research. For example: (1) The finding that repeated attempts to quit smoking are associated with greater success in quitting (e.g. Schachter, 1981) may be applied to the treatment of other drug users. (2) Substance abuse treatment and smoking cessation programs may become more alike. Smoking cessation programs will increasingly have to take into account other drugs used by the smoker, and may implement a more comprehensive multiple drug use approach. As the search for less expensive treatment methods continues, substance abuse treatment may increasingly resemble smoking cessation programs. (3) Studies that focus on smokers who quit smoking without formal treatment (e.g. Carmody et al., 1986) may be helpful in the study of alcohol abusers and drug abusers who quit on their own. (4) The decline in cigarette smoking offers an excellent opportunity to observe first-hand the transition of a drug from common availability to a drug which is widely disapproved of, and ultimately used only by a deviant minority. In some ways this parallels the decline in opiate use that occurred at the beginning of this century (Brecher, 1972).

Nicotine addiction

Smoking research will become more like research on alcohol and other drug addiction, as researchers increasingly think of smoking as nicotine addiction. When it was considered 'just a habit,' smoking seemed very different from other drug use. With increasing evidence that long-term tobacco use is largely due to the pharmacological effects of nicotine, it will be more common to compare smoking to other forms of drug use (e.g. Blakeslee, 1987).

Smoking as psychopathological behavior

As smoking declines, smokers will increasingly be viewed as psychopathological. Research suggests that smokers are more likely to be antisocial (Smith, 1970) and neurotic (Cherry and Kiernen, 1976), have a history of adolescent rebelliousness or deviance (Gritz and Brunswick, 1980; Powell, Stewart and Grylls, 1979), be impulsive risk-takers (Graham and Ekdahl, 1986; Smith, 1970), come from troubled families (Golding and Mangan, 1981), and have parents who smoke (Graham and Ekdahl, 1986). This negative social profile will be exacerbated by the tendency of these smokers to smoke heavily (Cherry and Kiernen, 1976), use other drugs (Thomas, 1973), and associate with other smokers (Eisinger, 1971). However, while smokers will increasingly be considered deviant because of growing public disapproval of smoking, and because smokers will act more like drug abusers, we do not suggest that smoking represents a distinct psychopathology. Rather, the public impression of psychopathology is likely to emerge from an interaction of social circumstances.

PUBLIC POLICY ISSUES

Nicotine as an addicting drug

The conception of smoking as nicotine addiction has yet to have its full impact on public policy, and has only recently begun to appear in the news media (e.g. Blakeslee, 1987). As the proportion of smokers declines, and smokers look more and more like other drug users, policy-makers may be more inclined to consider smoking as drug abuse. This may lead them to establish smoking policies which more closely resemble policies for alcohol and illicit drugs.

Policy-makers and the public may resist the notion that nicotine is an addicting drug because of a misconception about the nature of addiction. Smokers will not be seen as addicts if addiction is viewed as desperate drug hunger. Drug-seeking behavior is largely a function of availability. If heroin were made freely available addicts would not exhibit desperate drug-seeking behaviors, and their patterns of drug use would in many ways resemble those of tobacco users. Alternatively, when tobacco is scarce (as was the case, for example, in postwar Germany), smokers exhibit drug-seeking behavior which is very similar to that of other drug addicts (Brecher, 1972, pp. 220–228). Tobacco users appear to have about as much difficulty giving up cigarettes as heroin addicts have giving up heroin (Brecher, 1972, p. 217).

The growing conception of smoking as drug use is likely to influence policy toward tobacco cultivation. When smoking was considered 'just a habit' it was reasonable to treat it like food crops. In the future, tobacco producers will be seen as growers of a dependence-producing drug, similar to growers of other plants which contain controlled substances. The principal policy concern will be the pharmacological and toxicological impact of the crop, rather than its commercial value or the effect of tobacco prices on the livelihood of farmers.

Research on involuntary smoking

The growing evidence that involuntary smoking is harmful to health is already influencing public policy on smoking. The 1986 Report of the Surgeon General (US Department of Health and Human Services, 1986) which concluded that involuntary smoking causes lung cancer and other diseases, may ultimately have as great an impact on nonsmokers as the 1964 Surgeon General's Report had on smokers. If a new product in our immediate environment produced as many pollutants as cigarette smoke there would be a public outcry. Smoking used to be considered a serious health concern only for those who smoked; it was 'victimless' behavior. As attitudes toward smoking change in response to research results, there will be a greater awareness of the health risks to the smoker's spouse, children and co-workers. Information about the hazards of secondhand smoke has already become a crucial tool for nonsmoker's rights groups, and will promote the acceptance of public policies designed to protect nonsmokers from the hazards of smoking.

Government intervention and legal issues

Governments are likely to play a greater role in prevention, health promotion and legislation on tobacco use. As availability and prevalence decline, support for the prohibition of smoking in public places will grow. Governments have long tried to prohibit and punish tobacco use (Brecher, 1972, pp. 209–213), and restrictions on the availability and use of any drug generally reduces the consumption of that drug (Kalant and Kalant, 1971, pp. 101–111). However, even total bans have not eradicated smoking. In the past, when tobacco was prohibited or scarce, some people still went to extreme lengths to obtain it.

Governments will probably continue to show ambivalent attitudes toward smoking. Since tobacco products generate enormous tax revenues in many countries, it would be difficult for governments to adopt a unified policy on tobacco use. Agriculture and revenue departments will continue to tolerate tobacco use, while health departments will oppose it. As smoking declines, however, the influence of revenue and agricultural departments is likely to decrease. In the future, taxes on tobacco products will likely continue to increase. This should further reduce consumption, since tobacco tax increases can produce substantial reductions in cigarette consumption (Atkinson and Townsend, 1977; Lewit and Coate, 1982).

Issues related to tobacco control will become more important as the nonsmoking majority grows and imposes restrictions on the smoking minority. The decline in tobacco availability and the increased strength of dependence of the average smoker may promote more illegal behaviors, including black-market trading.

As government and private sector restrictions on smoking are implemented and enforced, civil liberties controversies related to smoking will increase (Hadaway and Beyerstein, 1987). The refusal of some employers to allow smoking on the job, or even to hire those who smoke, has already produced considerable controversy with respect to human rights issues.

There may be little increase in opposition to new smoking policies by smokers themselves, however. Many smokers do not oppose (and often welcome) restrictions on smoking, since they feel it provides an opportunity to reduce their consumption. Most of the opposition is likely to come from parties concerned with civil liberties (e.g. Hadaway and Beyerstein, 1987).

CONCLUSIONS

The decline in smoking will have many positive consequences, but some individuals will continue to suffer health damage from smoking, and tobacco use will increasingly be accompanied by social tension and ill-will.

At the turn of the century, government policy and public attitudes turned against the use of opiates. Prohibitions increased, use declined, and remaining users came to be seen as pathological (Brecher, 1972). A similar process is occurring today with the use of tobacco. During the next few years the profile of smokers will continue to change, as tobacco makes the transition from a substance that is widely accepted to a substance used by a minority of dependent users. Research on the decline in smoking, and the changing perceptions of smoking which accompany this decline, should enhance our understanding of the use of other substances of abuse. The problems associated with smoking used to be considered separately from those of other substance abusers. Scientific findings regarding these other forms of substance abuse had limited influence on either scientists or policy-makers in the smoking field. However, with the shift to thinking of tobacco as a drug that is highly addictive, tobacco will more often be included in policies and programs aimed at a range of addictive substances.

The challenge for researchers is to respond to the reduction of tobacco use with approaches tailored to the characteristics of current smokers. The challenge for policy-makers is to manage the decline in smoking in a manner that does not cause more social problems than it alleviates.

REFERENCES

Ashley, M.J., Olin, J.S., Harding le Riche, W., Kornaczewski, A., Schmidt, W., and Rankin, J.G. (1981). Morbidity patterns in hazardous drinkers: relevance of demographic, sociologic, drinking, and drug use characteristics. *International Journal of the Addictions*, **16**, 593–625.

Ashton, H., and Stepney, R. (1982). *Smoking: Psychology and Pharmacology*. New York: Methuen.

Atkinson, A.B., and Townsend, J.L. (1977). Economic aspects of reduced smoking. *Lancet*, **2**, 492–494.

Blakeslee, S. (1987). Nicotine: harder to kick than heroin. *New York Times Magazine*, 29 March, pp. 23–53.

Brecher, E.M., and the Editors of Consumer Reports (1972). *Licit and Illicit Drugs: The Consumers' Union Report*. Mount Vernon, New York: Consumer's Union.

Brill, A.A. (1922). Tobacco and the individual. *International Journal of Psychoanalysis*, **3**, 430–440.

Cahalan, D., and Room, R. (1974). *Problem Drinking Among American Men*. New Brunswick, NJ: Monograph of the Rutgers Center for Alcohol Studies.

Carmody, T.P., Brischetto, C.S., Pierce, D.K., Matarazzo, J.D., and Conner, W.E. (1986). A prospective five-year follow-up of smokers who quit on their own. *Health Education Research*, **1**, 101–109.

Cherry, N., and Kiernen, K. (1976). Personality scores and smoking behavior: a longitudinal study. *British Journal of Preventive and Social Medicine*, **30**, 123–131.

Clark, R. (1976). Cigarette smoking among teen-age girls and young women: summary of the findings of a survey conducted for the American Cancer Society. In: J. Wakefield (ed.), *Public Education About Cancer: Recent Research and Current Programmes*. Geneva: UICC Technical Report series, vol. 24.

Eisinger, R.A. (1971). Psychosocial predictors of smoking recidivism. *Journal of Health and Social Behavior*, **12**, 355–362.

Eisinger, R.A. (1972). Psychosocial predictors of smoking behavior change. *Social Science and Medicine*, **6**, 137–144.

Ferrence, R.G. (1988). The diffusion of cigarette smoking: an exploratory analysis. Doctoral dissertation, University of Western Ontario, Canada.

Forbes, W.R., Frecker, R.C., and Mastbakken, D. (eds) (1983). *Proceedings of the 5th World Conference on Smoking and Health*. Ottawa, Canada: Canadian Council on Smoking and Health.

Golding, J.F., and Mangan, G.L. (1981). Factors governing recruitment to and maintenance of smoking. Paper presented at the meeting of the International Congress on Drugs and Alcohol, Jerusalem, September.

Goldstein, P.J., Hunt, D., Des Jarlais, D.C., and Deren, S. (1987). Drug dependence and abuse. In R.W. Amler and H.B. Dull (eds), *Closing the Gap: The Burden of Unnecessary Illness*. New York: Oxford University Press.

Graham, K., and Ekdahl, A. (1986). *Addiction Prone: Evaluation of the General Substance Abuse Model by Comparing Correlates of Abuse of Four Common Substances*. Toronto, Canada: Addiction Research Foundation.

Green, D.E. (1977). Psychosocial factors in smoking. In: M.E Jarvik, J.W. Cullen, E.R. Gritz, T.M. Vogt and L.J. West (eds), *Research on Smoking Behavior*. National Institute on Drug Abuse Research Monograph No. 17. Washington, DC: US Government Printing Office.

Gritz, E.R., and Brunswick, A.F. (1980). Psychosocial and behavioral aspects of smoking in women. In: *The Health Consequences of Smoking for Women: A Report of the Surgeon General*. Rockville, Maryland: US Department of Health and Human Services.

Guildford, J.S. (1966). *Factors Related to Successful Abstinence from Smoking: Final Report*. Washington, DC: US Public Health Service.

Hadaway, P.F., and Beyerstein, B.L. (1987). Then they came for the smokers but I didn't speak up because I wasn't a smoker: legislation and tobacco use. *Canadian Psychology*, **28**, 259–265.

Health and Welfare Canada (1981). *The Health of Canadians: Report of the Canada Health Survey*. Ottawa, Canada: Minister of Supply and Services, Catalogue No. 82-538E.

Henningfield, J.E., Miyasato, K., and Jasinski, D.R. (1983). Cigarette smokers self-administer intravenous nicotine. *Pharmacology, Biochemistry and Behavior*, **19**, 887–890.

Herman, C.P., and Kozlowski, L. (1979). Indulgence, excess and restraint: perspectives on consummatory behavior in everyday life. *Journal of Drug Issues*, **9**, 185–196.

Jossa, D. (1985). *Smoking Behaviour of Canadians: 1983*. Ottawa, Canada: Minister of Supply and Services, Catalogue No. H39-66/1985E.

Kalant, H., and Kalant, O.J. (1971). *Drugs, Society and Personal Choice*. Toronto, Canada: Addiction Research Foundation.

Kozlowski, L.T. (1979). Psychosocial influences on cigarette smoking. In: *Smoking and Health. A Report of the Surgeon General*. Washington, DC: US DHEW, Publication No. (PHS) 79-50066.

Kozlowski, L.T. (1987). Less hazardous smoking and the pursuit of satisfaction. *American Journal of Public Health*, **77**, 539–541.

Kozlowski, L.T., and Herman, C.P. (1984). The interaction of psychosocial and biological determinants of tobacco use: more on the boundary model. *Journal of Applied Social Psychology*, **14**, 244–256.

Kozlowski, L.T., Jelinek, L., and Pope, M.A. (1986). Cigarette smoking among alcoholics: a continuing and neglected problem. *Canadian Journal of Public Health*, **77**, 205–207.

Lebovits, B., and Ostfeld, A. (1971). Smoking and personality: a methodological analysis. *Journal of Chronic Diseases*, **23**(10/11), 813–821.

Lewit, E.M., and Coate, D. (1982). The potential for using excise taxes to reduce smoking. *Journal of Health Economics*, **1**, 121–145.

McArthur, C., Waldron, E., and Dickinson, J. (1958). The psychology of smoking. *Journal of Abnormal Psychology*, **56**, 267–275.

McKennell, A.C. (1973). *A Comparison of Two Smoking Typologies*. Research paper 12. London: Tobacco Research Council.

Matarazzo, J.D., and Saslow, G. (1960). Psychological and related characteristics of smokers and nonsmokers. *Psychological Bulletin*, **57**, 493–513.

Mello, N.K., and Mendelson, J.H. (1986). Cigarette smoking: interactions with alcohol, opiates, and marijuana. In: M.C. Braude and H.M. Ginzberg (eds), *Strategies for Research on the Interactions of Drugs of Abuse*. National Institute of Drug Abuse Research Monograph No. 68. Washington, DC: US Government Printing Office.

Nesbitt, P.D. (1972). Chronic smoking and emotionality. *Journal of Applied Social Psychology*, **2**, 187–196.

Nuehring, E., and Markle, G.E. (1974). Nicotine and norms: the re-emergence of a deviant behavior. *Social Problems*, **21**, 513–526.

Powell, G.E., Stewart, R.A., and Grylls, D.G. (1979). The personality of young smokers. *British Journal of Addiction*, **74**, 311–315.

Prendergast, T.J., and Preble, M.R. (1973). Drug use and its relation to alcohol and cigarette consumption in the military community of West Germany. *Journal of Applied Psychology*, **37**, 54–56.

Reynolds, C., and Nichols, R. (1976). Personality and behavioral correlates of cigarette smoking: one-year follow-up. *Psychological Reports*, **38**, 251–258.

Rogers, E.M., and Shoemaker, F.F. (1983). *Diffusion of Innovations*, 3rd edn. New York: Free Press.

Schachter, S. (1981). Self-treatment of smoking and obesity. *Canadian Journal of Public Health*, **72**, 401–406.

Schmidt, W., and Popham, R.E. (1975). Heavy alcohol consumption and physical health problems: a review of the epidemiological evidence. *Drug and Alcohol Dependence*, **1**, 27–50.

Schwartz, J.L., and Dubnitzky, M. (1968). Requisites for success in smoking withdrawal. In: E.F. Borgatta and R.R. Evans (eds), *Smoking, Health, and Behavior*. Chicago, IL: Aldine.

Smith, G.M. (1970). Personality and smoking: a review of the empirical literature. In: W.A. Hunt (ed.), *Learning Mechanisms in Smoking*. Chicago, IL: Aldine.

Thomas, C.B. (1973). The relationship of smoking and habits of nervous tension. In: W.L. Dunn, Jr (ed.), *Smoking Behavior: Motives and Incentives*. Washington, DC: Winston.

United Kingdom Government Statistical Service (1981). General Household Survey: cigarette smoking, 1972 to 1980. *Office of Population Census and Surveys Monitor*, **2** (July), 1–7.

United States Department of Health and Human Services (1981). *The Health Consequences of Smoking: The Changing Cigarette*. A report of the Surgeon General. US DHHS, Public Health Service, Office of the Assistant Secretary of Health, Office of Smoking and Health, DHHS Publication No. (PHS) 81-50156.

United States Department of Health and Human Services, National Center for Health Statistics (1986). *Health, United States, 1986*. DHHS Publication No. (PHS)87-1232. Washington, DC: Public Health Service.

United States Department of Health and Human Services (1986). *The Health Consequences of Involuntary Smoking*. A report of the Surgeon General. Rockville, MD: US DHHS, Publication No. (CDC)87-8398.

United States Department of Health and Human Services (1987). *High School Senior Drug Use: 1975–1986*. US DHHS, Public Health Service, Rockville, MD: Press Office of the National Institute on Drug Abuse.

Warner, K.E. (1977). The effects of the anti-smoking campaign on cigarette consumption. *American Journal of Public Health*, **67**, 645–650.

Author Index

Subject Index

Attitudes (*cont*)
changing attitudes, 266–267
public attitudes, 13

Behavior
predicting from intentions, 303–305
role of current and prior behavior in
prediction, 303, 304, 307
self-report, 303, 304
Behavioral expectation, 304, 305
Behavioral intention, 266
Behavioral substitutes for smoking, 81
Behavioral tolerance, 38
see also Tolerance
Beliefs, 264–265
behavioral, 293–298, 305
differential, 295, 296
general, 308
measurement of, 193, 306
modal salient, 295
normative, 293–295, 297, 298
personal, 308
relationship with attitudes, 297, 298
salience, 298
salient, 291, 298, 305
salient behavioral, 291
salient normative, 291
of smokers and non-smokers, 294–299
strength of belief, 298
Benzodiazepines, 35
Beta-endorphin, 24, 26, 30, 31, 34, 36,
37, 42, 75
see also Opioids
Bias in research, 5
Bidirectional (or biphasic) effects, 7,
126, 127, 143, 147–151
Biobehavioral approach to smoking,
72–79
Biochemical markers, 202
Biofeedback, 128
Blackmarket trading, 345
Blood sugar, 33
Buprenorphine, 31
Butt nicotine, 104, 201, 210

Cannabis, 27
Calorie intake, 62–63
Carbon monoxide (in expired air), 203
CO boost 205, 207, 209, 210, 215, 216
COHb, 202, 203, 209, 210, 211, 213
Carboxyhemoglobin, 269, 276
Catecholamines, 32, 33, 177

Cessation, 21, 43, 44, 46, 47, 216,
315–322
behavioral techniques, 46
clinics, 45, 46
cognitive methods, 43
educational methods, 43, 44
social restraints, 43, 45, 46
see also Secondary prevention
Chewing gum, 12, 36, 39, 45, 60, 212,
213
Chlorpromazine, 35
Cigarette
consumption, 200, 209, 210, 211, 212,
213
craving for, 36
design, 280
Favors, 46, 47
holder, 200
manufacturers, 1, 267
nicotine aerosol, 47
safer, 46, 47
ultra-light, 205, 214
see also Nicotine, *and* Smoking
Civil liberties, 15, 345
Cocaine, 27, 41
Coffee, 339, 340, 342
Cognition, 22, 24, 25, 43
Compensation/regulation, 207, 209,
210, 211, 212, 214
see also Titration
Confidence (in ability to stop smoking),
307
Correspondence (among measures),
292, 304, 306, 308
Cortisol, 30, 32, 177
Cotinine, 202, 211, 215
Craving, 35, 36, 46
see also Abstinence, *and* Withdrawal
Cross-sectional switching design, 206

Decline in smoking, 338, 344, 345
Dependence, 57–64, 70, 142–145, 201,
210, 214
criteria for, 58, 72
definition of, 58
see also Nicotine
Deposition (of smoke particles), 203
Deprivation, 35, 130, 215
see also Abstinence, Craving, *and*
Withdrawal
Development (of smoking habit),
326–329